Also by David Maraniss

They Marched Into Sunlight: War and Peace, Vietnam and America, October 1967

When Pride Still Mattered: A Life of Vince Lombardi

First in His Class: A Biography of Bill Clinton

The Clinton Enigma

The Prince of Tennessee: Al Gore Meets His Fate
(with Ellen Nakashima)

"Tell Newt to Shut Up!" (with Michael Weisskopf)

Clem

The Passion and Grace of
Baseball's Last Hero

Simon & Schuster

ente

David Maraniss

NEW YORK · LONDON · TORONTO · SYDNEY

Insert photos: Neil Leifer: 1; Clemente Family Collection: 2, 3, 6, 7, 8, 9, 10, 11; AP/Wide World Photos: 4, 12, 28, 29; Photo by Sprinker 1960 ©1998 Point Four Sports, A Division of Point Four Ltd.: 5; *El Nuevo Día*: 13, 14, 17, 18, 19, 20, 21, 25; Ramiro Martinez Collection: 15, 22, 23, 30; Dwayne Reider Collection: 16; ©1991 Joel B. Levinson, Pittsburghscape: 24; Michael Pangia Collection: 26; Public Affairs Office, U.S. Southern Command: 27

SIMON & SCHUSTER
Rockefeller Center
1230 Avenue of the Americas
New York, NY 10020

For information about special discounts for bulk purchases,
please contact Simon & Schuster Special Sales at
1-800-456-6798 or business@simonandschuster.com

DESIGNED BY PAUL DIPPOLITO

Manufactured in the United States of America

10 9 8 7 6 5 4 3 2 1

Library of Congress Cataloging-in-Publication Data

Maraniss, David.
    Clemente: the passion and grace of baseball's last hero / David Maraniss.
        p.   cm.
    Includes bibliographical references and index.
        1. Clemente, Roberto, 1934–1972. 2. Baseball player—Puerto Rico—
    Biography. I. Title.

    GV865.C45M355 2006   2006042235
    796.357092—dc22
    [B]
    ISBN-13: 978-0-7432-1781-1
    ISBN-10:   0-7432-1781-0

In memory of Elliott Maraniss,

my wonderful dad,

the sweet-swinging left hander

from Abraham Lincoln High

Contents

Good actions ennoble us,
we are the sons of our own deeds.

—MIGUEL DE CERVANTES

Memory and Myth

THE FAMILIAR SOUNDS OF MODERN BASEBALL, PINGS OF aluminum bats punctuating the steady drone of a crowd, can be heard from the street a half-block away. It is late on a Sunday afternoon in February, overcast and drizzly in Carolina, Puerto Rico. Inside the stadium, there is a game going on, the Escuela de Deportiva against Bayamón. Nothing special, just teenage boys playing ball, the way they do every afternoon, and then the right fielder from Deportiva scoops up a base hit and fires to second, his throw a bullet—low, hard, right on the bag. Groups of men huddle in the stands, talking, laughing, playing cards, barely paying attention, or so it seems until the throw. It elicits a murmur of recognition, and suddenly they come alive, stirred by communal memory. All fires are one fire, the novelist Julio Cortázar once wrote. And all arms are one arm. The throw from right field reminds them of the original, the unsurpassable arm of the man for whom the stadium is named, Roberto Clemente.

Beyond the stadium, closer to the street, stands a cenotaph thirty feet long and seven and a half feet high. It is the nearest thing to a headstone for Carolina's favorite son. On its three panels the sculptor José Buscaglia has etched the stations of the cross of Roberto Clemente's thirty-eight years on this earth. In the far left panel, Roberto is a babe, held in the arms of his mother in the barrio of San Antón, and his father is seen working in the nearby cane fields. In the far right panel, Clemente passes from greatness into legend; first he is being honored for his three-thousandth hit, then his spirit is received by a figure of death in the Atlantic's watery grave, and finally his widow holds the plaque for his induction into the National Baseball Hall of Fame. But the center panel is the most telling. There, between scenes of Clemente batting, running, fielding, throwing, visiting hospitals, and consoling the sick and the poor, he is depicted standing regal and alone, holding a lamb.

1

Memory and myth are entwined in the Clemente story. He has been dead for more than three decades, yet he remains vivid in the sporting consciousness while other athletes come and go, and this despite the fact that he played his entire career in relative obscurity, away from the mythmakers of New York and Los Angeles. Forty public schools, two hospitals, and more than two hundred parks and ballfields bear his name, from Carolina, Puerto Rico, where he was born, to Pittsburgh, Pennsylvania, where he played, to far-off Mannheim, Germany. In the world of memorabilia, the demand for anything Clemente is second only to Mickey Mantle, and far greater than Willie Mays, Hank Aaron, Juan Marichal, or any other black or Latin players. Extraordinary as he was, Clemente was not the greatest who ever played the game, yet there was something about him that elevated him into his own realm. Much of it had to do with the way he died. He was young. He went down in a plane crash. His body was lost to the sea, never found. He was on a mission of mercy, leaving his family on New Year's Eve to come to the aid of strangers. In Spanish, Clemente means merciful. Some of it had to do with the way he looked and played on the ball field, No. 21, perfectly cut in his Pirates uniform, a portrait of solemn beauty, with his defiant jaw and soulful eyes. And much of it had to do with the way he lived. In sainthood, his people put a lamb in his arms, but he was no saint, and certainly not docile. He was agitated, beautiful, sentimental, unsettled, sweet, serious, selfless, haunted, sensitive, contradictory, and intensely proud of everything about his native land, including himself. To borrow the words of the Puerto Rican poet Enrique Zorrilla, what burned in the cheeks of Roberto Clemente was "the fire of dignity."

1

Something That Never Ends

IT WAS LONG PAST MIDNIGHT IN MANAGUA, NICARAGUA,
and Roberto Clemente could not sleep. Not sleeping at night was part
of his routine, the same wherever he went. At his apartment at
Chatham West in Pittsburgh, at his house atop the hill in Río Piedras,
Puerto Rico, on the team plane during late-night cross-country flights,
at road-trip hotels in Chicago, St. Louis, or Cincinnati—at each of
them equally he could not sleep. He might find rest after sunrise,
under the covers, with the air conditioner turned full blast and the
drapes shut and taped tight to the wall so no light could penetrate a
blackened room. Or he might doze off at work after lunch, in some
subterranean chamber of a stadium, dark and cool. In the old days at
Forbes Field, he often slipped away from his teammates before a game
and took a nap inside the vacant clubhouse of the football Steelers.
Left-handed pitcher Juan Pizarro, his countryman and occasional
teammate, found him there once and started calling him Old Sleepy
Head.

The hours from one to five in the morning were another matter.
Sleep rarely came to him then, and if by chance he did drift off, he
might be startled back into consciousness by a nightmare. In one bad
dream that had haunted him recently, he was hiding under a house,
feeling grave danger. In another, he was on a crashing plane. His wife,
Vera, knew all about these recurring nightmares. She knew that he
looked for omens and that he believed he would die young.

On this night, November 15, 1972, Vera was home in Puerto Rico
with their three young boys. She would join Roberto in Managua in a
few days. Until then he was on his own at the Hotel Inter-Continental.

3

His friend, Osvaldo Gil, had the adjacent room, and at Clemente's insistence they kept the doors open between the two so they could come and go like family. Deep into the night, they stayed up talking, Roberto down to his boxer shorts. That was all he would wear in the hotel room, his sculpted mahogany torso at age thirty-eight still evoking a world-class ballet dancer, with muscled shoulders rippling down to a narrow waist, thirty inches, the same measurement he had as a teenager, and powerful wrists, and hands so magical they were said to have eyes at their fingertips.

The two men would be defined by race in the United States, one black and one white, but thought of themselves only as fellow Puerto Ricans. They talked about baseball and their hopes for their team at the twentieth amateur world championships that were to begin in Nicaragua at noon that same day. A lawyer and Korean War veteran, Gil (pronounced "heel") was president of the Puerto Rican amateur baseball federation and had persuaded Clemente to come along and manage the team. Puerto Rico had finished third last time, and Gil thought all they needed was a push to get past the favored teams from Cuba and the United States and perhaps win gold. Clemente might make the difference.

So much had happened since Gil had first caught sight of Clemente more than twenty years earlier. Roberto was still in high school then, starring for the Juncos Mules in the top amateur baseball league in Puerto Rico. Most people who had seen him play carried some deeply ingrained memory, and Gil's went back to the beginning: He sat in the bleachers of the park in Carolina and watched this kid hum a throw from deep center field, the ball seeming to defy physics by picking up speed as it buzzed toward the infield and sailed over the third baseman's head into the stands. Even a wild throw by Roberto Clemente was a memorable work of art.

From there followed eighteen seasons in the big leagues, all with the Pittsburgh Pirates, two World Series championships, four batting titles, an MVP award, twelve Gold Gloves as a right fielder, leading the league in assists five times, and—with a line double into the gap at Three Rivers Stadium in his final at-bat of the 1972 season—exactly three thousand hits. The beautiful fury of Clemente's game had enthralled all of baseball. More than simply another talented athlete, he was an incandescent figure who had willed himself to become a symbol of Puerto Rico and all of Latin America, leading the way for the waves of Spanish-speaking baseball players coming North to the majors. And he was not done yet. At the end of each of the previous two seasons, he had talked of retiring, but he had at least two good years left.

Clemente would not be playing right field for this team. He was in Nicaragua only to manage. During practice sessions in Puerto Rico, he had underscored the distinction by showing up in civilian clothes. The job was not new to him, he had managed the San Juan Senadores in winter ball, but his players then had been professionals, including many major leaguers, and these were young amateurs. It was apparent to Gil that Clemente understood the potential problem. He was so skilled and brought such determination to the game that he might expect the same of everyone, which was unrealistic. Still, he was Roberto Clemente, and who wouldn't want him leading the Puerto Ricans against the rest of the world?

The simple life of a ballplayer is eat, sleep, fool around, play. Many athletes wander through their days unaware of anything else, but Clemente was more than that. He had a restless intelligence and was always thinking about life. He had an answer for everything, his own blend of logic and superstition.

If you want to stay thin, he told Gil, don't drink water until two hours after you eat rice so the food won't expand in your stomach. If you want to keep your hair, don't shower with hot water; why do you think they scald chickens in boiling tubs before plucking feathers at the poultry plant? If you want to break out of a slump, make sure you get at least three swings at the ball every time up. With a total of at least twelve swings in four at-bats a game, all you need is one good one to get a hit. So simple: to break a slump you have to swing at the ball. And it wasn't all body and baseball. Clemente could also talk politics. His sentiments were populist, with the poor. His heroes were Martin Luther King Jr. and Luis Muñoz Marín, the FDR of his island. He lamented the inequitable distribution of wealth and said he did not understand how people could stash millions in banks while others went hungry. The team president had to beg off, exhausted, or the manager would have yakked until dawn.

The next morning before breakfast, there was Clemente in the lobby, enacting his own modest wealth redistribution plan. He had instructed the cafeteria to give him a bagful of coins in exchange for a $20 bill and now was searching out poor people. A short old man carrying a machete reminded him of Don Melchor, his father. A boy without shoes reminded him of Martín el Loco, a character in his hometown of Carolina. When he was home, Clemente looked out for Martín and gave him rides in his Cadillac and tried to buy him shoes, but El Loco was so accustomed to going barefoot that he could not stand to have anything on his feet. Martín the Crazy is not that crazy, Puerto Ricans would sing. Of the needy strangers Clemente now encountered in Managua, he asked, *What's your name? Who do you work for? How many in your family?* Then he handed them coins, two or three or four, until his bag was empty. It became another routine, every morning, like not sleeping at night.

The Inter-Continental, a soulless modern pyramid that rose on a slope above the old Central American city, was enlivened by an unlikely alignment of visitors that week. Not only Clemente and his ballplayers were there but also squads from China and Japan, West Germany and Italy, Brazil and El Salvador, Honduras and Panama, Cuba and Costa Rica, Guatemala and the Dominican Republic, the United States and Canada. Then there was Miss Universe, Kerry Anne Wells of Australia, who won her crown days before at the pageant in Puerto Rico and had been flown across the Caribbean to Nicaragua at the same time as Clemente, creating a stir at Las Mercedes International Airport when the "two people who are news in any part of the world," as a report in *La Prensa* put it, arrived and posed for pictures in the VIP lounge. The photographs showed Clemente wearing a shirt collar the size of pterodactyl wings, while the beauty of Miss Wells, said to "exceed all words," thrilled fans who were "looking at her from head to toe and complimenting her in the most flowery manner"— such a polite description of catcalls. Also in the same hotel then was Howard Hughes, the billionaire recluse who had chosen Managua as his latest obscure hideaway. Hughes occupied the entire seventh floor in a luxury suite, but might as well have been in another solar system. The baseball folks heard that he was around but never caught sight of him. The story was that he sequestered himself in his spooky aerie, drapes drawn, ordering vegetable soup from room service and watching James Bond movies in the nude. No coins for the people from Mr. Hughes.

On the fifteenth, late in the morning, Clemente and his Puerto Rican team left the Inter-Continental for the opening ceremonies at the Estadio Nacional. There was a confection of Olympian extravaganza, baseball delirium, and military pomp, all orchestrated by Nicaragua's strongman, Anastasio Somoza Debayle, whose family owned much of the country and ran its institutions. For the time being, forced by the national constitution to cede the presidency to someone else, at least in title, Somoza controlled the government from his position as supreme commander of the Armed Forces. He also happened to be president of the organizing committee for the baseball tournament, which offered him an opportunity to bask in self-generated glory. *Novedades,* a journal that catered to his interests, declared that General Somoza's presence "gave a formidable support and shine to the event and confirmed the popularity of the leader of the Nicaraguan majority."

Fans more likely were clamoring to see Clemente, and to find out whether the scrappy Nicaraguan team, with the same underdog hopes as the Puerto Ricans, could stay in there with the Cubans, a sporting rivalry intensified by Somoza and Fidel Castro, the yin and yang, right and left, of Latin American dictators. So baseball mad was Managua then that thirty thousand people filed into the stadium and overflow throngs spilled into the streets outside, just to watch the opening ceremonies and a preliminary game between Italy and El Salvador. Black marketers had snatched vast blocks of seats in all sections of the stadium and were scalping them for as much as eighty *córdobas,* nearly triple the established price. Somoza and his wife, Mrs. Hope Portocarrero de Somoza, watched from the presidential box, not far from Miss Universe. A torch was lit, symbolizing the hope that baseball would become an official Olympic sport, then a procession of International Amateur Baseball Federation officials marched in, and gymnasts tumbled and cartwheeled, and beautiful young women in traditional dress pushed wooden carts, and Little Leaguers flooded the field, sixteen teams of nine, each team wearing the uniform of a country in the tournament.

After the visiting Panama National Guard military band played patriotic anthems, Somoza, wearing a light-colored sports suit and Nicaraguan baseball cap, descended from his perch and strutted onto the field. He stepped up to the pitcher's mound at ten minutes of noon. A swarm of reporters, photographers, and television cameramen closed in as *El Comandante* raised high his right hand and swiveled left and right, recognizing the applause. Most of the attention was directed not at him but at home plate, where a right-handed batter had appeared from the dugout, stretching his neck and taking his stance deep in the batter's box. It was Roberto Clemente, in full uniform. Everyone wanted a picture with him. It took fifteen minutes to clear the crowd. Finally, Somoza gripped the hardball and hurled it toward the plate. His house journal called the opening pitch "formidable." A less-flattering account came from Edgard Tijerino, a fearless little sportswriter from Pedro Chamorro's opposition newspaper *La Prensa*. "Obviously," reported Tijerino, "it was a very bad pitch."

Luckily for Somoza, Clemente did not swing. He loved to hit what others would call bad balls—*They're not bad if I hit them,* he would say—and had a habit in batting practice of ripping vicious line drives back through the box.

Clemente took to the people and sights of Nicaragua. He enjoyed strolling past the stalls in the central market and down narrow side streets where he picked out embroidered blouses and dresses for Vera made of the finest cloth. He had the hands of a craftsman and a taste for colorful art. But he never had much luck with baseball in Nicaragua. He had visited Managua once before, in early February 1964, when Nicaragua hosted the Inter-American baseball winter league series. Clemente led the San Juan Senadores, who were stocked with major leaguers, including his friends Orlando Cepeda, the slugging left fielder, José Antonio Pagan at shortstop, and Juan

Pizarro, the left-handed pitcher, but they failed to win the championship, and the lasting memory from that trip was of a fan heaving an iguanalike garrobo lizard from the right-field bleachers and Clemente blanching in fright.

This trip went no better. The Puerto Rican team started with convincing wins over China and Costa Rica, but then struggled the rest of the way, losing to the United States and Cuba and even the Nicaraguans, who prevailed 2–1 in eleven innings, largely on the brilliance of their pitcher, a future major league right-hander named Dennis Martínez. The team wasn't hitting, and Clemente became increasingly frustrated. How could players managed by Roberto Clemente not hit? From the dugout, he noticed a batter in the on-deck circle scanning the stands for beautiful girls. "Forget about the women, look at the pitcher!" he shouted. One of his better hitters struck out and threw his helmet, breaking it. For the rest of the game, Clemente kept pointing to the mound and saying, "There's the pitcher who struck you out—he's the one to be mad at, not your helmet." With outfielder Julio César Roubert slumbering in a zero-for-seventeen slump, Clemente invited him to breakfast at the Inter-Continental to talk hitting.

"Roubert," said the manager, repeating the theory he had presented to Osvaldo Gil late at night, "who do you think has more chances to hit the ball, the batter who takes three swings or the batter who takes one swing?"

"Three," said Roubert.

"Then take three swings!" ordered Clemente.

After the early losses, Clemente kept Gil up to talk about what went wrong and how to fix it. Gil eventually would excuse himself for a few hours' sleep, but Clemente could not rest. He found their driver and paid him to chauffeur him around and around through the dark streets of the city until dawn. That stopped when Vera arrived, but the sleeplessness continued. His longtime friend from Puerto Rico and the big leagues, Victor Pellot Power, known on the mainland as Vic Power, the classy first baseman for the Cleveland Indians from the late 1950s to early 1960s, was brought along to serve as trainer. In Puerto Rico, trainer is a term for an instructor in fundamentals. As the longtime manager of Caguas in the winter league, Power had more experience running a ball club than Clemente. But he had his own troubles in Managua. He had gone to a restaurant for a Nicaraguan *típico* meal, and got a bone stuck in his throat while eating a supposedly boneless fish. The incident prompted two trips to the hospital and a local doctor's suggestion to eat a pound of bananas, none of which helped much. With the disagreeable bone making him queasy, Power could sleep no more than Clemente. Early each morning, suffering together in the lobby, they read newspapers and talked baseball.

Power and Clemente were brothers in many ways. They were charismatic, black, Puerto Rican, from modest backgrounds, talented ballplayers with inimitable style. Power's pendulum swing at the plate, awaiting the pitch, the bat dangling vertically toward the ground, and his cool, jazzy, one-handed flair around first base were as distinctive as Clemente's neck gyrations, basket catches, and looping underhanded tosses back to the infield. Each man had fierce pride, but Clemente's was always on view, burning in his eyes, pounding in his chest, where as Power covered his with smiles, a rumbling laugh, and a signature response in his basso profundo voice to anything life brought his way, "Ohhhh, baby." Power seemed to have an easier time dealing with people, which made him the more comfortable manager. You want everyone to play like you play, Power cautioned Clemente. "To manage baseball, you have to know what you have. How they run, how they hit, what kind of temperament they have. You have to know who is Mickey Mantle, who is Billy Martin"—Mantle's hot-tempered Yankee teammate.

Clemente knew best of all who was not Clemente. One morning, reading *La Prensa,* he was shocked to see a column by Edgard Tijerino describing a throw from the outfield by Cuban Armando Capiró, "which was capable of making Clemente blush." Tijerino suggested a duel of arms between the two. This insulted Clemente, the very notion that anyone, let alone an amateur, might have an arm he would envy. Later that day, at the ballpark, he saw Tijerino before the game and summoned him to the dugout. It was the Nicaraguan sportswriter's first encounter with Clemente, but a scene that would sound familiar to many North American writers who had covered him over the years.

After the Pirates won the World Series in 1971, Clemente declared that the anger he had carried with him was gone at last, cleansed by a series that had allowed him to prove his greatness to the world. But some part of his proud disposition was immutable.

"Hey, why the hell did you compare my arm with Capiró's?" Clemente said urgently, his pain obvious. "I throw to get outs on third from the right-field corner in the huge Pirates stadium, and with Pete Rose sliding in. There is no comparison. You have to be more careful." Tijerino tried to argue, to explain himself, but ended up saying that Clemente was right. That night, when Gil entered Clemente's hotel room, he found him in his boxer shorts, as usual, still angry. Why did you do that? Gil asked. He could not understand why Clemente felt compelled to berate a local sportswriter about something so trivial. "When they say Babe Ruth hit over seven hundred home runs, I keep my mouth shut," Clemente explained, meaning that he was not a home-run slugger. "But when they talk about throwing the ball, I can't keep my mouth shut."

Days later, lobby-sitting with Vic Power early in the morning, Clemente read something else by Tijerino that set him off. The Dominican Republic had defeated Puerto Rico 4–1 the previous day, and in a strained effort to describe the brilliance of the Dominican pitcher, Tijerino had written, "Roberto Rodriguez, on an inspired night, was even en route to striking out the very Roberto Clemente . . ." Tijerino was in the press box that night when his colleague, Tomás Morales, told him to go down to the field because the Puerto Rican manager wanted a word with him.

When Tijerino approached, Clemente rebuked him sternly. "I bat against Roberto Rodriguez with a clean hand," he said. *Mano limpia.* He could hit the kid without a bat.

Tijerino was now "oh for two" with Clemente, but their relationship was not over. Perhaps the only thing that bothered Clemente more than being underestimated or misunderstood was not being given a chance to express himself. He had much to say, and in Nicaragua, Edgard Tijerino was the best means of saying it. One night Clemente invited the writer to his room at the Inter-Continental for a wide-ranging interview, greeting him in white pants and a flowery silk shirt.

Vera was seated nearby. "The dialogue with Roberto was agitated that night," Tijerino said later.

They talked about why the Pirates lost to the Reds in the playoffs that year, after winning the World Series a season earlier, and about which team was better between the two Pirates championship teams of 1960 and 1971. Clemente said the 1972 Pirates actually had more talent than either. Then the subject turned to the treatment of Latin ballplayers. Clemente was done blistering Tijerino for his sloppy comparisons. He had a larger target, the North American press. "I attack it strongly, because since the first Latino arrived in the big leagues he was discriminated against without mercy," Clemente said. "It didn't matter that the Latino ballplayer was good, but for the mere fact of him not being North American he was marginalized . . . They have an open preference for North Americans. Mediocre players receive immense publicity while true stars are not highlighted as they deserve." To make his point, Clemente talked not about his own long fight for recognition, but about Orlando Cepeda, his fellow Puerto Rican, and Juan Marichal, a Dominican, two stars now struggling at the end of their careers, whose flaws seemed more interesting to North American writers than their talents. "No one can show me a better pitcher than Marichal in the last fifty years," Clemente said.

Tijerino was sympathetic to the larger point, but believed objectively that Sandy Koufax was better than Marichal. "Koufax was a five-year pitcher," Clemente responded. "Marichal has a notable regularity. He is a pitcher forever." The problem, he said, was that Marichal would never be measured correctly.

Clemente took everything so seriously and would not give in, Tijerino wrote later. "Conversing with Clemente is something that never ends."

During his travels with the Pirates in the United States, Clemente had developed a routine of visiting sick children in National League cities. The hospital visits were rarely publicized, but ailing kids seemed to know about it everywhere. Before each road trip Clemente sorted his large pile of mail in the clubhouse and made a special stack for letters from children in cities where the Pirates were headed next. One morning in Nicaragua, he brought Osvaldo Gil and a few players along on a visit to El Retiro Hospital. There he met a wheelchair-bound twelve-year-old boy named Julio Parrales, who had lost one leg and mangled another playing on the railroad tracks.

Clemente could seem somber, reserved, cautious about letting strangers close to him, with pride bordering on arrogance. In Puerto Rico, some said he was *orgulloso*, meaning he had oversized pride of self. "Nobody buys Roberto Clemente cheap! I have my pride! I am a hero to my people!" he had harrumphed one midsummer day in 1967 at Shea Stadium as he angrily rejected a film company's offer to pay him a hundred dollars to hit into a triple play for a scene in *The Odd Couple.* But he was also intuitive, looking for connections, and if something touched him, he reacted deeply, immediately, and took you in as part of his family. It didn't matter who you were to the rest of the world—Jewish accountant, Greek pie maker, black postman, shy teenager, barefoot Puerto Rican wanderer—if Clemente saw something, that was that. Family was everything to him. When he saw Julio Parrales he knelt by the wheelchair and said that for the next world tournament Julio would be the team batboy. "Don't worry, we are going to help you," he vowed, and then turned to Gil and said they had to raise the $700 needed to enable Parrales to walk with prosthetic legs. Each player on the Puerto Rican team would end up chipping in $10, the Cubans would donate $50, and Clemente would provide the rest. But before he left the hospital, Clemente said he would see Parrales in the dugout the next time he was in Nicaragua.

The streets of Managua were festive as December arrived, a celebratory spirit intensified by three weeks of good baseball and the approach of the Griteria de Maria festival and Christmas season. The favored Cubans won the tournament, the decisive victory coming in extra innings against the Americans, but their only loss had been to the home Nicaraguans, a glorious upset that led to a wild night of firecrackers, rifle shots, and honking cars in the crowded streets. There was no celebrating for the Puerto Rican team, which finished in the middle of the pack, beating only teams that had no baseball tradition. Gil thought Clemente might be so upset that he would never want to manage again, but it seemed just the opposite. Clemente talked to him about what they had to do better next time, as though it were assumed that he would come back as manager.

Clemente would have to consult his wife about it, no doubt. He talked to her before he did most things, or so it seemed to Gil. "You ask your wife for advice too much," Gil told him one night. Clemente said he relied on her because she was settled, tranquil, even-tempered, and had a better sense than he did about whether people were trustworthy. Anyway, he needled Gil, the comment reflected the sort of stereotypical macho sexism that had held people down throughout history. "The way you think about women is what happened with the major leagues and black players," Clemente said. "They were afraid that if they let black players in, they'd take over. That's the way you are with women."

One day in the old city Clemente visited a luggage shop and bought a new briefcase made of alligator skin. The handle was ghoulish; styled with the head of a baby alligator. Back at the hotel, Vic Power boomed with good-natured laughter at his friend's purchase. Clemente worried that the briefcase looked too feminine and said he would cut off the alligator head. No, Power said, leave it like that. Maybe it would be good luck. A few days later, at Vera's suggestion, the Clementes took a side trip to Granada on Big Lake Nicaragua. When they entered a restaurant in the old colonial town, Roberto encountered another stranger with whom he connected immediately. It was a trained spider monkey who greeted patrons as they walked into the establishment.

"That's the monkey we need," Clemente told Vera. She knew he was serious. Before leaving Río Piedras, he had promised their youngest son, Ricky, that they would come home from Nicaragua with a pet monkey for him. Clemente found the proprietor and said that he wanted the monkey. But the owner was reluctant to part with it. "Anything you want, don't worry about the amount," Clemente insisted. "I need that monkey." The deal was done and he left with a new family member, a primate known thereafter as Teófilo Clemente.

Clemente flew back to Puerto Rico on December 8 bearing so many gifts that he had to call a driver to haul the cache from the airport. The monkey for Ricky, the briefcase with the little alligator head, dresses and blouses for Vera, presents for his parents and his three sons, Robertito, Luisito, and Ricky, and brothers, nieces, nephews, and friends. One of his prized gifts was a red and white hammock that he brought back for Rafael Hernández Colón of the Popular Democratic Party. To Clemente's delight, the young liberal, a protégé of Luis Muñoz Marín, had just been elected governor of the commonwealth. Red and white were the colors of his party, and of the Puerto Rican flag. Clemente had been invited to play a key role in the inaugural ceremonies coming up in a few weeks in Old San Juan, but after much deliberation respectfully declined, following the advice of Osvaldo Gil, who also supported Hernández Colón but said the partisanship might needlessly alienate half of Roberto's baseball fans.

All seemed well back home after that. Vic Power ate a juicy steak, and suddenly the bone problem in his throat disappeared. Clemente loaded his family into the car for a trip to see his parents at the house he bought for them on Calle Nicolas Aguayo in the El Comandante neighborhood of Carolina. All the boys excited, the great ballplayer exuberant, his magical fingers on the steering wheel, a Horner harmonica held by a neck brace humming and wailing at his lips, and the newest member of the family, the tailed one, Teófilo, screeching, dancing to the music, and scampering across the shoulders and legs of the little ones as the gold Cadillac Eldorado rolled down the streets of Roberto Clemente's hometown.

2

Where Momen Came From

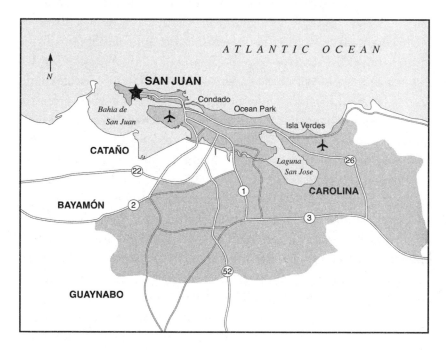

IT HAS RAINED A LOT SINCE THEN, AS THE PROVERB goes. This was the summer of 1934, a time of relentless heat and hardship in Puerto Rico. Twelve miles to the southeast of the capital city of San Juan, in Carolina's rural barrio of San Antón, a large family was about to grow by one. The household of Melchor and Luisa Clemente was crowded enough already. Luisa had two teenage children, Luis and Rosa Oquendo, from a first husband who died and left her widowed at an early age, and she and Melchor had produced four children of their own: Osvaldo, Justino, Andres, and Anairis. Three cousins also stayed with them in the five-room wooden house at kilometer seven on Road 887, and sugarcane workers stopped by every day for meals. With her mother pregnant again, the youngest girl, Anairis, announced that she wanted to have a little brother, but had one other wish. She hoped that he would come out white. On the Saturday afternoon of August 18, the baby was born, and Roberto Clemente Walker was soon presented to Anairis. "Here he is—a little dark."

The story has been told for seven decades, accompanied by laughter. Color of skin is noted in Puerto Rico—there is racism there—but it tends to be hidden and silent, with a history far different from the States. When Roberto was born in Carolina, a U.S. citizen by birthright, no laws on the island prohibited people of different shades from eating at the same restaurant, sleeping in the same hotel, or dating and marrying. Within five years of his birth, after a professional winter baseball league was formed, many talented players from the Negro Leagues, banned from organized ball in the United States, were hired to play for the San Juan Senadores and Santurce Cangrejeros and were hailed as stars by Puerto Ricans of all ages and colors. The elite of San Juan and Ponce tended to be white and boast of Spanish heritage, but being "a little dark" was not disqualifying.

Luisa's family, the Walkers, came from Loiza, the next town east from Carolina and the nave of blackness on the island. Runaway slaves, known as *cimarrones,* hid from the Spanish Army there in the dense, tangled mangrove swamps off the Atlantic coast, and formed their own community. In Puerto Rican folklore, there is a story that when slavery was abolished in 1873, a messenger bringing word to Loiza was killed in front of a big tree, and for years thereafter the tree dropped scraps of paper like leaves, pieces of a puzzle that former slaves tried in vain to fit together to decipher the lost message of freedom. For Luisa, the message could be found in her Baptist religion and favorite hymn, which she taught all her children. *Life is nothing. Life is fleeting. Only God makes man happy.*

Melchor Clemente, already fifty-one when his youngest son was born, grew up in Gurabo, called the city of stairs, in the interior foothills to the south of Carolina. In many ways he was a man of the previous century. Slavery had ended only ten years before his birth.

During his childhood, until he turned fifteen in 1898, Puerto Rico was still under Spanish domain. His relatives were poor farmers and sugarcane workers of black and Taino Indian blood. While Luisa had converted from Catholic to Baptist with her family as a child, Melchor was "not very Catholic," as his son Justino later described him. This meant that he was not particularly religious, though his given name came from the Three Kings, Melchor, Baltazar, and Gaspar, revered in Puerto Rico as magis of the Christmas story. Melchor Clemente's gift was not frankincense, gold, or myrrh, but sugar; he held a job as foreman for the sugarcane processing company, Central Victoria.

Sugar then was nearing the end of a four-century run as the economic mainstay of Puerto Rico. The first sugar mill had been built in 1523, only three decades after Cólumbus reached the island on his second voyage to the New World. More sugar was produced in Puerto Rico in the year of Clemente's birth than ever before, exceeding a million tons, but still the industry was dying. Devastating hurricanes, lower prices from world competition, deplorable working conditions in the fields, and a protectionist U.S. Congress—all were conspiring against it. In an effort to help mainland growers that year, lawmakers in Washington, treating Puerto Rico like a colony it could manipulate at will, passed legislation that set limits on exports, imposed higher taxes, and paid bonuses to landowners not to grow sugarcane. Jobs were still there, but work was seasonal and unpredictable, and most laborers were paid less than full-time scale. One study showed that in 1934 sugarcane cutters, with the most grueling job, averaged $5.76 a week. Foremen brought home twice that amount, but that still left Melchor Clemente little more than a dollar a week for each member of his extended family.

By the standards of Depression-era Carolina, the Clementes were not poor. They had food, shelter, electricity, clothing, and shoes. Rainwater for drinking was collected in a water box on the kitchen roof. Everything plain inside: iron beds, one bathroom, built of concrete; bare white walls, furniture of wood and *pajilla,* rolled corn leaf. Bedrooms overcrowded, some children sleeping in the living room. When they were old enough, ten or twelve, the children earned pennies bringing pails of ice water to workers in the canebrake behind the

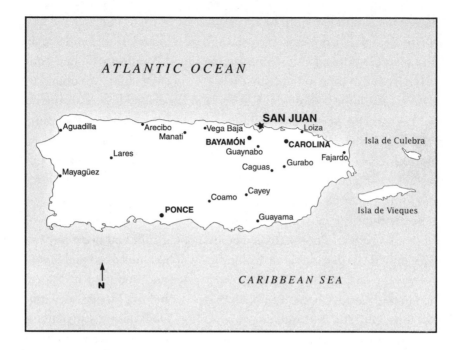

house. Luisa brought in extra money sewing and making lunches for Melchor's workers. A front room in the house served as a neighborhood grocery where they sold rice, eggs, milk, flour, and, on weekends, meat. Luisa was a dignified woman, correct and literate, reading her Bible, always finely dressed, and not bulky, but she had muscular shoulders and arms with which she could lift the carcass of a freshly slaughtered cow from a wheelbarrow and butcher it into cuts of beef. (A powerful right arm was something she passed along to her youngest son. When people later asked about his awe-inspiring throws from right field, he would say, *You should see my mother.* At age eighty, she could still fling a baseball from the mound to home plate.)

Roberto's earliest days were shaded by tragedy. He was still an infant when Anairis died from hideous burns. Luisa Clemente had two cooking stoves at her house, one in the kitchen, for family meals, and a larger one outside on the patio, where she cooked for the sugarcane workers. Known as a *fogón,* the outdoor stove burned firewood inside a pit made of three large rocks. One weekday afternoon, when only the women and children were in the house, Anairis was playing near the *fogón* and a can of gasoline spilled onto the fire and the whoosh of flames flashed onto her silk dress. Luisa took her to the municipal hospital in Carolina and stayed with her day and night. Little Anairis died three days later, burns covering 90 percent of her body. The hospital sent a man out to Central Victoria to give Melchor the sad news. The messenger's name was Flor Zabala, which meant nothing at the time, but later would prove to be a great coincidence. It was the father of Roberto's future wife, a woman he would not meet for another thirty years.

One husband lost, now a daughter. Luisa tried to hide her pain, but sometimes late at night her son Justino saw her crying alone when she thought no one was watching. Roberto was too young to know his sister, but for decades after her death she remained with him. *Here she is,* he would say. *I can feel Anairis at my side.* She was part of the mysticism of his life. Clemente was haunted by fire. He had been too young to help his sister, but years later, when he was twelve, he saved a man who had crashed in Carolina by running across a highway and pulling him from the burning wreckage of his car.

From a young age, Roberto had his own way of doing things. He was pensive, intelligent, and could not be rushed. He wanted to know how and why. His most common phrase was *"momentito, momentito,"* when he was interrupted or asked to do something. Time out. Wait a minute. He said *momentito* so often that Flora, one of the older cousins who often took care of him, shortened it and started calling him "Momen." To his family and Puerto Rican friends, at school and on the ball fields, Momen was his nickname from then on.

The sprawl of metropolitan San Juan eventually would reach Carolina and turn much of it into a noisy jumble of auto shops and storefronts, but it was a very different place, slow and pastoral, during Roberto's childhood in the thirties and forties. The choke of urban life seemed far away. There was an orange grove across the street from the Clemente house, and in the other direction, behind them, a lane led back to vast fields of sugarcane. Road 887 saw little traffic, so quiet that Roberto and his childhood friend Ricardo Vicenti, who lived across the way near the orange trees, spent much of their time playing improvised variations of baseball in the dusty street. Baseball was Roberto's favorite sport, his obsession, from an early age. "When I was a little kid, the only thing I used to do was play ball all the time," Clemente recalled during an interview decades later. "With a paper ball, with a rubber ball, with a tennis ball." Sometimes the ball was a tin can, emptied of beans or tomato sauce, or a lumpy sphere made of string and old rags. Often, they hit fungoes using a broomstick as the bat and a bottle cap as the ball. But it was always baseball. Rosa Semprit, a neighbor who walked by the Clemente house on her way to school, remembered that every time she saw Roberto outside he was throwing something; even if he was alone, he would be tossing a ball against a wall.

There was not that much else for a boy to do in the barrio of San Antón. The beaches of the Atlantic were ten miles north, and El Yunque, the exotic rainforest, stood fifteen miles further east. On a clear day, the breeze carried a scent of saltwater from one direction and the mountains were visible in another, but without a car both were too far away. Many years, the lone trip to the beach as a family came on the Fourth of July, when much of the neighborhood traveled by bus caravan to Isla Verde for the day. For local entertainment, movies were projected onto a wall inside a ranch house down the street. Children attended in packs and sat on hard wooden benches, laughing at grainy movies, a few from Hollywood but most in Spanish and produced in Mexico, black-and-white short films starring the comedian Cantinflas.

The adults walked to work. Melchor was a regular figure along the back roads, a short man with straw hat and machete, trooping miles at a time to the fields to the west or processing plant to the north, occasionally riding an old country mare. In later years, he also carried a .38 revolver and transistor radio wherever he went. Radios were a family trademark. Melchor was a man of habits, like his son. He was said to eat precisely eight hard-boiled eggs a day. He was gone from dawn until after nightfall, so his children did not see much of him, though Roberto, as an adult, spoke nostalgically of family gatherings that included Melchor. He grew up, Clemente once said, "with people who really had to struggle." His mother never went to a show, never learned how to dance. "But even the way we used to live, I was so happy, because my brothers and my father and mother, we used to get together at night and we would sit down and make jokes and eat whatever we have to eat. And this was something that was wonderful to me." His older brother Justino, known to the family as Matino, had one memory less wonderful. His father was loving, but also strict, and punished the boys with a horsewhip. Melchor gave his sons this advice about nonviolence: "Don't hit anyone, but don't let anyone hit you, either. I'd prefer to see you in jail than in a coffin." There was a tradition of dueling in Carolina that stretched back into the nineteenth century and was reflected in one of the town's old nicknames, *El Pueblo de los Tumbabrazos*—the town of those who cut off arms.

The old man knew nothing about baseball. The sport had reached the island from Cuba even before U.S. Marines came ashore in July 1898, but Melchor never had time for it as a young man and had not learned the basics. Once, watching from the stands, he felt sorry for his son for having to run all the way around the bases after hitting a ball while most of the other batters were allowed to return to the bench and sit down after sprinting to first base. But Roberto was not the first or only Clemente to love the game. Matino, who was seven years older, played first base in the top amateur league, a slick fielder and feared line-drive hitter. Roberto admired his older brother, and always insisted that Matino was the best ballplayer in the family but came along too soon, just at the cusp of the segregated era in professional baseball in the States. His career was cut short in any case when he enlisted in the U.S. Army in October 1950 and served three years, including eleven months in Korea with C Company of the 10th Engineers Combat Battalion of the 3rd Infantry Division. Matino was Momen's first baseball instructor, and he maintained that role, offering advice and counsel long after his little brother became a major league star.

Baseball was the dominant sport on the island, followed by boxing, horse racing, track and field, volleyball, and basketball. Soccer, by far the most popular sport elsewhere in Latin America, had not caught on in Puerto Rico, another sign of how it was influenced by the United States. The mainland seemed remote to young Clemente, and baseball there even more unreachable, but he followed winter league baseball in Puerto Rico religiously. In the San Juan area, loyalties were divided between the San Juan Senadores (Senators) and Santurce Cangrejeros (Crabbers), a split that in many ways mirrored the one between the

Yankees and Dodgers in New York. The Cangrejeros were grittier, beloved by cabdrivers, hotel workers, factory hands, and much like the Dodgers, they had a strong black following. Josh Gibson, star of the Negro Leagues, played for Santurce in the early years, followed by Roy Campanella, Ray Dandridge, Willard Brown, and Junior Gilliam, whose range at second prompted Cangrejeros fans to call him the Black Sea. But Clemente grew up rooting for the San Juan Senadores. His loyalties were shaped by his idolizing of Monte Irvin, San Juan's graceful outfielder. Irvin's color kept him out of the majors for most of his career, until 1949, when the Giants brought him up, but he was a star for the Newark Eagles in the Negro Leagues for a decade before that, and tore up the Puerto Rican winter league for several seasons in the mid-forties, when Clemente was eleven to fifteen, formative years for any baseball fan.

The Senadores and Cangrejeros played in the same stadium, Sixto Escobar (named for a bantamweight boxing champ), just off the ocean on Puerta de Tierra, the long finger of land leading to Old San Juan. The way the winter league worked, there were only three games a week, one on Saturday and a doubleheader on Sunday. Irvin said later that he enjoyed playing there because of the beauty of the island, the leisurely schedule, the excitement of the fans, the first-rate competition, and above all, the fact that "we were treated much better there than in the States." If a black American hit an important home run, fans might pass a hat through the stands to collect an impromptu bonus for the player. When they went out to eat in Old San Juan or the restaurant strip in Condado, they were treated as celebrities and offered meals on the house.

When he could, Momen caught the bus from Carolina on weekends to hang out at Sixto Escobar with swarms of other kids. Juan Pizarro, who lived much closer, near Loiza Avenue in Santurce, never had money to get inside, but shimmied up a palm tree to watch the games. Clemente sometimes had a quarter from his father. He used a dime for the bus and fifteen cents for a ticket. His goal was to get there early enough to watch Monte Irvin glide through the throng outside on the way to play. "I never had enough nerve, I didn't want to even look at him straight in the face," Clemente remembered. "But when he passed by I would turn around and look at him because I idolized him." Just by being there, hanging around, as shy as he was, Clemente eventually struck up a friendship with Irvin. And Irvin made sure that his young fan got in to watch the game, even without a ticket. "I used to give him my suit bag to carry into the stadium so he could get in for free," Irvin recalled. From a seat in the bleachers, Clemente studied everything about his hero: how he looked in a uniform, how he walked, how he ran, how he hit, and especially how he threw. More than half a century later, still trim, dignified, white-haired, Irvin could bring back that mentoring relationship in his mind's eye. "Yeah, I taught Roberto how to throw," Irvin said. "Of course, he quickly surpassed me."

By the time he was fifteen, Clemente was starring at shortstop in a softball league on a team sponsored by Sello Rojo, a rice-packaging firm. He was fast, had a gun for an arm, and surprising power for a lanky teenager. Sello Rojo (Red Seal) was coached by Roberto Marín, a rice salesman who became his baseball guardian. By the next year Clemente was also playing hardball, mostly outfield, for the Juncos Mules, a top amateur team in Carolina, and occasionally participated in track and field events at Julio Vizcarrando Coronado High School, running the 440 meters and throwing the javelin. The javelin, though he threw it only a few times, became an iconic symbol in the mythology of Clemente. It represented his heroic nature, since the javelin is associated with Olympian feats. On a more practical level it served to further explain his strong throwing arm.

Marín's former wife, Maria Isabel Cáceres, taught history and physical education at the high school and also watched out for Clemente. Cáceres developed a friendship with her student that deepened over the years, but her early impressions stayed with her. During the first day of class, when she invited students to choose seats, Roberto settled inconspicuously in the back row. He spoke quietly when called upon, not looking up. But "despite his shyness," she later wrote, "and the sadness around his eyes, there was something poignantly appealing about him."

While Cáceres noticed the sadness in Roberto's eyes, Marín focused on his baseball skills. As a bird-dog scout for Santurce, he passed the word to the owner of the Cangrejeros, Pedrin Zorrilla, known affectionately as the Big Crab. Zorrilla had grown up in Manatí, to the west of San Juan, and still spent much time there. He was always on the move around the island, looking for a ball game, searching for talent. In the fall of 1952, Marín told him that the next time the Juncos came to play Manatí, there was a kid that Zorrilla had to look at for his professional club. Zorrilla scribbled the name on a card and stuck it in his pocket. A few days later, he was in the stands watching a game. First he saw a Juncos player smack a line shot against the fence 345 feet away and fly around first and make a perfect slide into second. Later in the game, as he was talking with friends in the stands, he took notice when the same player sprinted back to the fence, grabbed a drive in deep center field, and made a perfect throw to second to double-up a runner.

"That boy, I must have his name," Zorrilla said.

"Roberto Clemente," came the answer.

"Clemente?" Zorrilla fished into his shirt pocket and pulled out the card. It was the name he had written down at Roberto Marín's suggestion.

When the 1952 season began on October 15, the youngest Cangrejero, freshly signed by the Big Crab, was Roberto Clemente, barely eighteen and still in high school. He was signed for $40 a week, and all he had to do was learn how to hit the breaking ball, low and away.

Less than a month later, on the Saturday of November 6, the Brooklyn Dodgers held a tryout at Sixto Escobar. On hand was one of Brooklyn's top scouts, Al Campanis, who was managing the Cienfuegos Elephants in Cuba that winter. Clemente was one of about seventy players at the tryout, and the obvious standout, throwing bullets from center to third and displaying excellent time in the sixty-yard dash. "If the sonofagun can hold a bat in his hands, I'm gonna sign this guy," Campanis said before Clemente stepped into the batter's box. On the mound was one of Zorrilla's crafty old pitchers, Pantalones Santiago. Clemente stroked line drives all over the field. When Campanis filled out the official Brooklyn scouting report, this is how it read:

SCOUT REPORT

Club **SANTURCE**   League   **PORTO RICAN**   Pos. **OF**   Age **18**

Hgt **5'11"** Wgt **175**

Bats **R** Throws **R**

Name   **CLEMENTE ROBERT**

Arm   **A+ GOOD CARRY**   Accuracy **A**

Fielding   **A GOOD AT THIS STAGE**   Reactions **A**

Hitting   **A TURNS HEAD BUT IMPROVING**   Power **A+**

Running Speed **+**   Base Running **A**

Definite Prospect? **YES**   Has Chance? _____   Fill-In? _____   Follow _____

Physical Condition (Build, Size, Agility, etc.)   **WELL BUILT—FAIR SIZE—**

GOOD AGILITY

Remarks: **WILL MATURE INTO BIG MAN.**

ATTENDING HIGH SCHOOL BUT PLAYS WITH

SANTURCE. HAS ALL THE TOOLS AND LIKES TO

PLAY. A REAL GOOD LOOKING PROSPECT! HE HAS

WRITTEN THE COMMISSIONER REQUESTING

PERMISSION TO PLAY ORGANIZED BALL.

Report By:

AL CAMPANIS

Clemente was "the best free agent athlete I've ever seen," Campanis would say later. Baseball was everything to Roberto then, but even though he had asked for permission to play, he was not quite ready to be signed. The phenom was still in high school, though not at Julio Vizcarrando, which would not let him attend school and practice and play for Santurce at the same time. He had transferred to the Instituto Comercial de Puerto Rico in Hato Rey, a neighborhood between his home and the stadium. It would be fifteen months between the time Campanis first scouted him and when Clemente formally signed a contract with a major league organization. By then he had earned his diploma from the technical school, and was doing a little better with the curveball low and away. And he was still only nineteen. Life was all possibilities: the only sadness in his life involved a girlfriend who stopped seeing him because her family thought his skin was too dark.

It was Clemente's way, throughout his life, to pay tribute to those who came before him. Blessings to his parents, he would say, and to his elders, and to his brothers. Along the path he took to northern baseball, several others went before him. The Three Kings, in a sense, were Hiram Bithorn, Luis Olmo, and Vic Power. Bithorn first, Olmo second, and Power down the line but before Clemente, and paving the way for him because of color distinctions that were made in the United States that had no bearing back on the island.

Clemente was seven years old when Hiram Bithorn, a right-handed pitcher, became the first Puerto Rican to play in the major leagues. Bithorn made his first start for the Chicago Cubs on April 21, 1942, against the Pittsburgh Pirates, five years before Jackie Robinson broke the color line. That Bithorn had white skin meant very little to fans in San Juan, where he had played with and against the Americans Josh Gibson, Monte Irvin, and Roy Campanella and the great Puerto Ricans Pedro Cepeda and Poncho Coimbre, all of whom had darker skin. But it meant everything to the men who ran organized baseball in the States. It was the only reason they let him play.

Bithorn was big and burly, a jolly giant and three-sport star in his native Santurce, excelling in basketball and volleyball as well as on the mound. The first story on him in the *Chicago Tribune* called him an "intriguing rookie," noting that his parents came from Denmark and that he liked pie and ice cream for breakfast. The sportswriters of San Juan thought he was "a little, if not wacky, okay, different," according to Eduardo Valero, who covered Bithorn for *El Imparcial.* Valero remembered the time Bithorn emerged from the dugout with an umbrella when the umpires were slow to stop play for rain. Bill Sweeney, who had managed him on the Hollywood Stars in the Coast League before his call-up to the Cubs, said the key to making Bithorn win was to yell at him in Spanish whenever he tried to throw sliders and forkballs. "Tell him to stick the slow stuff in the ashcan and throw like everything. You'll have to holler several times in every game, but he'll win with the high hard one," Sweeney advised. Bithorn's pale appearance did nothing to protect him from ethnic stereotyping. A Chicago writer, making the same point as Sweeney, said the trouble with Bithorn was that "fast pitching apparently doesn't appeal to his conception of Latin cunning." The press Americanized his first name, pronounced ee-rum, to the familiar "Hi."

The Cubs also had a rookie catcher from Cuba that year, Chico Hernández, and together he and Bithorn formed the second all-Latino battery in major league history, a quarter-century after the first pitcher-catcher duo of Cubans Adolpho Luque and Miguel Hernández played for the Boston Braves. At one point during the season, Bithorn and Chico Hernández decided to dispense with hand signs and simply call and receive pitching signs aloud in Spanish, assuming that opposing batters would be none the wiser. That worked fine until the Giants figured it out and sent their bench coach, the same Adolpho Luque, out to the third-base coaching box to intercept the verbal signs; suddenly Giants batters began cracking base hits.

The Cubs manager, Jimmy Wilson, was said to have a "soft spot" for Bithorn, fascinated equally by his attempts at English and his willingness to scrap with Leo Durocher of the Dodgers. During his sophomore season in 1943, the Cubs had more reason to be fond of Bithorn. He developed into a first-rate pitcher, one of the best in the National League. He pitched 249.2 innings that year, won eighteen games, fourth highest in the league, while losing only twelve, had an earned-run average of 2.60, and threw seven complete game shutouts. When the season ended and Bithorn returned to San Juan, he was greeted at the airport with a hero's welcome, paraded through the streets in a convertible, and handed the keys to the city. Then, asked to say a few words, Bithorn balked, explaining that he would rather face Mel Ott. That moment of glory, on the afternoon of October 26, 1943, turned out to be the high point of his career.

One month later, while managing in the winter league for San Juan, Bithorn received a draft notice and decided to enlist in the U.S. Navy. He served not quite two years, and came out a different man. When he arrived back in Chicago for the final weeks of the 1945 season, he was described as out of shape with "a sore arm and an unduly expansive waistline." He also was mentally troubled. His brother, Waldemor Bithorn, said that Hiram had suffered a nervous breakdown. In any case, his skills had vanished, and soon enough his major league career was gone, too. The Cubs cut him in 1946, after which he was picked up and released by the Pittsburgh Pirates and the Chicago White Sox. Bithorn scuffled through the minors, in Oakland and Nashville, and his prospects deteriorated from there. By 1951 he was umpiring in the Class-C Pioneer League on the West Coast, then went south to try a pitching comeback in Mexico.

Four days after Christmas 1951, Bithorn checked into a hotel in El Mante in northeastern Mexico. According to his family, he was on his way south to Mexico City to pick up his mother. The manager of the hotel, W. A. Smith, recalled that Bithorn arrived at three in the morning, and that when he checked out the next day he told Smith that he only had a single dollar. Smith told Bithorn to forget the charge, but instead Bithorn went out on the streets and tried to sell his car. He was stopped for questioning by a local cop, Ambrosio Castillo, who acted as though he were trying to inspect the car's registration but probably wanted to confiscate it for himself. The encounter ended, in any case, in violence. Castillo fired several shots into Bithorn, who was seriously wounded and died after being driven eighty-four miles over rough roads to a hospital in Ciudad Victoria. Doctors there issued a statement saying that he might have lived had he been treated earlier. Castillo claimed that he acted in self-defense, that Bithorn struck him and tried to escape. He also claimed that Bithorn's last words to him, after being shot, were "I am a member of a Communist cell on an important mission!" But Castillo's story eventually collapsed and he was sent to prison on a homicide conviction.

News of Hiram Bithorn's death reached home on New Year's Eve, 1951. December 31 . . . Then and later, in the history of Puerto Rico and baseball, it would be the darkest day. The Mexicans had buried him in an open grave, until Bithorn's family and all of Puerto Rico expressed outrage at his treatment. They had his body exhumed and placed in a double-sealed casket for the trip back to Puerto Rico. Before he was reburied on January 13, 1952, his funeral bier was placed on the field at Sixto Escobar and thousands of fans filed past to pay their last respects, including members of his old team, the San Juan Senadores, who played the rest of the season with black patches on their sleeves. Bithorn had died alone and destitute, an unknown stranger in a strange land, but his forlorn ending was transformed once his body reached Puerto Rican soil. He became a legend, a king in the mythology of baseball on the island—and all who came after him to play in the States, including Roberto Clemente, who began his professional career at Sixto Escobar the same year that Bithorn was buried, knew his story as the first among them.

One year after Bithorn made his debut with the Cubs, Luis Olmo was called up from the Triple-A Montreal Royals to play for the Brooklyn Dodgers. As the second king on the northern pilgrimage, his experiences, too, served as context for the later coming of Clemente. Olmo joined a crowded outfield in Brooklyn, with Augie Galan, Paul Waner, Dixie Walker, Joe Medwick, and Frenchy Bordagaray, but the Puerto Rican's talent won him more and more playing time, until by 1945 he was a team star, batting .313, leading the National League in triples with thirteen, and driving in 110 runs. Like Bithorn, Olmo grew up playing baseball in a place where skin color did not matter. But although he was considered white in the United States, and was allowed to play there before the race barrier was lifted, he was not free from the sting of prejudice. Something strange happened during the 1945 season that he would never forget. As he remembered it sixty years later, he was hitting well over .350 in July, using a heavy black bat. He considered the bat his magic wand, even though it was nothing special. He had bought it at a pharmacy near the apartment that he and his wife, Emma, rented at 55 Ocean Avenue in Brooklyn. One day in the dugout at Ebbets Field, manager Leo Durocher picked up the black bat, said that it was too damn heavy, and broke it in two. Why? Durocher could be volatile but he was far from racist and was obsessed with doing whatever it took to win. Yet in retrospect Olmo could think of only one reason that made sense to him: "They didn't want me to have a good season. They wanted Dixie Walker to beat me out and I was playing more than Dixie Walker."

That was not the first time Olmo felt discriminated against for being

Puerto Rican. In 1942, playing for Richmond in Triple-A, his manager, Ben Chapman, constantly made bed checks but only checked on Olmo. It seemed to Olmo that Chapman was determined to catch him with a woman, though it never happened. When the season was over, even though Olmo led the team in most offensive categories and excelled as an outfielder, Chapman gave the team's most valuable player award to someone else—himself. A few years later, when Jackie Robinson broke the color line and Chapman proved to be among the most virulent racists in major league baseball, Olmo was not surprised.

In a touch of irony, it was Jackie Robinson's benefactor, Branch Rickey, who caused Olmo the most grief after his breakthrough season in 1945. His salary that year was $6,000, and after his stellar play he asked for a $3,000 raise. Rickey, then Brooklyn's general manager, offered him an extra $500, but this was not a raise at all but rather the equivalent of the $500 bonus that had been handed out to every player on the team except Olmo. Take it or leave it, said Rickey, who was known as both the wisest and perhaps the cheapest man in baseball. Olmo left it. He decided to play in a new league that had begun in Mexico in direct competition with the majors. "They were paying good money in Mexico," Olmo recalled. "They paid me $20,000—more than three times as much as Rickey offered."

Induced by the higher salaries, and with no bargaining power of their own in that era, more than two dozen ballplayers left the States to play in Mexico. For their brazen act of independence, they were all suspended from baseball for five years. The winter leagues in Puerto Rico and Cuba had agreements with the majors, so the players were banned from those leagues as well. When the Mexican league folded in 1947, the vagabond players were left to scrounge in Venezuela, Canada, and an alternative league in Cuba. The suspensions were lifted after three years, and Olmo returned to the majors, along with Sal Maglie. He rejoined the Dodgers in time to play in the 1949 World Series against the Yankees, where he became the first Puerto Rican to hit a World Series home run. It came in the ninth inning against Joe Page, and was followed shortly by another homer by the great black catcher, Roy Campanella, his old teammate in San Juan. After the season, Olmo was traded to the Boston Braves. He played two years in

Boston, then one in Triple-A in Milwaukee, and his career in the States was over.

Olmo was hailed as another legend of baseball when he returned to Puerto Rico. He stayed with the game deep into middle age, joining Momen Clemente in the Santurce outfield one winter and also managing several teams and scouting for the Braves, who had moved to Milwaukee in 1953. He was a top-notch scout, bringing the Braves two talented young Puerto Ricans, Juan Pizarro and Felix Mantilla, and just missing on a third, Clemente.

When Puerto Ricans reenact the story of the Three Kings, one king is portrayed with dark skin. In the baseball story, this would be Victor Pellot Power. Seven years older than Clemente, Power signed with a major league club several years before him, and became the first black Puerto Rican to play in the American League. Power grew up in Arecibo, to the west of San Juan, though his family history traces back to slaves on the nearby islands of St. Thomas and St. John. His father, like Melchor Clemente, knew little of baseball and tried to discourage him from playing, but died of tetanus when Victor was thirteen. Three years later, when he was barely sixteen, Power was hailed as a baseball prodigy, playing in the Puerto Rican winter league for the Caguas Criollos, a club that would be his winter home for decades.

His name alone is a lesson in sociology. Pove was his mother's original surname, but during her youth, in the early days of U.S. control, Puerto Rican schoolchildren were taught in English, and a teacher changed the v to a w and added an r at the end and made her name Power. At home, in any case, he would be known as Pellot, since that was his father's surname, just as Roberto Clemente Walker was known as Roberto Clemente, not Roberto Walker. But during his first year north, playing in Canada, Power was introduced at a ballpark in French-speaking Quebec in a way that provoked laughter and some ridicule from the stands. He wondered whether fans were laughing because he was black, until someone told him that his name sounded like something bawdy in French slang—*pelote* means he who paws or pets women. From then on, when not in Puerto Rico, he went by the name Power. It was left to sportswriters to call him Vic, just as many called Roberto Bob or Bobby. And so the creation of Vic Power.

The social transition from Puerto Rico to the mainland was more difficult for Power than it had been for Bithorn or Olmo. "Here we were all together," he reminisced later in San Juan, speaking of people of different colors. "We went to school together. We danced together. A lot of black Puerto Ricans marry white women. When I get there—the States—I don't know what to do." What he did, often, was use humor as a shield to protect himself from deadly serious discrimination. His stories about how he confronted racism in the South have become a part of baseball lore, accurately reflecting social conditions in 1950s America even if some might shade into apocrypha. When a waitress told him that her restaurant did not serve Negroes, Power replied, "That's okay, I don't eat Negroes. I just want some rice and beans." Stopped by a policeman for crossing a street against the "Don't Walk" sign, Power explained that he thought street signs were for whites only, like all the other signs. There was nothing funny about the segregation that forced Power to sleep in a room above a black funeral parlor during spring training in Plant City, Florida, because he was not allowed to stay in the same hotel as his white teammates. But at least in retrospect, he transformed the scene into dark comedy. "People ask me what I learned from that experience and I say two things: that dead people don't snore, and that they don't get out of there. Because I was waiting for them upstairs with a bat, ohhh, baby. In Puerto Rico we believe that dead people might get you. I was a little bit afraid."

Along with Jim Crow segregation in the South, Power dealt with a more subtle form of prejudice during his baseball rise: the subjective standards of the New York Yankees. From 1951 to 1953, playing for Yankee farm clubs in Syracuse and Kansas City, Power was one of the best all-around players in the minor leagues. For two years, he was the lone black player on his team, and for the third he was joined by catcher Elston Howard. But Power was ready for the majors before the Yankees were ready for him. Word was that he was considered too flashy and socially daring to become the first black in pinstripes. Yankee officials were reluctant to call up a player who drove a Cadillac, listened to jazz, dated white women, and was unafraid to show his vibrant personality.

Power was the same man off the field as on. His style at first base was free and easy. He played far from the bag, always got there on time, and snatched the ball into his glove with a one-handed snap. It was a method that he had used effectively since his days in winter ball at Caguas, when his manager, none other than Luis Olmo, suspended him for ten days for refusing to follow instructions and catch with two hands. Olmo eventually relented, and so did all coaches thereafter, but not without some complaints. "They called me a showboat, but it was just the way I did it," Power recalled. "I told them, 'The guys who invented the game, if they wanted you to catch with two hands they would have given you two gloves, and I only had one glove.'" His trademark pendulum swing as he awaited a pitch was also as much about substance as style. "I had a weakness, and the weakness was I cannot hit the inside low ball," he later explained. "Now how am I going to manage that? What I would do was, I would keep the bat there, low and inside, and swing it back and forth, and people would say, be careful, he's a low-ball hitter, and they would pitch me high. Oh, baby. That was psychology."

After a third stellar season in the minors, when Power batted .331 and drove in 109 runs for the top farm club, the Yankees ran out of rationalizations for keeping him in the minors. But they chose instead to promote Elston Howard, reserved and unassuming, more the Yankee style—or at least more of what they seemed to want from a nonwhite player. Although the organization projected a public image of dignity and class, the Yankees of that era had their share of hard-partying roustabouts. With his deadpan sarcastic wit, Power took note of the contradiction: "They say they didn't call me up because I was going out with white women. And I told them, 'Jeez, I didn't know white women were that bad. If I knew that, I wouldn't go out with them.' I told them that they had a ballplayer in the organization, a white ballplayer, who would go out with black women. And they asked me who that guy was. It was Billy Martin. He was white. He was Italian. He was going out with black women. When they ask why I would say that, I say, 'Because I trade two of my black women for one of his white ones.'" On December 16, 1953, before he got a chance to play first base in Yankee Stadium, Power was traded to the Philadelphia Athletics.

Hiram Bithorn was dead by then. Luis Olmo, his major league career over, was back in Puerto Rico and scouting for Milwaukee. The Braves hoped Olmo could help them sign a nineteen-year-old kid from Carolina who was playing outfield for the Santurce Cangrejeros.

Five major league teams expressed some interest in Roberto Clemente: the Braves, Dodgers, Cardinals, Red Sox, and Giants. It was unlikely that Boston really wanted him, considering that they had no black players (and in fact were the last American League team to integrate in 1959 with Pumpsie Green). St. Louis was also an outside possibility, but New York, Brooklyn, and Milwaukee were serious suitors. All had connections. The Braves were represented by Olmo, who would play on the Cangrejeros with Clemente and had been one of the stars of his childhood. The Giants enjoyed a close relationship with Pedrin Zorrilla, the Santurce owner, and their major league roster included Clemente's childhood idol, Monte Irvin, as well as Ruben Gomez, a right-handed pitcher from Puerto Rico. The Dodgers claimed perhaps the closest connection to Santurce—Al Campanis was a frequent visitor to the Zorrilla home—and beyond that they were known in Puerto Rico for fair treatment of black players, many of whom had been playing winter ball on the island. When it came to bidding, the Braves offered Clemente the largest bonus. Most accounts say $25,000 to $35,000, although Olmo later claimed it was even more. But money alone was not enough. "He was very loyal to Pedrin and he wouldn't take it," Olmo recalled. If loyalty was a factor, of equal importance was Clemente's desire to play in New York, where he had friends and relatives in the large Puerto Rican community who could make him feel more at home.

That left the Giants and Dodgers. Any signing over $6,000 would designate Clemente as a bonus player, meaning a team would have to protect him on the major league roster or face losing him in a supplemental draft after his first year in the minors. The Giants, apparently concluding that Clemente needed at least a year of seasoning, kept their offer below the bonus line. Their scout, Tom Sheehan, hoped that Clemente would sign for a $4,000 bonus and begin in Class-A ball in Sioux

City, Iowa. Leo Durocher, the Giants' manager, later rationalized the low bid this way: "We offered him under the $6,000 bonus limit so he could go to the minors and mature there. We tried to do what was best for Clemente, but the Dodgers . . . dangled more money in front of him and you know what a kid his age does when money becomes a factor."

What the Dodgers dangled—a $10,000 bonus and $5,000 first-year salary—was far less than the Braves but enough to close the deal. Clemente wanted to play for the Dodgers. He had no way of knowing that they, on the other hand, had a covert motive in signing him. In their private calculations, even though their scouting reports on Clemente were great, they shared the Giants' assessment that he was not ready for the majors. Their plan was to send him to their top farm club in Montreal. As much as they coveted Clemente, part of their mission was simply to keep him away from the Giants. "We didn't want the Giants to have Willie Mays and Clemente in the same outfield and be the big attraction in New York," Dodgers executive Buzzie Bavasi said later. "It was a cheap deal for us any way you figure it." A cheap deal that was cheapened even more by the racial practices of that era. White bonus babies were being signed for an average of six times as much as their black and Latin counterparts.

On February 19, 1954, with his sons Roberto and Matino (just back from the Army), and Pedrin Zorrilla at his side, Melchor Clemente sent a telegram to Matt Burns, Brooklyn Baseball Club, 215 Montague Street, Brooklyn, New York:

I WILL SIGN A CONTRACT ON BEHALF OF MY SON ROBERTO CLEMENTE FOR THE SEASON 1954 FOR THE SALARY OF $5,000 FOR THE SEASON PLUS A BONUS OF $10,000 PAYABLE ON APPROVAL OF THE PRESIDENT OF THE NATIONAL ASSOCIATION. I WILL SIGN THE CONTRACT WITH THE MONTREAL CLUB OF THE INTERNATIONAL LEAGUE. SIGNED, MELCHOR CLEMENTE, FATHER, ROBERTO CLEMENTE, SON

One week later the signing was made public in a UP wire service report: "The Montreal Royals have signed Roberto Clemente, a Negro bonus player from Puerto Rico, General Manager Guy Moreau said today." Clemente would play center field for the Royals, the report added, "if Sandy Amoros, the league's leading hitter in 1953, moves up to the Dodgers." But more than the telegram or the public announcement, the true marker of Clemente's new status came when Hillerich & Bradsby, makers of Louisville Slugger bats for organized baseball, took note of the bonus baby and contacted him about his equipment needs.

His first bats were variations of a Stan Musial model, classified at headquarters in Louisville as M-117. The signature engraved on them read *Momen Clemente.*

3
Dream of Deeds

BEFORE MOMEN LEFT HOME TO PLAY BASEBALL IN THE
North, Melchor presented him with a going-away gift. It was a fine
brimmed hat, and the son thanked his father for it, not having the
stomach to say that he hated gentlemen's hats. His older brothers
Andres and Matino knew how he felt and teased him about the hat as
they drove him to the airport in San Juan, where he would catch a
flight to Florida, the first stop on his baseball migration. As they were
making their way from Carolina to the airfield, Roberto fidgeted with
the hat and then flung it out an open window. His brothers were
shocked. Even knowing how much he disliked it, they asked him why
he threw it away instead of just giving it to someone who needed it.
This was not like him; he was not wasteful or thoughtless. Roberto
explained that he did not want to get in trouble with his father. "Just
imagine that I become famous and the person that I give the hat to
tells everybody that it was my hat," he said. "Father will kill me." And
that is how he left the island: hatless, thinking of fame.

It is hard to imagine a more dazzling debut than his first game a few
weeks later as a Brooklyn Dodgers farmhand. CLEMENTE PACES ROY-
ALS TO WIN ran the headline after the opening day of spring training
for the Montreal Royals of the Triple-A International League. The wire
service account from Vero Beach on April 1, 1954, described Clemente
as an "18-year-old Puerto Rican bonus baby"—close, he was nineteen—and noted that along with two singles he pulled off one of the
rarest and most stirring feats in baseball, hitting and running his way to
an inside-the-park home run. From the box score in the *Montreal
Gazette,* the numbers indicated that he batted fifth, went three for four,

drove in two runs, made one outfield putout, was the only Royals starter to play nine innings, and moved defensively from center to left late in the 12–2 rout of the Civilians.

The opposing team, comprised of ex-servicemen awaiting assignments to Dodger farm clubs, was certainly below International League caliber. And this was, after all, April Fool's Day. How else to explain that Clemente's auspicious opener was less a foreshadowing of things to come that year than a cruel bit of false hope? Only three more times all season would he be featured in headlines or photographs of Royals games, and one of those was a picture of him twisting his ankle. He was treated more like baby than bonus, protected from the world, often hidden away in the dugout. Eight years earlier, Jackie Robinson had joined these same Royals in Montreal on his path to Brooklyn, and his every move was analyzed and recorded by the sporting press as he changed baseball forever. Clemente's coming was virtually ignored. His manager, Max Macon, assessed the team and its shortcomings almost daily in public, complaining about the first baseman's inept fielding, the overall lack of power, his hopes that the big club would send down some real talent, but he was mum on the potential of Clemente.

Momen was the youngest player on the Royals. He was the only Puerto Rican, and at season's start one of two blacks and two Spanish speakers. The other was Chico Fernández, a twenty-two-year-old shortstop from Havana. On top of that, during spring training in Florida, he found himself, for the first time, dealing with Jim Crow segregation whenever he left Dodgertown, where he was given a room and three meals a day. Even within the Vero Beach compound, he noticed how the black service workers were boarded onto buses and driven out of Dodgertown before sundown. Separated from the warm fold of his family in Carolina, Clemente felt isolated in an alien and at times malignant environment, a condition that accentuated his shyness. On the playing field, given a chance, he was daring, fierce, memorable, but now on most days he was tucked away, and what people saw was more like the reticent youngster with sadness around the eyes who sat in the back of Mrs. Cáceres's room, looking down, on the first day of history class.

*　　*　　*

The International Baseball League lived up to its name in 1954. Unlike the major league World Series, limited to one country in the world, this league was undeniably international. "There's never been such a league as this one," declared the writer Tom Meany in *Collier's* after spending the early part of the season traveling with the Royals and some of the other clubs. "All a ballplayer needs to get by in the International League is the ability to hit the curveball and to go without sleep. It also helps if he has a smattering of Spanish, a soupcon of French, a fondness for plane rides and the digestive processes of an anaconda." The eight teams included three in Canada: Montreal, the Ottawa Athletics, and the Jack Kent Cooke–owned Toronto Maple Leafs; as well as the Rochester Red Wings, Syracuse Chiefs, and Buffalo Bison of New York State, and two expansion franchises brought in that season, the Richmond Virginians and Havana Sugar Kings. The inclusion of a team from Cuba, where baseball was as much a national pastime as it claimed to be in the States, created a buzz in sporting circles, with some writers looking toward the day when Havana would field a team in the majors. Although that day did not come, the presence of the Sugar Kings in the International League served as an early landmark in the Latinization of North American baseball, a trend that would become more pronounced decade by decade for the rest of the twentieth century.

To call the IBL a minor league was somewhat misleading. It had been around for seventy-one seasons, going back to 1884, making it far older than the American League, which was established in 1900. And its talent pool, at a time when blacks and Latins were starting to get a chance, and when there were still only sixteen major league teams, was far deeper than minor leagues of later decades. The Toronto Maple Leafs alone boasted a roster that included twenty-two players with major league experience. Each of the eight teams had perhaps seven or eight players who would have been in the majors had they come up during the expansion era a generation later. The International League clubs had their own traditions and identities quite apart from their distant overlords. They played a schedule of 154 games, equal to the majors, and according to league secretary Harry Simmons, traveled by air 75 percent of the time. They even made personnel moves on their own now and then, but they were not independent. The daily reminder of that was the Montreal uniform, with the club name scrawled across the front in the cursive Dodger blue. The team's condition was still determined in large part by the decisions of Walter O'Malley, the Dodgers owner, and his baseball men in Brooklyn.

One of those men had just been promoted from Montreal after leading the Royals to the 1953 Little World Series championship. Walter Alston was now the rookie manager of the Dodgers. His third baseman, Don Hoak, also made the jump to Brooklyn, along with outfielder Sandy Amoros, who led the International League in hitting the previous year with a prodigious .353 average. Amoros, a Cuban, had continued his hot hitting with the Dodgers all spring, catching the attention of New York sportswriters. Dan Parker of the *New York Mirror* altered the pronunciation of his last name, moving the accent from the first syllable to the second (claiming "Poetic license No. 345-B") to make it fit a parody of "That's Amore." *"He's a new Brooklyn star and he's gonna go far, that's Amoros! For the latest of Bums fans are beating their gums, that's Amoros!"*

The one person not beating his gums happened to matter most—manager Alston. Dink Carroll, a columnist for the *Montreal Gazette,* astutely noted that "Wally Alston isn't particularly strong for Amoros, for one reason or another." The reason, Carroll suspected, was that Alston thought he saw a fatal flaw in his hitting star during the 1953 season with the Royals: when he got knocked down by opposing pitchers, he seemed to back off the plate and was afraid of the ball the rest of the game. This led Carroll to conclude that no matter how well Amoros played, he would be back in Montreal soon, which was just what Royals fans selfishly wanted.

Amoros was still in Brooklyn when the Royals, after a week of sloppy play and rain on the road, held their home opener against Syracuse on the last day of April at their bandbox stadium, Delormier Downs. It was a balmy spring day, with fans on the first-base side luxuriating in the afternoon sunshine. Montreal's mayor, Camillien Houde, threw out the first ball, and the Fusiliers de Montreal played the anthems, and the largest crowd at a home opener since 1946 (Jackie Robinson's brilliant debut) settled in for the game. The previous day's paper had not listed Clemente in the projected starting lineup, but there he was, wearing No. 5, trotting out to center field. This was the Vero Beach opener revisited—Clemente at his best in an 8–7 Royals win. He batted fifth, went three for four, drove in a run, executed a pivotal sacrifice bunt to set up the winning run in the tenth, and "made some sparkling catches in centre-field," reported Lou Miller, the *Gazette* writer.

After the first four games, Clemente was leading the team in batting, going four for eight. Then he disappeared again. Amoros was shipped down from Brooklyn, just as Dink Carroll had predicted, and Gino Cimoli arrived in a trade with the Cardinals organization, and veterans Dick Whitman and Jack Dempsey Cassini elbowed for playing time—and suddenly the outfield was loaded and Clemente became the odd man out. There was talk then and later about the racial politics of the situation. Some have asserted that the reason the Dodgers refused to protect Clemente, the bonus baby, by keeping him on the major league club all year, was that the team already had reached its limit of black players. The Dodgers had Jackie Robinson, Roy Campanella, and Junior Gilliam starting in the field, and Don Newcombe and Joe Black on the mound. There was a large dose of truth to the suspicion that unstated quotas existed then, but another baseball reality had a bearing on the story. Sandy Amoros, the black Cuban, was indisputably ahead of Clemente on the Brooklyn ladder after his outstanding year in Triple-A ball. It was Amoros, more than Clemente, who suffered because of the implicit quota, since he was more likely to be the fourth black in the Dodgers lineup. The first injustice was his demotion, and from there followed the outfield shuffling in Montreal that made less room for Clemente.

The reasons Clemente would not get much playing time in Montreal were also a mix of baseball practicality on the field level and duplicity from above. Who knows how much he would have played had he been white and not a bonus baby? If they were not huge talents, Whitman and Cassini were seasoned vets with a little major league experience. Whitman, then thirty-three, had played for the Dodgers after the war, and spent four years with the 83rd Infantry Division, winning a Bronze Star and Purple Heart in the Battle of the

Bulge. Nothing in the International League scared him. Cimoli could get hot for a few days and carry the club. Montreal had a first-place tradition, an expectation of success, and even if the Royals were a minor league team, winning was at least equal in priority to the development of raw prospects.

Any urge the Brooklyn organization felt to develop Clemente was overtaken by two seemingly contradictory notions that nonetheless each worked against the young bonus baby. The Dodgers wanted to hide him, but they also sensed that hiding him was impossible and whatever they did with him would only be to the benefit of some other team that drafted him. Their reasoning was illogical, their actions halfhearted, but the orders were to play him only occasionally. Max Macon, the manager, denied that he was being told whom to play, but few took that claim at face value. Glenn Cox, a pitcher on the team, said players always know about other players, and it was obvious to all of them that Clemente was something special and deserved more time. "Macon had orders, and that was that," said Bob Watt, who served as road secretary for the Royals. "Whenever we'd spot a scout in the stands, that would be the end of Clemente for that day. He never had the chance to show what he could do." The thinking in Brooklyn, Buzzie Bavasi acknowledged later, went like this: "Since we were going to lose him anyhow in the draft, why should we spend so much time developing him for somebody else? We used other players and Clemente went in only on defense in the late innings or played sparingly."

Clemente and Chico Fernández, the Cuban shortstop, lived in a rooming house a few blocks down Delormier Avenue from the stadium, the same place where Walter Alston had stayed the year before. Neither of them had a car, but they could walk to work, and got around town on the streetcar that ran up and down the avenue. Their rooms were in the French half of town, and the widow who ran the house spoke neither Spanish nor English. Her daughter was just starting to learn English and knew less than Clemente, who had studied English in high school but rarely used it in Puerto Rico. He could understand the language better than he spoke it. Fernández had picked up enough English phrases during his two years playing ball in the States to serve as a go-between. When Amoros joined them in May, the job more than doubled. Amoros barely tried to speak or understand English. If Max Macon, who knew a bit of Spanish from playing one year in the Cuban winter league, had something important to convey to Amoros, he went through his shortstop, as did the sportswriters. "Helluva ballplayer," Fernández recalled of Amoros. "But he didn't care that much" about communicating.

The rooming house offered beds but no meals. From the time they awoke, the players were on their own for food. Every morning, they ended up at the same breakfast joint, and ordered the same meal. Ham and eggs, said Fernández. Ham and eggs, echoed Clemente. If there were Cuban or Mexican restaurants in Montreal, they never found them. Now and then they made it downtown to clubs. On any scale measuring racial tolerance, Montreal in 1954 was closer to Puerto Rico than to Florida. With its cosmopolitan reputation, it had been the logical choice as the city where Jackie Robinson would break organized baseball's color line. But it was by no means free from prejudice. Clemente made friends with a young French-Canadian woman and left tickets for her to come to a game, but didn't leave them under his name because he wasn't sure how she would be treated. After the game, when they were talking outside the stadium, an older woman criticized them for socializing. During Clemente's first month in Montreal, several stories in the *Gazette* documented the frustrations of Charles Higgins, a thirty-one-year-old bricklayer, father of three, and World War II veteran of the Canadian Army, who was denied housing by forty landlords because he was black.

Fernández had been around the cities of North America before, but for Clemente everything on the road was new. Old hotels, food, accents, what people laughed at, or took offense at, the awkwardness of being separated from teammates to sleep on the other side of town in Richmond. At the Powers Hotel in Rochester, Clemente approached the traveling secretary in the lobby and softly asked for a loan. *Why do you need money?* Bob Watt asked. Clemente said he wanted to buy a shaver, a Remington electric. Watt teased him, but gave him the money. *Shy kid,* Watt thought. *Quiet. Never bothered anyone.*

For the most part, Clemente and Fernández were achingly lonesome for home, wherever they were: for chicken and plantains and black beans and sofrito and spiced pork, but only one of them was frustrated. Fernández was playing shortstop every day, making the plays. "Max was crazy about me," he said of the manager, who had coached him in Miami two years earlier. If Macon was crazy about Clemente, he never showed it. Not playing and not earning praise were as new to him as the language and the setting. "He was good, but, like me, desperate to play," Fernández said later. "And since he didn't play, he was real upset about it. It is lonely. When you are in some place for six months and not playing, that is bad. And he wasn't playing."

At night, Clemente would pour out his frustrations. It seemed that whenever he got a chance and played well, Macon benched him. Once they pinch hit for him with the bases loaded in the first inning. He got so disgusted he threw a bat onto the field. Fernández tried to explain. First of all, he said, there were so many good players in the Brooklyn system that it was hard for everyone. Rocky Nelson, Norm Larker, Jim Gentile, they all had been stacking up at first base because the Dodgers had Gil Hodges. At short, Fernández knew he had Pee Wee Reese blocking the way, and there was this phenom Don Zimmer out in St. Paul. *Same way in the outfield, Momen,* he said. And it was obvious that someone in Brooklyn didn't want him to play. *Max has gotta do what the big club tells him.* Clemente talked about going back to Puerto Rico. Fernández said it would be a big mistake. Neither of them could sleep much. They were both consumed by baseball. If Fernández wasn't hitting, his mind raced with worries about his slump. If he was hitting, he stayed awake yearning for his next time at bat. In his mind's eye, he practiced swinging from his new stance, over and over, the low crouch he had developed during the winter in Cuba. Clemente just wanted to get in the lineup.

After a mediocre first month, the Royals started to look formidable again by late May. A full complement of veterans bolstered the lineup, led at the plate by Amoros and slugger Rocky Nelson, who had been dropped by the Cleveland Indians. Delormier Downs, with its short porch in right, was made for the stocky left-handed slugger, who had cracked a record thirty-four homers in 1953. To strengthen the pitching staff, Ed Roebuck and Tom Lasorda had been sent down from Brooklyn, and Joe Black, struggling with the Dodgers, was also on his way. Lasorda had lost his spot on the big club when the Dodgers activated another bonus baby who, unlike Clemente, they kept on the twenty-five-man major league roster and did not try to hide in Canada. He was a left-handed pitcher named Sandy Koufax. Clemente was the team ghost, so deep in the dugout that he couldn't even get in a good scrap when the Sugar Kings arrived in Montreal for their first five-game visit.

Havana was stocked with Cuban players and managed by the Cuban Regie Otero. They had a fine time during the series razzing the two Cubans on the Royals, Fernández and Amoros, who played with many of them back home during the winter. A constant stream of profanity flew back and forth in Spanish, all of it beyond the comprehension of the International League umpires. Midway through the game on Thursday, May 27, Amoros was at the plate and made a half-swing at a pitch, which the umpire called a ball. Otero rushed from his dugout, furious, claiming that Amoros had gone around far enough for a swinging strike. After what was described as a "far from complimentary" exchange of suggestions between the batter and opposing manager, tempers remained edgy the rest of the game.

When it was over, according to Dink Carroll's reconstruction of the confrontation in his *Gazette* column, the Sugar Kings had to walk through the Royals dugout on their way to the clubhouse. As Mike Guerra, Havana's catcher, passed the Royals, he noticed that Macon and Rocky Nelson were standing sentinel in front of Amoros.

"What are you doing, trying to protect him?" Guerra asked.

"Why don't you mind your own business," Macon responded.

Guerra answered with a kick to Macon's shins.

Macon smacked Guerra in the nose, and they wrestled until they were separated. Later, as the Sugar Kings were loading for the trip back to their hotel, Guerra and manager Otero stood outside the bus, waiting to confront Macon again, but he slipped out a stadium door.

Ten days later, the Royals undertook their first trip to Havana. As part of the agreement that Sugar Kings owner Roberto Maduro had struck to gain his franchise, the seven other teams paid their own way to Richmond, the league's southernmost city on the mainland, and the Sugar Kings subsidized their flights from there. The schedule was drawn so that teams played a series against the Virginians on the way to Cuba. Late on the Saturday night of June 5, tired and famished, the Royals caught a bus from Parker Field out to the airport in Richmond. Frustrated to discover that the airport restaurant was already closed, Macon divided the team into two groups to scrounge for food at nearby roadside diners. But the four Royals with dark skin, Clemente, Amoros, Fernández, and Joe Black (he had joined the team that week), were denied service at the diners, so Macon picked up sandwiches and milk for them. After several delays, the charter flight left for Miami at 1:45 in the morning. It landed at dawn, and there was another three-hour delay before the fifty-eight-minute skip to Rancho Boyeros airport in Havana. When Clemente and his exhausted teammates slogged to the registration desk at the Hotel Nacional at 9:30, Macon informed them that they had three hours to rest before the bus left for the stadium and a Sunday doubleheader. Not that it mattered much to Clemente. He couldn't sleep anyway, and he was unlikely to play.

"They'll be calling us the Montreal Somnambulists," said Dixie Howell, the Royals veteran catcher and coach. Somehow, the zombies from the North managed a split, winning the second game behind the two-hit pitching of Joe Black. Amoros, Cimoli, Whitman, and Cassini shared outfield duties, and the bonus baby never got off the bench. The crowd at Gran Stadium was large and buoyant: twenty thousand fans whistling, jeering the umpires, chanting "Sol! Sol! Sol! Sol! Baby!" to the insistent rhythm of conga drums and marimbas. In the press box, writers sipped espresso cups of Cuban coffee and downed bottles of "one-eyed Indian" (Hatuey) beer as they looked down on the field and beyond to the old city washed in faded yellow and ivory. Nothing unusual for Clemente and the Latin players, or for Anglo teammates who had played in the winter leagues. Tommy Lasorda, a born ham, would even delight the crowd by doing a little wriggle to the rhythm before he went into his windup on the mound. But for those experiencing baseball in the Caribbean for the first time, it all seemed exotic and a bit dangerous, reinforcing stereotypes. "The Cuban fan is a complete extrovert and does everything but get right into the ball game,"

Dink Carroll observed after his first day at the park. "After watching them for a while, it's easy to believe a paragraph we read in a local publication: 'In Cuba people talk about two things: politics and baseball. These are passionate topics leading often to violent discussions.'"

Butch Bouchard, a former Canadiens hockey player and Montreal restaurateur who came South with the team for a vacation, joked that if Cubans got into hockey "There'd be nobody alive when the game ended."

When Mickey McGowan, a writer for the *Montreal Star,* noticed a stirring in the crowd after a loudspeaker announcement, he blurted out, "What is it? A call for the militia?"

Collier's Tom Meany had to explain that it was merely notice of a gift giveaway for kids who attended the doubleheader the following Sunday.

Walter O'Malley, the Dodgers' owner, was also on the scene. After taking in Joe Black's impressive performance, he skipped the rest of the games to go deep-sea fishing in the Gulf with Bud Holman, his pal from Eastern Airlines. Not a bad place to hang out for a few days. The Hotel Nacional, sitting on a hill overlooking the blue-green Caribbean, was all comfort and ease, the good life, with two swimming pools, sweet flowering bushes, a putting green, high-ceilinged rooms with fans and air-conditioning, rum, beer, and beautiful women. One night, after the game, Rocky Nelson strolled through the lobby chomping a Cuban cigar, rounding up teammates for poker. They hooked Max Macon and drained his wallet until he was almost broke. According to Glenn Cox, the manager pushed back from his seat at the table, held up his last $10 bill, shouted "You guys aren't gonna get this!" and went over to the bathroom and flushed it down the toilet. Then he said: *No more high-stakes poker on the road.*

Havana was not home for Momen, but it was close enough. There was even a Morro Castle, jutting into the sea, a fortress much like El Morro at the tip of Old San Juan. Clemente made friends with the jack-of-all-trades for the Sugar Kings (publicist, radio announcer, promotions director, and road secretary), the gregarious Ramiro Martínez. It was Martínez who branded the logo for the Sugar Kings, a cartoon character shaped like a baseball named Beisbolito. He also came up with the idea of publicizing the new team by flying a plane over Havana and dropping thousands of matchbook sewing kits that featured Beisbolito on the cover. Years later, after Fidel Castro took power in Cuba and the baseball franchise fled to New Jersey, Martínez would settle in Puerto Rico and remain close to Clemente, whom he called "the top personality I ever met in my life." At first, he knew him only as a talented, lonely young man. The highlight of the trip for Clemente came when Chico Fernández picked him up at the hotel and drove him over to the Fernández house: the big family, the teasing and laughing, the mother making a home-cooked meal—it reminded him of Carolina.

In the six-game series, the Royals won three, lost two, and tied one. The final game was scoreless in the tenth inning when they had to call it so the Royals could catch their plane back to Montreal. Joe Black had pitched nine more shutout innings. Over the entire series, Clemente never played. Too many scouts in Havana was the word.

Scouts and baseball officials were always roaming the International League circuit. A week after the Royals returned home from Havana, Dodgers personnel man Andy High visited Montreal to assess the talent. Rumors were going around that another organization had offered the Dodgers $150,000 for Amoros. "It isn't hard to believe," High told the Montreal press. The baseball men in Brooklyn hadn't given up on Amoros, he insisted. They didn't think he was much of a fielder, and his arm was weak, but he sure could hit the ball hard. It took Duke Snider a few times to make the big club, too, High pointed out.

The writers asked him about Don Hoak, the former Royal who was starting at third for the Dodgers in place of the injured Billy Cox. High had nothing but praise. "Hoak is a dynamic type of player," he said, and would stay in the lineup as long as he was hitting. They also loved the way he charged slow-hit grounders and fielded them with his "meat hand." Still, Cox remained the best-fielding third baseman in the league, even if he was colorless and backed up on hard-hit ground balls.

What about Chico Fernández? Would he ever hit big-league pitching?

"Chico doesn't have to hit too much," High said. "I guess you've noticed that he's changed his stance this year. He's crouching. That's something he developed in the winter league in Cuba. I remember I was watching him with Fresco Thompson this spring training in Vero Beach. The first time he came to the plate and went into that crouch, Fresco said, 'Ho, ho, take a look at this! We've got a new hitter.' But he makes some great plays in the field. We don't teach young ball players to go after a ball with one hand; they do that by themselves. But they're apt to make those seemingly impossible plays because they practice that way."

There was more talk about Don Zimmer and Moose Moryn, Dodgers prospects in St. Paul. Not a word about Roberto Clemente. Better not to put his name in the papers.

A month later, after a long road trip, the Royals came back to town and found Dodgers front-office men Buzzie Bavasi and Al Campanis waiting for them. During the final road stop in Toronto, Max Macon had been kicked out of a game for the third time that year, and was about to be suspended and fined for almost coming to blows with home-plate umpire Carlisle Burch. But Bavasi and Campanis had other concerns. The Dodgers were going nowhere, lost in the whirlwind of Willie Mays and his Giants. Tommy Lasorda had just been recalled to help the pitching, and they were looking again at Joe Black. They were also worried about the frustrations of their Latin players. Amoros was discouraged. Fernández wondered whether he would ever get a chance. And Clemente wanted to go home.

It was Campanis who had first seen his uncommon talent during that tryout at Sixto Escobar two years earlier and had stamped Clemente for greatness. How could he be great if he didn't play? *Don't leave*, Campanis urged him. *Trust us. You'll get your chance.* The next night, in a mess of a game that the Royals lost 22–4, Clemente was inserted into the lineup in the second inning, replacing Whitman, and got two hits in three at-bats. He played some more during that series against the Maple Leafs, but then, with Bavasi and Campanis gone, it was back to the bench.

The effort to hide Clemente from the world, or more specifically from the last place Pittsburgh Pirates, who would have the first selection in the supplemental draft at season's end, was ineffective. Branch Rickey, who ran the Dodgers organization for most of the 1940s, had moved on to Pittsburgh at the start of the fifties, where he had struggled to lift a pathetic Pirates club out of the National League cellar. Although there had been no notable success at the big-league level to show for it, Rickey was starting to accumulate talent, with the help of two superb scouts who had come with him from Brooklyn, Clyde Sukeforth and Howie Haak. They were opposites in personality: Sukeforth a modest, efficient, polite New Englander, Haak (pronounced Hake) a prodigiously profane baseball addict who chewed tobacco from the moment he got up and could keep a wad going in his mouth while eating scrambled eggs. But they were two of the best talent evaluators in the game. With Rickey's intimate knowledge of the Dodgers and their system, and with his scouts at his call to go wherever he needed them, there was no way a prospect like Roberto Clemente, dangling out there, ready to be drafted at the end of the year, was going to escape their notice. At various times during the summer, Rickey dispatched Sukeforth and then Haak out to report on Montreal's bonus baby.

As Sukeforth later told the story, he checked on the Royals during a series against Richmond. Just observing Clemente in outfield practice, when he unloosed one stunning throw after another, and at the plate during batting practice, when he kept drilling shots back through the box, was enough. It hardly mattered that Macon kept Clemente on the bench.

Before he left town, Sukeforth approached the Montreal manager and said, "Take care of our boy!"

"You're kidding. You don't want that kid," Macon answered.

"Now, Max. I've known you for a good many years," the scout said, softly chiding Macon. "We're a cinch to finish last and get first draft choice. Don't let our boy get in trouble."

Not long thereafter, Rickey sent Haak up to Montreal to double-check. Haak, with his belly paunch, slicked-back gray hair, and pants that constantly drooped down a flat rear, drove to Montreal nonstop in his beat-up old car with a spittoon next to the driver's seat. He would drive anywhere to see anyone, and was known for being able to size up a player in a minute or two, thumbs-up or thumbs-down. As Haak later recounted the scene in writer Kevin Kerrane's delicious book of interviews with baseball scouts, *Dollar Sign on the Muscle*, Rickey instructed him to watch the Royals without specifically stating what player to scout. "I knew who it was, though. Another Pirate scout [Sukeforth] had already been up to Montreal and he'd raved to me about this kid the Dodgers had hid out there. . . . When I walked into the Montreal clubhouse, I said hello to Max Macon, the manager, and he said, 'You son of a bitch, what're you doing here?' I said, 'I came to talk to you.' He said, 'You're fulla shit. You're here to look at Clemente. Well, you aren't going to see him play!'"

Macon kept Clemente in the dugout again, but Haak outmaneuvered him. He met Clemente after the game and found the young outfielder in a perplexed mood, steamed again about being consigned to the bench. With that psychological opening, Haak told Clemente that he should bleeping stay where he bleeping was and keep bleeping quiet, because the bleeping Pirates bleeping wanted him. The Dodgers might not bleeping appreciate him, Haak said, but Mr. Rickey and the Pirates sure as bleeping did. And if they drafted him, he'd be playing in bleeping Forbes Field next bleeping year.

For a few weeks after Haak's visit, Clemente found more playing time in left, center, and right. On August 14, his picture made the papers, but not the way he would have wished. The photograph showed No. 5 being lifted to a stretcher and carried off the field after he twisted his ankle stepping in a hole near the pitcher's mound as he ran in from left at the end of the sixth inning. It turned out to be a minor sprain, and he was eager to show his manager that he could run without trouble. Two days later, on the road, he was back in the starting lineup, and his throwing arm was the headline after a game against the Maple Leafs: CLEMENTE'S TOSS HELPS ROYALS DEFEAT TORONTO. Here was the true harbinger of things to come, the thrill of a pure Clemente moment. He was playing right field that night, where he belonged. Bottom of the ninth, two out, Toronto's Connie Johnson on second base, Ed Stevens raps a single to right, Clemente charges hard (he said he was always blessed with the ability to run fast in a crouching position), scoops the ball on the run, and catapults himself into the air as he unleashes a perfect overhand peg to the plate. Game over.

At year's end, his statistics were meager. Games Played: 87. At-bats: 148. Home Runs: 2. RBI: 12. Batting Average: .257. But all the numbers said less than that single throw from right ending an otherwise routine game in the middle of August.

Clemente played on several winning baseball teams during his career, but none with more appeal than the team he joined when he came back to Puerto Rico after that frustrating 1954 season in Montreal. Even the batboy on that year's winter league edition of the Santurce Cangrejeros had enormous talent. He was a gangly, bowlegged teenager named Orlando Cepeda, son of the legendary Pedro Cepeda. Orlando, known later as the Baby Bull, would go on to a Hall of Fame career himself, but now he was just glad to be rubbing shoulders with his elders. During practice every morning at Sixto Escobar, when the Santurce outfielders practiced charging the ball and throwing it in, Cepeda stationed himself near the pitcher's mound to take their throws. Who was out there throwing to him? Fifty years later, in a deadpan voice, he brought back the names. "Oh, couple guys. Willie Mays in center and Roberto Clemente in left or right."

Mays and Clemente, side by side, roaming the same outfield. That possibility was what drove the Dodgers to sign Clemente in the first place, at least in part—to keep him away from Mays and the New York Giants. But it was no problem in Puerto Rico, no nightmare for the Dodgers, only a baseball fan's delight. Clemente was all fire when he got home, not so much rusty from disuse in Montreal as raging to play and to overcome the injustice of his lost, lonely season. If Mays drew most of the attention, Clemente would make it impossible for people not to notice that he was out there, too.

This marked Santurce's seventeenth season, and for Pedrin Zorrilla, the founder and owner, in many ways it was the culmination of a life's work. Pedrin was the son of a poet, the impassioned romantic Enrique Zorrilla of Manatí, who loved his country and its people.

Foreigners: make space
Because here, the Puerto Rican troubadour
Will sing with noble valor
Land, blood, name and race.

But he had no time for baseball and wanted his son to have nothing to do with it, either. The old poet even sent Pedrin off to boarding school in the States with the intent of keeping him away from the dissolute life of an athlete, but it was of no use. Manatí was a place for intellectuals, proud of its reputation as the Athens of Puerto Rico. People there lived for their *juegos florales,* poetry pageants. But when Pedrin had his own Dream of Deeds (the title of his father's most famous poem), he dreamed only of baseball. He started the Cangrejeros with no money, rounded up a first team that included many of his friends, and from there built a dynasty.

Over the years, Zorrilla had lured many great players from the North, but none with the major league glamour of Willie Mays, who less than a month before his arrival had led the New York Giants to victory in the World Series against the Cleveland Indians—and had imprinted his image into the American sporting consciousness forever with his dashing over-the-head catch of Vic Wertz's drive into deepest center field. In baseball-mad San Juan, Mays was embraced joyously. More than a thousand fans waited in the rain on the gray Saturday morning of October 16 when he arrived at Isla Grande airport, many disbelieving that he was coming, and once he truly arrived, uncertain that he would stay. They quickly took up chants of his trademark greeting, "Say, Hey!" and developed their own Spanish variation, "Ole, Mira!" Like Clemente in Montreal, Mays felt lonesome in San Juan, hating the empty feeling of returning to his spare apartment near the stadium. But he was not among strangers. The manager, Herman Franks, was the third-base coach for the Giants. Santurce's star pitcher, Puerto Rican Ruben Gomez, was also a Giants teammate, and several American blacks on the team—pitcher Sam Jones, outfielder Bob Thurman, and third baseman Buster Clarkson—knew Mays from the barnstorming circuit.

Clemente admired Mays, but did not worship him. He preferred the other black Giants outfielder, Monte Irvin, his childhood hero. Some observers would later assume that Clemente learned his basket catch from Mays when they played together that winter. Not so. Clemente had been making basket catches, with the web facing up instead of forward, since his softball days, a style common among Puerto Rican outfielders. Luis Olmo was making basket catches years before Mays came along. Olmo held his basket near his naval; Mays at his hips, and Clemente drooped the glove even lower. On days when Olmo started for the Cangrejeros that winter, they had perhaps baseball's one and only all-basket outfield. Pete Burnside, a pitcher on the team, later told baseball historian Thomas E. Van Hyning that he sensed "a friendly rivalry" between Mays and Clemente, who were "trying to outdo each other on the field." Mays and Gomez, the Giants teammates, also had a bit of a rivalry, apparently, and got into a fairly heated shoving match one day during practice, an incident that Zorrilla desperately tried to downplay for fear that apoplectic Giants officials might spirit Mays off the island before he got injured.

At eleven on the Monday morning of November 22, while the front-running Cangrejeros were practicing on an off-day in Puerto Rico, representatives of the sixteen major league teams gathered in Room 135 of the Biltmore Hotel in New York for what was known formally as the Major-Minor League Rule 5 Selection Meeting. This was the draft of minor league players who had not been protected by the big clubs. The order of selection for two rounds ran from worst record to best, starting with the worst team in the National League, the Pittsburgh Pirates, and ending with the best team in the American League, the Cleveland Indians. Branch Rickey's son, Branch Rickey Jr., a club vice president, was there representing the Pirates. He carried in his briefcase scouting reports from Sukeforth and Haak, as well as detailed instructions from his father.

Ford Frick, commissioner of baseball, began the proceedings and called on the Pirates for their selection. What was described as "a gasp of surprise" swept through the room when Rickey Jr. announced the first choice: Roberto Clemente. It might have been a surprise to major league sportswriters, who knew nothing about him and quickly looked up his modest statistics in Montreal, but it was an obvious choice to baseball men in the room. Many of them acknowledged afterward that the young Puerto Rican was the top name on their lists. It is always interesting, in retrospect, to examine a group of names from the past, at a moment of hope and promise, and see if any survived the fate of athletic oblivion. The other ballplayers picked that day included Mickey Grasso, Art Ceccarelli, Parke Carroll, Bob Spicer, Jim King, Vicente Amor, Glenn Gorbous, Jerry Dean, John Robert Kline, Joe Trimble, Roberto Vargas, and Ben Flowers. Some of them can be found in the Baseball Encyclopedia. And then there was Clemente, who came to the Pirates for a mere $4,000 drafting fee. "He can run and throw—and we think he can hit," Rickey Jr. told the press.

Herman Franks's lineup card for Santurce was packed with five fearsome hitters: Mays, Clemente, Thurman (known as "Big Swish"), Clarkson (team RBI leader with sixty-one), and George Crowe (first baseman who would make it to the majors in 1956)—a group that came to be called "The Panic Squad." He also had scrappy young Don Zimmer at shortstop, Valmy Thomas and Harry Chiti behind the plate, and aging local stars Olmo and Pepe Lucas St. Clair coming off the bench. "I always said that was the greatest winter league team ever assembled," Zimmer recalled a half-century later. "Can you imagine Mays, Clemente, and Thurman in the outfield? And Orlando Cepeda just hanging around, a big kid stumbling all over himself because he was growing so fast." As they ran away with the winter league pennant, Mays, with a .395 average, was the most valuable player and star, but Clemente shone nearly as bright. He hit .344 and led the league in hits (ninety-four) and runs scored (sixty-five). The Crabbers ended the season in mid-February by winning the Caribbean World Series, which was held that year in Caracas. Zimmer, Mays, and Clemente were the stars in Venezuela, with Clemente rapping two triples, his specialty, and scoring eight runs, including one dash from first to home on a single by Mays to win the fifth game. Zorrilla, the Big Crab, said the fury and pride with which Clemente ran the bases was something that he would never forget.

In the end, it was not the stirring Caribbean series that Clemente would remember from that winter, but another series of events that occurred earlier, on the last two days of 1954. On the weekend after Christmas, Santurce was playing three games down in Ponce, over the mountains on the southern coast. When the road trip was over, because of a family emergency, Roberto did not take the team bus home but instead drove back with his brothers, Andres and Matino. Their oldest sibling, Luis Oquendo, Luisa's firstborn, a school teacher then thirty-eight, for months had been suffering from terrible headaches, occasional seizures, and sudden loss of sight. After several examinations, doctors diagnosed a brain tumor, uncertain whether it was malignant. On December 30, a Sunday, they operated on his brain. His brothers were still in Ponce. With Momen at the wheel, driving the 1954 blue Pontiac he had bought with his bonus money, they sped north to see Luis as soon as the game was over. At eleven at night, as they were driving through the dark mountain streets of Caguas just past the Gautier Benitez School, another car barreled through the intersection from the side, running a red light, and smashed into them. Andres and Matino were unhurt. Roberto wrenched his neck and spine, but insisted that he did not need treatment. The car was dented in the front but still drivable, and soon they were back on the road.

When they reached Doctor's Hospital in Santurce, the news was bleak. Luis's tumor was malignant and advanced. He was conscious but groggy when his brothers entered the room. Momen flicked on the lights, but Luis said he wanted it dark. He died the next day, at noon. The date was December 31.

4

The Residue of Design

RIDICULING THE PITTSBURGH PIRATES WAS ONE OF THE simple pleasures of the national pastime in the first half of the 1950s. *The Boy Buffoons of Baseball, Life* magazine called them. "The atrocities they committed under the guise of major league baseball were monstrous," wrote Marshall Smith. "Pirate pitchers threw the ball in the general direction of home plate and ducked. Pirate batters missed signs as blithely as they missed baseballs. Pirate fielding was so graceful that the team gave the opposition four or five outs per inning. Sportswriters accused Pirates of running the bases with their heads tucked under their arms." When the club's top minor league manager wanted to scare one of his underachieving players, he threatened to send him up to Pittsburgh. The Pirates were bound for the cellar every year; the only tension came with guessing how many games back they might finish. In 1952 when they were accused of fielding a team of midgets, infielders so short that balls bounded over them for doubles, they ended up fifty-four and a half games behind the Brooklyn Dodgers. All of this was overseen by Pittsburgh's esteemed general manager, Branch Rickey.

In Pittsburgh, some skeptics said, Wesley Branch Rickey finally met his match—or worse, let the game pass him by. For more than four decades, since he had graduated from Michigan Law and got into baseball management, Rickey, an erudite Presbyterian from Lucasville, Ohio, had been regarded as the one true genius of the sport. Red Smith, the New York sportswriter, called him "a giant among pygmies." Before coming over to run the hapless Pirates in 1950, at the seasoned age of sixty-nine, he had built two of the century's dominant

National League clubs, first the Gas House Gang in St. Louis, and next what would become the Boys of Summer in Brooklyn. His place in history was assured by a single bold act, breaking the color line with the signing of Jackie Robinson, but there was far more to him than that. It was as a measure of respect that he became known as the Mahatma. He was cool and manipulative in his transactions, meticulous with his records, formal and pompous in his speech, stingy with his money, always curious and innovative, brutally sharp in his assessments, and interested equally in a player's psychological disposition and his ability to learn an elusive hook slide.

All events in Mr. Rickey's world could be studied, categorized, and explained. Good things did not fall upon people, or baseball clubs, by accident. He was a man of sayings, and his most famous phrase came at the end of this thought: "Things worthwhile generally don't just happen. Luck is a fact, but should not be a factor. Good luck is what is left over after intelligence and effort have combined at their best. Negligence or indifference or inattention are usually reviewed from an unlucky seat. The law of cause and effect and causality both work the same with inexorable exactitudes. *Luck is the residue of design.*"

And what was his design for the Pirates? "The Pittsburgh club was in last place on merit and not by mishap or circumstance," Rickey said when he took over, and when they got better it would not be through luck. He doubled the number of minor league affiliates and started stocking them with young players, underscoring his belief that, in baseball, the surest way to get quality was through quantity. He spent what to him seemed like a huge sum ($900,000) on prospects, most of whom flopped. He worked to rid the team of popular players who in his opinion could never take the Pirates to a championship, Ralph Kiner prime among them. Kiner, the slow-footed slugger who won four straight home-run titles, was not only beloved in Pittsburgh but was also a duck-hunting companion of the owner, John Galbreath. But Rickey was so determined to trade him that he wrote Galbreath an eight-page, single-spaced letter on March 25, 1952, enunciating "twenty-four reasons why Ralph Kiner was useless to the Pittsburgh Pirates." Within a year, Kiner was a Cub. And with his sharp-eyed talent men, scout Haak and coach Sukeforth, Rickey plucked young players from other clubs, none more important, in the long run, than the twenty-year-old outfielder, Roberto Clemente.

In the mythology that later enveloped the Clemente story, there is a commonly recounted scene of Rickey blessing him at the dawn of his career. It supposedly took place in the winter league in Puerto Rico in 1953. According to the story, first told by San Juan sportswriters and repeated through the years, Rickey caught sight of Clemente at a Santurce game, was stunned by his skills, called him over to talk, asked him a few questions, and ended the conversation by telling the young man to find a girl and settle down to the business of baseball because he was destined to be a superstar. But Rickey was an inveterate memo-keeper; his dictated observations and handwritten notes were typed out by his personal secretary, Ken Blackburn, after virtually every game that he attended. And the documents point to another less-glowing account.

With aide-de-camp Blackburn at his side, Rickey flew south in January 1955 for a scouting swing through Cuba and Puerto Rico (which in Blackburn's transcriptions was often spelled the way Rickey said it, Puerto *Rica*). In Cuba, on January 18 and 19, Rickey watched two games between Havana and Cienfuegos. His notes show that he was impressed with young players in the St. Louis Cardinals chain, especially Don Blasingame (" . . . a pest at the plate. He should become a good base on balls man, and his power is ample. He is no puny in any respect.") and Ken Boyer. ("I saw the best ballplayer on first impression that I have seen in many a day. Boyer by name . . . Never loafs. Has big hands and knows what to do with them . . . He is a line drive hitter deluxe. The newspapermen down here are raving about the outfielder Bill Virdon, saying, in effect, unanimously, that Virdon is the greatest player ever to be in Cuba etc. etc. I will take Boyer.") With those three players coming up, Rickey concluded, all the Cardinals needed was a top-flight pitcher to contend against the Dodgers, Giants, and Braves.

The next week he was in San Juan, taking in a game at Sixto Escobar between Santurce and Ponce. He kept his own scorecard and dictated his game notes to Blackburn, though he complained that he was "disturbed by dignitaries so much during the game" that his notes were not as sharp as normal. "The Ponce team is managed by Joe Schultz Jr. and Santurce by Herman Franks—both really two kids who came up with me," Rickey began his Memorandum of Game. Schultz and Franks were both old catchers who had played for the Cardinals. "I have had interviews with both boys, and Schultz is to have breakfast with me in the morning."

Then, one by one, Rickey analyzed all the players he had seen on both teams. His comments on the Cangrejeros were often blistering. Luis Olmo, he observed, "pinch hit for Lopez and looked lazy, overweight, indifferent, helpless." (It is well to remember that Rickey and Olmo had a falling out back in the mid-forties, when Olmo, insulted by Rickey's salary offer after his best season with the Dodgers, bolted to an upstart Mexican League.) Willie Mays did not play that day, resting for the winter league playoffs, which were to begin in a few days. Rickey's most in-depth assessment was done on the young man who moved over from left to center, Roberto Clemente. He must have begged dignitaries away whenever Clemente was in action.

Two months earlier, the Pirates had made Clemente the first overall selection in the Rule 5 draft. He was Pittsburgh property, and bound by rule to stay with the big club in 1955. From the content of Rickey's notes, it appears that this was the first time he had seen Clemente play. The language does not correspond to the legend of Rickey observing Clemente in 1953 and telling him that he was destined for superstardom. He saw a few things he loved in the young player, but more flaws. The memo began:

> I would guess him to be at least 6' tall, weight about 175 pounds, right hand hitter, very young. I have been told very often about his running speed. I was sorely disappointed with it. His running form is bad, definitely bad, and based upon what I saw tonight, he had only a bit above average major league running speed. He has a beautiful throwing arm. He throws the ball down and it really goes places. However, he runs with the ball every time he makes a throw and that's bad.

Rickey had his own scouting vocabulary. One of his favorite baseball words was adventure. In this regard, by his standards, Clemente was no Willie Mays.

He has no adventure whatever on the bases, takes a comparatively small lead, and doesn't have in mind, apparently, getting a break. I can imagine that he has never stolen a base in his life with his skill or cleverness. I can guess that if it was done, it was because he was pushed off.

Later, Rickey thought he saw that same timidity in the field:

> The most disappointing feature about Clemente is his lack of adventure—of chance taking. He had at least two chances tonight to make a good play. He simply waited for the bounce. I hope he looks better to me tomorrow night when Santurce plays San Juan—the final game of the regular season and the city championship of San Juan is at stake. Perhaps this boy will put out in that game.

When Clemente was hitting, Rickey found more to like. With the cool detachment of a cattle appraiser, he reported:

> His form at the plate is perfect. The bat is out and back and in good position to give him power. There is not the slightest hitch or movement in his hands or arms and the big end of the bat is completely quiet when the ball leaves the pitcher's hand. His sweep is level—very level. His stride is short and his stance is good to start with and he finishes good with his body. I know of no reason why he should not become a very fine hitter. I would not class him, however, as even a prospective home run hitter.

From his observations in San Juan, Rickey reached a disappointing conclusion. He believed that the bonus baby he had swiped from the Dodgers was not ready for the big time:

> I do not believe he can possibly do a major league club any good in 1955. It is just too bad that he could not have had his first year in Class B or C league and then this year he might have profited greatly with a second year as a regular say in Class A. In 1956 he

can be sent out on option by Pittsburgh only by first securing waivers, and waivers likely cannot be secured. So, we are stuck with him—stuck indeed, until such time as he can really help a major league club.

There are several things to keep in mind when reading that critical assessment of Clemente made a few months before the first game of his major league career. First, though Rickey was astute, he made mistakes. Three years before he compiled his report on Clemente, he had observed a Pirate minor league pitcher named Ron Necciai and declared: "There have only been two young pitchers I was certain were destined for greatness, simply because they had the meanest fastball a batter can face. One of those boys was Dizzy Dean. The other is Ron Necciai." All baseball lovers know Dizzy Dean. Necciai won exactly one game in the major leagues. Second, despite those rare raves, Rickey tended to look for a player's faults, and was merciless in doing so. Of Tony Bartirome, a prospect in 1955, he wrote: "A puny hitter. He never will go major." (Perhaps Rickey had forgotten, but he had called up the 5'9" Bartirome briefly to start 135 games at first base in 1952 as part of the midget infield.) A pitching prospect named Jackie Brown was lucky not to see Rickey's private assessment of him: "Brown was born prematurely, and has never caught up. I don't think he ever has a thought. He has never related an incident in his life, never told a story in his life, never had a belly laugh in his life. He would be incapable of comprehension to so deep a point." Could Rickey be any crueler? Yes. In another report he noted that Brown "is also afflicted with rectal warts."

It also must be said that Rickey's scouting report on Clemente was not completely inaccurate. Clemente did have an odd running style, and looked a bit faster than he really was. While he never stole many bases, though, he was regarded as a smart base runner and thrilled fans with his dashes from first to third and second to home. The prediction that he would become "a very fine hitter" turned out to be a severe understatement. As to power, Rickey was at least half right. Clemente never was a big home-run hitter, though on occasion he could hit mammoth shots, and he frequently drove the ball deep into the gaps for doubles and triples. Based on Clemente's statistics in 1955 and the next few years, Rickey's assessment that he needed a few more years of seasoning was within the realm of debate. But where Rickey was most mistaken was in his conclusion that Clemente's game lacked adventure. It was true that he did not steal many bases, but to think of him as timid was wildly off the mark. Clemente in the field, sprinting in and sliding across the grass to make a catch; on the base paths, legs flying, arms pumping furiously as he ran out every ground ball or raced from first to third; at the plate, daring a pitcher to get it by him no matter where he threw it—everything about his play evoked a sense of adventure. An essential fact of which Rickey seemed unaware when he wrote the scouting report is that Clemente had been in a car accident less than a month earlier and was suffering from neck and back troubles that would plague him off and on for the rest of his life.

On his way back to Pittsburgh from the Caribbean scouting mission, Rickey stopped in Fort Myers, a city on the Florida Gulf Coast that was preparing a new training camp for his Pittsburgh club. The Pirates had been spring vagabonds in the years of Rickey's reign, moving from San Bernardino in 1952 to Havana in 1953 to Fort Pierce in 1954, but now they were ready to settle down. The Fort Myers Chamber of Commerce had recruited them with a sweet offer. Here was a new stadium and clubhouse at Terry Park, constructed with $80,000 in city and county funds. Here was a guarantee from local businessmen of two thousand Grapefruit League season tickets worth $30,000. Here was a fleet of new Pontiacs from baseball booster Al Gallman, a local car dealer, for the use of club officials. Town leaders would even send several hundred citizens up to Pittsburgh for Fort Myers Day during the regular season and fill the Forbes Field outfield with a tractor-trailer's worth of free coconuts. It might seem like small stuff compared with the desperate inducements Florida towns would throw at major league teams decades later, but it was enough to get the job done in 1955. The only possible drawback Pirates officials could think of was that there was no top-flight racetrack nearby for the thoroughbred horses of Mr. Galbreath.

Rickey arrived at Terry Park on the morning of January 29 to find another baseball legend waiting for him. "God bless you, Connie," he said in greeting. "I'm sure glad to see you." It was Connie Mack Sr., who had managed the Philadelphia Athletics for half a century, from 1901 to 1950, and was now ninety-two. The Athletics had trained in Fort Myers in the late 1920s, and Mack still spent the winters there with his son. He was perhaps the only person alive who knew more baseball than Branch Rickey, and he had come out to the park to show his compatriot around. Together the Mahatma and the Tall Tactician, with a hundred years of baseball experience between them, but both dressed like bankers, inspected the clubhouse, the infield, and the fences (set deep, 360 down the lines and 415 in center to give the feel of spacious Forbes Field up North). Rickey was impressed by the smoothness of the infield dirt and the luxurious green outfield, and decided that the team should stay off the main diamond and play only on the practice field for a few weeks, at least until owner Galbreath arrived. The clubhouse met his exacting standards. He said it was better than most clubhouses in the majors, and he was especially satisfied with the color choice for the shower room, a shade of light green that he considered good for morale.

After the brief tour, the two venerable baseball hands sat in the sun and talked. Len Harsh, the young sports editor of the local paper, the Fort Myers *News-Press*, stood nearby, awed by the great men, and eavesdropped on their conversation. Rickey and Mack chatted like old codgers who had seen it all. Who lost more stock in the Wall Street crash of 1929. The peaks and valleys of their careers. Mack had ended his baseball years in a valley, a long string of losing seasons for his once champion Athletics, and now Rickey was hoping to avoid the same fate. As the conversation ended, he invited Mack to throw out the first pitch at the preseason opener, then left to go deep sea fishing with a local doctor. He would return to snowy Pittsburgh for ten days to get the team's affairs in order before flying South again to the sunshine and the start of camp.

The sportswriters who covered the Pirates were waiting for Rickey when he got back to Pittsburgh. They were hungry for news about his scouting trip, especially his assessment of the young Pirate who was tearing up the winter league for Santurce. Was Clemente really that good? asked Jack Hernon of the *Pittsburgh Post-Gazette*. Without going into the precise critical analysis of his scouting report, Rickey put the best light on it while saying that he was not sure. "The boy is a great prospect, just as I was told. But you must remember he is only twenty years old and had almost no competition last season at Montreal. He is a big boy. He can run, throw, and hit. He needs much polishing because he is a rough diamond. He might go to town, but you can't tell. He might (make it) but he'll have his hands full." Hernon wrote up the story for his paper and the *Sporting News* before leaving for Fort Myers with his writing brethren, Al Abrams, the *Post-Gazette* sports editor, Les Biederman of the *Press*, and Chilly Doyle of the *Sun-Telegraph*. None of the old boys would be Roberto men, as it turned out, and Hernon least of all.

Clemente reached Fort Myers on the last day of February, fresh from his star turn with Willie Mays in the Caribbean series. Even though he was a rookie, he reported with the other veterans because his spot on the roster was assured by his Rule 5 draft status. This was his second preseason in segregated Florida, but in many ways it proved more difficult for him than his first camp at Dodgertown.

There was no dormitory housing for the team, and while the white players were put up at the Bradford Hotel downtown, Clemente and other black prospects were shuttled off to board in private homes in the historically black Dunbar Heights neighborhood across the railroad tracks on the east side of town. Dunbar was its own world, and though some back streets were unpaved and strewn with shacks that lacked indoor plumbing and electricity, there was also a bustling black merchant class along Anderson Avenue, where residents shopped at B&B grocery, ate at Clinton's Café, and took in movies at the King Theater. Many of the residential streets in Dunbar Heights were named for citrus fruits. Clemente found a room at the home of Etta Power, widow of Charley Power, who lived on Lime Street. Lime and the next street over, Orange, were alive with children who tagged after Clemente whenever he was in the neighborhood. Jim Crow segregation was everywhere: in the schools, gas stations, hotels, restaurants. The white players and their families relaxed at beaches and pools where black teammates could not go. There was a golf outing at Fort Myers Country Club—Bob Rice, the traveling secretary, nearly got a hole-in-one on the water hole—but Clemente and the black Pirates were not allowed to play. There was a designated "colored night" at the Lee County Fair when white residents stayed away.

If blacks wanted to watch the Pirates, they were penned in their own pavilion section of the bleachers at Terry Park. The bathrooms and water fountains at the ballpark were labeled *Whites* and *Colored.*

Before the first intrasquad game on March 2, Branch Rickey, wearing his signature polka-dot bow tie and straw hat, delivered a long lecture to the players. He told them about what would be expected of them in training camp, and his aspirations for the season, and then briefly discussed the realities of race in Fort Myers. This was the South, he told them. They were all Pittsburgh Pirates, but upon leaving the confines of the field, conditions were beyond the team's control. God knows it was damnably wrong, he said, but so it was. There would be no trouble here. The ladies and gentlemen of Fort Myers were peaceful citizens. Then Rickey left the clubhouse and walked over to the box seats, which were only folding chairs, and took his place in the front row amid a lineup of luminaries that included Connie Mack Sr., owner Galbreath, and Benjamin F. Fairless, the soon-to-be-retired president of United States Steel.

Far to the side, in a section cordoned off for customers who did not have white skin, Pat McCutcheon, the No. 1 baseball fan on Orange Street in Dunbar Heights, found a seat in the bleachers and began urging the team on with his foghorn voice. As it turned out, most of the cheering that day, black and white, was for Clemente. In the sixth, he fired a throw to third that would have nailed a runner if only the third baseman had been ready. Then in the seventh he made two consecutive shoestring catches, the first on a dead run, the second while sliding gracefully to his right, and two thousand fans roared and rose for a standing ovation as Clemente galloped to the dugout after the third out. "The sight of him in spring training encouraged all of us," said Bob Friend, the pitcher. "After all the lean years, to have a player of that talent on our team was pretty heady stuff."

Beautiful weather, buoyant crowds, good play—it all seemed so free and easy, but of course it was not. Fort Myers in the mid-fifties might have seemed serene to the businessmen who ran it and to the visiting sportswriters from Pittsburgh ("a beautiful little Florida town," Al Abrams wrote), but to young Clemente the prevailing culture was an affront. At home in Puerto Rico, his family seldom talked about race. It was not an issue when he played baseball in the winter league, but here it was unavoidable. Three memories from that first Fort Myers spring stayed with him. He remembered the subdued behavior of black players who feared they might be cut or sent to the minors for the smallest act of asserting themselves. He remembered the way blacks were kept on the bus whenever the team stopped to eat on the road. And he remembered, or thought he remembered, a derogatory description of him that appeared in the local paper. Years later, in a reflective interview with Sam Nover, a Pittsburgh broadcaster he trusted, Clemente said: "When I started playing in 1955 . . . every time I used to read something about the players, about the black players, [the writers] have to say something sarcastic about it. For example, when I got to Fort Myers, there was a newspaper down there and the newspaper said, PUERTO RICAN HOT DOG arrives in town. Now, these people never knew anything about me, but they knew I was Puerto Rican, and as soon as I get to camp they call me a Puerto Rican hot dog."

It is not clear where Clemente saw that derogatory reference. A study of every edition of the Fort Myers's newspaper in 1955 from before training camp opened until the team headed North shows no story or headline where Clemente was called a hot dog. In his "Keeping Score" column, Len Harsh once called him "a fiery young Puerto Rican," and another time said he "has some rough edges that need to be smoothed out" but Harsh liked Clemente and was invariably complimentary. The front section of the paper was indeed full of racist stereotypes. The January 22 front page, published more than a month before Clemente arrived, featured two stories that belittled Puerto Ricans. CRAZY PUERTO RICAN GIVES COPS WILD RUN read the headline of the first story, about a young man who led local police on a high-speed chase through town. The second story, under the headline NUDITY BANNED FOR PUERTO RICANS, reported on the agricultural town of Immokalee, to the southeast of Fort Myers, where the constable announced that he was banning the practice of letting Puerto Rican toddlers run around without clothes. "In accord with the custom, brought from the island and long practiced by Spanish and Indian forebears, Puerto Rican migrant workers here have been letting their toddler-sized children play up and down the streets naked as jay-birds," the report said. "Constable Joe Brown told parents the kids better wear pinafores, shorts or at least bikini-style diapers. He acknowledged that in his hometown of Tampa Cuban kids go without clothes but only in the Latin neighborhoods where there are no objections." This was the social atmosphere of 1955 Florida, and Clemente hated it.

Could it have been a Pittsburgh paper that called him a hot dog? The archives show no such reference there, either, though some descriptions came close. In one of his columns, Al Abrams wrote: "From the standpoint of showmanship and crowd appeal, this Clemente will be the right Forbes Field ticket. The dusky Puerto Rican . . . played his position well and ran the bases like a scared rabbit. It seemed that every time we looked up there was Roberto showing his flashing heels and gleaming white teeth to the loud screams of the bleacher fans." Abrams most likely was unaware of how loaded those words might seem to his subject, meaning it only as high praise, and certainly not trying to imply that he was turned off by Clemente's flair. So it was close, but still no hot dog. Perhaps a heckler in the stands or a sportswriter after a game called Clemente a hot dog for making a basket catch and he conflated that oral account with a newspaper story he didn't like. In any case, he was deeply troubled by the stereotypes and sought out more experienced Latin players to see how they felt. Carlos Bernier and Lino Donoso, who were trying to make the Pirates, urged him to contain his anger. His friend Vic Power, who arrived in Fort Myers with the Kansas City Athletics, told him about an incident where the team bus had been pulled over by cops and Power had been dragged off because he had taken a Coca-Cola from a Whites-only roadside service station.

The message, according to Clemente was the same. "They say, 'Roberto, you better keep your mouth shut because they will ship you back,'" But Clemente did not want to stay silent. His sense of fairness overtook his innate shyness. "This is something that from the first day, I said to myself: 'I am the minority group. I am from the poor people. I represent the poor people. I represent the common people of America. So I am going to be treated as a human being. I don't want to be treated like a Puerto Rican, or a black, or nothing like that. I want to be treated like any person that comes for a job.' Every person who comes for a job, no matter what type of race or color he is, if he does the job he should be treated like whites."

As much as the sport itself, it was the issue of basic human dignity that drove the *Pittsburgh Courier* in its intense coverage of the Pirates camp that spring. With a vibrant sports section featuring columns by Wendell Smith and Bill Nunn Jr. and cartoon sketches by Ric Roberts, the *Courier,* Pittsburgh's black weekly newspaper, reported on the integration of major league baseball with a depth and passion that equaled any other publication in America. Al Dunmore, the paper's correspondent covering the Pirates in Fort Myers, filed regular dispatches on the ups and downs of the team's non-white prospects. In the headline jargon of black newspapers of that era, these players were often called "tans." Along with four minor leaguers who had been in Fort Myers for Mr. Rickey's training school earlier in February, there were six major league prospects in camp that year, the most in the team's history: Curt Roberts, a second baseman, pitchers Lino Donoso and Domingo Rosello, and outfielders Carlos Bernier, Roman Mejias, and Roberto Clemente.

It seemed to the *Courier* correspondent that only Clemente, among the six, was secure in his position with the club. "The highly publicized Roberto Clemente must be retained a full year as a drafted player," Dunmore stated in an early spring training report. And from his observations, the young Puerto Rican's play merited a job in any case. "Clemente is just about everything promised, lacking only major league polish," he wrote. The artist Ric Roberts, in his first sketch of the spring, drew "Rookies and Robins," a collection of promising black rookies, with Clemente prime among them. There he was in Pirates uniform, charging a ball in right field at full speed, with a balloon caption of him saying, "EXTRA BASE? NO!" Certainly no hot-dog portrayal from the *Courier.*

If the Courier men were impressed, old man Rickey remained uncertain about the prize he had snatched from the Dodgers. On the afternoon of March 23, he sat in the stands at Terry Park and kept up a running commentary as the Pirates played the Chicago White Sox on Merchant Appreciation Day. The day before, Clemente had poked his first home run of the spring, and against the White Sox he cracked out two singles and a triple. But Rickey was concerned. He thought that Clemente's running was improving after days of tutoring from coach George Sisler, who taught the rookie how to take sharper turns around the base paths. But at the plate, Rickey observed, Clemente seemed off balance, stepping away from the ball, trying to pull it too much. It could be a fatal flaw, Rickey feared. "I will not be surprised if Mr. Clemente gets to the place where he will be permitted only to play against left-hand pitchers. When the pitchers in the National League know his terrific weakness on sidearm pitching, he will not get anything else to hit." He asked Sisler to work his magic on Clemente at the plate.

Most of the attention in the *Courier* all spring was directed not at Clemente and the question of whether he could hang in there against sidearming righties, but on Curt Roberts and concerns about whether he could keep his job at second base.

Roberts was another of the baseball elders who paved the way for Clemente, a lineage that began with his fellow Puerto Ricans, Hiram Bithorn, Luis Olmo, and Vic Power. Only a year earlier, seven seasons after Jackie Robinson joined the Dodgers, Curtis Benjamin Roberts made history in Pittsburgh by becoming the first black Pirate. None other than Mr. Rickey, the engineer of baseball integration, had recruited Roberts, who like Robinson had played in the Negro American League for the Kansas City Monarchs. But Roberts was no Jackie Robinson. He was an unprepossessing middle infielder from the East Texas timber town of Pineland with a slick glove but not much of a bat. Listed at 5'8" but probably at least two inches shorter, Roberts played three years with the Pirates' minor league affiliate in Denver. During his stay in the minors he was switched from shortstop to second base and earned the admiring nickname "Little Man" from his manager, Andy Cohen, who was Jewish and sympathetic to the black ballplayer's situation. Roberts had good range, excelled at charging slow-rolling grounders, and led minor league second basemen in fielding percentage and assists.

By the time he reached Pittsburgh in 1954, Roberts had received the Rickey tutorial on how to survive in the dominant white sports culture, advice that boiled down to three words: ignore the abuse. Easier said than done, of course. Christine Roberts, the player's wife, told *Pittsburgh Post-Gazette* writer Ed Bouchette that when she attended games at Forbes Field she heard constant shouts of "Knock the nigger down!" and "Hit him in the head." It got so bad that she preferred sitting in the upper deck. "The people in the front were the most vicious. They wanted to make sure [Curt] heard them." But she never turned to look at the bigots. "I had to ignore them like Branch Rickey told us," she said.

Roberts began his major league career with a bold stroke. With a bitter April wind slicing across the diamond as the Pirates opened at home for the first time in sixty-one years, he belted a triple in his first at-bat off the accomplished Phillies right-hander Robin Roberts, leading the woeful Pirates to an unexpected victory. He went on to start 134 games that year under Fred Haney, the rookie manager, with mixed results. In the field, some local writers said he was smoother than any Pirate second baseman in decades. But at the plate his average was a meager .232. It was his inability to hit that found him fighting for his life in the spring training camp of 1955, a struggle chronicled in detail by the *Courier.*

ROBERTS PLAYS BALL IN SPITE OF RUMORS, read an early headline from spring training. "The pre-spring ballyhoo about Gene Freese with the Pirates hasn't fazed little Curt Roberts in his bid to retain the second-base job on the club. The little fellow with the slick glove has been his usual self hounding ground balls around second," correspondent Dunmore wrote. Freese, who came from Wheeling, West Virginia, considered Pittsburgh's southern backyard, was nearly as short as Roberts (his common nickname was Augie, but college teammates called him the Microbe). But he had more pop in his bat. After starring in the minors for the New Orleans Pelicans, he came to spring training with glowing publicity. As Dunmore described Freese, he seemed "desperate in his madness to take over the job." He had also impressed the starting shortstop and quiet team leader, Dick Groat, just back from two years in the Army, who invited Freese to room with him. But Roberts was "a determined little cuss" who would not give up without a fight, Dunmore said. In his next article under the headline NINE MORE HITS ALL HE NEEDED, Dunmore noted that with those extra nine hits Roberts would have been a .250 hitter the previous year instead of "a wretched .232" and wouldn't have to worry about losing his starting role. Branch Rickey himself had made the pronouncement that "all Roberts has to do is hit .250."

What a fine line between success and failure those nine hits were, as Dunmore presented the dilemma: "Sixteen times did enemy gloves rob him of potential hits. Five times was he called a dead duck at first when in the opinion of his mates, at least, he might have been given the nod."

In the larger scheme of baseball, the battle for the second-base job on a perennial last-place team was not much of a story. But from the perspective of the *Courier* and its readership, Curt Roberts and all his hopes and sufferings were telling drama. "Back in Pittsburgh the question of Curt, with reference to the immediate future, is household conversation," Dunmore wrote. "Day by day the question mounts: Did Curt play yesterday?" The question mounted, if nowhere else, back at the *Courier*'s office on Centre Avenue in the Hill District of Pittsburgh, and perhaps in black neighborhoods in eight other cities where editions of the influential weekly circulated. One day, Dunmore confronted manager Haney about Roberts's lack of playing time. His report on the interview was filed under the headline WE ASK HANEY "WHY?" Haney explained that hitting was not the only weakness he saw in Roberts; he also questioned the strength of his arm on relay throws from the outfield. Then Dunmore went to the white sportswriters—Hernon and Biederman and Chilly Doyle—and asked them why they were ignoring Roberts: "Pittsburgh reporters, questioned about a charge that they were 'freezing' Roberts out"—wordplay on the last name of the second-base competition—"said they could write little about a man they didn't see play. They said that even during the winter the Pirates talked about Freese in discussing spring plans." In the end, Roberts made the regular season roster, but lost his starting job.

From the perspective of the black newspaper, this was unfortunate, but only a lost battle in a larger war for racial equity that was being won, however slowly. In the same edition that announced pitcher Lino Donoso's demotion to the Hollywood Stars and Roberts's place on the bench, the *Courier* ran a story accompanied by a Ric Roberts sketch about the economic gains blacks had made in baseball. PAID 45 TAN STARS SUM OF $1,596,500 trumpeted the headline. The paper's study of salaries paid Jackie Robinson and the forty-four blacks who followed him into the majors from 1947 to 1955 showed that they had been paid an aggregate sum of more than a million and a half dollars. If Robinson had remained with the Kansas City Monarchs, the *Courier* estimated, his total pay over seven years would have been no more than $35,000. Instead, with the Dodgers, he had earned a total of at least $252,000. Behind Robinson in the salary rankings, a list that included active and retired black players, were Larry Doby of the Indians, $182,000; Roy Campanella of the Dodgers, $125,000; Satchel Paige of the Indians, $105,000; Luke Easter of the Indians, $103,000; Monte Irvin of the Giants, $97,000; Saturnino Orestes Arrieta Armas (Minnie) Minoso of the White Sox, $77,000; Hank Thompson of the Giants, $76,000; Don Newcombe of the Dodgers, $73,000; Sam Jethroe of the old Boston Braves, $57,000; and Willie Mays of the Giants, $40,000. The twenty-eight veteran black ballplayers in the league were expected to earn $445,000 in 1955. If thirteen rookies stuck with their clubs, the total would jump to $549,000.

Roberto Clemente did not add much to the total. On February 3, while he was still in San Juan, he had signed his first major league contract for $6,000.

When the decade started, the Pirates asked for patience. It was a five-year plan, fans were told. Then it was Operation Peach Fuzz, the force-feeding of young players who were not ready. As the fifth season approached, Rickey was feeling the harsh sting of skeptics. "I am by no means perfect," he wrote in a private memo in his own defense. "I am not a baseball God. I have never pretended to be so. I do not claim perfection. Far from it. But I am not God damned and I will never be. No series of articles from writers anywhere can divert me from the job at hand or dull the edge of my courage to do the things I think ought to be done to bring a great team to this town. Cicero had his Cataline, Abraham Lincoln had his Vallandigham, and even ordinary individuals like myself can have detractors." But the future will answer all critics, Rickey said. And the future was now. Nineteen fifty-five, he boasted, would be the time when "the bells will start ringing as the red wagon comes down the street. That's when the Pittsburgh folks will shout, 'By George, this is it!'"

In fact, once the team went North, the fifth season of Mr. Rickey's five-year plan was over almost as soon as it began. The Pirates lost their opener at Ebbets Field in Brooklyn and never looked back. They just kept on losing, eight losses in a row. A few games were close. The scoring totals for those opening eight against the Dodgers, Giants, and Phillies were: Opponents 54, Pirates 16. Rickey's judgment that Clemente would have trouble with right-handed pitchers was passed along to Fred Haney, the manager, who kept him on the bench as the season began, despite his productive spring. It was not until the fourth game that Clemente made his debut, on the afternoon of April 17 at Forbes Field against the Dodgers. Johnny Podres—a southpaw who later that year pitched Brooklyn to its finest hour, shutting out the Yankees in the seventh game of the World Series—was on the mound when Clemente rapped a bounding shot to the left side of the infield. Shortstop Pee Wee Reese knocked the ball down but could not make a play at first. A ground ball single in a losing game with a lame last-place team; no way to know then that someday people would look back on that hit as a piece of baseball history.

In the clubhouse under Forbes Field, dank and ancient, Clemente was given a locker next to another rookie, none other than Gene Freese. There was no animosity between them, although Clemente felt that Curt Roberts had not been given a fair chance to keep his second-base job. Freese liked to tease Clemente about the rats that roamed the encrusted tunnel between the clubhouse and dugout. Had 'em for pets down in West Virginia, he would say, knowing that Clemente could not stand the sight of them. Clemente and Freese were not strangers. They had competed against each other in the Puerto Rican winter league. Freese had played for the San Juan Senadores in 1954, and had made the All-Star team, where he met Clemente and Willie Mays. One of his proudest moments, as he would recall it decades later, came before the All-Star game when several players took part in a sixty-yard dash. There is no official record of the event, but by Freese's account Hal Jeffcoat won, George Freese, his brother, playing for Mayagüez, finished second, he came in third, and trailing behind them were the Santurce club's two speedsters, Mays and Clemente. "They would look fast, but in a straight dash, we beat them," he said.

It was typical of Pittsburgh teams of that era that Freese was best known for an oddity. To have brothers Gene and George Freese on the same team was uncommon enough, but the Pirates took it a step further. They also had Johnny and Eddie O'Brien, who were not only brothers but identical twins. No team before or since had the brother act going quite like the 1955 Pirates, though the Giants later would have three brothers Alou. And the O'Briens provided another curious dimension. If the team lacked talent in baseball, it could field one powerhouse basketball squad. The O'Briens, known as the Gold Dust Twins, had led the Seattle University Chieftains to the NCAA basketball tournament in 1952 before being recommended as baseball players to Branch Rickey by Bing Crosby, who was vice president of the Pirates board of directors. (On stationery with a Bing Crosby/Hollywood logo, the crooner wrote Rickey: "I think you'll agree that they are colorful performers and one boy has decidedly good form and a hook slide.") Then there was Dick Groat, the shortstop, who had been an All-American guard at Duke. And for a front line the Pirates could send out Dick Hall and Nellie King, both 6'6" (a center's height in those days) and 6'4" Dale Long. All good for a winter recreation league, but not of much use at Forbes Field.

Gene Freese, playing second base and then moving to third, got off to a great start. It seemed that any ball that blooped off his bat fell in front of the outfielders. No such luck for Clemente, who after a hot first two weeks began lashing the ball right at someone, making him so frustrated that he broke several batting helmets. If a white player broke a helmet, he was considered a fierce competitor; when Clemente did it some teammates and sportswriters thought it was another manifestation of showboating, like his basket catch. (Breaking helmets was a mixed blessing for the man upstairs. It cost the team money, yet profited Branch Rickey at the same time. The fiberglass and plastic batting helmet was one of his innovations, and Rickey and his friends and family owned a company, American Baseball Cap Inc., which manufactured them under Patent No. 2,698.434, issued January 4, 1955. Clemente later would give testimonials to the helmet's effectiveness.) The general impression in the locker room was that the Puerto Rican kid barely knew any English because he didn't speak that often and when he did, in his soft, tenor voice, his words were heavily accented. Local sportswriters, when they quoted him, spelled his comments phonetically, a practice that infuriated him. But he was learning the language quickly from a wide variety of sources, ranging from the cute inanities of television cartoons to the piercing profanities of the locker room.

He called Freese "Magoo," as in Mr. Magoo, because Freese liked to talk like the blind-as-a-bat cartoon character. "Hey, Magoo," he blurted out one day in the clubhouse. "How come you Magoo get fucking bloop hit and I hit line drive out?"

Freese had an answer. "You got an unlucky number, Clemente," he said.

His number was thirteen. "Hey, Hoolie!" Clemente called out to the locker room attendant. "Find me another shirt!" A legend grew later that Clemente had counted out the number of letters in his first name, last name, and mother's maiden name, Roberto Clemente Walker, and had used the total for his new number. In fact, it was just random: No. 21 was available.

Every two weeks of the season, the *Courier* ran a special box called "What They Are Doing," which listed the batting statistics of the black starting players in both leagues. A month and a half into the season, Clemente's name was in the top-ten batters on the paper's list. His pal Vic Power was number one, sprinting to a .359 average in Kansas City, just ahead of Elston Howard, the man the Yankees chose to make their first black player instead of Power. Roy Campanella was tearing up the National League with ten home runs and thirty-nine runs batted in. And then came a trio whose names would be linked many times over the years as they combined to form an All-Star outfield that could not be surpassed: Willie Mays of the Giants, Henry Aaron of the Braves, and Roberto Clemente of the Pirates. Clemente had been at-bat 134 times and was hitting .284 with three homers and sixteen runs batted in. He had been hitting well over .300 until falling into the first slump of his career.

Two weeks later, after another hot streak, he was playing well enough that the *Courier* spread a headline across the top of the sports page: CLEMENTE MAY BRING "ROOKIE OF THE YEAR" LAURELS TO PIRATES. The article by sports editor Bill Nunn Jr. noted that there had been "something different" about the previous season—it marked only the second time since Jackie Robinson broke in that "a Negro didn't win either the Baseball Writers' Association or *The Sporting News* National League 'Rookie of the Year' award." Robinson, Don Newcombe, Sam Jethroe, Willie Mays, Joe Black, and Junior Gilliam had all won in recent years. Then along came Wally Moon of the St. Louis Cardinals, who beat out Hank Aaron and Ernie Banks in 1954. In Pittsburgh, Nunn said, "they think they might have the man" to restore the tradition. "A 20-year-old rookie outfielder who came to the Pirates by way of the Brooklyn Dodgers farm club at Montreal, Roberto Clemente has proved thus far to be one of the classiest rookies in the loop. He's the gem many experts claim may eventually lead the Pirates to the gold that goes to those teams ending in the first division. Although he speaks only a little broken English, there is nothing about the bat Clemente's been carrying around which doesn't put him near the head of the class when it comes to being heard. As this is being written, the speedy Puerto Rican is batting a very respectable .302." And the Pirates, as that was being written, were already dead ducks, twenty games under .500 at 21–41.

One phrase in Nunn's glowing account—"he speaks only a little broken English"—reflected Clemente's precarious position in Pittsburgh. He was black, yet as a Spanish-speaking Puerto Rican was somewhat removed from the indigenous black community of Pittsburgh, and even further removed from most of his white teammates, separated by language, race, and age. The Pirates might have been mediocre, but they were for the most part an easygoing lot. Many of the single guys lived in the same apartment complex and went to the same bars. They thought Clemente was shy and wanted to be by himself. They could not see the world through his eyes: the meaning of his family life in Carolina with Don Melchor and Doña Luisa and all of his older brothers and cousins, the pride he felt for his island, the matter-of-fact racism he had encountered every day in Florida, the social isolation of being a Spanish-speaking black kid in a clubhouse of older white men, athletes who seemed from another place and generation, including one, Sid Gordon, who was born when the United States entered World War I. Only a few people were hostile; Elroy Face, the effective little fork-balling relief pitcher and hillbilly musician, had no use for Clemente from the beginning. Jack Hernon, the *Post-Gazette* sportswriter, for various reasons, felt the same. Most of the guys were cordial, but still there was a distance. "He was very quiet. A gentleman. Always complimentary," Nick Koback, a rookie catcher, said of Clemente. "Sometimes he would come out on the field and bullshit with me. He'd say, 'Hey, you—strong guy!'"

Pittsburgh was advanced well beyond Fort Myers on racial issues, but blacks, who according to census data comprised about 16.7 percent of the population (less than most other major Northern cities), were for the most part confined to the Hill District and Homewood and efforts to move out at times met ugly acts of resistance. GO TO HILL! NEGRO FAMILY TOLD blared a headline in the *Courier* that summer over a story about the Sanford family, Mahlon and Beatrice and their thirteen-year-old daughter Mary, who were threatened with violence when they moved from the Hill to a rental house in the town of Glenfield. On the door of their house, where windows had been broken by vandals, the Sanfords found a scrawled note that read: *Nigger—don't let the sun set on you here. Your place is the Hill District. Don't mar our town.* Clemente did not face anything as nasty as that, but like Curt Roberts a year earlier, he heard racist bench-jockeying from opposing teams during games. Roberto had the same urgent will and strong sense of self as Jackie Robinson, and it was as hard for him as it had been for Robinson to follow Mr. Rickey's advice to ignore the abuse.

In the working-class neighborhoods of the old city, there was still much resistance to integration, even on the ball field. Richard Peterson, who grew up on the South Side and went on to become a professor of English and a lyrical essayist about Pittsburgh sports, was just starting to play an outfield position on his high school team that year and later recalled that he was looking for a Pirates outfielder to be his new hero. Clemente would have been the one, except for his race. "The only problem was Clemente himself," Peterson noted a half-century later in a column in the *Post-Gazette*. "I was living on the South Side, at that time a shot-and-a-beer neighborhood defined by its ethnic enclaves, its steel-mill mentality and its deep distrust of minorities. My working-class father and his beer-joint buddies, while diehard Pirates fans, believed that black ballplayers were ruining baseball, and I was my father's son. I had plenty of help in my early prejudice against black ballplayers."

Clemente's first friend in Pittsburgh was Phil Dorsey, who worked at the Post Office and had served in an Army Reserve unit with Bob Friend, the starting pitcher whose name matched his personality. After Friend introduced him to Clemente in the clubhouse after a game, Dorsey gave the right fielder a ride back to his stuffy little room at the old Webster Hall Hotel. Soon they developed a routine, with Dorsey, when he was off work, driving the carless Clemente to and from games and out to eat. The life of a ballplayer comes with oceans of free time, and Dorsey helped Clemente fill them. They played pool and penny-ante poker and ate Chinese food and went to the movies. Clemente loved westerns, and would memorize lines from them as a way to learn more English. (Years later, in the clubhouse several hours before a game, a teammate saw Clemente standing in front of a mirror with a young Latin player, helping the newcomer with English by having him repeat a phrase from *The Lone Ranger*: "You go into town, I'll meet you at the canyon.")

Realizing that Clemente was miserable at the hotel, a setting so depressingly different from his home life in Puerto Rico, Dorsey found an apartment that Clemente could share with Roman Mejias, the other

Latin on the club. But Mejias stayed up late and made a lot of noise with the hangers when he put away his clothes, and part of the building turned out to be a brothel. Finally, Dorsey set up Clemente with his friends Stanley and Mamie Garland, a childless black couple who had an extra room available at their trim red-brick house at 3038 Iowa Street in Schenley Heights, a middle-class black neighborhood up the hill from the University of Pittsburgh. Mr. Garland worked at the Post Office with Dorsey, and his wife held a supervisory job at Allegheny General Hospital.

The Garlands had let rooms to college students before, but never to a major league ballplayer. Mamie Garland had qualms about the idea. Roberto was young, single, and gorgeous. Women jostled to get near him before and after every game, and one of Dorsey's roles became that of the gatekeeper for Clemente's women. Mrs. Garland, before taking in Clemente, wanted to get it straight that there would be no women in the house. Clemente assured her that he did not like to party at home and that he was quiet and always trying to get his rest. He was a very peaceful person, he said. She would have no problems with him. It was just a room at first, nothing more. He went out for meals. But Mamie Garland was a good cook, and the aromas drifting up to his room from her kitchen were too much for him. One day he stocked her freezer with steaks and other cuts of beef that he had brought home from the butcher shop. They are for you, he told Mrs. Garland, as she recalled the story. Do what you want with them. But I'd like to eat at the table if it's okay with you because I smell those steaks that you prepare. I would appreciate it if you would fix one for me. Please, one of these days, fix one for me. From then on, he ate at the table with the Garlands, and the bond deepened so that he would call them his parents in America and they thought of him as their son.

Looking south and downhill from the rear window of the Garland house, beyond the treetops, Clemente could see the Pitt skyscraper, the Cathedral of Learning, and to its right his baseball cathedral, Forbes Field, which was only a short if steep walk down the curving streets. Around the block on Adelaide was the house of singer Billy Eckstine's sister. Bill Nunn Jr., the sports editor of the *Courier*, lived four blocks away on Finland, across from the Williams Park reservoir, and nearby on Anaheim, Dakota, Bryn Mawr, and Cherokee were many of the city's leading black judges, ministers, and nightclub owners. A quarter-mile down the slope to the north ran Centre Avenue, with the *Courier* offices and presses taking up a half-block at the corner of Francis Street, across from the YMCA, whose pool tables served as a social hub for the Hill, and beyond that came Wylie Avenue and an undulating three-block stretch of nightclubs surrounding the Crawford Grill No. 2, where Jackie Robinson, Roy Campanella, Junior Gilliam, and Don Newcombe would go when the Dodgers came to town, and where the musicians entertaining on weekends included John Coltrane, Mary Lou Williams, and Art Blakey. The Crawford Grill had been founded by Gus Greenlee, who also owned the Pittsburgh Crawfords baseball club in the Negro National League and made his money running the local numbers racket along with Boogie Harris, the brother of Charles (Teenie) Harris, the talented photographer for the *Courier.*

The black Pittsburgh that Clemente entered was a small, tight world. He became a familiar figure on Wylie Avenue, according to Nunn, who ran with the ballplayers when he was not at the office putting out the paper, but as a black Puerto Rican who spoke another language Clemente was somewhat apart from the crowd. The Latino population in Pittsburgh then was minimal, less than 1 percent. "I think it was always tough for Clemente," Nunn remembered. "For years in the black community there was a little tension with blacks from other countries. There were no Puerto Ricans in Pittsburgh to speak of, not like New York. The thing here was steel mills, which didn't draw workers from the Caribbean." Nunn noticed that when Clemente went out his female companions were as often white as black. "Some of the black women just didn't understand him," Nunn said.

In 1955, with no help from the baseball team, not yet, the city of steel was undertaking what civic leaders called the Pittsburgh Renaissance. Mayor David Lawrence, with the cooperation of the corporate elite, had already pushed through smoke ordinances to clean the air, which had grown so thick during the industrial frenzy of World War II that a photograph showed cars driving through town at noon with headlights on. Now they were cleaning the rivers, clearing land, razing buildings, and remaking downtown and nearby neighborhoods, for better and for worse; better for some businessmen and merchants, largely worse for displaced residents. Pittsburgh was a city of neighborhoods, with a rich ethnic mix. Every immigrant group was said to have its own hill, and newspaper. Along with the three dailies and the black-owned *Courier,* there was also the Jewish *Criterion,* the *Sokol Polski* weekly, the Italian *Unione,* the *Nardoni Slovu* for Ukrainians, and the Serbian *Daily.*

It was only at the top that everyone appeared the same. Margaret Bourke-White, the great *Time-Life* photographer, came to Pittsburgh and took a picture of the manufacturers and financiers who ran the city in the mid-fifties. They posed inside the Duquesne Club on Sixth Avenue, some standing, others settled comfortably in plush leather chairs, with portraits of successive generations of Mellon men looking down from the back wall. Gray and black suits, dark ties, crossed legs, manicured fingers, scrubbed faces, hair combed back—here was the power of Pittsburgh assembled for an executive session of what was known as the Allegheny Conference: United States Steel, Pittsburgh Plate Glass Company, Westinghouse Electric Corporation, Mellon National Bank, Mine Safety Appliances Company, Allegheny Ludlum Steel Corporation, Aluminum Company of America, Consolidation Coal Company, Gulf Oil Corporation, H. J. Heinz Company, Jones & Laughlin Steel Corporation, Fisher Scientific Company, Duquesne Light Company, Oliver Tyrone Corporation, Carnegie Institute, Mellon Institute. World-class fortunes were made in Pittsburgh, most from the days when it was called "hell with the lid off."

A losing baseball team played a minuscule role in the economy of Pittsburgh, but it was one of the few institutions that everyone in the city could get behind. Old Forbes Field, built in 1909 and named for a general in the French and Indian War, was easily accessible by bus and trolley. It was located in the Oakland neighborhood, at the edge of the University of Pittsburgh, two miles east of downtown along Forbes Avenue. Across the street, visible over the left-field fence, were the

trees of Schenley Park, where the city had just unveiled a new eighteen-foot-high statue of Honus Wagner, shortstop for the first seventeen years of the century, the first and then the greatest of all great
Pittsburgh Pirates. Most of the 34,361 seats inside Forbes were afford-
able for steelworkers as well as executives. Bleacher seats along the
left-field line went for a buck. General admission seating in the lower
and upper decks of right field cost $1.40. The most expensive season
ticket package, known as Plan E, which included field level box seats
for seventy-seven games plus a throw-in of sixty-six general admission
tickets, went for $143. It was almost enough to draw crowds, but that
was something only a better team could make happen. Attendance in
1954 had been the worst since the war years, and 1955 was showing little improvement, under a half-million for the entire home season.

For those who did attend, the rookie stationed in right field offered
full entertainment value, whether he was hitting or in a slump. Opposing teams kept trying to run on him, and consistently ran themselves
out of innings as he compiled eighteen outfield assists. Deep in the
summer, Monte Irvin, Momen's childhood hero, was sold by the
Giants to their minor league club in Minneapolis, his career nearing an
end. At about the same time, Clemente—beset by nagging injuries:
the wrenched spine and neck from the car accident, a sore ankle, a
banged-up shin—fell into a slump that would find him struggling at
the plate for the rest of the season, with his average eventually dipping
to .255 (with five home runs and forty-seven runs batted in). The
Pirates would slip with him, finding solace only in the fact that they
avoided losing a hundred games. But there was something about
Clemente that went beyond results. His little underhanded flips and
basket catches, the way he ran hard and threw harder and swung hard-
est, even the élan with which he wore the traditional cut of the white
Pirates uniform with black sleeves, all of this was absorbed and appreciated by patrons who sat down the right-field line, and by the knothole gang youngsters and families who gazed down on him from the
stands above the high right-field wall.

From the beginning, there was a bond between Clemente and
many baseball fans, especially kids. If they were not bound by prejudice, if they could appreciate Clemente for what he was, they were his.

As Branch Rickey said, the law of cause and effect and causality both work the same with inexorable exactitudes. Sportswriters would almost always frustrate Clemente; either they couldn't see his perspective or he didn't think they could. The system, whatever it was, whatever was holding him back—that ticked him off. Seeing other people get more recognition upset him. The stereotypes of Puerto Ricans made him mad. Being told where he couldn't sit or eat or sleep infuriated him. All of that angered him so much he once called himself a double nigger, resorting to a word that also irritated him. But the fans were something else. As a young ballplayer, lonely and burning, he found relief with the fans, and after games, with no wife or children to go home to, Momen loved nothing more than to stand surrounded by admiring strangers—*momentito, momentito*—and sign his autograph in a sweet-flowing cursive scrawl on their scorecards and baseballs for as long as they wished.

5

¡Arriba! ¡Arriba!

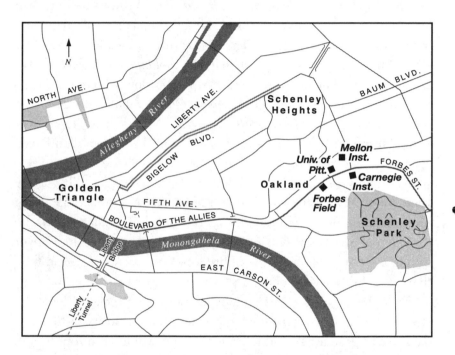

BOB PRINCE, THE PLAY-BY-PLAY ANNOUNCER ON PIRATES radio and television broadcasts, had a nickname for everyone. That included Prince himself, who was known in Pittsburgh as "the Gunner." Where that nickname came from is a matter of dispute; either it was descriptive of his announcing style or—an equally likely story—his friends started calling him the Gunner after an unhappy husband pulled a gun on him for talking to the man's wife. With his deep, raspy voice, goofy, bespectacled face, skinny legs, ugly plaid sport coats, unbridled home-club shilling, keen sense of humor and intelligence, and bottomless supply of nicknames, metaphors, jinxes, good-luck charms, and idiomatic sayings, Prince was not just the voice of the Pirates, he was in many ways their creator. Baseball teams live in the public imagination, and the Pirates came to life as imagined first by Bob Prince.

At his side in the broadcast booth was Jim Woods, who in Prince's world was called Possum. For those who grew up listening to Prince, there were phrases that transcended cliché because they were embedded so deeply in the cultural fabric of Pittsburgh during that era. *We had 'em all the way.* Said only after a tense game when it seemed that the Pirates would lose. *You can kiss it good-bye.* Prince's defining call for a home run. *How sweet it is!* Proclaimed after a particularly satisfying victory or winning streak. The bases were not loaded but *F.O.B.,* full of Bucs. A ball was not barely foul but *foul by a gnat's eyelash.* He also had colorful names for the players. Bill Virdon, who roamed center field in wire-rimmed glasses, was *Quail.* Smoky Burgess, the rotund catcher, was *Shake, rattle, and roll.* Vernon Law, the clean-living Mormon pitching ace, was *Deacon.* Third baseman Don Hoak, aggressive and fearless, was *Tiger.* Bob Skinner, the lanky, sweet-swinging lefty who played left field, was *Dog,* or *Doggie.* Little Elroy Face, the forkball artist who had an unhittable season in 1959, going 18–1, was *The Baron of the Bullpen.* He tried calling Dick Groat, the captain and shortstop, No. 24, *Double Dozen,* but that name never caught on. Dick Schofield, the utility infielder, was *Ducky.* And then there was Roberto Clemente.

From the beginning, the Gunner seemed to appreciate Clemente, at first as a circus barker might appreciate the virtuosity of his most dazzling trapeze artist, and later as a friend would admire a friend. There was rarely tension between the two, as there was between Clemente and many members of the press. Prince was among the few people who could call him Bob or Bobby with no hard feelings. He also called him Roberto often enough. And when Clemente entered the U.S. Marine Corps Reserves near the end of the 1958 season and took basic training at Parris Island with Platoon 346 of the 3rd Recruit Battalion, he came back to find Prince saluting him as Private Clemente, the leatherneck. But whenever Clemente approached the plate, Prince greeted him with a phrase that came to define their relationship. *¡Arriba! ¡Arriba!* He had heard Lino Donoso, a Spanish-speaking teammate, say it to Clemente once, early in his career, and liked the sound of it. Translated, it means something like Get there! Go up! Arise! Let's go! The etymology goes back to the Latin words for reaching shore. *¡Arriba!* The double r's would trill on Prince's tongue with fluid, exaggerated delight.

In the early winter of 1960, at the dawn of the sixties decade, Prince and the Pirates and all the baseball world were still waiting for Clemente to get there. At age twenty-five, after five full seasons in the major leagues, he remained a player with more promise than results. He had batted over .300 only once, during his sophomore season in 1956. His third year had been almost a complete washout; he was disabled by a painful back and spine and hit a meager .253 with thirty runs batted in. At the close of the 1958 season and into the following preseason his baseball had been interrupted by the Marine Corps training, and for much of that time he was plagued with a sore right arm. He had played for three managers already—Fred Haney, Bobby Bragan, and Danny Murtaugh—and feared that they had misinterpreted his pride and perfectionism as malingering, not realizing how much he was hurting. On the field, he was such a dashing ballplayer—*¡Arriba!*—yet the cold numbers were unimposing. In no season had he driven in more than sixty runs or hit more than seven home runs. Even his stunning arm in right field had a downside; along with high assist totals and highlight reel plays came too many errors. All these deficiencies had been pointed out by general manger Joe L. Brown when he offered Clemente a contract of $27,500 plus bonuses for the 1960 season.

On February 26, 1960, after signing for a sixth season with the Pirates, Clemente wrote Brown a letter and included it with the agreement he sent back to Pittsburgh. The typewritten letter, composed by Clemente in English, unpolished but improving, was his answer to any and all criticism.

> *Dear Joe,*
> *Here is the 1960 contract.*
> *I want to tell you that last year I played most of the season sick. Just because when I said when my arm was sore nobody believed it and I*

*played that way until I almost lost my arm. I think that if somebody is
sick you should know if he can't play or not, but with me is different.
Is different occasion I can't see where I stand with Pittsburgh club
when I said that something is wrong with me.*

Clemente had played fewer games in 1959 (105) than in any previous
year. Murtaugh, who took over as manager midway through 1957,
Clemente's worst season, was a hard-charging Irishman who wanted
his men to play hurt and wasn't particularly interested in explanations.

*Okay, I was the player who make more errors. I can play like
Skinner and make one error or nothing and Virdon and make not so
many assists and I'd be way ahead, too. So Please don't count those
errors because playing safe everyone can field .1000.*

Clemente made thirteen errors in 104 games in right field and had a
fielding percentage of only .948 in 1959. His attempt to contrast his
play with left fielder Bob Skinner and center fielder Bill Virdon was
not entirely on the mark. Clemente had ten outfield assists in 1959,
below his totals of previous years, while Skinner had nine assists and
Virdon sixteen. While Skinner was clearly less adventurous in the field
than Clemente, Virdon covered as much ground and took nearly as
many chances, yet had a fielding percentage of .979. Most of Clemente's errors were on wild throws, often to third base. Some fans
with seats in the third base boxes brought gloves to games with the
specific hope of catching an errant heave from Roberto.

*With the RBI if I hit third I can get some but not hitting seventh
with nobody on base. Well, I think that is all for now. My car leaves
the 26th for Miami. I would like the 28th to pick it up in Miami.
With best regards.*

Roberto Clemente

In 1954, when Momen left Puerto Rico for his first spring training, he
was still a naïve teenager, healthy, happy, and hungry for fame. Now,
six years later, he returned to the mainland struggling to find a com-

fortable mental equilibrium. The fire inside him burned hotter than ever. He was still trying to show the world the full measure of his talent and character. At the time he wrote his letter to Brown, he felt in the best physical condition of his career and had just finished a stellar season in the Puerto Rican winter league. He had batted .334, trailing only his pal Vic Power, and drove in forty-two runs, only eight fewer in four dozen games than he had knocked home in all of the previous year for Pittsburgh.

Clemente's slow rise and seeming readiness to break through at long last in 1960 mirrored the frustratingly slow ascent of the ball club. A decade had passed since Branch Rickey unveiled his five-year plan for pennant contention in Pittsburgh. Rickey had come and gone, no longer even a consultant to the club. He had spent the final years of the fifties obsessed with a new idea—to create a third major league, the Continental League, which would never come to fruition but would help major league expansion. His successor was Joe L. Brown, who had been trained by Rickey and was the baseball-loving son of comedian and actor Joe E. Brown. The younger Brown had been focused on baseball since age eleven when he traveled and trained with the old San Francisco Missions and Hollywood Stars. By twenty he had his first pro front office job with Lubbock in a low Class-D League, and from then on relied more on hard work and talent than celebrity connections to make his way up the ladder, becoming general manager at AAA New Orleans and then Rickey's successor after only one year in the front office of the big club. As much as he admired Rickey's brain, Brown realized that the Mahatma had failed in Pittsburgh and that a new course had to be followed. He brought in more veteran talent and paid the players better. "Mr. Rickey was penurious with salaries; if he could save a thousand or two, he did it," Brown recalled. "I made a decision to pay them even more than they were worth . . . I felt the players should have somebody who believed in them, and one of the best ways to show a man is worthy is to put it in his paycheck." By 1960, ten years into the rebuilding program, Brown's reconfiguration of the Rickey plan had finally molded a balanced team that was ready to contend.

The acquisition of Virdon from St. Louis in 1956 had solidified the outfield, but the key trade occurred in January 1959 when Hoak, Burgess, and little left-handed pitcher Harvey Haddix arrived from the Reds in exchange for John Powers, Jim Pendleton, Whammy Douglas, and the slugger Frank Thomas. Burgess did not like to run and was adequate behind the plate but could hit in his sleep. Hoak, the hard-living, hard-playing prototype, who had married a popular singer from western Pennsylvania named Jill Corey (her real name was Norma Jean Speranza), quickly emerged as a team leader and one of Pittsburgh's most popular players. And Haddix became the ideal third man in the rotation behind the rock-solid twosome of Law and Friend. Surpassing Face's record-smashing win-loss percentage in 1959, that season's most amazing feat was Haddix's twelve-inning perfect game against the Braves at Milwaukee County Stadium. Lew Burdette had also shut out the Pirates for those twelve innings, while giving up thirteen hits, and Haddix ended up losing the game, in the thirteenth, when Hoak made an error on a Felix Mantilla grounder, Hank Aaron walked, and Joe Adcock lofted a home run (that was ruled a double because of a base-running mistake). Haddix had pitched possibly the best game in major league history and had only an L to show for it, as well as a secure place in the annals of bad luck. But the game brought more notice to the Pirates, who had been National League afterthoughts for so long. After dismal seasons in 1956 and 1957, they were now demanding attention, not just individually but as a team. They finished second in 1958 and fourth in 1959 and played the two seasons a cumulative sixteen games over .500. As the 1960 season approached, Pittsburgh seemed ready to fulfill its promise.

The regular season started on the road, with an odd one-game series in Milwaukee. The Pirates treated it more like an exhibition game, and lost 4–3 when Face gave up a two-run home run in the bottom of the eighth. Clemente had two hits and a run batted in, but it was not enough. No big deal, said the Baron of the Bullpen, joking that he had already matched his loss total for the previous year. On the charter flight back from Milwaukee, Dick Groat told the beat reporters: "This is a ball club that will make its presence felt this summer—and you can mark that down in your notebooks for rehashing 'round about the end of the season."

Two days later came the home opener, a day game, a 1:30 P.M. start, on a weekday, Thursday, April 14. Day and time seemed to make no difference in workaday Pittsburgh; whenever the game was played it would draw a packed house. In many ways, the first Pirates home game of the sixties decade was a scene from baseball past. Tribes of businessmen in gray and brown suits; crowds hopping off the No. 64, 66, and 68 streetcars on Forbes Avenue; the congenial black preacher greeting patrons near the third-base entrance, sermonizing on his quarter-bags of neatly packed peanuts. Not long after the gates opened at eleven, a sellout crowd of 34,064 started massing into Forbes Field, greeted by a ragtime band, Benny Benack and the Iron City Six, who had anointed themselves the club's musical mascots. For the first time, Pirates fans would hear a tune that would become the season's baseball anthem.

A face in the crowd at the home opener, making his way by streetcar from Squirrel Hill, was twelve-year-old Howard Fineman. He was the son of Mort Fineman, a shoe sales representative, who during his college years had peered down on Bucs games in the stadium below from the aerie of a library carrel on an upper floor of Pitt's Cathedral of Learning; and the grandson of Pirates fan Max Fineman, the patriarch who at age nine ran alongside the baseball parade heading to the wondrous new Forbes Field for the 1909 World Series and was hoisted up by one of the players and carried the rest of the way in an open convertible. Grandfather and father had each seen the Pirates to glory. The youngest Fineman was ready for his turn, and the herald of better things to come; the inane words of Benny Benack's ditty would stick with him for the rest of his life: *Oh, the Bucs are going all the way, all the way, all the way. Oh, the Bucs are going all the way, all the way this year. Beat 'em, Bucs! Beat 'em, Bucs!*

As it turned out, it did not take long for the Pirates to make their presence felt. They won the opening game against the Cincinnati Reds 13–0 with Vernon Law pitching a complete game shutout, giving up seven hits and no walks. Second baseman Bill Mazeroski, lean and mean after a pudgy and disappointing 1959 season, hit a home run and drove in four runs, but the star of the game was Clemente, who went three for three and drove in five, smacking two doubles, a single, and a long sacrifice fly that would have been a home run in any other park but was hauled in by Vada Pinson near where the batting cage was stored at the 457-foot sign in deepest left center. Hal Smith, Pittsburgh's backup catcher, who had been acquired from Kansas City during the off-season, had by then become one of the right fielder's biggest fans. "If you play in 140 games," Smith told Clemente, "we'll win the pennant." *¡Arriba!* Clemente was on his way.

During an Easter Sunday doubleheader against the Reds a few days later, a season-long pattern first became apparent. "It was magical," Bob Friend recalled years later. "You could sense it even then." Friend pitched the first game and won 5–0, another complete game shutout, with Clemente belting a two-run home run to clinch it. In the second game, the Reds were leading 5–0 going into the bottom of the ninth. The game seemed over. Reds manager Fred Hutchinson brought in a second-line reliever to finish it off. Then the Pirates scored a run, and got two more runners on, and Hal Smith smacked a three-run homer to draw them within one. Another Pirate reached base, and Bob Skinner stepped to the plate, shrouded by early evening shadows. In the gloaming, Skinner said he couldn't see the ball, but his swing was smooth and level and he caught a pitch in his bat's sweet spot and it clanked off a pipe on top of the right-field screen for a game-winning two-run shot. Minutes later, in the visiting dressing room, chairs and food trays started flying as manager Fred Hutchinson pitched a fit. In the locker room next door, Skinner was surrounded by well-wishers. Reflecting the journalistic mores of that era, a *Post-Gazette* writer had no qualm reporting that Skinner "took a congratulatory pounding from players, newspapermen, club officials and others . . ." The story also quoted Clemente going on excitedly about his teammate's game-winning clout. "I bet you that Doggie's ball, she bent iron bar over the right-field fence. That's how hard he hit son-mo-gun."

Within a week, in the midst of a nine-game winning streak, the Pirates had claimed first place, a lofty position they would hold most of the season, dropping to second for a few days in May and only once after that, for a single day in July. It was the quintessential team effort, with strong pitching, led by Law, Friend, and Face, and supplemented by Haddix and Vinegar Bend Mizell, obtained from the Cardinals in a crucial trade in late May. There was timely hitting up and down the lineup, including a career year from shortstop Dick Groat and clutch performances from Hoak, first baseman Dick Stuart, Skinner, Maz, and catchers Smith and Burgess, but Clemente was the driving force behind the team's rise. From that first game, when he knocked home five runs, he was the team's top run producer all season. He drove in half as many runs in the first thirty games as he had in all of 1959. He was hot all of May, when he was named the National League's player of the month for batting .336 and driving in twenty-five runs in twenty-seven games. Throughout the long season what stood out most was Clemente's consistency. From the opening game to the final out, his batting average never dropped below .300. His final average was .314. He had no long hitless slumps, his worst lasted only four days, and no long hitting streaks, either, but a succession of short ones—nine games once, eight games three times, six games once, five games twice. And with that steady hitting he more than doubled his power totals, finishing with sixteen home runs and ninety-four runs batted in, the team high.

His fielding was as daring as ever, but far more consistent than 1959, when his ten assists and thirteen errors were cited negatively by general manager Brown during contract talks. This time Clemente had nineteen assists and only eight errors, and he won as many games with his glove as with his bat. It was not just all natural talent with Clemente; he worked diligently at the craft of fielding. He spent countless hours before games studying how balls caromed off the right field fence at Forbes Field and other National League stadiums. And he combined that studiousness with fearlessness. Danny Murtaugh would say for the rest of his career that the best catch he ever saw was made by Clemente on August 5 that year in a home game against the San Francisco Giants. In the seventh inning, Willie Mays hit a line shot to the right-field corner that Clemente, running full speed, caught just as he was crashing into a brick abutment on the unpadded wall. He bruised his knee and cut his chin, needing six stitches, but held on to the ball and saved the game for Mizell, who won 1–0.

Clemente and Murtaugh had an uneasy relationship over the years, but during 1960 the manager found little to criticize in his right fielder. If there were years when Murtaugh thought Clemente should play more even if he was hurt, this was not one of those years. Clemente played 144 games, 4 more than Hal Smith said they would need to win the pennant.

The Pirates were as consistent as Clemente. They had winning records against the Reds, Cubs, Phillies, Giants, and Braves and were all even, eleven and eleven, with the Dodgers and Cardinals. They had winning records at home and on the road, in day games and night games, against righties and lefties, in nine-inning games and extra-inning contests. They won a majority of the games played every day of the week except Monday, when they went six and six. Their longest losing streaks were four games (twice), while they rolled off winning streaks of nine straight in April, six straight and five straight in May, five straight in June, seven straight in August, and six straight in September. And they also had some magic. Starting with that incredible opening-week comeback against the Reds, they won twenty-eight games that they were trailing in the sixth inning, and twenty-one of those times they staged their winning rallies in the last inning. Clemente was second on the club, behind slugger Stuart, in last-inning game-winning hits.

Throughout the season, the *Pittsburgh Courier* kept close watch on all forty-eight black players in the National League and fifteen in the American League. One of the paper's weekly features was a guest column by a major leaguer, usually cobbled together by Bill Nunn Jr. after an interview. Gene Baker, the veteran utility infielder for the Pirates, who had missed all of the 1959 season with an injury, wrote about how the Pittsburgh front office put him to work as a scout when he was out of action. It was Baker who spent several weeks tailing the Kansas City Athletics and made the key recommendation that the Pirates pick up reserve catcher Hal Smith. "I'm one of those optimists who like to think that the day will come when Negroes are accepted in front-office jobs the same as they are on the playing field," Baker wrote. Al Smith, the White Sox star outfielder, wrote about how much things had improved for black players since the days of Jackie Robinson and Larry Doby. Bill White of the Cardinals wrote that if he had to do it over again he would complete his college education before going into baseball. Willie Kirkland of the Giants wrote about how he was signed off the sandlots of Detroit for $2,500. Don Newcombe, in Cleveland after an illustrious career pitching for the Dodgers, compared the two leagues and said the American League had nothing to match the power of Ernie Banks, Willie Mays, Hank Aaron, Frank Robinson, Orlando Cepeda, old Stan Musial, and Frank Howard. In June it was Roberto Clemente's turn for the guest column.

Nunn published the verbatim transcript of Clemente's tape-recorded comments, using the phonetic spellings that so irritated Clemente when they were done by the mainstream white press. A few weeks earlier, a society note in the paper had taken a jab at Clemente, questioning whether he preferred whites to people of his own race. Clemente lived in Schenley Heights and spent most of his off-hours in the Hill District, but was never fully at home, and occasionally had been the subject of unkind whispers. Coming from Puerto Rico, where segregation was not an overt matter, he had been quoted as saying that he did not want to be treated as a Negro, but by that he meant that he was not accustomed to being discriminated against, not that he disliked blacks. With the column, Nunn gave his friend the opportunity to respond.

"Som' Co-lored people I understand saying 'Clemente, he do not like co-lored people,'" the column began. "This is not the truth at all. Look at me. Look at my skin. I am not of the white people. I hav' color the skin.

"That is the first theeing I straighten out. I like all the people, both co-lored and the white; and since I am co-lored myself, in the skin, I would be seely hate myself.

"Thees' people tell me I don't like colored people. Well, I use this time to tell deeferant. I like myself, so I also like the people who are like me."

Clemente turned to the baseball season. "I hit real good," he noted.

I hit many what you call the "bad bol" pitches, and get good wood. The bol' travel like bullet. That remind me, I hit 565 foote hum-rum in Chicaga, last year; the bol' disappear from centerfield, and Raj Hornsby tell me it longest drive he ever saw hit out of Wrigley Field.

The bol' feel good on the bat but I feel bad at heart, when no writer with our team play up the big drive. I feel effort not appreciated.

Next came a discussion of ball parks, with Clemente saying he liked Forbes Field best for both batting and fielding. His least favorite was Sportsman's Park in St. Louis, and next worst was Candlestick in San Francisco. "Pretty seats and grass but poor playing in tricky wind," he wrote. As for his play this year, he attributed it to his better health. He felt better, he said, than any time since his rookie year. And he saw the team coming together at last.

We have the best . . . hitter in the clutch; none better than Bob Skeener. I tell him they bring in southpaw lefty, and that they lefty mean him trouble. Skeener merely wave hand, then step in and hit line drive for the extra bases.

Don Hoak he player we hav' to hav' in line-up. He solid everywhere. If he out of line-up, Pirates hurt plenty. Everybody got specialty, Groat best hit-run men in baseball.

We have good speerit on Pirates thees' year. Ev'rybody hungry for winning, to get more money. Everybody try little harder and make it harder for the other team.

Ev'rybody work with Manager Murtaugh and the coaches because we hungry to win ball games and fly pennant flag in Forbes Field. If nobody get sick, we make it a race all the time. Thank The Courier very much.

As the season neared its final month and the Pirates looked like pennant winners, talk inevitably intensified on the question of who was the most valuable player. The Pirates had several candidates, including Groat, the quiet captain who led the league in hitting; Tiger Hoak, their gutsy clubhouse leader, the player Clemente himself cited as being indispensable; Deacon Law, on his way to winning twenty games, and Clemente, excelling at the plate and in the field. Les Biederman, the beat reporter for the *Pittsburgh Press,* made it known that he favored Groat, even though Groat had only two homers and barely half as many runs batted in as Clemente. In talking to sportswriters in Los Angeles, Biederman took his campaign a step further, not only pushing Groat but telling his colleagues that Clemente and Hoak, but especially Clemente, did not deserve consideration. By the time the club arrived in San Francisco, word of the sportswriter's actions reached Clemente, leaving him distraught. He had been on another tear, knocking out twenty-two hits in fifty-eight at-bats during the fourteen-game road trip, including five home runs and fifteen runs batted in. He had been lighting the way for his teammates all season, and still Biederman was down on him? On the plane from San Francisco to Chicago, the first leg of a long red-eye flight home, Clemente shared his feelings with Rocky Nelson, the old first baseman, a friend since Clemente had played with him on the Montreal Royals. Nelson had heard about Biederman's anti-Clemente whisperings, and had read other stories in the papers that seemed to ignore Clemente's role on the team, and he thought it was all unfair.

As the team waited for a change of planes in Chicago at five in the morning of September 1, Nelson sought out *Post-Gazette* beat writer Jack Hernon to make Clemente's case. Hernon was no real fan of Clemente's either, but listened and took notes. "There's one thing I can't understand," Nelson said as he approached Hernon. "I've read many stories about who is the most valuable player on the Pirates. But never see the name of Roberto mentioned. I don't know how he can be overlooked when you talk about players on the club. Actually, there is no one player that can be classed as the most valuable, in my opinion. There are about five fellows on this team we couldn't get along without. I mean individually, there's Dick Groat and Don Hoak and the Deacon and Elroy and Clemente. But he doesn't get a call. He's been consistently around .320 all season. He has hit more home runs than ever. He just might be the only player here to drive in over a hundred runs. And certainly he is the best right fielder in the league. Sure, those others are valuable to the team, but no more valuable than Clemente. He's won more games for us with his bat, with his arm, and with his speed on the bases. What more can you ask a player to do to be recognized? If Roberto beefs about not being mentioned, I wouldn't blame him. He's done as much as any other player on this team to keep us in first place."

Hernon acknowledged that Clemente was "Mr. Clutch" on the ball club during the first two months of the season. He remembered Groat telling him once in the locker room how Roberto's eyes "lit up" when he came to the plate with men on base. The other teams seemed to recognize this, Hernon added, by making him the target of brush-back pitches later in the season. But as for himself, Hernon preferred Don Hoak.

The following week, sensing the press box preference for the other players, the *Courier*'s Nunn took up Clemente's cause. "To me, just based on what was right, it was Clemente," Nunn said decades later. "And most guys that really knew baseball felt the same way." In his column, Nunn noted that Clemente had far more home runs and runs batted in than Groat and that he was the best right fielder in the league whereas Groat was in the middle rank of National League glove men at shortstop. "Groat supporters will loudly proclaim that there are intangibles going for their guy which don't show up in the records," Nunn observed. "Having watched both players over the season I would have to say, and very definitely, that this is a two-way street, on which Clemente can walk with pride."

There was nothing easy about winning a pennant that year in the eight-team National League. Series after series, the heavy hitters came at you: Mays and Cepeda and Alou; Musial and Boyer and White; Aaron and Mathews and Adcock. The Pirates had been lucky all year, but in the season's final two months they began to hurt. The first injury was hidden from the public and press for six weeks. On August 13, after defeating the charging Cardinals, Hoak, Friend, Virdon, and Gino Cimoli, (the fourth outfielder, and another former teammate of Clemente's in Montreal back in 1954), went to relax at a friend's back-yard swimming pool in the Pittsburgh suburbs. As Hoak was pulling himself from the pool, he ripped his right foot on the ladder. A large gash opened between his second and third toes, and the bleeding would not stop until a doctor arrived and sewed it up on the spot, without anesthesia. Not for nothing was he called Tiger. The players vowed not to tell anyone about the incident, and Hoak played the next day in a doubleheader, but was hobbling slightly for the rest of the year.

Less than a month later, as the Pirates were playing the Braves in a crucial series at Forbes Field, Dick Groat froze on a high, hard, inside fastball from Lew Burdette in the first inning. At the last nanosecond, Groat raised his left hand to protect his head, and the ball struck him an inch above the wrist. Groat insisted on staying in the game, but the intense pain forced him into the dugout in the third inning, when he was replaced by Ducky Schofield. Officials urged Groat to leave immediately so that he could have his wrist examined, but he wanted to wait until the end of the game. He watched both Clemente and Schofield rap out three hits as the Pirates came from behind to win, 5–3. The X rays showed a fracture that doctors said might keep him out for four weeks, possibly even forcing him to miss the World Series. Groat's prognosis brought a telegram from Vice President Nixon, whose presidential campaign against John F. Kennedy had just been stalled by a ten-day hospitalization for an infected knee. "I was very sorry to hear of your accident," Nixon wrote. "While I will be able to campaign with a bum knee you can't play with a broken wrist." Of more importance to the Pirates, the season's magic dust settled on Schofield, the light-hitting utility man, who suddenly perfected a stunning impersonation of Groat, coming up with key defensive plays and timely hitting game after game.

The same day's paper that carried the grim news of Groat's injury also had front-page stories on Hurricane Donna, which was bearing down on Florida and the East Coast. Donna had already ripped through Puerto Rico, killing more than a hundred people in flash floods, but reports of when and where were sketchy. When a concerned Clemente finally reached his family, he learned that everyone was okay. His brother Matino was more worried about whether Momen was growing tired at the end of a long season and starting to pull off the ball. His batting average had slipped below .320 and his run production had slowed as well. A week later, with the temperatures in Pittsburgh dropping into the fifties in the wake of the hurricane, Clemente came to life with a two-run homer against the Giants. That same day, the Pirates announced that World Series tickets would go on sale in a few days, and the *Post-Gazette* began running a Pennant Fever thermometer illustration on the front page that showed the magic number of games the Pirates needed to clinch the pennant.

Friend pitched a three-hitter against the Dodgers, the thermometer dropped to ten. A few days later, on September 18, Deacon Law won his twentieth, and Clemente made a dazzling catch in the second inning of the second game of the doubleheader, diving to his left to snare a ball off the bat of rookie Bobby Wine with two men on, helping Vinegar Bend Mizell roll to a three-hit shutout—and the Braves and Cards lost and the number dropped to five. They started resodding Forbes Field for the World Series, painted the left-field wall, and constructed new digs for the national press and photographers. The Bucs swept a pair from the Cubs and the magic number was now two. Clemente was superstitious. He thought that Benny Benack and his Iron City Six had become a jinx; when he saw them play the Pirates lost. He didn't want them to go to Milwaukee for the three-game series. Hal Smith kept the team loose, playing his harmonica on the bus to the ballpark. The Pirates lost the first game, and then the second, but the Cardinals also lost and the magic number was one. The good news was that Groat had taken the cast off his wrist and said that he was ready to make a comeback.

The final game in Milwaukee was Sunday, September 25. The Pirates were winning 1–0 late in the game. Clemente was at the plate. Paul Long was announcing with Bob Prince in the broadcast booth. "One to nothing, the Pirates lead on the strength of a home run by Bill Mazeroski. Back in the fifth inning. Otherwise, it's been a real pitching duel between the great lefthander Warren Spahn and the great lefthander Harvey Haddix. Right now it's one to nothing, the Pirates lead . . ."

Bob Prince interrupted. "They've just won it! It's all over! The Pirates win it!"

Just as Prince makes the announcement, Clemente slaps a hard single to center. He began the season hitting and kept hitting to the end. *¡Arriba! ¡Arriba!* In Pittsburgh, thirty-three years of frustration are over. The Pirates have arisen. Families celebrate and head for the airport to await the arrival of their heroes. City officials make plans for a torchlight parade down Fifth Avenue and Grant Street and prepare for a welcome-home crowd of a hundred thousand that will celebrate long into the night. "The Pirates have won the National League pennant on the basis of the Cardinals losing to the Chicago Cubs at Wrigley Field. It's all over," Long continues. "And the crowd here knows it. A lot of transistor radios here. And the applause has gone up . . . And somehow this crowd . . . now they're making the announcement on the loudspeakers. The Cubs have beaten the Cardinals, and the Pirates have won the National League pennant!"

6

Alone at the Miracle

THE LAST TIME THE PIRATES PLAYED IN A WORLD SERIES, in 1927, the opponents were the same New York Yankees. Then the American League champions terrorized opposing pitchers with a lineup of Babe Ruth and Lou Gehrig, Bob Meusel and Tony Lazzeri, now it was Mickey Mantle and Roger Maris, Yogi Berra and Moose Skowron. Murderers' Row old and new, one baseball legend long established, another in the making. The formula was identical in either case: audacious power, solid pitching, pinstripes, intimidation, all rendered glorious by the self-centered hyperbole of New York and its sporting press.

Part of the lore of the 1927 Yankees was a boast that the Pirates, after watching the famed sluggers take batting practice before the series opener, felt so overmatched they folded and lost four straight. Harold (Pie) Traynor, Pittsburgh's Hall of Fame third baseman, had bristled at that story for decades, insisting that it was apocryphal. By Traynor's account, the Pirates were in the clubhouse poring over a scouting report when the Yankees took their pregame cuts. Whatever prodigious shots Ruth and Gehrig stroked during batting practice, the Pirates saw none of them. But the debunking of this myth did not sit well with baseball's commissioner, Ford Frick, for the particular reason that it was Frick himself, as a young sportswriter for the *New York Journal,* who had spread the story in the first place.

The 1960 Pirates were rated 13–10 underdogs by the bookies, but seemed even less likely than their predecessors to be awed by New York, even though these Yankees had won their last fifteen games of the season heading into the World Series. "We'll fight 'em until our teeth fall out and then we'll grab 'em with our gums," snarled Don Hoak, sounding like the former boxer and inveterate scrapper that he was. It was the nature of this team, Hoak said, that they would always rise to the challenge of the better opponents. Virgil Trucks, the batting practice pitcher, told anyone who approached him in the days before the series opener that Pittsburgh was the most relaxed team he had ever seen. Relaxed and gabby. When it came to quotable quotes, Pittsburgh was a gold mine for visiting sportswriters. Hoak, shortstop Groat (recovered from his wrist injury and ready to play), outfielder Gino Cimoli, trainer Danny Whelan, ace Deacon Law, pudgy old Smoky Burgess (who talked so much behind the plate Richie Ashburn once beseeched the ump to shut him up before Ashburn bopped him over the head with his bat), Vinegar Bend Mizell, the big galoots at first, Dick Stuart and Rocky Nelson, and the story-spinning dark Irishman, manager Danny Murtaugh (prone to blabbing about anything but the game itself)—they all were go-to guys on deadline. The *Post-Gazette*, further short-cutting the process, enlisted Hoak, Groat, and Law to write stories during the series, or at least columns published under their by-lines.

Everyone was in on the action, it seemed, except the Pirate in the middle of the lineup who roamed right field. Roberto Clemente was indisputably an important member of the team, yet also in many ways alone. At the end of his sixth and finest season, he was still separated by culture, race, language, and group dynamics. He was the lone black player in the starting lineup and a Spanish-speaking Puerto Rican, while none of the sportswriters for the major dailies in New York or Pittsburgh were black or spoke Spanish. Life is defined by images, especially public life, and the Pirates image was that of a band of scrappy, happy-go-lucky, fearless, gin-playing, hard-drinking, crew-cut, tobacco-chewing white guys. Where was the place in that picture for the proud, regal, seemingly diffident Roberto Clemente? He had led the team in runs batted in and total bases, finished second in batting average, hits, game-winning hits, runs scored, home runs, and triples, had the best arm on the team, played with style and every bit as much grit as Hoak or Groat, yet now was the invisible man. In the run-up to the World Series, the writers of Pittsburgh and New York, for all their overwrought coverage of the spectacle, gave Clemente barely a passing glance.

A notable exception, as usual, was the *Pittsburgh Courier,* the black weekly that had been paying close attention to Clemente all season. On the weekend before the series opener, sports editor Bill Nunn Jr. saw Clemente on the street in Schenley Heights, the middle-class black neighborhood where they both lived, and asked him how he felt about facing the mighty Yankees. The Pirates would win, Clemente assured him, his words echoing Hoak and Trucks. Although the Yankees had more power, he believed Pittsburgh was the better team, stocked with hard-nosed players who could not be intimidated. "We've been a relaxed team all season and I expect us to be the same in the Series," he said. "Pressure didn't get us down during the National League race. We fought off Milwaukee, St. Louis, and Los Angeles without cracking. Now that we've come this far, we aren't going to look back now." In Clemente's estimation, the Braves, not the Yankees, were the second-best team in baseball. "If the Braves had won the pennant, they would have been good enough to beat the Yankees, too." As for playing in Yankee Stadium, Clemente said he would not be haunted by the outfield ghosts of Ruth and DiMaggio, but he was concerned about the late-afternoon shadows. He had played there in the second 1960 All-Star game and found the ball hard to follow.

Aside from Nunn's interview, the other notice Clemente received before the series was negative. Someone had leaked a scouting report from the Yankees suggesting that the most effective way to pitch him was inside. "Knock him down the first time up and forget him," was the dismissive summary. Clemente laughed when asked about it, but the report bothered him. Like many black stars of that era, in a tradition that went back to Jackie Robinson, he got brushed back nearly every series, and he suspected that opposing pitchers chose him for retaliation in part because of the color of his skin. They'd been knocking him down all season in the National League, Clemente observed, and he'd still gotten his share of base hits. During one sequence that season, so memorable that pitcher Bob Friend could recall it forty-five years later, Clemente was hit in the stomach by Dodgers fireballer Don Drysdale but came back the next at-bat and cracked a home run over the right-field fence.

Another scouting report got in more digs. It was by Jim Brosnan, a pitcher who had gained renown for *The Long Season,* a pathbreaking journal-style sports book that provided a revealing glimpse inside his 1959 season with St. Louis and Cincinnati. In the wake of that successful book, Brosnan had been commissioned by *Life* magazine to analyze the series lineup of the Pirates, a team he had faced many times. (Ted Williams, just retired from the Red Sox, wrote *Life*'s scouting report on the Yankees.) After stating that Clemente "dislikes knockdown by close pitch" and that the best way to pitch him is to "jam him good," Brosnan added a caustic and contradictory conclusion. "Clemente features a Latin-American variety of showboating: 'Look at *número uno,*' he seems to be saying . . . He once ran right over his manager, who was coaching third base, to complete an inside-the-park grand-slam home run, hit off my best hanging slider. It excited fans, startled the manager, shocked me, and disgusted the club." Here was precisely the sort of characterization Clemente had battled since he arrived at Fort Myers for his 1955 rookie season. Then the phrase that bothered him was "Puerto Rican hot dog." Now came Brosnan, a respected opponent, far from a redneck, blithely referring to his *Latin-American variety of showboating.* Clemente's mad dash around the bases, the anecdote Brosnan employed to make his point, might have inspired a different interpretation had it been Don Hoak or Dick Groat or years later Pete Rose. Rather than the showboating of a flashy Latin, it would have been viewed as the indomitable spirit of a tough competitor.

This was nothing new for Clemente. It angered him but did not distract him. He still had the Pittsburgh fans on his side—they had voted him their favorite Pirate—and friends were coming from Puerto Rico to see the World Series. Among those making the trip was his mother, Doña Luisa, who had never flown before. She was weakened from the flu, but came anyway, willing herself to be healthy enough to watch Momen play. Don Melchor was equally proud of his son but deathly afraid to fly, so he would not budge from the house in Carolina. He could follow the series from there; all the games were to be broadcast in San Juan on radio and television with Spanish-language announcers. Accompanying Doña Luisa to Pittsburgh was Momen's older brother, Matino, a former ballplayer who had followed the rise of the Pirates on the radio all summer, keeping mental notes on Roberto's play and writing or calling him several times with batting tips. When Matino arrived in Schenley Heights, Clemente gave him some tips of his own on which streets and bars in Pittsburgh were friendly and which ones to avoid.

A fellow named Ralph Belcore was the first out-of-towner to make it to Pittsburgh for the World Series. He came by bus from Chicago toting a stool and a bag of sandwiches and camped outside Forbes Field five full days before standing-room-only tickets went on sale. Belcore was the definition of a baseball fanatic, but in Pittsburgh that week he was just one in the crowd. The city had lost itself with these Pirates. Bands of businessmen crowded the congested streets of the Golden Triangle wearing gold-banded black derbies, walking past block after block of gold-and-black-draped stores with BEAT 'EM, BUCS! signs in the windows. City Hall printed thousands of placards with the familiar slogan translated into seven languages. Carnegie Library came up with its own variation—BEAT 'EM, BOOKS! At the Central Blood Bank of Pittsburgh the sign read BLEED 'EM, BUCS!

Local radio stations incessantly blared out Benny Benack and the Iron City Six's throbbing theme song. The Bucs were going all the way, over and over again. A correspondent for the *New York Times,* filing the first dispatch from alien territory, haughtily described a "carnival atmosphere . . . that one would never experience in sophisticated New York." The Pittsburgh newspapers were all Pirates all the time, from the front page to editorials to society to sports, inspiring Red Smith of the *New York Herald Tribune* to praise the city for focusing on what truly mattered during a week when presidential candidates John F. Kennedy and Richard M. Nixon were debating on television and Soviet Premier Nikita Khrushchev was visiting the United Nations. "In New York," Smith wrote, "the cops picked up a diplomat wallowing hip-deep in smuggled heroin. At the United Nations, Nikita hollered at Dag and Hammarskjöld yelled back and Nehru had a thing or so to say about the future of civilization. Rockets whirled through space, snooping into affairs on the moon, Lyndon [Johnson] called Nixon a fool and Nixon said Kennedy was another. Only in Pittsburgh, it seemed, did they preserve a sense of proportion. Announced the eight-column banner on page one: YANKS, BUCS IN LAST WORKOUT. It was comforting to find a town that puts first things first."

So, first things first. The final workout before the opener was held on a bright October afternoon. Sunlight glanced off the bright white flannels of the Pirates as they took fielding practice. Danny Murtaugh, surrounded by a posse of national sportswriters, entertained them with stories about his Irish family. "When the kid brother gets a job, the brother-in-law quits his. That's the way it is in my family," Murtaugh said as a way of answering a question about how many ticket requests he was getting from relatives. Asked if he had any surprises planned for New York, he said, "Just to win." Soon the Yankees emerged in their gray flannels and Roger Maris muscled into the batting cage, shirtsleeves rolled up over bulging biceps, and began bombing one pitch after another into the right-field stands. The Pirates were in the clubhouse by then, just like their forebears thirty-three years earlier, going over a scouting report prepared by Howie Haak. The Yanks effin' feasted on high ball pitches, Haak said, so keep the damn ball low and outside. A telegram had been taped to the clubhouse wall from the old man, Branch Rickey, gone from the Pirates but still their godfather. It read simply:

> I WOULD RATHER HAVE YOU
> BEAT THE YANKEES THAN
> ANY OTHER TEAM IN THE WORLD.
> AND YOU CAN. AND YOU WILL.

The Pirates would need a healthy Vernon Law if they were to have any chance of that; accordingly much of the focus was on the Deacon's right ankle. He had pulled a tendon in a moment of joy, slipping on a wet dressing room floor as he celebrated with his teammates in Milwaukee after they had clinched the National League pennant. The club tried to hide the injury, but it became obvious a week later when the Braves came to Pittsburgh to finish the season and bombed Law for eight runs and ten hits before he could escape the third inning. There was a day or two when the Pirates were uncertain whether their twenty-game winner could start the series opener, but Law insisted that he was ready, and trainer Whelan said the ankle had not swelled and was bothersome only when twisted a certain way. It did not hinder Law's normal delivery.

Law had the stuff to baffle the Yankees, a sinking fastball and curves of various speeds, all delivered with pinpoint control. Early in his career, he had impressed old Branch Rickey with the "change of pace on his fastball with a wiggle-waggle, half fadeaway rotation." Law had walked only forty-one men in 272 innings all year. He also had the tenacity, despite his reputation as a clean-living elder in the Church of Jesus Christ of Latter-day Saints who did not drink, smoke, or curse (once, at his most vituperative, he shouted "Judas Priest!" at an ump and almost got tossed). Nor did he throw at batters' heads, or so it was said. At a Bucs Fan Club luncheon before the series, Murtaugh jokingly dismissed that last claim. "So I'm talking to one of my pitchers and I says, 'Look, when the other pitcher comes up there I want you to knock him down.' And my pitcher [Law] was one of those fellows who is well versed in the Bible and he tells me, 'Skip, turn the other cheek.' So I looked at him and said, 'All right with me. I'll turn the other cheek. But if this guy don't go down it's gonna cost you a hundred bucks.' So he looked at me and said, 'They that live by the sword die by the sword.'" Even if that was no more than Murtaugh blarney, it captured Law's spirit; he was fire and brimstone on the mound and a fierce competitor. New York had a pitcher of equal big-game stature, Whitey Ford, but the Yankees manager, Casey Stengel, for reasons known only to him and those who could translate Stengelese, chose instead to go with right-hander Art Ditmar, who in fact had won more games that season but was not in Ford's class.

Another perfect autumn day washed over Forbes Field for the opener. The upper deck was dressed in red, white, and blue bunting. In the box seats behind third, Joe Cronin, the American League president, pointed to a screen across the diamond behind first and said he was responsible for it; they installed it after he had made one too many wild heaves into the stands as a rookie shortstop for the Pirates in 1926. A communal gasp sounded from the capacity crowd as a parachutist soared down from the blue sky above, but Jack Heatherington of Mc-

Keesport, who had made the sky-jump after losing a bet that the Pirates would *not* win the pennant, was off-mark again, landing not on the field but on a nearby roof. This was no year to underestimate anything in Pittsburgh.

In the Pirates' dressing room before the game, Murtaugh adhered to his regular season routine, pulling out a scorecard and going over the Yankee lineup hitter by hitter. "Any questions?" he asked when he was done. His team had none. Then "go get 'em," he said. No need for a pep talk, Captain Dick Groat thought. Everyone understood what this series meant. Writing a column for the *Post-Gazette* under the impressive byline . . .

By Dick Groat
PIRATE SHORTSTOP AND NL BATTING CHAMPION

. . . Groat confessed that while he tried to tell himself it was just another game and that there was no reason to be nervous, he had "a peculiar feeling" in the pit of his stomach in his first at-bat and his nerves would not settle for the first few innings.

Law and the Pirates had reason to be anxious in the top of the first when Maris, acting as though it were still batting practice, deposited a home run over the right-field fence, but they got out of the inning with no more damage and swiftly went at Ditmar. Bill Virdon singled and stole second. Groat, nerves and all, doubled him home. Bob Skinner singled in Groat and also stole second. Dick Stuart was retired for the first out, then up came Clemente, batting fifth instead of his usual third, because Murtaugh thought he might have trouble with the six-foot-two 195-pound right-hander. Here was Clemente's first appearance on the World Series stage, the first by a Puerto Rican hitter since Luis Olmo played left field for the Dodgers in 1949 against the Yankees. Doña Luisa and brother Matino were watching from seats behind the screen. The old man was listening on the radio back in Carolina. With the count at two balls, two strikes, Ditmar came inside with a fastball and Clemente stroked it over second for a single, driving in Skinner with the third run. Ditmar was done for the day, yanked by Stengel after throwing only eighteen pitches and getting a lone out.

The first-inning rally showed the Pirates would not be intimidated. It was Stengel who looked anxious, with his quick hook. This was not what most experts expected. Shirley Povich, the venerable sportswriter for the *Washington Post,* thought it was "like the patient examining the doctor for symptoms." By the top of the second, with New York still trailing 3–1 and third baseman Clete Boyer coming to the plate with runners at first and second, the impatience bordered on panic. Boyer was called back to the dugout, and at first he assumed that Stengel had a tip for him on how to bat against Law, but the manager's only instruction was for Clete to find a seat on the bench. Dale Long was sent up to pinch-hit. First game, second inning, Boyer pulled for a pinch hitter on his first at-bat—an uncommon baseball humiliation. Clemente, in right field, knew the feeling; long ago, he had been taken out for a pinch hitter in the first inning with the bases loaded, but that was during his first year in pro ball with the Montreal Royals, when the Dodgers were trying to hide him. As it turned out, Long hit a long fly to Clemente in right, who gathered it in and unloosed a bullet throw to second, nearly doubling Berra.

Stengel's desperation was for nothing. The game essentially was over after a brilliant defensive play by Virdon in the fourth inning. Law was struggling as he worked his way through the new Murderer's Row. Maris walked, Mantle singled, and Yogi Berra, playing in his record eleventh World Series and still feared by the Pirates as the Yankees' toughest clutch hitter, cracked a drive to the deepest expanse of right center. Clemente, racing over from right, and Virdon, at full sprint from center, simultaneously reached the spot where the drive was headed. Clemente, called for it, certain that he could make the catch, and so did Virdon, who "had a beam" on it all along. There was such a roar in the stadium that neither could hear. They brushed against each other, Virdon's spikes cutting the back of Clemente's right shoe, and just as Clemente pulled up, the No. 21 on his back facing the infield, Virdon leaped and snared the ball with his outstretched glove as he neared the light green wall. Writers who had not seen Virdon field were stunned. Murtaugh in the dugout, Law on the mound, and regular observers of the Pirates were elated but not the least surprised. They considered Virdon the nearest thing to Willie Mays in center, perhaps even his equal, and with Clemente patrolling beside him any ball hit to center or right might be caught if it stayed in the park. The Yankees were deflated, and even when Moose Skowron singled to drive in Maris, Murtaugh did not consider taking out Law, who got out of the inning maintaining the lead, which was soon extended in the bottom half when Bill Mazeroski hit a two-run homer for the Pirates.

During the early innings, Elroy Face and his teammates in the Pirates relief corps, unable to get a clear view of home from the bullpen, had raced into the clubhouse when the Yankees were up so they could scout the hitters on television. Everything about the five-foot-eight, 155-pound Face was compact and efficient, including his preparations. He needed only three to four throws to get loose, and rarely bothered to warm up until he saw his manager ambling toward the mound in a late inning. In the eighth, with Law holding a 6–2 lead but looking tired and feeling soreness in his right ankle, Murtaugh made his move. Two gestures signified that he wanted Face. One was simply to hold his hand up to his face; the other was to stick out his right hand, palm down, waist high. Face had a rubber arm and could relieve for two and occasionally three innings, day after day, relying on his specialty pitch, a forkball. Thrown with two fingers spread like fork prongs wide apart over the top of the ball, the forkball was an early variation of the split-fingered fastball that became popular four decades later. (When Steve Blass, a latter-day Pirate pitcher and announcer, asked him to describe the difference between the two pitches, Face replied, "Oh, about four million dollars.") When Face came in, it was a done deal. No trouble in the eighth. In the ninth, he gave up a two-run homer to Elston Howard, but got left-fielder Hector Lopez to ground into a game-ending double-play, Maz to Groat to Stuart, and the Pirates, 6–4 winners, hollered and whooped as they bounded up the underground ramp to their dusty old dressing room.

The Yankees were grouches after the game. They had banged out thirteen hits, more than they had in any game during their season-ending fifteen-game winning streak, yet lost. How could this happen? Boyer made no effort to hide his rage over being yanked before his first chance to bat. Ditmar was despairing over not finishing the first. Mantle, called out on strikes twice, thought one of them was a bad call. Second baseman Bobby Richardson criticized the Pirates infield, notorious for its concrete-like hardness. And Stengel, in his inimitable way, lodged the same complaint. "If they want to I guess they could have the groundskeeper plow it up pretty good because he could get a plow here where they have all the steel to make one but they don't want it," he said. Stengel also took a shot at Clemente, who had grounded into a fielder's choice in the fifth but stayed on first while second baseman Bobby Richardson chased after Skinner on a rundown between second and third. Was this the lack of adventure that Branch Rickey had mentioned during his first scouting report on Clemente in San Juan in January 1955? "Where was the man who hit the ball?" Stengel asked. "He's the fastest man, ain't he? Now if that play had decided the game, they'd all be asking why he didn't go to second. And if I was the manager I wouldn't have an answer." No one asked Clemente about it. In the locker room, he sat alone while the writers gathered around Virdon, Maz, Law, Face, and Bob Friend, who would be starting the next day.

It rained all that night in Pittsburgh and into the next day. By 12:26 P.M., only thirty-four minutes before Game 2 was to begin, the skies were dark, a tarp covered the infield, the players were lounging and playing quick rounds of gin in the clubhouse, and fans were taking shelter under the overhang. But Commissioner Frick, protected by raincoat and hat and working a walkie-talkie with his staff, said the weathermen promised him that sunshine was coming, and within twenty minutes his confidence was rewarded. Stengel presented a starting lineup with veteran catcher Berra playing left field for the first time in his World Series career. His pal Joe Garagiola, who grew up with Berra in St. Louis and had dinner with him in Pittsburgh the night before, thought the talkative Yogi, so accustomed to conducting a running commentary with the home plate umpire and opposing batters, would be "lonely out there with no one to talk to."

Bob Friend, the eighteen-game winner, who threw what was known as a heavy ball, with a fastball reaching ninety-two miles an hour, took the mound for the Pirates, and the home crowd settled in feeling optimistic. Warming up, Friend realized that he had "tremendous stuff," and he felt powerful and in the groove through the opening innings. "The ball was moving all over the place." He had six strikeouts in four innings and it seemed only accidental that he was trailing 3–0. One Yankee run was unearned and another came on a bounding double by Gil McDougald that third baseman Hoak insisted was foul. Fans and writers second-guessed Murtaugh after he removed Friend in the bottom of the fourth for pinch hitter Gene Baker, who rapped into a sharp double play, and at the time Friend himself was distraught. The Yankees weren't really hitting anything, he thought, and he was just getting warmed up. But decades later, the event distanced by time, Friend gave his manager a reprieve. "I don't blame Danny for taking me out," he said. "Danny did the right thing."

There could be no right thing for the Pirates in this game. The Yankees went on a tear after that, pounding out nineteen hits, one short of the World Series record of twenty by the 1921 Yankees and 1946 Cardinals; and sixteen runs, only two less than the record set by the Yankees against the Giants in 1936. They turned the game into a romp in the sixth, sending twelve batters to the plate and scoring seven runs on the way to a 16–3 victory.

In the mess of this slaughter, one sportswriter shouted from the press box, "Bring in Yellowhorse!"—a lament so evocative that several colleagues stole the quote and attributed it to an anonymous fan. Mose J. Yellowhorse, a full-blooded American Indian from Pawnee, Oklahoma, known affectionately as Chief, possessed the most felicitous name in Pittsburgh Pirate history, if not the best record. He pitched two seasons, 1921 and 1922, and won a total of eight games. Perhaps his best move in the majors, according to baseball historian Ralph Berger, came when he and shortstop Rabbit Maranville made some barehanded grabs of pigeons fluttering outside the sixteenth-story window of their road-trip hotel. *Bring in Yellowhorse!* The Chief was sixty-two years old in 1960 and fishing in retirement back in Pawnee, but certainly could have fared no worse that day than the relief quintet of Green, Labine, Witt, Gibbon, and Cheney. Once his sluggers gave him an edge, Stengel became a relentless bench jockey from the shadows of the visitors' dugout, directing a nasal torrent of sarcastic jibes at Smoky Burgess and the procession of hapless Pittsburgh firemen. When Hoak, from his position at third, would shoot a stern look at him, Stengel would "just look at me," Hoak recalled, "throw his hands in the air, and shrug, as if to say, 'What's going on? Why the dirty look, Hoak?'"

Clemente, batting third for the Pirates, had two hits, as did each of the next four men in the lineup (Nelson, Cimoli, Burgess, and Hoak), but Bob Turley, the Yankees starter, was able to scatter thirteen hits and allow only three runs from the losing side. The batting star of the game was Mickey Mantle, who drove in five and clouted two homers, including a tape-measure blast that he hit right-handed. The ball landed in an area over the right-center field vines that had been reached only by lefty sluggers Stan Musial, Duke Snider, and Dale Long. A city policeman who happened to be standing near where the ball came down helped estimate its distance at 478 feet. Handsome Mick was an irresistible story line in the press box. Stengel talked about how he played on one leg and about how he laboriously taped his aching legs for an hour before each game. "He'll always be a hero in our book," wrote David Condon of the *Chicago Tribune.* "He had human faults, but he has super human courage."

Mantle also had more baseball common sense than most sportswriters. Arthur Daley of the *Times,* in prose only slightly more dismissive than his peers, wrote that "the Pirates may never recover from the humiliation of their horrendous rout. It was one that didn't just jar them to their shoe tops. It had to penetrate deeper, all the way to the subconscious, and create a fear complex that could destroy morale." The Mick would have none of that. He understood the rhythms of the game, and the dangers of depleting energy in a one-sided contest. To Mantle, the home runs were a waste, since they came in a blowout. "I wish I could have saved them for a time when they meant something," he said.

With the series now moving to New York, the Pirates left Pittsburgh at six o'clock that night, flying the same United Airlines charter they had used all season. The pilot, Captain Joe Magnano, was from Long Island and had grown up a Yankees fan, but came to identify with the Pirates. Law, Burgess, and Cimoli were interested in flying and were always hanging around the cockpit. Clemente was among those who hated to fly and tried, usually in vain, to sleep on the plane so he wouldn't have to brood about every thump or bump. The Yankees, at Stengel's insistence (he wanted to "ride herd" on them, it was said), traveled by train, reserving five Pullman cars in the Pennsylvania Railroad's *Pittsburgher* express. The sportswriting tribe tagged along, as did a few hundred boisterous Pirates fans, who upon arrival in New York found themselves virtually alone in the belief that the series would last enough games for a return to Forbes Field. Al Abrams, the *Post-Gazette* sports editor, strolled into the lobby of the Commodore Hotel to see a tabloid headline about Game 2—MURDER IN PITTS-BURGH. "Every time I go outside the hotel," he noted, "I hear dire consequences for the Pirates." When the teams worked out at Yankee Stadium on Friday, the off-day, there was no front-page headline, though Red Smith might have appreciated this priority: Khrushchev moved out of the Waldorf-Astoria, making room for the World Series headquarters. There was no citywide delirium like in Pittsburgh; a World Series was considered an annual event in New York, but still by eight on the morning of game day there were three thousand people waiting in line for bleacher seats, and five hours later the stadium was filling with seventy thousand fans.

With Clemente on the Pirates and countryman Luis (Tite) Arroyo pitching in relief for the Yankees, the series was drawing great interest in Puerto Rico and all of the Caribbean. The North American press tended to treat the Latin contingent as fodder for lighthearted comedy. There was nothing malevolent about this, but it reflected the attitudes of the time and the fact that Spanish-speaking players and their culture were still regarded as oddities. Clemente was quoted in the locker room before the third game telling his teammates how thrilled he was that his family and friends in Puerto Rico could see him play on television for the first time. "I shave, put on cologne and powder so I smell good for television," he reportedly said. As the game was getting under way, with Vinegar Bend Mizell starting for the Pirates, there was guffawing in the press box about what Al Abrams called a "crisis" faced by Latin American journalists, who struggled with the pronunciation of Mizell's colorful appellation. Vinegar Bend was the name of the hamlet where he grew up in rural Alabama. "So they just called him Wilmer," Abrams reported.

The pronunciation problem was resolved soon enough in any case, since Mizell lasted only a third of an inning. He gave up four runs on three hits before Murtaugh replaced him with Clem Labine, who proved no more effective than he had been in Game 2. It was 6–0 at the end of one, and 10–0 by the end of four. Pirates pitchers consistently fell behind in the count and ended up grooving fastballs for the Yankees to feast on. Gino Cimoli, playing left, tried Ring Lardner's favorite Alibi Ike complaint, that the sun was in his eyes, but teammate Rocky Nelson shut him up by noting that Cimoli had no excuses since he was usually turned away from the sun looking at balls soar over his head. By the middle innings, binoculars turned from the field to the stands for celebrity spotting. Herbert Hoover, the former President, showed up in the fourth wearing a gray fedora, taking his seat in time for another Mantle home run. He was barely noticed, which someone noted was an improvement on his World Series appearance at Philadelphia's Shibe Park during the depths of the Depression in 1931, when he was roundly booed. Jawaharlal Nehru, the prime minister of India, appeared in the sixth. It was appropriate, Red Smith observed, that a "man of peace" would not arrive until the "carnage was over." One fan supposedly mistook Nehru for a hot dog vendor in his white cap. Mildred McGuire, a fan from Wayne, New Jersey, seated nearby, reported that he spoke perfect English. Though Mantle had four hits including the home run, the stars for the Yankees this time were Whitey Ford, who tossed a complete game shutout, and second baseman Bobby Richardson, who drove in six runs, four of them on a fly ball that reached the close, cozy corner of the left-field stands for a grand slam.

Clemente kept his hitting streak alive by singling with two out in the ninth, and flashed his fielding brilliance a few times with rocket throws from right and a difficult catch of a Maris line shot to right center. All piddling and forgettable when your team gets drubbed 10 to zip. "That game didn't make me feel any younger," said Danny Murtaugh, who had turned forty-three that day. In the press box, there was a rush to bury the Pirates. The lone writer who thought Pittsburgh still had a chance was Don Hoak, who in his column after the game declared: "If you quit on the Pirates now there's a very good chance you'll have to eat your words in a few days."

For the critical fourth game on Sunday, October 9, the Pirates were able to turn again to Vernon Law. The Deacon and Mrs. Law had been unable to attend church that morning, much to his dismay, but they prayed in their hotel room at the Commodore. For all of his devotion, Law was not the proselytizing sort, never bugged his teammates to stop doing this or that, and never tried to pretend the Lord was on his side, or taking any side at all in a sporting event. "We prayed that no one on either side would get hurt and that everyone would do as well as they possibly could," he reported. "We did not pray for victory because that would be a selfish prayer."

The way the first inning started, it looked as though Law could have tried some selfish prayer. Bob Cerv cracked an inside pitch to left for a single and Tony Kubek followed by doubling a low, outside pitch to left, the forty-ninth and fiftieth Yankee hits of the series. Hoak approached the mound from third and said, "Deacon, we've been pitching that Kubek wrong. The reports on him are wrong. Let's pitch him up and in instead of down and away." Law was so accustomed to Hoak's yammering that he paid little attention. But he nodded and registered the suggestion, which was what he was thinking anyway. And he "wasn't too worried," he reported later, about having runners on second and third, because he knew that if he got Maris out he could walk Mantle and try for a double play. That was precisely what happened, with Berra grounding to Hoak for an around-the-horn twin-killing that ended the inning. Law coasted until the fourth, when Moose Skowron homered to give the Yankees a 1–0 lead.

At the same hour, the Steelers of the National Football League were hosting the New York Giants in Pittsburgh. In the second quarter, as the Giants were driving, quarterback George Shaw approached the line of scrimmage to take the snap and was startled by a thunderous roar echoing through the stands of Pitt Stadium. Over thousands of transistor radios, NBC announcers Chuck Thompson and Jack Quinland had just reported that Vern Law had doubled in the tying run at Yankee Stadium in the middle of a three-run rally for the Pirates. As two more runs scored, the roar at Pitt Stadium grew louder, confusing Shaw so much that a referee eventually had to call time. Pennsylvania Governor David Lawrence, the former Pittsburgh mayor who also scribbled a column for the *Post-Gazette* that week, was in the Pitt Stadium crowd, listening on his own portable radio, and chronicled the eeriness of hearing a hometown throng "cheer at the same time the Giants were moving against our Steelers."

Law kept the Yankees off the board in the fifth and sixth, but by the seventh the pain in his ankle was so intense that he could barely land on it. Skowron, first up for New York, lined an opposite field double that bounced into the right-field stands, and McDougald slapped another single to right. Clemente scooped up the ball and fired a dead-true, no-bounce strike to the plate, a throw that Red Smith described as "low and baleful." The third-base coach, Frank Crosetti, keenly aware of Clemente's arm, had held Skowron at third or he would have been moose meat. Richardson then bounced a grounder to Maz, who stepped on second but had a slight hitch getting the ball out of his glove, allowing Richardson to beat the throw and barely avoid a double play. No-touch, they called Maz, for the way he could turn the double play seemingly without ever touching the ball, but in this case his touch was uncertain. Skowron came home, making the score 3–2. John Blanchard, another left-handed Yankee slugger, pinch hit for the pitcher and singled to right, sending Richardson to second. That was enough for Murtaugh, who walked slowly to the mound to get his ace. Before taking the ball, he placed his hand out, palm down, waist high, and in came Face. Photographers captured the transition, a classic tableau of baseball courage. In the background, the little reliever stood on the mound, rubbing the ball and talking to Smoky Burgess, as Law, his work done, his glove dangling from his pitching hand, limped slump-shouldered toward the dugout. His arm felt like he could go eighteen innings, Law recalled—he had indeed pitched eighteen innings in a game several years earlier—but "the leg was beginning to pain me something awful late in the game and I'm glad Face was ready to do the job."

One out, men on first and second, here came the forkball, and there it went, soaring off the bat of Bob Cerv, arcing toward the fence in deep right-center, a virtual duplicate of the ball Berra had struck in the opener. And here came Clemente again, racing from right, and Virdon flying in from center, and Virdon leaping and bringing the ball in with both hands, then falling against the wall at the 407 mark but holding on. Richardson tagged and went to third, but died there when Kubek bounced out. And that was the last threat against Face, who shut down the Yankees for two and two-thirds innings, the final out coming on a fly to Clemente in right. Series tied, two games apiece.

Bob Friend was ready for Game 5 on Monday, but Murtaugh decided to go with Harvey Haddix, his little lefthander, which caused some grumbling among the locals in the press box but not in the club-house. Why gamble with Friend rested? a writer deigned to ask. "What the god damn hell are you talking about?" responded Tiger Hoak, never at a loss for words, or expletives. "It's no god damn gamble. That god damn little shit has a heart as big as a god damn barrel!" It was a sun-splashed day, and the little guys made it look easy. Haddix and Face, again, combined on a five-hitter, striking out seven and never really seeming in danger. When Face was on the mound, the Crow, as Yankees third-base coach Crosetti was called, would usually study his finger work in the glove and yell out, "Here it comes!" when he could detect a forkball. Hoak, at third base, was on to this and came up with a foil, yelling, "Here it comes!" on every pitch. But in this fifth game Hoak could see that Face was unhittable, so he didn't even bother yelling. Another two-and-two-thirds, this time with no hits.

The Bucs had ten hits, including a key run-scoring single by Clemente off his countryman, Arroyo, who thought he had made the perfect pitch and threw up his arms in exasperation as the ball screamed toward the outfield grass. Clemente had now hit safely in all five games, and was starting to get a bit of recognition for his play. In the locker room after the game, which the Pirates won 5–2, Ted Meir of the Associated Press decided to step away from the crowd and write something about Roberto. "The unsung star of the World Series?" his report began. "That phrase could well apply to Roberto Clemente, the Pittsburgh right fielder with the rifle arm." Scores of reporters, Meir observed . . .

> . . . surrounded pitchers Elroy Face and Harvey Haddix after Pittsburgh's 5–2 victory over New York Monday. Off to one side Clemente sat in front of his locker—alone.

Yet here was the player whose bullet throwing arm had stopped the Yankees from taking an extra base on hits to his territory, a feat that contributed mightily to Pittsburgh's three victories.

He beamed as his throwing arm was compared to the famed one of Hazen (Kiki) Cuyler, who played the same right field for the Bucs in 1925 when they won the World Championship by beating Washington and Hall of Fame pitcher Walter Johnson.

"Sure," Roberto grinned happily. "Nobody can run on me." Clemente put the fear into the Yankee base runners in the first game at Pittsburgh. In the second inning, after Yogi Berra and Bill Skowron had singled with none out, he gathered in pinch hitter Dale Long's fly and just missed doubling Berra at second with a rifle peg.

"We discovered then," Yankee manager Casey Stengel said later, "that they have a good right fielder."

Meir wrote that Clemente had made the last putout in the fifth game and had given the ball to the Pirates owner, John Galbreath. "My son's wife is expecting a baby any day in Columbus, Ohio," Galbreath said. "If it's a boy, that ball will be his first present." (The ball remained with the Galbreaths and forty-five years later Squire Galbreath, the grandson born just after the World Series, kept it in a display case at the family estate, Darby Dan, near Columbus, Ohio.)

The focus of the world seemed to shift back to Pittsburgh that night. The Yankees, Pirates, and John F. Kennedy all were coming to town. Kennedy arrived first for an appearance at Gateway Center, where thousands jostled for viewing position to see the Democratic presidential candidate, at one point bursting through the police lines. (Most of the Pirates were Republicans—Bob Friend would later serve as a delegate for Kennedy's opponent, Nixon—but Clemente was a staunch Kennedy man.) At the Penn-Sheraton Hotel downtown, Kennedy issued what was described as his strongest-ever speech in support of civil rights. Then came the Yankees, who drew only a sprinkling of autograph seekers at the airport. "I understand we made a lot of people happy here and they're glad to see us back," Casey Stengel said as he stepped from the plane. An hour later, when the Pirates charter eased toward the terminal, the players peered out portholes to a stunning sight—more than ten thousand fans cheering behind the gate along a line that stretched ten deep for a quarter of a mile. Kennedy and Nixon held little interest for this crowd. MURTAUGH FOR PRESIDENT signs were more prominent. Such was the reception for a team that in the first five games of the World Series had been outscored 34–17, outhit 61–42, outhomered 8–1, trailed in total bases 95–59, and in team batting average .325 to .245. All true, and yet only one statistic mattered. The Pirates led the Yankees three games to two.

Stengel had a decision to make on whom to start in the sixth game, and explained his reasoning in a way only he could articulate. "I asked my players if they wanted Ford to start and they all did except six or eight; they was the other pitchers which wanted to start themselves." Whitey was tired, his fast ball had little zip and his curve wasn't breaking much, but most pitchers would give anything for his problems. With his day-old blond stubble and crafty determination, he tossed another complete game shutout, throwing only 114 pitches and inducing the Pirates to hit into seventeen ground outs and three double-play grounders. Clemente singled in his first at-bat to keep his string alive, but spent the rest of the game chasing down singles and doubles. "The fellow who did the most throwing than any other Pirate was Roberto Clemente," reported the game story in the *Times*. "So many hits whistled into his territory that he was forever firing the ball into the infield." It was another rout, with the Yankees banging out seventeen more hits and Bobby Richardson again stealing the show from the sluggers, driving in three more runs for a record total of twelve for the series. The final score was 12–0, yet somehow to the Pirates it seemed like no big deal. "All three of our defeats have been shellackings but that doesn't hurt our pride one bit," Hoak observed. "When you've had the tar kicked out of you, you don't lose sleep replaying the game."

They had lost three games by a composite score of 38–3, yet they had the Yankees right where they wanted them. Vern Law was ready for the seventh game, with Face backing him up, whereas Stengel had used up Ford and had no one comparable to Law available, facing a choice among Bob Turley, twenty-two-year-old rookie Bill Stafford, and little Bobby Shantz. "I've got to talk to Turley and see how he feels," Stengel said. "He did a lot of warming up in the bullpen [during game six] and I want to make sure he isn't too tired."

The thirteenth of October was another dreamy day in western Pennsylvania, with a summery haze and temperatures in the low seventies. It was a weekday in Pittsburgh, a Thursday, yet the city had the feel of an August vacation weekend. Thousands of children stayed home from school to watch the final game of the World Series on television. Hordes of businessmen and government workers also contrived excuses to play hooky. "Our *other* grandmother died," read a sign in the county clerk's office. "We've gone to bury her with the Yanks."

Most fans were not so confident about which team was to be buried. Of the three games the home crowds had witnessed at Forbes Field, the Yankees had won two, and by the monstrous scores of 16–3 and 12–0. During the sixth-game trouncing, demoralized Pittsburghers started streaming out of the stadium in the third inning and the stands were half-empty by the seventh. Those holding tickets for the decisive seventh game arrived in a subdued mood. Benny Benack and his Iron City Six set up outside the stadium at the corner of Boquet and Sennott and valiantly tried to energize the faithful, but people seemed reluctant even to shout "Beat 'em, Bucs!" There was a sense that the Bucs had gone a long, long way already, but maybe they would finish one game short of all the way. The Yankees certainly felt that way. Two of their stars, Mantle and Berra, were quoted in the *Post-Gazette* that morning saying that they had the far superior team, and would still have the better team even if by some fluke the Pirates happened to win. Their comments further stirred the Pirates. "We'd read the *Post-Gazette* . . . you bet we did," Don Hoak reported from the clubhouse.

Casey Stengel chose a symbolic way to inform Bob Turley that he was starting the seventh game. He never spoke directly to the pitcher, but after the team bus pulled up to Forbes Field from the downtown

Hilton and Turley reached his locker, he found a baseball inside one of his spikes, placed there by third-base coach Crosetti. "It was a brand-new ball and that was the tip-off that I was to be the starter," Turley explained during batting practice. "Sure, I had an idea I would be it, but you never can tell with Casey." Perhaps Casey couldn't tell about himself, either. From Turley's first pitch, he had both Stafford and Shantz warming up in the bullpen. "It was something less than a rousing vote in Turley's skills," observed Shirley Povich of the *Washington Post.*

Murtaugh stocked his lineup with left-handed hitters, including Skinner, who had been out for most of the series with a sore thumb, and Rocky Nelson, who took over at first for Dick Stuart, slump-ridden with only three hits, all singles, in twenty at-bats. The move paid quick dividends in the first inning when Skinner walked with two outs and Nelson then homered to right to give the Pirates a 2–0 lead. Redemption of this sort had been a long time coming for Glenn Richard Nelson. Since making a major league roster in 1949, he had played for the Cardinals, Pirates, White Sox, Dodgers, Indians, Dodgers again, Cardinals again, and finally the Pirates a second time, with long spells in the minors all during that stretch. Rocky was a nomadic baseball lifer, so attached to the game that during one of his minor league stints he got married at home plate. Thirty-five and balding now, he was the oldest of the Pirates, called "Old Dad" by his teammates. Clemente had first played with him in 1954 on the International League's Montreal Royals, where Nelson was the reigning home-run champ and a fan favorite but annoyed manager Max Macon with his lackadaisical fielding. He had what was called minor league power and hit more round-trippers in one season at Montreal than in his full major league career. His trademark was his odd stance—body turned, front foot facing the pitcher, bat held high, posture so formal and rigid that writers called it the John L. Sullivan stance, evoking the old boxer's pose. After years of frustration it served its purpose this one magical time, delivering a crucial early blow to the cocksure Yankees.

When Smoky Burgess led off the second with a shot into the right-field corner, his slowpoke gait and Maris's quick recovery holding him to a single, the edgy Stengel had seen enough. He ambled out to the mound, mumbled something to himself, and "out came Turley like a loose tooth," as Red Smith reported. In came the rookie Stafford, who walked Hoak on four pitches and gave up a bunt hit to Mazeroski to load the bases. Vern Law, unable to duplicate his hitting magic of Game 4, bounced into a double play, pitcher to home to first, but then leadoff man Virdon singled to right-center to make the score 4–0. The fan anxiety that had enveloped the stadium before the game suddenly lifted. Up four, the Deacon on the mound, it all looked good for Pittsburgh.

Through four innings, Law had allowed only one hit, a single by Hector Lopez, but it was obvious that he was in pain every time he put weight on his ankle. In the fifth, Moose Skowron led off with a home run that fell just inside the foul pole in the right-field stands. Law retired the next three batters with no trouble, but when he started the sixth by giving up a single to Richardson and walking Kubek, Murtaugh came to get him. "I knew his ankle was hurting him and he might have injured his pitching arm if he'd stayed in any longer," Murtaugh explained later. "Winning a World Series is important but not at the cost of ruining a pitcher like Vernon Law." In fact, Law would go on to pitch for another seven seasons in his fine career, but never again win twenty games or approach the level of dominance he reached in this series, when he battled the Yankees on one leg and left every game with his team in the lead.

There's no tomorrow is the old seventh-game cliché, and Murtaugh used it on his pitchers before the game, saying they should all be ready in the bullpen. Bob Friend, Harvey Haddix, and all the others were available, but when Law had to come out, even though it was just the sixth inning, Murtaugh had only one thought in mind. He brought in Face one last time. Perhaps it was once too many. Face had gone more than two innings in each of the previous two wins, and his arm was shot. He retired the first batter, Maris, on a foul out, but then Mantle bounded a single up the middle, scoring Richardson, and Berra crushed a three-run home run that landed barely fair in the upper deck in right. In an instant, the Pirates had lost the lead and the Yankees seemed transformed again into the murderous bunch of games two, three, and six.

Face got out of the inning after that and the next inning and a half were uneventful except for one move that seemed utterly insignificant at the time. Burgess singled in the Pirates half of the seventh and left the game for a pinch runner, who was stranded. When the Yankees came to bat in the eighth, Hal Smith replaced Burgess at catcher. Face, still plugging away with no strength or stuff, retired Maris and Mantle, then ran into trouble again. Singles by Skowron and Johnny Blanchard and a double by Cletus Boyer—the same Boyer who had been humiliated by Stengel in the first game—brought in two more runs, giving the Yankees a 7–4 lead going into the bottom of the eighth. All of this was mere prelude to the dramatic final act.

Since their early-inning explosion, the Pirates had been tamed by New York's own little giant, lefty Bobby Shantz, who had encountered fifteen batters and given up only one hit and a walk. Up first for the Pirates now was Gino Cimoli, pinch hitting for Face. As he described it later to the *Post-Gazette*'s Myron Cope, Cimoli felt "slightly weak at the stomach" as he plucked his bat from the rack and walked to the plate. He worked the count to two and two, staying off Shantz's pitches that hit the low, outside corner of the strike zone, and then found one more to his liking and dropped a single into right field between Maris running in and Richardson hustling out. Next up was Virdon. On the second pitch, he cracked a two-hop grounder to shortstop Kubek. "Oh, heck, a double play," Virdon thought to himself as he ran to first. But on its last hop on the infield apron, the hard surface the Yankees had been complaining about all series long, the ball took a bad bounce, higher than Kubek expected, and struck him in the throat. In excruciating pain, he fell to the ground and the ball rolled free. Two on, no out instead of two out, bases empty. In the press box, the *Post*'s Povich recalled the famous pebble play of the seventh game of the 1924 World Series when Earl McNeely of the Senators grounded to third but the ball struck an infield pebble and bounded over New York third baseman Freddie Lindstrom's head, allowing the winning run to score. The way the ball bounces: so *that's* what the cliché meant.

The game stopped and attention turned to the fallen Kubek. Stengel made the long walk from the dugout to check on his young shortstop, who had celebrated his twenty-fourth birthday earlier in the series. Kubek was spitting blood and couldn't really talk, but signaled to Stengel that he wanted to stay in the game. It was a gutsy request, but Stengel ignored him and took him out, and soon he was being transported to Pittsburgh's Eye and Ear Hospital, where Dr. H. K. Sherman determined that he had internal bleeding and a severely bruised vocal chord and needed to stay overnight for observation. Joe DeMaestri was sent in to play short. Now it was Shantz facing Dick Groat, who had struggled during the series with only five hits in twenty-seven at-bats. Shantz decided to pitch him inside, not wanting the skilled batsman to poke the ball to right. He came inside three straight times. By the third pitch, Groat had adjusted, and pulled the ball down the third-base line, past Boyer, for a run-scoring single. Stengel decided Shantz was through, and replaced him with Jim Coates. Everyone knew the next batter, Skinner, would bunt, and he did, dropping the ball down the third-base line, moving the runners up to second and third. Rocky Nelson had another chance at heroics, but failed to reach the right-field porch this time, instead lofting a routine fly ball to Maris.

Two out, men in scoring position, Roberto Clemente stepped to the plate. Coates decided to pitch him outside, hoping to get the free-swinger to lunge at a bad pitch. Clemente, in his eagerness, flailed at three straight outside pitches and fouled them off, breaking his bat in the process. He strolled back to the dugout for another Frenchy Uhalt model. In the radio booth, NBC's Chuck Thompson was calling the play-by-play. "In typical World Series fashion this one appears to be going right down to the wire," he said. "Now Blanchard pumpin' out the sign to Coates, who wigwags with that glove just a bit. He wants to see the sign again. Now Coates is into the move, the one-two to Clemente."

Thompson's voice quickened. "He swings . . . ground ball . . . slowly hit off the first base side. Charging is Skowron. He makes the pickup. There'll be no play and the run scores!" A thunderous roar filled Forbes Field, and Thompson waited for the decibels to lower slightly before continuing. "Clemente hit a slow roller down the first-base way, wide of the bag, about ten or twelve feet to the right, or to the second-base side. Skowron came charging in, made the pickup on the ball.

Had no chance of a play at the plate because Virdon broke with the crack of the bat. And then realized that he couldn't get over there in time to get Clemente at first base. So the infield hit by Clemente has driven in the sixth Pirate run. Down to third base goes Groat. Two outs. It's the Yankees seven, the Pirates six. And the batter will be catcher Hal Smith."

The New York writers went into a tizzy over this play. Where was Coates? they wanted to know. He should have been at the bag to take Skowron's throw, complained Arthur Daley, but "was probably so busy trying to figure out what his share of the winners' purse would be that he forgot to cover the bag." Clemente, racing down the line, was certain that he would have beaten any throw to the bag, and many observers agreed. Coates did not delay leaving the mound, but had to circle around Skowron on his way to the bag. In any case, the Pirates were still alive, sending up Hal Smith, the backup catcher who had replaced Burgess in the seventh. "Smith steps in with two down, runners at first and third, and this ballpark is going crazy," Thompson reported. An electric current seemed to run through the stands of Forbes Field, every fan plugged in, wired, lit up, a sensation that only late-inning October baseball could create. In downtown Pittsburgh, crowds bubbled on the sidewalks outside department stores showing the game on televisions in their display windows. All work stopped. Thompson returned to the microphone . . .

"Coates into the set . . . he throws . . . takes a strike right down the pike. And Smitty was giving it a good look. One strike to the right-hand batting Hal Smith. Clemente hit a little dribbler off the first-base side, wide of the bag at first and legged it out for a base hit. And Virdon was able to score the sixth run. Now the one-strike pitch coming to Smith. It's high, a ball. One ball, one strike. Well, the Pirate opportunity in this inning came about on the bad-hop ball that hit Kubek in the throat and knocked him out of the ball game. Now the one-one pitch to Smith. There it is. Swing and a miss, strike two. He really pulled the trigger. One ball, two strikes to Hal Smith. He gave it the big ripple, the Sunday punch, and couldn't find it. The tying run is at third base in the person of Dick Groat. The go-ahead run is at first base in the person of Roberto Clemente. And now the set, the one-two pitch to Hal Smith."

On the mound, Coates had decided to climb the ladder, hoping that Smith would swing at a high hard one. "Coates throws," announced Thompson. "He started to swing and held back. And took it high for a ball. A checked swing. Ball two. Two and two now. And for just a split-second every move in the Pirate dugout came to a stop on that call out there at the plate. It was a high pitch and Smith held back on the swing. So the count at two and two."

At the plate, Smith stood ready, whispering a quiet mantra to himself. *Meet the ball. Meet the ball.* "Coates into the stretch. He sets. And the two-two to Smith. He swings." Anyone listening on the radio could hear the sharp crack of the bat. "A long fly ball deep to left. I don't know, it might go out of here! It is going . . . going . . . gone! Forbes Field at this moment is an outdoor insane asylum! We have shared in one of baseball's great moments!"

Smith liked to golf low pitches and could tell by the "feel" that he had connected. Coates could tell, too, and threw his glove in the air in disgust. As Smith rounded first base and saw Berra and Mantle stop in their tracks and the ball soar over the 406 sign and far beyond into Schenley Park, he had to fight off the urge to turn a celebratory somersault. Stengel had crab-walked out of the dugout by then and was signaling in Ralph Terry from the bullpen. Coates departed, head down, and Stengel followed behind, his team now losing 9–7. Hoak flied to left, and the Yankees came in for their last at-bat.

Haddix and Friend had been warming up in the bullpen for the Pirates. "You're the one," Haddix said, and Friend hitched his pants and marched to the mound. He had been the loser in games two and six, but here was his chance to make amends. He had a rubber arm and wasn't feeling tired. You can rest all winter, Murtaugh had told him. It was all happening so fast now, and here he was, facing the top of the order. Four pitches later, there he went, heading toward the dugout, distraught, having given up singles to Richardson and pinch hitter Dale Long. Now Haddix was the one. Hoak looked over from third and thought Haddix looked "as cool as fish on ice." Lefty against lefty, he got Maris to pop up to the catcher. But Mantle, batting right-handed, smashed a line drive to right-center, sending Richardson home and Long to third. The stadium fell silent. Gil McDougald went in to run for Long, representing the tying run at third. Berra, the feared clutch hitter, slashed a sharp drive to the first-base side. Rocky Nelson, never known for his fielding, snared the ball on a short hop, saving a double, and made a split second decision. Should he throw to second to try for a first-short-first double play or step on the bag for a sure out and then throw to second to try to get Mantle on a tag play? Step on the bag, Nelson said to himself, and as he touched the bag and turned to make the play, where was Mantle? Not heading toward second but sliding back into first. Nelson was frozen in surprise. Mantle swerved to avoid the tag in a brilliant bit of base running. In retrospect, it was apparent that Nelson could have tagged Mantle first and then stepped on the bag for an easy, game-ending double play, but both players were reacting on instinct, and Mantle's instincts were superior. The tying run scored from third and the game was still on. The next batter, Skowron, hit into a force play at second, and the Pirates raced to their dugout. Nine-nine, bottom of the ninth.

Mazeroski was first up for Pittsburgh.

That was the brilliant last line of Red Smith's column the next day.

Maz was made for Pittsburgh. He grew up nearby, in Wheeling, West Virginia, and was tough, quiet, modest, ethnic, the son of a coal miner who had lost a foot in a mining accident and died young of lung cancer. For five seasons, since he came up at age nineteen, Maz had struggled to fulfill his potential as a boy wonder. He was up one year, down the next, but had rebounded from a dismal 1959 season to help lead the Pirates to the pennant this year, at age twenty-four, fielding brilliantly and hitting .273 with eleven home runs and sixty-four runs batted in. Like his counterpart on the Yankees, Bobby Richardson, he could seem lost in the lineup until a tense moment arose, and then his teammates were encouraged to see him walk to the plate.

Now here he stood, No. 9, waiting for Ralph Terry, his jaw working a wad of tobacco. Dick Stuart, the slumping but dangerous slugger, had lumbered out to the on-deck circle, ready to pinch-hit for the pitcher. Stuart was certain that he would hit a home run to win the game. In the dugout, Bob Friend stared down at his spikes, swearing at himself, brooding about his pitching and not getting the job done. Vern Law was hoping, even praying, that all would turn out right. Clemente sat nearby. He was scheduled to be the fifth batter that inning. He was preparing himself mentally for the possibility of coming to bat with two outs and two on. In the radio booth, Chuck Thompson had almost exhausted his superlatives with all the dramatic plays he had called in the last twenty minutes.

"The last half of the ninth inning," Thompson began prosaically. "Changes made by the Yankees: McDougald goes to third base. Cletus Boyer moves over to play shortstop. And Ralph Terry of course on the mound will be facing Mazeroski. . . . Here's a ball one, too high now to Mazeroski. The Yankees have tied the game in the top of the ninth inning. A little while ago, we mentioned that this one in typical fashion was going right down to the wire. Little did we know. Terry throws . . . here's a high fly ball going deep to left. This may do it. Back to the wall goes Berra . . ."

Third baseman McDougald is still looking toward home plate as the ball sails over his head. The third-base and left-field umpires, neatly aligned along the line, are also looking in. This clout does not have the towering parabola of Hal Smith's, but the ball keeps going. Murtaugh thinks it will be caught. So does Bob Friend. Mazeroski is not sure, barely looking, sprinting hard to first, no easy home-run trot. From the Pirates dugout, Ducky Schofield, the reserve infielder, watches Berra retreat to the wall and look up, ready to play the ball off the wall. Then Yogi turns and bends and slumps, his knees almost buckling. And it is over.

Behind the ivy wall, the square Longines clock reads 3:37 P.M. Murtaugh wants to kiss his wife. Unbelievable, thinks Friend. "It is . . . over the fence, home run, the Pirates win!" shouts Chuck Thompson. A staggering roar shakes the stands. "Ladies and gentlemen, Mazeroski has hit a one-nothing pitch over the left-field fence at Forbes Field to win the 1960 World Series for the Pittsburgh Pirates . . ." Ralph Terry throws his glove and stalks from the mound. He has no idea what kind of pitch it was, he will say later, only that it was the wrong one. Maz is dancing, leaping high, like he's riding an imaginary bronco, waving his helmet instead of a cowboy hat; now prancing around second and taking the joyous homeward turn at third. The diamond is madness, fans rushing forward, a raving, wild-eyed convoy, a boy reaches out, and then another, men in suits and shirtsleeves scramble into the action, city cops and state troopers with billy clubs race-waddle in from the left-field side, the Pirate dugout empties and forms a buzzing, delirious hive, bobbing behind the plate, waiting, fortunes changed in a second; and now the final steps, the crew-cut hero arriving with all of Pittsburgh in loving pursuit, and the ump clears the way, arms out, and Maz takes a final leap on the plate and disappears, everyone grabbing, pounding, like going fifteen rounds with Floyd Patterson, he thinks, but he's too happy to feel the pain, and Clemente and a few teammates try to protect him as they bounce back to the dugout and through the underground dimness to the dressing room.

The field is left to the fans, hundreds of them, running aimlessly, singing endless choruses of what Red Smith now calls "the tinny horror entitled 'The Bucs Are Going All the Way.'" A man in a brown suit brings out a spade and literally digs up home plate and walks away with it. Life is a series of sensations, and here is an unforgettable one for all Pirates fans. For the rest of the afternoon and late into the night, the streets belong to the people. Everything upside down, an act of rebellion at the dawn of the sixties, the establishment losing a first round.

Bob Prince, working the television broadcast with Mel Allen, missed calling Maz's home run. The Gunner had left the booth early to reach the dressing room in time for postgame interviews. There was a noisy, bustling traffic jam inside the clubhouse door, making it almost impossible to get through. John Galbreath and his son Danny needed an eight-man police wedge to join the celebration. Cimoli, Stuart, Hoak, Face, Mizell, all drenched in champagne, came rushing over to douse the owner. Prince groped around for interviews.

"Beat 'em, Bucs!" Cimoli shouted into the microphone. "Can't beat our Buccos, tell you that. Yes, sir, we got 'em, we got 'em. They broke all the records and we won the game."

"Here's the president of the ball club, Mr. John Galbreath," Prince said.

"I just want to ask you one question that you asked me," Galbreath said, his voice urgent and hoarse. "Have we paid our debt to this city, the people of Pittsburgh?"

"I think you have," Prince said. "And you've given your voice to it, too, haven't you?"

"I'll give it all I've got," Galbreath said.

"You wouldn't trade a Kentucky Derby for this, John," Prince added, referring to the owner's obsession with thoroughbred racing.

"You, you're trying to get me where I'm vulnerable," Galbreath responded.

By the time Bill Nunn Jr. reached the dressing room, his friend Clemente was sitting alone in the corner, "happy but unconcerned with all the fanfare." He had been the only player to get a hit in all seven games. He had performed flawlessly in the field. His dribbling hit and dash to first base in the eighth inning had kept Pirate hopes alive. Now he said he planned to use his World Series money to buy a house for his mother in Carolina. "It's something I've always wanted to do for her after all she's done for me," he said. "I can't wait to see the joy on her face the first time she sees her new home." Nunn noticed that Clemente had showered and was packing his large duffel bag as champagne flew around him.

"What's the hurry?" the *Courier* editor asked.

Clemente was slipping a glove into the bag. "I catch plane at six o'clock for New York," he answered. "I stay there tonight and then I head for home."

"What about the victory party they're holding for the team? You certainly belong in that group," Nunn said.

"I don't like those kind of things," Clemente said. "There is not fun for me. Last one I went to all I did was stand in a corner."

A teammate handed Clemente a cup of champagne. He smiled and took a sip, then gestured to his friend Diomedes Antonio Olivo, the forty-one-year-old Latin pitcher, a legend in the Dominican Republic, who did not make the World Series roster but threw batting practice for the Pirates. Olivo, who spoke no English, would accompany Clemente to New York and back to the Caribbean. Nunn noticed that Clemente "paid special attention to a box he had next to him. In it was a trophy voted to him by Pirates fans as the most popular of all Pittsburgh players."

Olivo was ready to go. Clemente turned to Nunn and asked if he could give them a ride to the airport. On the way out, Clemente shook hands with Gene Baker, then slipped from the clubhouse and took a side exit, hoping to avoid the crowds. In an earlier conversation, he had told Nunn that he was worried the Pirates would not reward his excellent year with a sufficient raise. "It looks like everything is going to be all right next season," he said now. He had talked to Joe Brown the day before, and Brown had told him there would be no contract trouble. The general manager also asked him not to play winter ball when he got home to Puerto Rico.

As soon as they emerged from the stadium someone shouted, "There's Clemente!" and soon a crowd engulfed them. They walked a few yards, then were stopped again by another adoring throng, the jubilant scrum inching along toward Nunn's car. It took nearly an hour. By that time Clemente was radiating happiness. The fans of Pittsburgh, he said, made everything worthwhile. They were the reason he was glad the Pirates won the World Series. They were the best fans in the world.

7
Pride and Prejudice

IN THE SEASONAL MOVEMENTS OF ROBERTO CLEMENTE'S baseball life, October was the month of return. He not only could go home again, he loved to go home to Puerto Rico. Delayed ten days by the World Series, Clemente's homecoming in October 1960 was unlike any he had experienced before. His countrymen had followed the dramatic seven-game series between the Pirates and mighty Yankees with an intensity perhaps matched only in Pittsburgh and New York. All seven games were broadcast in Spanish over WAPA radio in San Juan, and the newspapers provided in-depth coverage, much of it focused on the Pittsburgh right fielder. Almost every day, his photograph appeared in the sports sections under captions like . . . *Roberto Clemente . . . throw saves run.* His batting averages for the season (.314) and series (.310, with a hit in every game) could be cited by most every fan on the island. And now, on the afternoon of October 16, as he stepped down the portable stairs leading off the Pan Am jet that had carried him home, he was greeted as the triumphant son.

Handmade welcome-home placards bobbed in the milling crowd of several hundred people that awaited him on the tarmac. The sign that captured Clemente's feelings read simply *La Familia.* He embraced his father, kissed his mother, and hugged his brothers and various cousins, nephews, and nieces who came out to see him, but family in this case went beyond blood relatives. His family was all of Puerto Rico. The words of the poet Enrique Zorrilla, father of his baseball patron, Pedrin Zorrilla, were Clemente's now: *My pride is my land/ For I was born here/ I don't love it because it is beautiful/ I love it because it is mine/ Poor or rich, with burning/ I want it for my own.* And his land wanted him, in a way that North America, despite his connection with Pittsburgh fans, seemingly could not. Clemente was on the ground only a minute when he was swept up by the adoring mob, raised high into the air, and carried on shoulders toward the airport gate, a ragtag band of horns, drums, and whistles lending a surging salsa rhythm to the jubilant parade.

There was only one small note of disappointment. When a local sportswriter asked Clemente whether he intended to play winter baseball, he paused and answered, "I don't know yet." Those four words were grist for an ongoing conversation. The winter league in Puerto Rico was struggling enough already, as Ponce, Mayagüez, and San Juan all had lost money the previous season. The future looked no more promising despite the virtual collapse of the main competition, the Cuban winter league, under the weight of the Castro revolution. Ballparks in Havana, Cienfuegos, and Marianao were going dark night after night. "Be a patriot and go to the ball games," Cuban government broadcasts urged, but the campaign was flopping. All the baseball equipment that came from the United States had been embargoed, and of more significance so had the talented U.S. ballplayers. Following the lead of the International League's Havana Sugar Kings, who fled for Jersey City in July 1960, soon after Castro took over, the major leagues now were also abandoning Cuba. Winter league teams that traditionally fielded eight major leaguers apiece had zero since commissioner Ford Frick imposed a ban on Cuban play. That meant even more Americans would come to Puerto Rico, but the teams there still relied heavily on the draw of local stars, none of whom glowed brighter than Clemente. Four days after his arrival, Clemente's ambivalence remained a major story. In a television interview with Pantalones Santiago, the colorful old pitcher who had thrown to him during his first professional tryout in 1952, the twenty-six-year-old Clemente lamented that he was so tired he could "hardly lift a bat." Maybe he would suit up later in the season, he said, if he felt better.

During his first month in Puerto Rico, Clemente attended almost nightly banquets in his honor, large and small. He received the *Star* trophy as the outstanding Latin American ballplayer in the major leagues. He brought his full Pirate uniform home from Pittsburgh with him, and began wearing it at baseball clinics he held for boys in towns around San Juan. Joe L. Brown, the Pirates general manager, came down on a sunny scouting mission and the local papers reported rumors that he had signed Clemente to a big new contract. The *San Juan Star,* citing "a source which is right at least half the time," said Clemente had been signed for $40,000, which was termed "a considerable sum even if some jockeys and some professional wrestlers make more." In fact, Clemente had not yet signed, and the amount he eventually agreed to was less than the reported figure. According to documents filed with the National League and eventually archived at the National Baseball Library at the Hall of Fame in Cooperstown, Clemente's 1961 one-year contract paid him a salary of $35,000 plus a possible bonus if he avoided winter ball.

The favorite phrase of San Juan sportswriters during Clemente's period of inactivity that winter was that he was "resting on his World Series laurels." Resting, perhaps, but not peacefully. On a physical level, he was an insomniac who rarely slept. And mentally, he was churning more than usual. The satisfaction he drew from starring on a championship team was tempered by a long-simmering frustration over his place in the major league firmament. Hank Aaron of the Braves and Frank Robinson of the Reds, the other great right fielders in the National League, had been dominant from the start, but it had taken Clemente six long seasons to make his breakthrough, longer than the career of the average player. Even Orlando Cepeda of the Giants, the former Santurce batboy, who idolized Roberto as a big brother, seemed to have surpassed him, hitting for a higher average, stroking nearly twice as many home runs, and driving in nearly as many runs as his Puerto Rican elder in only half as many big league seasons. To watch Clemente play was an aesthetic experience. He was an expressionist art form all his own, yet something had been holding him back. Was it his inexperience in the early years, or the reality of his uneven play, or the misperceptions of managers and sportswriters, or the lingering effects of the 1954 traffic accident, or the extra pressure of being a Spanish-speaking black Latin, or bad luck, or some combination of all of those?

Whatever the cause, the most profound effect came on November

17, when the vote for the National League Most Valuable Player award was announced. His brother Matino had predicted that Clemente would win, but Momen knew better. He told Matino about how Les Biederman, the influential beat writer for the *Pittsburgh Press*, had been dismissive of Clemente when talking to his brethren in other National League towns, and talking up other Pirates. The winner was indeed a Pirate, but not Clemente. It was Dick Groat, the shortstop, who led the league in batting with a .325 average, but hit only two home runs with fifty runs batted in. Groat was a studious player, a college man from Duke, a favorite with the writers, and respected as a quiet leader by his teammates. He was a popular choice, compiling sixteen of twenty-two first-place votes and finishing more than a hundred points ahead of the next player, but was he most valuable? When Groat had missed the last three weeks of the season with a wrist injury, Ducky Schofield had filled in well enough that the Pirates just kept winning. The second place vote-getter also was a Pirate, again not Clemente. It was third baseman Don Hoak, the club's tobacco-spitting vocal sparkplug, whose statistics (.282 average, sixteen homers, seventy-nine runs batted in) were good but unexceptional. After that were the league's two perennial stars, Willie Mays and Ernie Banks. Next? Finishing fifth was not Clemente but Lindy McDaniel, a St. Louis relief pitcher with a 12–4 record. Tied for sixth were Ken Boyer of the Cardinals and yet another Pirate, Vernon Law, ace of the pitching staff, who would win the Cy Young award as the best pitcher. Finally, down in eighth place, there was Clemente, with 62 points from the writers, 214 fewer than Groat.

With Clemente, this was a matter of pride. No doubt he would have been pleased had he won the award, but it was finishing eighth that wounded him deeply. He felt alienated, marked as different. Groat was a Pittsburgh area boy. Hoak had married a Pittsburgh area girl. The MVP vote, Clemente believed, was confirmation that Pittsburgh writers had campaigned against him. "The writers make me feel bad when you don't even get considered," he said. Before the vote, he had been brooding; afterward, he was enraged. He carried the slight with him for the rest of his career, for better and worse. He brought it up every year during contract negotiations with Joe L. Brown, the first in a perennial litany of perceived inequities. "There was this burr under his saddle," Brown said later. "I said, 'Bobby, you're too big to be concerned about that. You are a great player and nobody can take that away from you. Your best years are ahead of you. You played on a World Championship team and were a big part of our winning. If someone screwed you, tough luck. You are still great." All true, but the pain stayed with Clemente, and it was this pain that drove him forward—to prove his doubters wrong.

Soon enough that winter, Clemente felt ready to lift a bat again and was back in uniform for the San Juan Senadores, the favorite team of his childhood. The Senadores were the third club of his winter ball career. He had played for the Santurce Cangrejeros for four and a half seasons, until founding owner Pedrin Zorrilla, out of money, had been forced to sell the franchise two days after Christmas 1956, bringing to a sad and sudden end a remarkable two-decade run from Josh Gibson through Willie Mays. As Zorrilla's son, named Enrique in honor of his poet grandfather, later explained: "My father was a boy in a man's body. He loved the game and couldn't bear the thought of losing his team. But he couldn't bear the thought of trading ballplayers to get the money to pay his debts." Zorrilla conditioned the team's sale on a promise from the new owners that they would not dump players to reduce the debt, but that promise was broken in a single day. The first action the new owners took was to sell Clemente, Juan Pizarro, and Ronnie Sanford to the Caguas Criollos for $30,000. The initial public reports said the sale of Clemente had been arranged with Zorrilla's knowledge. By his son's account, this infuriated the Big Crab. "That is a time when my father later told me he regretted the way he acted in a way. He stormed out of the house, went to the new owner and told him, 'You take it back and tell the truth or I am not responsible for what I can do.' He regretted saying that. But it was important for him for the truth to be known. That day on local radio at noon everything was cleared up and it was said the deal was made after the club's sale, without his knowledge. But that is how the great Roberto Clemente went away from Santurce."

Caguas, an interior mountain city fifteen miles south of San Juan, was never more than a sideshow for Clemente. He led the league in hitting for the Criollos, but had no real commitment to playing there, even though his manager was Vic Power, his fellow major leaguer. Power and Clemente were fast friends off the field, but there was always some competitive jousting in the manager-player relationship. In his good-natured way, Power essentially accused the proud Clemente of manipulating his image. "At the start it was kind of hard because he was hurt all the time. His neck hurt. His back hurt," Power recalled. "When I told him, 'Okay, I'll put someone in for you,' he'd say, 'No, let me play.' And then he played. And every time he played hurt, he got two hits. I was wondering, one time when I played him if he went 0 for 4, and the press asked him, 'Hey, what's the matter?' and he would say, 'Well, I told the manager I was sick.'" Power, in other words, thought Clemente slyly used his ailments to place himself in a no-lose situation. If a Pittsburgh sportswriter had expressed the same thought, an icy stare or severe lecture would come his way, but Power could tease Clemente, no hard feelings.

The difference was a matter of culture and familiarity. Power had endured the same slights and had been stereotyped in the same ways. Between the two of them, there was no fear of being misunderstood, but at the same time Clemente couldn't fool Power, or bluff him, or intimidate him—they knew each other too well. Away from the ballpark, Momen and Vic enjoyed hanging out—together and with young women, the pursuers and the pursued—in Caguas, San Juan, and all points between. Clemente had classical style and good looks, but Power was more freewheeling, their different personalities most obvious at the dance halls. Power, all loose limbs, loved the salsa and merengue. For Clemente, those moves were too fast, undignified, not cool enough, and he wasn't any good at them. He liked the boleros, the slow dances. Sometimes, Power said, Clemente would go after his girls, but no problem, he had so many he could share them. One night on a double date, Roberto took out a girl who had to be home by midnight. When they were an hour late, she told Clemente that her father would be waiting outside with a shotgun. As they approached her house, Clemente pretended his car had run out of gas. He even forced Power to get out and push. Anything to avoid the censure of an elder.

After spending parts of two campaigns with Power in Caguas,

Clemente was traded to San Juan, which would remain his home team for the rest of his career. It was for the Senadores that he finally lifted his bat in the winter of his rage, after the 1960 World Series and the eighth-place finish for most valuable player. The rejuvenation of a struggling San Juan team was immediate with Clemente in the lineup. The Senadores swept to the regular season championship, won the league playoffs, and then flew south to Venezuela in February 1961 to represent Puerto Rico in the InterAmerican series, a makeshift tournament designed to replace the Caribbean World Series, which had been scrapped because of the political situation in Cuba. San Juan was a formidable team, with Clemente banging away and Tite Arroyo, the proficient Yankee reliever, on the mound, and the regular season lineup was fortified for the tournament by two additions from Santurce, Clemente's friends Orlando Cepeda and Juan Pizarro. In a short series, though, one great pitcher can always make the difference, and the Valencia team from Venezuela had that one unhittable ace just coming into his own—young Bob Gibson of the St. Louis Cardinals, who shut out San Juan 1–0.

All of this, in any case, was just prelude for Clemente, preparation for a season on the mainland that would make him impossible to ignore any longer.

Momen arrived at Pirates camp to train for the 1961 season on March 2, a day late. He and Tite Arroyo had been delayed entry from Puerto Rico to Florida until tests came back proving they did not have the bubonic plague, a few cases of which had broken out in Venezuela during the tournament.

On the day he reached Fort Myers, free from the plague, a story ran on the front page of the *New York Times* under the headline: NEGROES SAY CONDITIONS IN U.S. EXPLAIN NATIONALISTS' MILITANCY. One of the key figures quoted in the story was Malcolm X, the Black Muslim leader, who in the *Times* account was referred to as Minister Malcolm. Interviewed at a Muslim-run restaurant on Lenox Avenue in Harlem, Malcolm X said the only answer to America's racial dilemma was for blacks to segregate themselves, by their own choice, with their own land and financial reparations due them from centuries of slavery. He dismissed the tactics of the civil rights movement as humiliating, especially the lunch-counter sit-ins that were taking place throughout the South. "To beg a white man to let you into his restaurant feeds his ego," Minister Malcolm told the newspaper.

This was fourteen years after Jackie Robinson broke the major league color line, seven years after the U.S. Supreme Court struck down the separate-but-equal doctrine of segregated schools, five years after Rosa Parks and Martin Luther King Jr. led the bus boycott in Montgomery, four years after the Little Rock Nine desegregated Central High School in the capital of Arkansas, one year after the first lunch-counter sit-in in Greensboro. Year by year, the issue of race was becoming more urgent. The momentum was on the side of change, but the questions were how and how fast. In baseball, where once there had been no black ballplayers, now there were a hundred competing for major league jobs, and along with numbers came enormous talent, with ten past and future most valuable players among them. Yet every black player who reported to training camp in Florida that spring of 1961 still had to confront Jim Crow segregation. Even if their private emotions were sympathetic to Malcolm X's rage at having to beg a white man to let you into his restaurant, the issue in baseball was necessarily shaped by its own history. Having moved away from the professional Negro Leagues and busted through the twentieth century's racial barrier, black players did not view voluntary resegregation as an option, and separate and unequal off the field was no longer tolerable.

Wendell Smith, the influential black sportswriter who still had a column in the weekly *Pittsburgh Courier* but wrote daily now for the white-owned newspaper *Chicago's American,* began a concerted campaign against training camp segregation that year. On January 23, a month before the spring camps opened, Smith wrote a seminal article that appeared on the top of the front page of *Chicago's American* headlined NEGRO BALL PLAYERS WANT RIGHTS IN SOUTH. "Beneath the apparently tranquil surface of baseball there is a growing feeling of resentment among Negro major leaguers who still experience embarrassment, humiliation, and even indignities during spring training in the south," Smith wrote. "The Negro player who is accepted as a first class citizen in the regular season is tired of being a second class citizen in spring training." Smith added that leading black players were "moving cautiously and were anxious to avert becoming engulfed in fiery debate over civil rights," but nonetheless were preparing to meet with club owners and league executives to talk about the problem and make it a front-burner issue for the players association.

In a drumbeat of stories for *Chicago's American* and columns for the *Courier,* Smith documented the life of black players in Florida. While his scope was national and his campaign was for all of baseball, he often focused on the travails of black players on Chicago's American League team, the White Sox, who trained in Sarasota. Those players included Minnie Minoso, Al Smith, and Juan Pizarro, Clemente's friend and sometimes teammate in Puerto Rico, who had been traded from the Braves. "If you are Minoso, Smith or Pizarro . . . you are a man of great pride and perseverance . . . Otherwise you would not be where you are today, training with a major league team in Sarasota, Fla.," Smith wrote in a *Courier* column. "Yet despite all your achievements and fame, the vicious system of racial segregation in Florida's hick towns condemns you to a life of humiliation and ostracism." Among the indignities, he wrote:

> You cannot live with your teammates.
>
> You cannot eat the type of food that your athletic body requires.
>
> You cannot get a cab in the mornings to take you to the ball park, unless it happens to be Negro-driven.
>
> You cannot enter the hotel in which your manager lives without first receiving special permission.
>
> You cannot go to a movie or night club in the heart of town, nor enjoy any of the other normal recreational facilities your white teammates enjoy so matter of factly.
>
> You cannot bring your wife and children to the town where you are training because accommodations are not available where you are imprisoned.
>
> You cannot, even if there are facilities, take them to

the town's sprawling beaches or parks, unless, of course, they are designated as "Negro."

You cannot do anything that you would normally do in any of the major league cities where you make your living during the summer.

You are quartered in a neighborhood that ordinarily you would be ashamed to be seen in.

You are horribly embarrassed each day when the bus returning the players from the ball park stops on "this side of the railroad tracks" and deposits you in "Colored Town," and then proceeds on to the plush hotel where your white teammates live in splendor and luxury.

You suffered a bruised leg sliding into second base, but you cannot receive immediate treatment from the club trainer because he is living in the "white" hotel. If he can get away during the night and come to your segregated quarters, he will, of course; but for obvious reasons, he prefers to wait until daylight.

Your wife cannot call you in case of emergency from your home because the place where you are incarcerated does not have phone facilities available at all times.

That is what it is like to be a Negro big leaguer in Florida during spring training . . . And the story has been only half told.

The spring training headquarters for the White Sox was the Sarasota Terrace Hotel, which banned journalist Smith and the black players. When Smith pressed the owner, a building contractor named James Ewell, to explain his policy, Ewell said he was following the social practices of the Sarasota community. Also, he claimed that if he opened his establishment to blacks he would lose contracting work: "My clients throughout Florida and other sections of the south would reject my business, I believe." The White Sox situation was made more interesting by the fact that the team's president, Bill Veeck, had been in the forefront of integrating baseball and was not oblivious to the plight of his black players. Veeck had found another place for them, the DeSoto Motel, which was run by Edward Wachtel and his wife, Lillian, a white Jewish couple from New York, who had retired to Florida and wanted in their own "quiet" way to break the segregation policies of their new home. For this gesture, the Wachtels received anonymous bomb threats, hate mail, and late-night telephone calls warning that crosses would be burned on their lawn. Their modest green-and-white one-story motel was located in a white neighborhood on Route 301 a mile or so from the rest of the team. The DeSoto was clean but modest, with far fewer services than the Sarasota Terrace. The neon sign out front boasted HEATED * AIR CONDITIONED * OVERNITES * EFFICIENCIES.

Veeck had tried to balance the conditions by hiring a cook, maid service, and transportation to and from the ball park. On the road, he had made the bold stand of pulling the White Sox from a hotel in Miami because it rejected his black players. Still, it wasn't until Wendell Smith began his incessant campaign that the White Sox took the final step of leasing their own hotel in Sarasota so the entire team could stay together.

Down at the Pirates training camp in Fort Myers, where conditions were worse, *Courier* sports editor Bill Nunn Jr., a journalistic disciple of Smith, was determined to lend his voice to the integration campaign. From his first day in town, Nunn began interviewing players and club executives for a full-page story. There had been few advances since 1955, the first Pirates camp in Fort Myers, when young Clemente was sent off to a rooming house in the Dunbar Heights section of town where he had to eat and sleep apart from his teammates. Including top minor leaguers, there were now fifteen black players in the Pirates camp, led by Clemente and Gene Baker, a veteran infielder. In interviews with Nunn, both expressed their disgust. "We live in a world apart down here," Baker told Nunn. "We don't like it and we've voiced our objections. We only hope we get action." At the ball park during the day, Baker said, he enjoyed talking to teammates Don Hoak and Gino Cimoli about their shared passion, greyhound racing. But when they went to the dog track at night, Baker had to go through the entrance marked "Colored" and sit apart from them.

Clemente was described as "bitter" about the situation. Here he was, a star player on the world champions of baseball, a reservist in the U.S. Marine Corps, still treated like a second-class citizen. "There is nothing for us to do down here," he told Nunn. "We go to the ball park, play cards, and watch television. In a way it's like being in prison. Everybody else on the team has fun during spring training. They swim, play golf, and go to the beaches. The only thing we can do is put in time until we head North. It's no fun."

Later, when asked to list his heroes, Clemente would place Martin Luther King Jr. at the top of the list. He supported integration, the norm in Puerto Rico, and believed in King's philosophy of nonviolence. Yet in some ways his sensibility brought him closer to Malcolm X. He detested any response to Jim Crow segregation that made him seem to beg. In his early years with the Pirates, whenever the team stopped at a roadside restaurant on the way to or from a spring training away game, the black players would remain on the bus, waiting for white teammates to bring out food for them. Clemente put a stop to it by telling his black teammates that anyone who begged for food would have to fight him to get it. As he recalled the scene later, he went to Joe L. Brown, the Pirates general manager, and said the situation was demeaning. "So I say to Joe Brown, 'We won't travel anymore with the bus. If we can't eat where the white players eat I don't want to go with the bus.' So Joe Brown said, 'Well, we're going to get a station wagon for you fellows to travel in.' And [now] we're traveling in a station wagon." That still left a long way to go to reach equality.

During the first week of exhibition games, Nunn interviewed Brown and asked him why he allowed the team to be divided by segregation. The general manager said that he had met with the Fort Myers town fathers, who told him local law prohibited the mingling of races in hotels or motels, but that he felt he was making progress in getting them to change their practices. "I talked to all of the city officials about this situation of separate quarters for our players this year. I didn't go to these men to make demands," Brown said. "I explained our problem to them and told them we wanted integration at all levels for our players. I was pleased with the reception I received. The city officials listened to my complaints and appeared receptive. They didn't make any promises but I believe they are just as eager to have this problem solved as we are." Integration would take time, Brown told Nunn. He considered it a step forward that city officials even agreed to talk about it. Brown was a Californian who had no use for segregation, but he also was a businessman who did not want to alienate the Fort Myers establishment. "Frankly, we have no real complaints against the city of Fort Myers," he concluded. "We have been treated wonderfully since coming here. The facilities are good and I've heard no objections from the Negro members of our club on the segregation issue."

That last comment reflected a common attitude among baseball executives, and many sportswriters, who were so lulled by their own comfortable situations and the lazy ease of their sport in springtime that it was difficult for them to see the reality. When the Fort Myers Boosters Club held a Pirates Welcome Luncheon at the Hideaway, the guest list included Brown and manager Danny Murtaugh, Pennsylvania Governor David Lawrence, Ford Frick, the baseball commissioner, Warren Giles, the president of the National League, and several heroes of the World Series, but not Clemente, who could not get into the building unless he worked as a waiter or dishwasher. That same day, at ten in the morning, a forty-three-minute highlight film of the World Series was shown at the Edison Theater downtown, and notices announced there was no charge and "the public is invited—men, women and children." As long as they were white. When the Fort Myers Country Club sponsored its annual Pirates Golf Tourney, the *News-Press* listed the foursomes, comprised of players, coaches, businessmen, and sportswriters. Brown and Murtaugh played, along with Groat and Friend and Schofield and Stuart and twenty more members of the Pirates organization. The Pirates were described as acting "like boys let out of school." When the golfing was done, they were all served "a bountiful buffet dinner." Clemente and his black teammates were back in Dunbar Heights.

In the bonhomie of the occasion, no one noticed who wasn't there. Ducky Schofield, the utility infielder, was perhaps typical of white Pirates who were not racist but also did not seem to take into account how social conditions might have deeper effects on black teammates. When asked later whether Clemente was disliked by some of the

Pirates of the late 1950s and early 1960s, Schofield said: "I'm sure there were some who didn't like him. . . . Maybe it was because he didn't put forth a whole lot of energy as far as being one of the guys. I think he pretty much stuck to himself quite a bit. In those days, guys ran in groups. Guys would eat together, have a couple of beers. Not that he had to do it, but I never saw him do it."

Exclusive events like the Fort Myers welcome luncheon and golf outing were held in spring-training towns throughout Florida. But unlike previous springs, this time they were loudly criticized. The most attention was drawn to St. Petersburg, which called itself the capital of the Grapefruit League as home to the Yankees and Cardinals. Both teams had been staying at segregated hotels, the Cardinals at the Vinoy Park and the Yankees at the Soreno, but under pressure from the local NAACP and black players, the system was finally being cracked. When Soreno's management refused to change its policy, the Yankees picked up and moved across the state to Fort Lauderdale, and in the aftermath, St. Pete officials were so worried about losing baseball entirely that the Cardinals were finally allowed to house their entire team in the same hotel. Small victories of that sort were being won here and there, rivulets in the mighty stream of civil rights. On March 13, in Miami Beach, Floyd Patterson defended his heavyweight boxing crown in a title match with Ingemar Johansson, and along with Patterson's victory the most newsworthy aspect of the fight was that, at the champ's insistence, the color bar was lifted in the Convention Hall. "Negroes were spotted freely among the predominantly white crowd in all sections," the *New York Times* reported, and "so far as could be noted, no incidents arose from the integrated set-up." It was an off-day for the Pirates, and third-baseman Don Hoak, who had been a decent amateur boxer, covered the event for a Pittsburgh newspaper. Yet in Sarasota and other spring-training cities, black ballplayers wanting to watch Patterson were not allowed into the whites-only theaters.

Change was slow, and did not occur unprovoked. One of the pivotal events that spring came when the chamber of commerce held a Salute to Baseball at the St. Petersburg Yacht Club. Bill White, the Cardinals first baseman, blasted the lily-white event as a symbol of baseball's capitulation to Southern racism. His words echoed across the state and nation. "I think about this every minute of the day," White told Joe Reichler of United Press International. "This thing keeps gnawing at my heart. When will we be made to feel human?"

For Clemente, already simmering over the personal slight of the MVP vote, the second-class treatment he encountered in Florida as a star player on a World Championship team only stoked his fire. He was a baseball player, not a journalist or politician, and it was on the baseball diamond that he expressed himself most often. In his first batting drill of the spring, he cracked a relentless volley of blistering line drives and then slammed two balls out of the park, and it seemed that he never stopped hitting from there. The most anticipated exhibition contest of the spring was a rematch with the Yankees, a game that drew a standing-room-only crowd of 5,351 to Terry Park. In the second inning of a game the Pirates won 9–2, Clemente started the scoring with a towering home run to left. It was just a solo homer in a meaningless spring game, but it was also a statement: Clemente was not to be ignored. Several factors were coming together to transform him from a dangerous hitter with weaknesses into a great hitter who was essentially unpitchable.

George H. Sisler, the sweet-swinging Hall of Fame first baseman, deserved a generous share of credit. Gorgeous George, who hit for a .340 career average from 1915 to 1930 and twice batted over .400, had been working as a special assistant with the Pirates throughout Clemente's first six seasons. Even now, as he was turning sixty-eight, he still knew how to help good hitters improve, and he thought Clemente was on the verge of becoming the best hitter in the National League. Sisler's first breakthrough with Clemente had been teaching him to stop lifting his head, or bobbing it, as he strode into the swing. By holding his head still, and keeping it down, Clemente could train his eye on curveballs as they broke down and away, pitches that gave him trouble earlier. As a slashing line-drive hitter himself, Sisler also helped Clemente work on staying back on the ball and keeping his hands in, close to the chest, a technique known as swinging from the inside out. Sisler had no problem with another aspect of Clemente's hitting that others criticized, a tendency to swing at bad balls; what was important, he thought, was having an idea of what pitches you could hit, and in that regard he considered Clemente uncommonly intelligent at the plate.

Paradoxical as it sounds, another factor in Clemente's development as a hitter was his aching back, which had bothered him off and on since the December 30 traffic accident in Caguas in 1954. There were times when the injury was debilitating, particularly during the 1956 season, when he developed a pinched nerve, but most of the time he could play through it. In a sense, it proved to be long-term pain for long-term gain. The pain that occasionally knifed into the lower left side of his back forced him to slow his swing—perhaps a mere nanosecond slower, but enough to prevent him from trying to pull every pitch—again, the weakness that Branch Rickey at first feared would be his undoing. Instead, he started hitting the ball more to center and right. "I learned to go with the pitch," Clemente said later, out of physical necessity. That might explain why at times during his career when he was feeling free and easy, without pain, he might end up swinging so violently his head would bob and he would lose his balance and virtually whirling-dervish his way to the ground; but conversely, whenever his teammates heard him moaning about a bad back, they joked to themselves that the opposing pitcher was in trouble and a four-hit day was in the offing.

A third element in Clemente's refinement as a hitter involved his selection of bats. Early in his career with the Pirates, he used thirty-two and thirty-three-ounce M117 (Stan Musial) model Louisville Sluggers, and then S-2s, which were first made for Vern Stephens, the power-hitting shortstop who played most of his career with the St. Louis Browns and Red Sox in the 1940s and early fifties. But by 1961 he was using much bigger and heavier bats, mostly thirty-six inches and thirty-four to thirty-five ounces. The models were U1s, named for one Bernard Bartholomew Uhalt, known to his friends as Frenchy. The major league career of Frenchy Uhalt amounted to fifty-seven games with the Chicago White Sox in 1934. His bat seemed to have very few hits in it—five doubles, one triple, thirty-four singles—yet it made a significant contribution to the history of baseball as the model favored by Roberto Clemente. What was most notable about the U1 was that it didn't have a knob, but instead tapered out at the bottom. It felt exactly right in Clemente's sensitive hands, and the extra weight, like his bad back, had the effect of forcing him to hit more straightaway and to right.

To Clemente, a bat was not just a bat, it was an instrument that had to meet his exacting standards. "He probably knew as much about timber as anyone," recalled Rex Bradley, the Hillerich & Bradsby executive in charge of Louisville Slugger bat sales to major leaguers. "He knew if he had a good piece of bat. He would bang them together and see if they sounded good. He could tell from the sound." Wood was not only essential to Clemente's profession, it was also his hobby. During the off-season in Puerto Rico, he loved nothing more than combing the Atlantic beach from Punta Cangrejos to Punta Maldonado in search of driftwood he could use to make lamps and furniture. As an amateur carpenter, he studied the hardness and grains of different woods. He once sent a note to Bradley stating that he wanted "no red wood"— which meant no wood from the heart of the ash tree, which was a darker color. "He wanted the widest grains, always," according to Bradley. "And he knew the wide grains came in the summer growth, he was that precise."

With all this—with pure talent, with pride and will fueled by the need to prove his doubters wrong, with the expert instruction of Hall of Famer George Sisler, with the beneficial swing adjustments arising from his bad back, and with the comfort of the heavier, knobless Frenchy Uhalt bats, Clemente came blasting into the prime of his career.

In baseball, as in so many other ways, 1961 launched the sixties decade on its stunning trajectory. Life reinvented, and seeming so much larger. Two more teams were added to the American League: in Washington (again, a reborn version of the old last-place Senators) and Los Angeles. The National League had the Mets and Colt .45s in gestation, a year from taking the field. In persuading major league owners to grant Houston a franchise, Judge Roy Hofheinz had already wowed them with a model he had built of the world's first domed stadium.

With its expansion teams, the American League had scheduled the longest regular season in major league history, extended to 162 games. Was it a prefiguring of the antiestablishment mood that emerged later in the decade, or just plain madcap hopelessness, that found the Chicago Cubs that year rejecting the concept of a single manager and instead delegating authority to a succession of feeble coaches? The Yankees still wore pinstripes, but Casey Stengel, the Ol' Perfessor, was gone, Mickey Mantle told the press he would assume a stronger leadership role, and the new boss, Ralph Houk, said his team looked lean and mean. The big bats started booming in April. By the end of the month, Mantle had fourteen home runs and his outfield mate, Roger Maris, had twelve, and the pursuit of Babe Ruth's record was on. Six months later, Maris held the record, sixty-one, ahead of Mantle's fifty-four, and four other Yankees, Moose Skowron, Yogi Berra, Elston Howard, and Johnny Blanchard, finished with more than twenty home runs each. Even taking into account the two additional teams, 1961 was prodigious, the year of the homer. The 2,730 total home runs in the two leagues were nearly five-hundred more than any previous year.

The Pittsburgh Pirates were a very small part of all this. After being picked by a majority of sportswriters to repeat as National League champs and rampaging through spring training, they finished April three games over .500, but then remained stuck at that mediocre level throughout the first half of the season. They looked more and more like the overmatched team that was walloped by the Yankees in three losing World Series games rather than the gutsy club that prevailed in the other four. Groat, the MVP, had fallen back to being a slightly-better-than-average performer. Law, the reigning Cy Young winner, tore his rotator cuff and pitched only eleven games. The pennant-fever magic of southpaw Vinegar Bend Mizell vanished. Elroy Face, the tough little relief pitcher, won only a third of his games, going six and twelve, only two years after compiling an astounding .947 winning percentage by winning eighteen and losing one. The one player who was even hotter than he had been in 1960 was Clemente. By July 10, after a torrid week in which he stroked thirteen hits in twenty-seven at-bats, including one five-hit game and another four-hit game, he was leading the league with a .357 average. With the soaring average came newfound power, with twelve home runs and fifty-four runs batted in—statistics so strong that his peers voted for him to start in right field at the July 11 All-Star game held at Candlestick Park in San Francisco.

The All-Star setting offered Clemente another chance to shine before a nationwide audience, and he seized the opportunity. He played the entire game in right field, slashed a triple to right-center off Whitey Ford in the second, knocked in an early run with a sacrifice fly, and then, in the bottom of the tenth, after Henry Aaron singled and Willie Mays doubled, he drove in Mays from second with the winning run in a 5–4 game. From what Jackie Robinson started in 1947, here was a benchmark of black accomplishment in the major leagues, an All-Star team with Aaron, Mays, and Clemente in a row. The rosters that day presented in stark relief the different racial histories of the two leagues. The American League had only one black player, Elston Howard, who entered the game as a defensive replacement and had no at-bats. The National League fielded five black starters—Maury Wills at shortstop, Bill White at first, Orlando Cepeda in left, Mays in center, and Clemente in right, with Aaron, Frank Robinson, George Altman, and Johnny Roseboro coming off the bench. Those nine players combined for nine of their team's eleven hits and drove in all five runs. Clemente at last was voted most valuable player, for one game.

In the locker room afterward, he was beaming about his game-winning hit off knuckleball pitcher Hoyt Wilhelm. The national press corps gathered around as he described the decisive moment. The Associated Press account quoted Clemente as he sounded, or as the reporter thought he sounded, using exaggerated phonetic spelling. (In the *Post-Gazette*, this account ran under the headline I GET HEET, I FEEL GOOD). "I jus' try to sacrifice myself, so I get runner to third if I do, I feel good. But I get heet and Willie scores and I feel better than good," Clemente was quoted as saying. "When I come to plate in lass eening, with Mays on second and nobody out, I ask myself, 'Now, what would Skipper [Murtaugh] want me to do?' He want me to hit to right side to send Willie to third so he could score on grounder or fly ball. So I say, 'I 'ope that Weelhelm peetch me outside, so I could hit to right,' but he peetch me inside and I meet it and hit it in right field. Willie runs to third and to home plate and the game is over. That make me feel real good. Just like when Pittsburgh won the World Series."

Most of the press pack then moved on to the locker of Stu Miller, the little relief pitcher who had stolen the show with a comic absurdity. Before throwing his first pitch in the ninth inning, with the National Leaguers clinging to a 3–2 lead, Miller balked when the vicious winds at Candlestick literally blew him off the mound. The balk moved American League runners up to second and third, and the tying run then scored on an error by third baseman Ken Boyer, one of three errors in the wind-ravaged inning. For most of the press, Miller and the wind were the stories of the day. The *San Francisco Chronicle* ran a boldface banner headline above the masthead on the front page: HOW WIND CONQUERED MIGHTY ALL-STARS. Noting the seven errors in the contest, *Chronicle* sports editor Art Rosenbaum said the winds turned the game into "a Mickey Mouse comedy." As much type was devoted to mustard-stained hot-dog wrappers that swirled around the field in the late innings as to the play of the National League's right fielder.

But for those who stuck around his locker afterward, Clemente had more to say. In the AP story, it all came out, the combustible mix of pride and anger that had been churning inside him for months, in words that out of context seemed to walk a fine line between righteous plea and egotistical rant. At least the quotes this time were not presented in condescending phonetics. "I am hitting for higher average than last year and have more home runs than last year at the time of the All-Star game," Clemente said. "I had best year in majors last year and I was the league's most valuable player but I didn't get one first place vote [Not so, he did receive exactly one first-place vote]. The papers gave it to Groat, but I drive in more runs, and I hit more balls and I helped win more games. I know Groat is a Pittsburgh boy, but the writers made me feel bad . . . I talked to other players in the league and they all told me I was most valuable. This year, the players voted me on the All-Star team and I am feeling very good that I did not let them down."

The next morning in the *Post-Gazette*, sports editor Al Abrams took note of Clemente's explosion and came to his defense. The column reflected one of the curious aspects of Clemente's relationship with

Pittsburgh sportswriters. He was often madder at them than they were at him. Even those reporters who had the toughest time with him could be seen trying, in perhaps limited ways, to consider his perspective. Abrams had always been more sympathetic than most. "Clemente happens to be an outspoken lad, a trait that I admire in him," Abrams wrote. "This goes for Jimmy Piersall, too. The colorful and at times zany Cleveland Indians star told off Paul Richards because the American League's All-Star manager did not name him to the squad this year. More Clementes and Piersalls would liven up baseball, a sport that needs livening up in more ways than one."

There was one other aspect to that midsummer classic in Candlestick Park that went unmentioned at the time but sticks out in retrospect. With one out in the ninth inning, National League manager Danny Murtaugh called in Dodger lefthander Sandy Koufax, who gave up a single to Roger Maris before being yanked for Miller. The only thing notable about Koufax's cameo role was that this marked his first All-Star appearance. Clemente and Koufax had been equally slow to mature, each taking six long years after making the majors in the 1955 season. Koufax's progression actually had been the more gradual of the two; he went 2–2, 2–4, 5–4, 11–11, 8–6, and 8–13 before breaking loose in 1961 with eighteen wins and a league-leading 269 strikeouts. And now here they were, reaching their primes together at the dawn of the sixties decade, and there was a magic to these two radiant athletes, the twenty-six-year-old black Latin hitter and the twenty-five-year-old Jewish pitcher, that would set them apart from the crowd. And if, back in 1954, the Dodgers had not tried to hide Clemente in Montreal, but kept him on the twenty-five-man roster as they did Koufax, the two would now be playing on the same team.

A trivial manifestation of the everything-bigger movement of the early sixties was that the major leagues experimented with holding two All-Star games every summer. The second game of 1961, played at Fenway Park in Boston on July 31, was a dud, a 1–1 tie called because of rain after nine innings. But the event was not an entire waste. It brought the player representatives to Boston, and the next day they met and discussed the *Chicago's American* campaign against segregation at Florida spring training sites. Bill White of the Cardinals and Bill

Bruton of the Tigers presented the issue to their fellow players, with support from the association's attorney, Robert Cannon. White was insistent that the players not "pussyfoot over this thing." Most white major leaguers, he told Wendell Smith before the meeting, probably "don't realize how bad things are for us in Florida. After all, the only time they come in contact with us is at the ball parks. We want them to know exactly what the situation is. We are sure they will sympathize with us." At the meeting, the players adopted a resolution demanding an end to training camp segregation and calling on all major league owners to take steps to deal with the problem before the World Series in October. Clemente was not the Pirates player representative, but he made his strong views known to his teammate, Bob Friend, who supported the resolution.

The Pirates were a mess the second half of the season. After a disastrous stretch in July when they lost eleven of thirteen games, they fell below .500 and never recovered, eventually finishing the season with a 75–79 record—eighteen games behind the Cincinnati Reds of Frank Robinson and Vada Pinson. Things got so bad during the second-half slide that Jack Hernon wrote a game story with the most honest and reader-defying lead of all time—"Philadelphia, August 7—It was a dull game." Period, paragraph. And that was a rare game that the Pirates actually won. Not that the sporting world was paying much attention to Pittsburgh—or any team in the National League, including the Reds. The media focus every day that August and September was on Maris and Mantle and their relentless pursuit of Ruth's magic sixty.

The virtuosity of Roberto Clemente went virtually unnoticed outside Pittsburgh, but those scorching line drives he thwacked during the first day of spring training just kept flying off his Frenchy Uhalt bat month after month. After he won a game in San Francisco with a grand slam, Danny Murtaugh, for the first time, started comparing his right fielder with the best in the game. "Clemente's quite a player, isn't he?" Murtaugh told the press. "He's as good an outfielder in right field as . . . Willie Mays is in center. There isn't anything he can't do." With a month and a half to go, Clemente picked up the one-thousandth hit of his career. A few days later, Al Abrams was speculating that he might even challenge Arky Vaughan's record, set in 1935, for the best single season batting average for a Pirate, .385. The only thing holding Roberto back, Abrams wrote, was that he tended to tire out in the final month. The Pittsburgh writer attributed that late-season tendency to the fact that Clemente played winter ball every year and never got sufficient rest. "Why a brilliant performer such as Clemente is permitted to take part in outside baseball action is beyond our thinking."

One night that August on a road-game flight, Clemente sat on the armrest and talked for forty-five minutes with Hernon, the beat writer with whom he had an uneasy relationship. In his "Roamin' Around" column, Hernon quoted verbatim the right fielder's stream-of-consciousness monologue. Clemente told stories about how he almost quit in 1957 when he was hurting, and how his father, Don Melchor, lost thousands of dollars once when someone stole a money box from his house in Carolina, and how he had invested some of his own money in real estate back home. When Clemente was on a roll speaking in his second language, there was a bit of Casey Stengel to him, the poetry of run-on thoughts. "Sometimes I get mad at people," he said. "But only once here in Pittsburgh. That when I was hurt and everyone call me Jake [to Jake is a verb used by athletes to connote someone who is not trying and making excuses]. I don't like that. I want to play but my back hurt lots of times and I can't play. Then that year in St. Paul when I threw the ball in exhibition game the elbow started to puff up. That when some people write that I was in a fight with Face [the relief pitcher, who never got along with Clemente] in St. Louis. You know that not right. You can still feel the bone chip in my elbow," he continued . . .

> That's why I throw the ball underhanded sometimes. That way it don't hurt my arm. If I throw real hard lots of times overhand in game, the elbow hurts and swells up.
>
> The back is okay too. Sometime it hurt me when I run. But I find out it is bad disc. If it goes out on the right side I can push it back in easy. But if it hurts on

the other side sometimes I have to work long time to
get it back in place.

I have friend in Puerto Rica [the way Hernon
spelled it, apparently implying that Clemente pronounced it that way, or at least that Hernon thought he
did] who studied to be a doctor but not finish. He has
lots of money now and just likes to work as doctor
sometimes. He has helped lots of fellows playing winter ball in my home. He fixed me up . . .

I think my friend in Puerto Rica can help Vernon
[Law, out with the torn rotator cuff]. He can tell when it
hurts without touching the spot. He do that with me
just in exercise he asked me to do. I make face once
and he said, "You have a bad disc." And he right. I
think he can help Vernon, but no one listen to me and
do anything.

The bone chip in his elbow finally did what National League pitchers
could not, shutting Clemente down for the last five games of the season. By then, his statistics for the season included 201 hits and a
league-leading .351 average. Along with the Silver Bat for being the
league's best hitter, he also was voted a Gold Glove as the best right
fielder.

This was not just Clemente's rise, but all of Puerto Rico's. It had
been exactly twenty seasons since Hiram Bithorn took the mound for
the Chicago Cubs and became the first Puerto Rican to play in the
major leagues. Within two decades, the island had reached a point of
baseball excellence. Not only had Clemente captured the batting title
but Orlando Cepeda ended the season as the National League leader
in home runs, with forty-six, and runs batted in, with 142. Never
before had a player from Puerto Rico led the league in any hitting cat-
egory, and now they had won all three. Back home, people were calling it the Puerto Rican triple crown. And there was more—Tite
Arroyo, the left-handed reliever on the unbeatable Yanks, had had the
lowest earned-run average in the majors and led the American League
in saves with twenty-nine, and Juan Pizarro was excelling, too, going

14–7 with the White Sox. San Juan was ready to celebrate. Even Cantalicio, the impish cartoon character for Corona Beer, got into the act, with Spanish-language ads that ran in *El Imparcial* and other newspapers: *Corona Beer joins the joy of our island in the triumph of our Puerto Rican baseball stars, leaders in the recent big league season: ROBERTO CLEMENTE and ORLANDO CEPEDA, winners of the triple crown; TITE ARROYO, leader in ERA in both leagues, and TERRIN PIZARRO, who had his best year in the big leagues. Congratulations from Corona . . . to our most outstanding ballplayers.*

On his way out of Pittsburgh, Clemente paid special tribute to George Sisler and another Pirates instructor, Bill Burwell, for their encouragement. "They helped me all season by giving me confidence," he said. "They kept telling me I could hit for high average—even .400—and that made me feel good." He also talked again about how his hurt feelings had motivated him. "I was mad [from] last year. I played as well as anyone on our team and I didn't receive one MVP vote. Don't get me wrong, I didn't say I was the best last year or that I should have won the MVP award. But nobody seemed to care about me. But you win the batting title yourself. They can't take that away from you."

The Sportswriters Fraternity of Puerto Rico cared enough about Clemente to send a delegation of scribes, Juan Maldonado, Tito Morales, and Martinez Rousset, to New York to meet him and Orlando Cepeda and escort them back to the island for a festive homecoming. The triple crown kings arrived in San Juan on Pan Am Flight 211 at 2:35 on the afternoon of Monday, October 9 and looked out at a swarming sea of fans. Packs of schoolchildren were there, along with businessmen, families, airport employees. People sat on every available ledge, legs dangling, and stood shoulder to shoulder on the roof of the terminal. It took nearly an hour for Clemente and Cepeda to make their way from the plane through the joyous crowd. Clemente, who had undergone minor surgery on his elbow, kept his right arm at his side and waved with his left. He seemed "almost puzzled by the hugeness of the thing," reported the *San Juan Star.* "But even this shy young man loosened up after being kissed by three pretty young things representing a beer company." The streets of Santurce and San Juan resounded with cheers as Roberto and Orlando, Momen and Pedruchin, rode in open convertibles along a circuitous route to Sixto Escobar stadium, where they were met by a roster of public officials and another boisterous crowd of several thousand fans. The mayor declared the ballplayers honored citizens, and Martiniano Garcia, owner of the Ponce baseball team, made the formal introductions, calling it "a day of glory for Puerto Rico." Cepeda spoke first, and was brief. He said that he loved Puerto Rico now more than ever.

Then Clemente took the microphone. If it was beyond the thinking of Pittsburgh sportswriters why the great Pirates right fielder would play winter baseball in Puerto Rico, here was the answer. He was home again. His parents and brothers were standing nearby, and off to the side were Pedrin Zorrilla, the Big Crab, who had signed him to his first contract, and Roberto Marín, the first coach to believe in him, and Pancho Coimbre, one of his heroes, a great black Puerto Rican hitter who had played too soon, before major league baseball integrated. Clemente often connected his own history to the struggle of his people, and here was a moment of triumph for them all. He was speaking in his own language, and his words were eloquent. "In the name of my family, in the name of Puerto Rico, in the name of all the players who didn't have a chance to play for Puerto Rico in the big leagues, I thank you," he said. "You can be sure that all the Puerto Rican players who go to the States do their best."

8

Fever

ON A DECEMBER DAY IN 1963, TWO CARS CROSSED PATHS
on the streets of San Juan. In one, Orlando Zabala, on leave from the
U.S. Army, was driving his younger sister Vera back to their parents'
house in Carolina. In the other, Roberto Clemente was cruising into
town in his big white Cadillac. As the cars passed, Vera caught a brief
glimpse of the great baseball star and felt a nervous flutter in her chest.
She said nothing, and tried to remain expressionless, knowing that her
protective brother would not approve.

A month later, after the New Year and Three Kings Day, Vera
Zabala left the house to go to Landau's drugstore on the far end of the
central plaza in Carolina. She was twenty-two, a business administration graduate of the University of Puerto Rico, and an administrative
assistant at GDV, the government bank. Her appearance was entranc-
ing: statuesque, with radiant black hair, smooth coffee skin, high
cheekbones, and dark, dancing eyes. On her way to the pharmacy, she
noticed a car slowing and the driver looking at her. It was Clemente.
Always careful to convey an all-business demeanor as she walked, Vera
tried to appear even more serious, aware that she was being observed.
To her surprise, when she entered the drugstore, Clemente was
already there. How he had parked his car so fast and slipped inside,
she would never know, but he was sitting near the counter, reading the
paper with his legs crossed, a study in nonchalance. For some reason,
no one seemed to be working at the pharmacy, and Vera, feeling a bit
afraid, wanted to leave.

"No, no, don't leave," Clemente said. "The owner will be back in a
few minutes."

Vera kept silent, pretending she was searching for something on the shelves.

"Are you from Carolina?" Clemente asked. "Because I never saw you before. Never!"

"Yes, sir," Vera answered.

Clemente pressed forward with his interrogation. "I cannot believe you are from Carolina because I never saw you before. What is your last name?"

"Zabala," she said.

"Zabala." Clemente paused. "Are you related to Rafael Zabala?" Rafael Zabala was a baseball player for the Caguas Criollos. He was Vera's distant cousin.

"Yes, we're related, but we don't know each other," she said.

Oscar Landau, the pharmacist, finally returned, and Vera was able to buy what she needed and leave. As soon as she was gone, Clemente pumped Landau for more information. Who was this striking young woman? Could Landau help set up a date? That would be difficult, Landau said. Her father was very strict. You never see her around town. She is working at a bank, and when she comes home you don't see her at the movies, at the plaza, anywhere. If you want to see her, you have to go to her house.

That made Clemente more determined. He contacted a friend from Carolina, Natin Vizcarrando, son of the poet Fortunato Vizcarrando, who lived near the Zabalas. Any chance for an introduction? That would be difficult, Natin said. Her family protected her like a jewel. Clemente next called Mercedes Velasquez, who lived two houses from the Zabalas and taught at the high school. Everyone in town respected the Velasquez family. After work one evening, Mrs. Velasquez summoned Vera, her former student, to her house and said, "Vera, Roberto Clemente is driving me crazy. He is calling me twenty times a day. He wants to meet you."

"One of these days," Vera said. She had a sense already that Roberto Clemente would be the love of her life, but she was afraid to rush it. He was the famous one; better to see how much this mattered to him.

A week or so later, Mrs. Velasquez came to the Zabala house with an invitation. Some friends were going with Clemente to watch him play a baseball game for the San Juan Senadores at Hiram Bithorn Stadium, and they were wondering if Vera and her older sister, Ana Maria, would like to come. (The new Bithorn stadium, named in honor of the first Puerto Rican major leaguer, had opened in Hato Rey in 1962, replacing Sixto Escobar.) Ana Maria, who never married, was even stricter than their parents, and immediately suspicious. The teacher had never asked them to a baseball game before, why now? Ana Maria said she didn't want to go, but since it was with a group, and the outing seemed harmless, it was decided that Vera could attend. On the day of the game, Clemente came to pick her up in his white Cadillac. Vera wanted to sit in back, but Roberto insisted that she ride in front. She kept quiet as they drove toward the stadium.

"Don't you talk?" asked Clemente.

"No," she said. "I don't talk much."

The intricate courtship had only just begun.

At the stadium, Clemente excused himself and went to the locker room while Mrs. Velasquez led the group to reserved seats below the grandstands. Clemente's teenage nephew, Paco, was there, and it was obvious that Clemente had assigned him to look after Vera. Every few minutes, he would ask, "Do you want something to eat or drink?" Once, Clemente emerged from the dugout with a teammate, looked into the stands, and pointed out Vera. That was all he did on the field; the game was rained out.

When Clemente and the others started making plans to go to a restaurant, Vera said she had to return home. It was three in the afternoon, Clemente argued. They could go and still get her home in plenty of time. "No, no, no," she said. "My parents will be listening on the radio and know that it was postponed." Her father, Flor Zabala, was a big Senadores fan, though the rest of the family rooted for the Santurce Cangrejeros. Vera herself knew little about baseball; she had not followed winter ball or Clemente's career in Pittsburgh. But she knew she had to go home. They drove back to Carolina, where she told her parents that the game was rained out and that the group was gathering at Mrs. Velasquez's house, where she would like to join them. When she got there, everyone was circled around Roberto Clemente in the living room, listening as he went on and on about his bad back and stiff neck.

Orlando Zabala, the Army sergeant, came home at about this time looking for his sister. "Where's Verín?" he asked, using her diminutive nickname. Sister Ana said she had gone to the Senadores game but it got rained out and now she was at her old teacher's house with the ballplayer Roberto Clemente. Orlando drove around the block and parked his car on the street outside Mrs. Velasquez's front window. Vera noticed him, excused herself, and quietly stepped outside. "I'll give you five minutes to get back home," he told her.

At the bank the next day, Vera picked up the ringing telephone and it was Clemente on the other end, asking whether she would like to go to lunch. The sound of his voice made her anxious. "Sorry," she said. "I'm busy. Maybe some other time." And she hung up on him.

A few days later, the persistent Clemente turned to his niece Rafaela to make the call. Fafa, as she was known, was so nice that Vera could not think up an excuse and accepted the invitation to lunch. Somehow, word spread through the bank about the date with the famous ballplayer and coworkers teased her all the next morning. *Vera, it's ten-thirty! Vera, it's eleven!* At noon, they left their desks to get a look. Vera persuaded one woman to stay back and walk to the lobby with her. "And there he was, all dressed up. A nice suit," she recalled. "And then he sent for his car. He had the white Cadillac. I was so nervous. He opened the car door for me. The Cadillacs in those days were very wide, and I pushed against the door to be as far away from him as possible."

Lunch was at the San Juan Hilton, on the terrace, and Clemente did most of the talking, spending an hour to say in various ways that he wanted to visit Vera at her home and meet her parents. She kept saying that she wasn't sure; they were very strict, very mean. When talking to him, she used the formal pronoun *usted*, rather than *tú*.

A bouquet of flowers came for her at the bank the next day. They went to lunch again, and a third time, and then Clemente had to leave with the Senadores for the 1964 InterAmerican baseball winter league World Series, which was being played in Managua. This was Clemente's first visit to Nicaragua, the trip where a fan in the right-field stands threw a garrabo lizard onto the grass and made him jump in fright.

When he returned home to Puerto Rico, he took Vera to the Hilton terrace again, and this time brought out a surprise box.

"I don't even know you," Vera said when she opened the box and saw a ring.

He just wanted to make certain that the ring fit, Clemente said. And now he had to meet her parents. She relented, and the meeting was arranged.

As it turned out, the fathers knew each other, Flor Zabala and Melchor Clemente. They had both worked in the sugarcane industry, and it had been Flor, long ago, who had been sent from the hospital in Carolina to Central Victoria to tell Melchor that his daughter Anairis had died of burns. Melchor was known as something of a character in Carolina, and Roberto tried to break the tension with Vera's father by telling a few jokes at his old man's expense. There was a joke about Don Melchor in the bathtub, and another about him watching a ball game. Vera eavesdropped nervously from the next room. Roberto had stationed his niece Fafa in a car down the street in case he had to run. Finally, after Clemente had exhausted his routine of lame father jokes, Mr. Zabala reproached him.

"I don't know what you're doing here," he said. "You are a famous person, a famous baseball player. And I'm sure you know girls more beautiful than Vera and with more money. We are a very humble family."

"You are right," Clemente answered. "I can walk down to the corner and probably get ten girls. But I don't care. The one I love is here."

The conversation then turned to practical negotiation, with the strict father and earnest suitor now bargaining over visiting arrangements like two owners trying to work out a season's schedule. Mr. Zabala set precise times when Clemente could visit his daughter. Twice a week, before sundown. Clemente pleaded for more, noting that he had to leave to play ball in the States in a few weeks. No way, said the old man. Clemente brought up the wedding and all the plans that had to be made. No reason to rush, said Vera's father. No hurry for weddings here.

There were more lunches and visits twice a week, and once Clemente overstayed his allotted time on a Sunday morning and Mr.

Zabala expressed his displeasure by loudly thumping his Bible down on a table when he got back from church. Soon enough, the ballplayer was gone, off to Fort Myers and spring training. He wrote Vera every night from his room at Pirate City, the dormitory the team bought so that all the players, black and white, could stay together. There was so much work to do to plan a wedding, Clemente wrote. Come to the States so that we can talk more about it.

Time was of the essence to Roberto Clemente. In those first months of courtship, when Vera thought she hardly knew him, he told her that he felt an internal clock for everything in his life—playing baseball, starting a family, fulfilling his nascent dream of a sports city for poor Puerto Rican children. Life was a fever; no time to waste.

Ten years had passed since he had autographed his first Louisville Slugger at the 1954 training camp with the Montreal Royals. Where was he now in his baseball rise? Further along as a player than leader. He was only twenty-nine, yet a nine-year veteran of the major leagues, and though it had been slow in coming his status as a first-class talent was now firmly established. He was the right fielder with the golden arm, and the only question about his batting was how many points over .300 he would finish each season. He fell to .312 in 1962, then went up to .326 in 1963. The Pirates were still in transition from the team that had won the World Series only four seasons earlier. Groat and Hoak were gone, and Law, Friend, and Face were pitching in the late shadows of their careers. Maz was an anchor at second, and young Wilver Stargell, playing left field, was about to blossom, but Clemente was the undisputed star of the team. His influence in the clubhouse was still evolving.

To Steve Blass, a rookie pitcher from the hamlet of Falls Village, Connecticut, the 1964 Pirates were like "a wonderful baseball school—if you wanted to learn something, keep your mouth shut." Law, Friend, Face, Maz, Stargell, Clemente—but Clemente stood apart from the rest. Even more than Danny Murtaugh, the manager, he was the person to whom you had to prove yourself, but he also seemed more intimidating. "I didn't dare go near Clemente," Blass recalled. "He was this rather stern, imposing, all-work, very professional figure. I said to myself, 'If I'm going to validate myself here I better make sure he knows I'm capable and not just some asshole kid coming up.'"

Blass knew about Clemente's skills, especially his fearsome throwing arm, long before he ever saw him play. As pitchers moved up the Pirates' minor league system on their way to the majors, they were given special tutoring on what to do if there was a base hit to right field with nobody out. In that situation, they were instructed to run toward the first-base dugout and plant themselves about twenty-five feet behind the first baseman on a line with the right fielder. Why back up first on a single to the outfield? The coaches pounded in the answer: Because when you get to the big leagues, Clemente's out there in right. With that gun of his, he's likely to throw behind the runner.

First base that year was manned mostly by another young Pirate, Donn Clendenon, a lanky athlete who played basketball at Morehouse College and considered baseball his third best sport, even behind football. Clendenon's father had helped teach Roy Campanella how to catch and had "pushed baseball down the throat" of his son so much that he played the game more out of obligation than love. In the field for the Pirates, Clendenon had to remain constantly on guard for those rifle throws behind the runner, and he was both awed and annoyed by Clemente's tremendous arm. The ball would come in low and screaming, and if it took a short hop, Clendenon said, "it would just eat me alive." In a different way from Blass, he also felt that Clemente in the early years was somewhat apart from the team. The six-foot-four first sacker had been reporting to spring training with the Pirates since 1960, though he didn't make the final roster that year and only began getting significant playing time in 1962 before becoming a starter in 1963. But during that period he thought that Clemente, as the team's black star, could have been more nurturing of him and other young black players. "When I got there, initially, he didn't come to my assistance," Clendenon said in retrospect. "I just thought he could have done more. He kept kind of a low profile."

Clendenon was only a year younger than Clemente, born in the summer of 1935, yet if baseball lifetimes are measured in seven-year cycles, it had taken him a full baseball lifetime longer than Clemente to make the majors. He got a late start for the best of reasons, he was a college graduate, but after signing with Pittsburgh in 1958, he felt that his rise was slowed for the worst reason—a racial quota. "After two or three years, I found that the Pirates had a two-person quota [of minority players]—Roberto Clemente and a Spanish-speaking roommate. It was evident," Clendenon insisted later. The second black Pirate would be either Roman Mejias, a Cuban, or Joe Christopher, from the Virgin Islands, Clendenon said. If this was not precisely true, the statistics were close enough to explain why Clendenon could have felt that way. At various times during the seasons, the Pirates had five black players in 1958, six in 1959, six in 1960, and eight in 1961—but in each of those years only Clemente and one other position player, either Mejias or Christopher, were on the squad all season or played in sixty or more games. The others, for the most part, were up for little more than baseball's proverbial cup of coffee in September.

At the same time, Pittsburgh's minor league clubs during the late 1950s and early sixties were "jam-packed" with black players, as Clendenon put it. The minor league bundling was a reality hard to ignore, whether it was the result of a racial quota at the top, which Joe L. Brown, the general manager, denied, or simply because the Pirates were signing increasing numbers of black players at a time when the major league squad already was stocked with World Series–quality talent. Another black Pirate who came into his own in 1964, Bob Veale, the big left-handed pitcher, recalled playing for the Wilson Tobs (Tobacconists), the Pirates farm club in the Carolina League, in 1959. By Veale's account, the team had so many black players that many Southerners assumed it was a Negro League outfit. The Tobs had a rivalry that year with the Raleigh Capitals, who were led by a future Hall of Fame outfielder named Carl Yastrzemski. "There used to be an old white gentleman waiting in the stands in Raleigh before we got there," Veale remembered. "We would come riding in on the bus, and he would shout out, 'Here comes Wilson and all that black magic!'"

In any case, by the time Clendenon, Veale, Stargell, and other black Pirates finally started making the Pittsburgh club in the early 1960s, in the post–World Series years, they brought with them varying degrees of pent-up frustration. Clendenon, for one, was hoping that Clemente would protect him and counsel him on how to survive and thrive in the majors. When that didn't happen immediately, he instead turned to veterans on other teams like Willie Mays and retired trailblazers like Jackie Robinson and Joe Black. Clendenon shared a house with Stargell and Veale at 428 Dakota Street in Schenley Heights that year, not far from Clemente, but did not hang out with him.

By 1964 Clemente was in the early stages of his emergence as a leader. He had become a big brother of sorts to other Caribbean players, not just on the Pirates but throughout the league. Tony Taylor, a Cuban who played second base for the Philadelphia Phillies, said that he and other Latin players would go out to eat with Clemente whenever they were in the same city, and that he revered Clemente, as much for the way he behaved as the way he played. "He'd try to help you and talk to you about the way to play baseball and the way to handle yourself in society and to represent your country," Taylor recalled. "He was the type of guy who would just sit with you and talk, do this, do that. In my life, besides my mom and father, I'd met no person who meant so much to me. People say he was moody, he was this and that. But he would say the truth. He told you the truth. He never tried to hide anything from anybody."

On the Pirates, Clemente took Manny Mota under his wing that year. Mota was a Dominican outfielder who was starting to get some playing time in his third major league season. He was far slighter than Clemente, only 5' 9" and 160 pounds, and displayed little power, but shared that rare skill of being able to get wood on almost any ball. Like Clemente, who excelled in the Puerto Rican winter league before shining in the majors, Mota had led his Dominican league in hitting two winters in a row before gaining notice up North. He had been traded from the Giants to Houston to Pittsburgh within two seasons, devalued because it was thought he lacked power. Clemente identified with the struggle and became Mota's closest friend and adviser on the Pirates. At the stadium every day before games, they could be seen working on hitting, bunting, fielding, and throwing. "He's always been a good hitter," Clemente said of Mota at midseason, pushing his cause to skeptical Pirate beat writers. "He can hit big league pitching if he's given the chance." Mota eventually proved his friend and mentor right, playing fourteen seasons with a career average over .300. And Clemente would do it again a few years later, working to transform another Dominican Pirate, Mateo Alou, from a mediocre pull hitter into a first-rate spray hitter.

Clemente would always have some sharp angles to him, not the easy, steady-as-you-go personality of the traditional clubhouse captain. He was shy, yet bursting with pride. He was profoundly humble, yet felt misunderstood and undervalued. Even when he wasn't angry at a sports writer or feeling some perceived slight, it could be hard to tell by looking at him in the clubhouse. Television sportscaster Sam Nover, during an interview, told Clemente that some members of the press "come away from seeing you for the first time in the locker room and say, 'Clemente's a mean man. He frowns. The man never smiles'"— and then posed the question: "Is the shape of your face such that you never smile too often?" Clemente took the query seriously, and noted that some teammates had a physiognomy that made them look like they were laughing even when they were mad, whereas his was the opposite. "Now you might think I am serious when I am not serious," he said. "This is the way that I am. And I like to be that way because sometimes you are smiling and then the next time you don't see me smiling and say, 'Hey, what's wrong with you?' So now, I am natural. That is the way I am. Nobody can say Roberto is mean. I might look mean but I really respect people."

That Clemente defined himself as Puerto Rican, rather than by the color of his skin, also might have shaped Clendenon's perceptions. "He kept saying, 'I no black,'" Clendenon recalled. In fact, Clemente was proud to be a black Puerto Rican, yet never wanted to be categorized or limited by race. When he talked about the issue, especially in English, his comments occasionally were seen as rebukes of blackness, which they were not. The *Pittsburgh Courier* made that mistake in 1960, but later realized that it had misinterpreted Clemente's intent and his remarks. The clearest account of his perspective on being both Puerto Rican and black came in the wide-ranging interview with sportscaster Nover. "I am between the worlds," he said. "So anything I do will reflect on me because I am black and . . . will reflect on me because I am Puerto Rican. To me, I always respect everybody. And thanks to God, when I grew up, I was raised . . . my mother and father never told me to hate anyone, or they never told me to dislike anyone because of racial color. We never talked about that. As a matter of fact, I started listening to this talk when I came to the States."

That leads to another way of looking at Clemente and his slow evolution as a leader in the States: language. After a decade in North America, Clemente knew English and the idioms of baseball, including the lexicon of profanity. He knew how to use variations of the all-purpose word fuck as a noun, verb, and adverb in any sentence. ("You pitch me the fuck inside and I hit the fucking ball to McKeesport.") Clendenon suspected there were times when Clemente pretended that he couldn't understand something in English "because he didn't want to deal with something." That is certainly probable, but more often Clemente wanted to speak English and insisted on doing so. It was his fear of being misinterpreted that could make him seem reserved and defensive, especially when writers lurked in the clubhouse. "I always had a theory that here was a very bright man who had taken verbal risks with English before and had been burned and didn't care for that to happen again," Blass recalled. "I think the writers relating what he said in pigeon English was actually secondary to the fact that he had concepts that he was trying to convey and wouldn't be understood because his English wouldn't convey it as well as his Spanish. And I think that frustrated him."

Don Leppert, a backup catcher who arrived in Pittsburgh in 1961, the season after the World Series victory, said later that he was amazed by the gap between Clemente's talent and his public recognition, and attributed that to the language barrier. Leppert placed the blame largely on the baseball writers who covered the Pirates. His locker was near Clemente's and Leppert felt frustrated by the way some writers portrayed his teammate. "They tried to make a buffoon out of him," Leppert recalled. "I was sitting there one night when Biederman [Les Biederman of the *Pittsburgh Press*] was asking Clemente something, and Biederman had a little smirk on his face. I went off on Biederman: 'Why the hell don't you ask him questions in Spanish?' I didn't endear myself to Biederman, but didn't give a rat's ass, either. They tried to take advantage of every malaprop." Clemente said as much himself once to Pittsburgh writer Myron Cope. "I know I don't speak as bad as they say I speak," Clemente told Cope. "I know that I don't have the good English pronunciation because my tongue belong to the Spanish. But I know where the verb, the article, the pronoun, whatever it is, go. I never in my life start a sentence with 'me.' I start with 'I.' The sportswriters [make it] 'me.' 'Me Tarzan, you Jane.'"

And finally there were lingering questions about Clemente's aches and pains and his constant physical laments. Since his third season, 1957, when he had suffered through a year-long slump that he attributed to an undiagnosed malaise (eventually, it was determined to be a lower-back condition), he had been unable to shake the reputation of being an oversensitive hypochondriac. In the long run, this perception was utterly contradicted by his enduring statistics; he would break Honus Wagner's cherished record and play more games in a Pirates uniform than any player in Pittsburgh history. In the medium term, the perception would be contradicted by his determined clutch play, month after month, year after year. As Clemente himself put it one day, "Hypochondriacs cannot produce. I fucking produce!" But in the short run, whenever he took two or three days off to rest his troubled body, his behavior was deemed by some to be too sensitive and unbefitting a team leader. He probably didn't help his own cause by talking so much about his ailments, but that reflected his desire to be perfect more than a need for excuses. His physician in San Juan, Dr. Roberto Buso, said that Clemente's sensitive personality included a low threshold for pain. "If his back hurts he worries and then it becomes a vicious circle leading to more things," Buso once explained. "If he has a little diarrhea he worries that he has a little stomach difficulty." Pittsburgh, with its blue collar ethos, a milltown whose mythic figure was a giant named Joe Magarac, who by legend made steel with his bare hands, was a particularly difficult atmosphere for someone as sensitive to all things and especially pain as Clemente.

His relationship with Danny Murtaugh had been uneven precisely because of this sensitivity. Since taking over the Pirates in mid-season 1957, Murtaugh had occasionally criticized Clemente for not playing. The manager's admiration for Clemente as a magnificent player had

grown year by year, yet he never stopped sticking in the needle. It was
nothing personal; that happened to be Murtaugh's personality. The
"whistling Irishman" would say what was on his mind and then forget
it. Clemente's personality was altogether different. Whatever was said
about him hurt, and kept hurting. Mazeroski, who enjoyed a smoother
relationship with Murtaugh, thought their manager didn't think twice
about how to handle Clemente or would have done it better. "Roberto
just wasn't the type of guy you just took off and embarrassed in front of
the team," Maz said later. "He'd crawl in a shell and the more Murtaugh hollered at him, the more moody he got." Their periodic difficulties had busted into the open during a road trip in May 1963.
Clemente had been groaning about his physical ills during a three-day
series in Los Angeles, when he had played poorly and asked for a day
off as the Dodgers had swept the Pirates, and Murtaugh, feeling
grumpy about the losses, confronted Clemente when they reached
Houston. "You let me know when you're ready to play again," Murtaugh said. "You're making too much money to sit on the bench. The
next time you feel like playing you'll play and you'll play every day
until I say you won't play."

Clemente, acutely conscious of his dignity, felt insulted by the
reproach. "You talk like I don't want to play baseball," he told Murtaugh.

He ended up playing 152 games that season, but the story of the
encounter seeped into the press and became part of the mythology of
Clemente's fragility. Mazeroski, for one, thought the undeserved reputation was linked to the language problem. "When he was hurt he had
trouble explaining himself because of the language problem and everyone thought he was jakin'," Mazeroski later wrote about Clemente in
Sport magazine. "I don't think he's ever jaked. He just could do things
when he was hurt as well as the rest of us could when we were healthy
and people would see this and decide that he was dogging it."

All of this—pride, shyness, culture, language, preoccupation with
his physical condition, anger over being underappreciated, even the
shape of his face—could make Clemente seem guarded and at times
unapproachable. Roy McHugh, a talented columnist for the *Pittsburgh
Press*, had decided to write his first piece about Roberto early in the
1964 season after Clemente had blasted a tape-measure home run over

the left-field wall at Forbes Field. In the clubhouse after the game, McHugh asked Clemente if it was the longest ball he had ever hit. Clemente took offense at the innocent question. It reminded him of all the other long balls he had hit that got no notice, going back to a home run at Wrigley Field in 1959. "It was like throwing a lighted match into a can of gasoline," McHugh said later. "He blew up, shouting, a torrent of words. He went on for five minutes before I could get in another word." Clemente had nothing against McHugh, but the question unwittingly hit a sensitive spot. McHugh, who was predisposed to like Clemente, or at least to present him accurately, decided to choose another subject for his column, and for several years thereafter tended to stay away from the Pirates right fielder, thinking he was too difficult.

Yet Clemente could be thoroughly engaging when he was around people who made him feel comfortable, including not only friends, family, and fellow Latin ballplayers, but also children, taxi drivers, old people, clubhouse attendants—anyone who seemed to have the soul of an underdog. "He would extend himself more to somebody who seemed unsure than to a cocky writer or player," pitcher Blass noticed. In the same locker room where his vibes held sportswriters at bay, he was a magnet for the children of other players. He kept a jar of honey in his locker—he took a spoonful before games to relax—and shared it with the kids. Jim Marshall, a utility infielder for a few seasons in the early sixties, remembered that whenever he brought his young son Blake into the locker room, "he always ran for Roberto, sitting on his knee, the two of them eating honey." Tony Bartirome, the pint-sized former first baseman who began working in the Pirates' training room in 1964, recalled that reputations did not always reflect reality. Some established older white stars who were portrayed as "great guys" by the press virtually ignored the clubhouse staff, but not Clemente. In the daily give and take, he would tease them, ask about their families, offer his folklore medical advice, tip them generously. "Everybody in that clubhouse, we loved him," Bartirome said.

During the first half of the 1964 season, several nights a week, Clemente had been calling Vera Zabala from Pittsburgh or one of the National League road cities. He was always making plans, pressing the issue of marriage. He finally persuaded Vera to come to New York for the All-Star game in July, accompanied by Ana Maria, her protective older sister, and his mother, Doña Luisa. The combination of chaperones was enough to get the visit approved by Vera's father and brother, and the three women flew to New York on July 6, the day before the game at Shea Stadium. They were picked up at the airport by Carlos and Carmen Llanos, longtime family friends from Carolina who now lived in the Bronx. Throughout Clemente's major league career, the Llanoses provided him a place to stay and relax when he came to New York, and eased his homesickness by plying him with good humor and Puerto Rican food and seasonings.

The Pirates were in the middle of another middling season, but had four players on the National League team: Clemente, Mazeroski, Stargell (hot in the season's first half with eleven homers and forty-eight runs batted in; just starting to show his slugging potential), and old Smoky Burgess, the butterball catcher who was still a dangerous hitter, even at age thirty-seven. Among the four, only Clemente, leading the league again with a .345 average, had been elected to the team as a starter; the others were added to the roster by the National League manager, Walter Alston. A noteworthy feature of the game that year was that the rosters were stocked with more Latin players than ever before. The group again was led by Clemente. It also included a trio of Cubans, rookie outfielder Tony Oliva, shortstop Leo Cardenas, and right-handed pitcher Camilo Pascual; the Venezuelan shortstop Luis Aparicio (who wouldn't play because of a groin injury); Dominican ace Juan Marichal (in the second year of a stunning seven-year string in which he averaged twenty-two wins a season); and two of Clemente's Puerto Rican friends, Orlando Cepeda of the Giants, starting at first base for the National League, and pitcher Juan Pizarro, enjoying his best season for the White Sox in the American League. Long since a star in his homeland, Pizarro was finally getting some recognition up North. He had won eleven games already that year on his way to a nineteen and nine record.

Clemente started the All-Star game in right field and batted leadoff for the National League. This was the summer of the World's Fair in New York, and the area around the new ballpark in Flushing Meadows was awash with foreign tourists, Midwestern family vacationers, and hard-core metropolitan baseball fans. Al Abrams rode the subway out to Shea, and noted in his *Post-Gazette* column that "judging by the aroma in the crowded trains, some of the great 'unwashables' in history were among the passengers today." It was a hometown crowd, with a smattering of LET'S GO, METS! signs, and the largest pregame ovations went, in order, to Ron Hunt, scrappy second baseman for the Amazin' Mets; Casey Stengel, the comic-foil old manager of the inept new club; and Sandy Koufax, the favorite son who had come home from the golden West. As Vera, Ana, and his mother watched from the stands, Roberto got one hit in three at-bats, singling in the fifth inning and racing around to score on a double by his former teammate, Dick Groat, who was now playing shortstop for the St. Louis Cardinals. As it turned out, Clemente's late-inning replacement in right, Johnny Callison of the front-running Phillies, cracked a three-run home run with two out in the bottom of the ninth to give the National League a 7–4 win, a victory that at long last evened the all-time match between the two leagues at seventeen wins apiece. Here, it seemed, was the culmination of a sociological as well as sporting trend. At the close of the 1940s, the American League had to that point dominated the midseason exhibition, winning twelve of the first sixteen contests. Since then, the National stars shone brighter, in large part because of the league's tradition of aggressively recruiting black and Latin players.

In his ellipses-dotted "Sidelights on Sports" column the next day, Abrams took special note of the Pittsburgh contingent: "There were stars in Wilver Stargell's eyes as he took the field with his National League teammates for batting practice. 'I'm excited,' the husky Pirate youngster admitted. 'I don't think I've ever been as excited about anything as I am today' . . . Roberto Clemente, Bill Mazeroski, and Smoky Burgess, old hands at this sort of thing, took things in stride . . . Clemente's mother watched her talented son play. It was her first All-Star game. She saw Roberto perform in the 1960 World Series . . ."

Clemente and his women guests caught a flight to Pittsburgh immediately after the game; he had to get right back to work. The Pirates were not afforded the traditional extra day off after the All-Star break, but instead a makeup game was scheduled the next night against the Cincinnati Reds, an odd one-game series to open a nine-game home stand. Baseball officials were still adjusting to the complications of fitting the expanded ten-team leagues into 162-game schedules. With great care, Clemente had already worked out his own schedule. He needed Vera around to continue their discussions about an off-season wedding, and nothing could go wrong beforehand. He had rented an apartment in Pittsburgh for the week, where he would sleep, while the women would stay at his normal lodging with Stanley and Mamie Garland. The Garlands showed great kindness to Vera, and the obvious regard they had for Roberto helped persuade sister Ana Maria of his worthiness. Vera was touched by his courtesies and graciousness. She realized for the first time how big a star he was in the States, yet celebrity didn't seem to change his manner. The trip was a success: Vera knew that she wanted to marry him, and she returned to San Juan with two more engagement presents, a watch and a collar of pearls, and a wedding date in November.

The remainder of the 1964 season offered much excitement, but not for the Pirates. From five games above the .500 mark at the All-Star break, they sputtered slowly downhill, finishing with two fewer wins than losses. Since the World Series glory of 1960, they had come in sixth in 1961, eighteen games in back of the Reds; fourth in 1962, eight games behind the Giants; eighth in 1963, twenty-five games behind the Dodgers (shades of the pathetic early fifties); and now sixth again, trailing St. Louis by thirteen games. The closest sniff the Pirates got to the pennant race this time was during four days in September, between the twenty-fourth and twenty-seventh, when they dropped five straight home games to the charging Cardinals, helping lift St. Louis over the free-falling Phils. It was, all in all, another year of mediocrity at Forbes Field, except when a ball was hit to right—baseball ecstasy, Clemente charging, scooping, unwinding overhead, the arm!—or when he made his way to the plate, his reluctant, creaky, slow-motion advance evoking the delicious contradiction of a rapacious hitter who nonetheless resembled, as Pittsburgh writers joked to one another in the press box, a condemned man heading toward the electric chair. "Roberto has been a dominant force in the Pirates' attack," Abrams wrote during the dog days of summer. "We shudder to think where the club would be without him."

There were wins and losses of other sorts when the games were done. After seven and a half seasons at the helm, with that one unforgettable 1960 season and fifty-eight more total wins than losses, but two final losing seasons, Danny Murtaugh stepped down as manager. He was replaced by Harry (the Hat) Walker, the old Cardinals outfielder from the Deep South city of Pascagoula, Mississippi, son and brother of ballplayers called Dixie. The Hat was known for his skills as a teacher and for having a mouth that would never shut.

Luck is the residue of design, Branch Rickey once said. And now the Mahatma's own grand design was nearing an end. After leaving the Pirates at the end of the fifties decade, he had found a sinecure with his first team, the Cardinals, as an adviser, and tried not very hard to repress the occasional feelings of envy or schadenfreude that seeped into his mind as he watched Joe L. Brown run his Pirates up to the heights of the World Championship and then slowly down the hill again. The Cardinals now had capped his long and eventful career by catching the Phillies and then outplaying the Yankees in a classic seven-game World Series, but in truth the old man had little to do with it.

Rickey scouted for general manager Bing Devine (indeed considered himself still the boss and tried to tell Devine what to do) and wrote his acerbic memos to the end. (At a Minnesota Twins game with secretary Ken Blackburn at his side, he said of slugger Harmon Killebrew, who must have reminded him of Ralph Kiner: "The high hard inside pitch he misses . . . Strikes out a great deal. I would not be interested in obtaining his contract in any kind of a possible trade. I don't want him at the price." And of pitcher Jim Kaat: "Looks like an athlete and acts like one. He can throw hard and he has a good curve—a corker most of the time. Stress does not agree with him. He is a young chap and ought to become a fine pitcher.") Rickey also entered the personnel fray during a crucial stretch of the season as an intermediary between Dick Groat, brought over from the Pirates a season earlier, and the laconic manager, Johnny Keane, for whom Groat had no baseball respect. At a private huddle in August, as the Cardinals were about to make their move, Rickey tried to persuade Groat to agree to a trade, to no avail. In fact, Rickey had opposed the acquisition of the quick but slow-footed shortstop in the first place. Groat was stunned by the trade attempt and said that he just wanted to win. He thought if Keane were replaced by Red Schoendienst, the talented Cards would find their way. Groat went on to hit .292 and play almost every day in his last fine season, and the Cards won everything despite Groat's dismal assessment of Keane, who was appreciated by other Cardinals, especially black stars Bob Gibson and Bill White.

During the World Series, Rickey cordially invited Brown, his disciple and successor, to breakfast. They had talked baseball, as always, including the future of the Pittsburgh club. Brown's decision afterward to replace Murtaugh with Walker prompted one final polite memo from Rickey. "Dear Joe," he wrote. "I think you have made the very best choice for your manager. I know that Danny had good reason for resigning and it was undoubtedly good judgment for him to do that. Harry is a student of baseball and he has had enough managing experience to keep him out of the experimental class. He knows how to handle his manpower. You will surely get good field results from him."

Brown responded with a handwritten note:

Dear Mr. Rickey,

Thank you for your thoughtful note about Harry Walker . . . I was certain Harry was a good choice at the time of his appointment, and after spending four days and nights with him in Florida, I am more positive than ever. [The new coaches] Hal Smith, Clyde King, John Pesky, and Alex Grammas, who have been added to Harry's staff . . . are all personable, aggressive, intelligent, experienced, ambitious, comparatively young, and mindful of the necessity for continuing instruction.

You were nice to have us for breakfast at your lovely home during the Series. It was good to see you, Mrs. Rickey and Auntie looking so well and in good health.

Rickey was fired by the Cardinals soon after, and within a year he was dead. An irreplaceable if difficult baseball life extinguished at age eighty-three. As he would describe it, the laws of cause and effect worked this one last time with inexorable exactitude.

Roberto Clemente's season ended with another win. He finished the year with 211 hits and a batting average of .339, high enough to bring home his second Silver Bat as the league's leading hitter.

Here, in Carolina, was a day to honor the meaning of home. All morning and into the slow, sweet Saturday afternoon, townspeople had celebrated like it was the festival of a local saint, and as evening approached on November 14, 1964, they congregated in the central plaza outside the San Fernando Church for a final act of worship. Thousands of *carolinenses* jammed the streets of the quadrangle plaza and elbowed for viewing position under rows of neatly pruned laurel trees. The evening light glowed soothingly on the church's soft pastels. Inside, three hundred guests sat on hard pews, under the high dome, flowers everywhere. At age thirty, after a decade as a rising star in the major leagues up North, Momen Clemente was getting married. The weight of his achievements in Puerto Rico and the states was evident in the invitation list. There sat Luis Muñoz Marín, the longtime progressive governor of the island. Nearby were general manager Brown and Howie Haak, the brilliantly profane scout, a tobacco plug removed from his jowl for this special occasion. The Clemente family came in, parents Melchor and Luisa and brothers Matino, Osvaldo, and Andres, and various cousins, nieces, and nephews, along with the adopted Pittsburgh parents, the Garlands, Phil Dorsey, and what amounted to a couple of pickup teams of fellow ballplayers.

Clemente looked as princely in his black tuxedo as he did in the cool white and black of his Pirates uniform. Before the service, as he stood in the sacristy fidgeting, someone approached and wondered whether he was nervous. That was never the right question to ask him. He might be quick to say what was nagging him, and something always was—lack of sleep, pain in the lower back, headache, sore leg—but very rarely would he confess to feeling nervous. "Never," he said this time. "I feel great!"

A friend seized the chance to needle the proud Clemente. "Then why don't you spit out the gum you're chewing?" he asked.

Vera Christina Zabala, wearing a dress of Italian silk satin, the sleeves embroidered in white porcelain beads and diminutive pearls, was escorted down the aisle by her father, Flor Manuel Zabala. The matron of honor was Mercedes Velasquez, the neighbor and teacher who a year earlier had complained that Roberto had been driving her crazy by relentlessly trying to press her into service as a matchmaker. Myrna Luz Hernández was the maid of honor, and another Velasquez, Clemente's friend Victor, stood as best man. When it was time for vows, the audience strained to hear. Tito Paniagua, covering the ceremony for the *San Juan Star,* noted that Clemente, though his voice was soft, said *"acepto"* just loud enough for Father Salvador Planas "who called the play, to make it official."

Joyous organ music filled the church as the wedding party spilled out to the plaza, where the outdoor crowd, still in the thousands, broke their silence with a thunderous roar as though *El Magnífico's* magic arm had nailed another runner at third. The caravan of sedans, led by police escort, weaved through the streets of Carolina toward the reception at the clubhouse of the Phi Eta Mu fraternity in Cupey Bajo, which overflowed with more than eight hundred guests.

A year earlier, when Vera's father first met the famous ballplayer, he had wondered why someone who could choose from scores of women had settled on his daughter. The same question seemed to be on the minds of several women Clemente had befriended in Pittsburgh and other National League cities. One woman in New York, not realizing that the marriage had already taken place, sent Clemente a letter that he kept and later showed to Vera. "Dear Roberto," it began. "What do I have to do to get you to write? I waited for you to come to New York and you didn't even try to call me. I'm going mad not knowing what you're doing or when you're getting married. If there's something I could do to stop you I would. But you haven't even given me the chance . . . You don't understand what the whole thing is doing to me. I've never needed anything as much as I need you . . . Roberto, I love you as always. You know I'll be yours no matter what happens."

The Puerto Rican winter league had begun, but Clemente was in no rush to get back to baseball. He and Vera took a honeymoon in the Virgin Islands, then spent the Christmas season between their parents' houses and a three-acre farm he was renting in the countryside south-west of Carolina. Vera quickly discovered that Clemente was a home-body who was happiest when he was fiddling around the house. He liked to repair equipment, clear brush, and mow the lawn. In his role as a country squire, he proved both skilled and accident prone. One day that December while he was cutting grass, a rock flew up from his mower and struck him in his right thigh, causing a bruise so deep and persistent that by mid-January he was put in the hospital and Dr. Buso performed a minor operation to drain blood from the leg.

As he was recovering from the operation in February, Clemente organized a group of Puerto Rican and Cuban all-stars to play a series against the best Dominicans. If nothing else, the three-game series played in Santo Domingo, the Dominican capital, gave an indication of the progression of baseball hotspots in the Caribbean. First Cuba dominated, then Puerto Rico, and now the DR. Clemente put himself in center, and his team also included major leaguers Juan Pizarro, José Pagan, Cookie Rojas, and Sandy Alomar, but they were outmatched by a Dominican squad that had Juan Marichal on the mound and the three Alou brothers, Felipe, Mateo, and Jesus, in the field. For the third game, Clemente yanked himself from the starting lineup. He said that he felt tired. He entered the game in the seventh inning, only because the fans expected to see him play, and of course, as he usually did when he was feeling poorly, rapped out a hard single. That was the lone game the Puerto Ricans won. By the time they returned to San Juan, he was feeling even weaker.

In sickness and in health; during her first three months as a bride, Vera saw the strength and vulnerability of her husband. He went to bed and stayed there, his fever rising every day. At times he appeared to be in a stupor, unable to talk. At other times he seemed on the verge of delirium. The nurses gave him sleeping pills, but no medicine short of general anesthesia seemed capable of getting him to sleep.

What was wrong? At first the doctors suspected he might have picked up a paratyphoid infection from some hogs at his country farm. They put him in the hospital again. He became morbid. He would die young, he told Vera. She should remarry. God forbid, don't talk about that. Don't talk about sad things, she answered. His brothers Andres and Matino came to visit and tried to lighten his mood, mocking his fatalism. When your ass becomes so skinny that the back pockets of your pants come together, then you're dead, Andres joked. The diagnosis remained uncertain, but now it was thought he had contacted malaria during his barnstorming tour in the Dominican Republic. This was not hypochondria, or Clemente just being sensitive. He lost five, ten, fifteen, twenty, twenty-three pounds, until finally the fever broke. By the second week in March, he was out of the hospital. He changed his diet and started drinking fruit cocktail milkshakes made with egg yolks, banana ice cream, orange juice, a peach or pear, and crumbled ice.

With the Pirates already training in Fort Myers, general manager Brown began calling Clemente every day to check on his condition and find out when he might report. Then, one evening, Brown and his wife, Virginia, who went by the nickname Din, were injured in a traffic accident as they were returning to Fort Myers from dinner in a nearby town. Din was badly hurt, with several broken bones. The next time Brown called Clemente it was from his wife's bedside at the hospital. Din was crazy about Roberto, who always treated her with warmth and kindness.

"Din is hurt but is anxious to know how you are doing and when you'll be able to come," Brown told Clemente.

"I'm two or three days away, I think I can come Friday," Clemente responded. "How is Din doing?"

"She's right here, would you like to talk to her?"

"Yes."

"How are you, Roberto?" Din said softly.

"Din, so sorry you had this accident," he said.

"I'm doing better, how are you?" she answered, turning the attention away from her own battered body.

"Well," said Clemente, "I got this touch of diarrhea."

Din laughed when she recounted the conversation to her husband. Classic Clemente, Joe Brown thought.

A few days later, Clemente was ready to return to Florida for his twelfth baseball spring. Andres and Matino drove him to the airport, as usual. Florida was still not the most inviting place for Clemente and his new bride, so Vera would join him later in Pittsburgh. As the boys walked toward the gate, Andres said that his little brother would be too puny to bring home another Silver Bat that year.

Momen stopped, grabbed the back pockets of his pants, and squeezed them together, laughing at the sign of death.

9
Passion

EVERY MOVE CLEMENTE MADE WAS STUDIED BY HIS admiring fans at Forbes Field. Bruce Laurie, who landed in Pittsburgh in 1965 as a graduate student in history, might show up at the stadium in the fifth inning and take a freebie seat in the right-field stands, sharing his beers with the usher. For his baseball satisfaction, all Laurie needed was to observe Clemente up close, all "bone and sinew with long arms that looked longer still because of the Pirates' sleeveless shirts." And then, at some point, the thrill of the throw—with a motion faster than any Laurie had ever seen "and overhand, with an exaggerated follow-through, so that when he wound up . . . he looked like a dervish expelling a cannonball." Many players have one memorable trait; Clemente's every action on the diamond had its own singular style. The writer Michael Chabon, who grew up in Pittsburgh, said it was hard *not* to look at Clemente; he attracted one's attention like a glint on a telephone wire. Howard Fineman, another denizen of the right-field stands, memorized his hero's intricate routine at the plate until it was etched into his teenage brain as surely as the capitals of the fifty states or the chronological order of the Presidents. In retrospect, Fineman would think of Clemente taking a turn at-bat as "positively Iberian, a bullfighter, the great test of wills," so serious in every detail that it was thrilling yet almost comic. And here it was:

Clemente would never smile preparing for a plate appearance. When he approached the rack inside the dugout, his attitude was that of a surgeon toward his instruments or a toreador toward his swords. He knew these bats, these Frenchy Uhalt models. He had studied them from the moment a new shipment came in during spring training. He was as tuned to them as he was to his body, and his choice might depend on his mood, or the fitness of his lower back, or the pitcher on the mound, or something he saw in the grain of wood. Not ready yet to decide, he would haul two or three bats out to the on-deck circle, carrying them all in one hand. Then he would kneel, left knee bent at ninety degrees, right knee touching the ground, posture erect, the bats draped elegantly against his thigh. One by one, he would pick them up, heft them, as he stared at the pitcher, and wipe them with his rag. Here was the serenity of Clemente, before the storm. From his right-field perch, Fineman relished this moment, knowing what was to follow. At last it was Clemente's turn to hit, and he would now make his final selection ceremoniously, this piece of wood, of the three, had made the cut; the others, unlucky, left behind as orphan scraps to be retrieved by the batboy. Then the famed dead man's walk to the batter's box.

On the way, as he approached the plate, he would rotate his neck from side to side, then twist it back, so many kinks to unloosen. Of all the sequences in the ritual, the neck move was the most regal. The poet Tom Clark would draw upon this memory above all others:

> *won't forget*
> *his nervous*
> *habit of*
> *rearing his*
> *head back*
> *on his neck*
> *like a*
> *proud horse*

And now the care of his habitat. Like an animal preparing his ground. Or maybe fortifications, that is the metaphor that popped into one observer's head—a French general preparing his fort. He would hold his bat with his left hand and raise the other toward the ump—*momentito, momentito* for Momen—as he rearranged dirt and dust with his polished leather shoes, spikes gleaming, until it was just right. By now the pitcher was ticked. But there was little in the way of filibustering from then on, no constant stepping out of the box and repeating a superstitious ritual after every pitch, aside from the occasional revolving of the neck. When his workplace was ready, he would take his stance, left leg coiled, hands back, stance way off the plate, back near the line, beseeching the ball, bring it on. He would take the first pitch, almost always, in order to calculate the timing and motion, but then let it rip. And for someone not known as a slugger, what a rip it was. Jim Murray, the *Los Angeles Times* sports columnist who made his living off metaphors, wrote that Clemente "had a batting style like a man falling down a fire escape." His swing, Bruce Laurie thought, was the mirror image of the throw—"a great swirling motion in blinding speed that routinely dislodged his batting helmet." Both Laurie and Fineman felt this odd sensation, a ripple of joy even in a Clemente swing and miss. There was such pent-up intensity in the moment that it seemed to Fineman that Clemente's "entire being was at stake with every pitch." One image that stuck was of him flinging himself and the bat toward a high-outside pitch and literally leaving his feet altogether to make contact, stroking a shot down the right-field line.

Donn Clendenon and other teammates would joke that there were three great left-handed pull hitters in the National League who scared the hell out of every first baseman: Willie McCovey, Billy Williams, and Roberto Clemente, who, of course, was no lefty at all.

In repose, there was a grace and beauty to Clemente. "Compact, flawlessly sculpted, with chiseled ebony features and an air of unshakable dignity," Roy McHugh reflected later. "He carried himself—everybody noticed this—like royalty." At times, as Clemente posed on second after a double, McHugh thought of "Michelangelo's statue of David—David wearing a baseball uniform." But in action everything changed; Clemente was all fury and agitation. A writer once described Willie Mays as liquid smooth. With Clemente, there was a liquid nature to his eyes and body, but only until he ran; then it was gone. Steve Blass and his Pirates teammates took goofy joy in watching Clemente run. He ran everything out, first of all, full speed, head down, every feeble tap back to the pitcher, and he worked so hard at running. They would tell him he looked like a broken windmill, every limb rotating a different direction. Clemente didn't actually run, they would say, he galloped. To Richard Santry, another teenager who sat in the right-field stands at Forbes Field during those years and spent the entire game watching Clemente, he ran "like he was running away from the bulls in Spain, like a crazy man." Fineman also was struck by Clemente's urgency. He seemed to run as though "his pants had been set on fire by the flames of hell itself"—and that is the point. He was not running, he was fleeing. When Clemente was on the go, it seemed not so much that he was trying to get to a base as to escape from some unspeakable phantasmal terror.

During the first two months of the 1965 season, Clemente's first notion was to escape Pittsburgh itself. He was still weakened from his bout with malaria, and the team seemed even punier, with Willie Stargell, the only legitimate long-ball threat in the lineup, also somehow sapped of strength. After opening the season with five wins in their first seven games, the team struck out on a brutal road trip that took them to five cities, covering 7,585 miles in planes that were in the air for a total of twenty-one and a half hours, including one particularly long and dis-combobulating haul on a chartered prop that took six hours and twenty-five minutes to get from Los Angeles to St. Louis. Clemente was exhausted by the trip, and needed a rest. After two losses to open the series, with the team now dropping ten of its last eleven games, the new manager, Harry Walker, went on a postgame rampage in the visiting clubhouse, flinging cups, papers, and trays around his cubicle and denouncing his players with what one writer described as "the most earthy and sulphuric language at his command." The pitching was okay, Walker said, but the hitting was horseshit, and he was especially concerned about what he feared was a "defeatist attitude." The whole team was playing like crap, he said, from the lowest scrub to the top star. He thought Clemente's hands were slow, and that he needed some rest and maybe lighter bats. For the Sunday doubleheader, Walker sat Clemente on the bench and sent left-handed hitting Jerry Lynch out to right. Lynch got hot immediately, banging out four hits in seven at-bats that day, though the Pirates lost both games. Before leaving town, Walker had an interview with a St. Louis radio station during which Clemente's benching was mentioned. Yes, Roberto had malarial fatigue, Walker said, but great players—he said Stan Musial and Ted Williams came to mind—played even when they were ailing.

Lynch stayed hot as the team reached Chicago, smashing two home runs in the first game and going two for three in the second. Now it was Clemente's turn to erupt. His irritation at Walker's comments, his persistent psychological soreness over being underappreciated, his passion to be the best, and perhaps some hurt pride in seeing Lynch excel in his place—all combined to send him into a sudden fit. "I want to be traded from this club and I don't want to play for this manager anymore," Clemente said in the visitors' locker room on May 5. He appeared to be talking to Les Biederman of the *Pittsburgh Press*, who had asked him how he was feeling. But this was not a muttered aside. It was a shout that any writer or player within earshot heard. And to emphasize the point, he walked up to Al Abrams of the *Post-Gazette* and said, "Put what I said in your goddamned newspaper!" Abrams not only obliged, his story ran on the top of the front page under the blaring headline:

CLEMENTE IRKED,
SAYS, "TRADE ME"

In what Abrams described as a "fit of temperament," Clemente had popped off in the clubhouse in front of newspapermen and teammates, demanding a trade. The star right fielder had "appeared moody and sullen," the story noted, and "hadn't been very chummy with his teammates, either, the past few days." Walker was not around to hear the tirade, and expressed surprise when reporters asked him about it. "If Clemente wants to be traded, he hasn't said a word to me about it," he said. "I don't know what he has in mind." The manager said he talked to Clemente before the St. Louis doubleheader and explained that he was resting him because he appeared tired and the team needed another lefty bat in the lineup. When Joe L. Brown was reached by telephone that night back at his home in Pittsburgh, the general manager said he knew nothing; Walker had not bothered to call him about it, so he thought it must be unimportant. Brown, after dealing with

Clemente for a decade, had by then developed a deep respect for him. He considered Clemente prickly and "very, very sensitive," Brown would say later, yet Clemente's sensitivity was not selfish egotism, it was a "huge sense of self-worth, of social self-worth. That he was as good as anyone who ever lived. That people should recognize that he was a special person. He didn't lord it over anybody, he just believed it."

The next morning, still in Chicago, Walker summoned Clemente to his room at the Knickerbocker Hotel, and they emerged with the classic sporting-tiff resolution. It had all been a misunderstanding. "We had breakfast together and we understand each other," Walker told the press. The great right fielder would be welcomed back in the lineup whenever he was ready. Walker even posited that the air clearing could do everyone some good. "This might be the thing we just need to snap out of this damn slump," he said. "I know Roberto will be all the better for it." Later that day, when Clemente reached the stadium, a swarm of reporters encircled him. He was reluctant to talk at first, still in a gnarly mood, but eventually could not keep quiet. "You just blow off steam when you can't play," he told a reporter for the Associated Press. "I don't want to be traded. I want to play—but not bad ball." Then he blew off more steam. There was always steam inside him, the heat of years of feeling misunderstood. "The newsmen blow up everything bad about me and when I am good, they give me like this," he said, pressing his hands to within an inch of each other. "I lose twenty-five pounds from malaria in Puerto Rico and maybe even should not play any spring training. I am now a hundred and seventy-eight pounds—seven pounds under my playing weight last season. I feel okay, but not up to par."

The notion that Clemente had been misunderstood did not sit well with Abrams, who was among those who heard him. "Denials to the contrary, Roberto Clemente did pop off Wednesday afternoon here and say that he would like the Pirates to trade him to another club. There are at least twenty-five witnesses, most of them his teammates, who heard the outburst in the visitors' dressing room at Wrigley Field," Abrams wrote. There was a notable ambivalence in Abrams's response, common among the Pittsburgh writers who dealt with

Clemente on a regular basis. None of the reporters hated Clemente; they didn't launch public vendettas against him, they just lived with his unpredictable temperament, at times trying to soften it, at times irritating it. Abrams again called Clemente "moody and sullen," but also took up part of his defense. He noted that he had publicly hailed Clemente as "the best player in the major leagues" for leading the majors in hitting over five seasons. But, he concluded, "if Clemente continues to feel that everyone is against him, myself included, for writing a story that should be printed, there's nothing I can do about it. And I can't care less."

Walker had it just about right, as it turned out. The controversy lifted the club out of its malaise. With Clemente restored in the lineup, batting third, along with a hot Maz at second and big Stargell finally clouting the ball again, the Pirates soared in late May and ran off twenty wins in twenty-four games. Day after day, Clemente strolled slowly to the plate, prepared his ground, stood deep in the box and away from the plate, and attacked the ball. Thirty-nine base hits in ninety-three times at-bat during the winning streak, a .419 pace. Johnny Pesky, one of Walker's coaches, told Biederman of the *Press* that the only hitter he had ever seen get solid wood on the ball time after time as much as Clemente was his friend Ted Williams.

The malarial funk was long forgotten and Clemente was back in the batting race. He kept hitting through July and August, distracted only by the birth of his first son, Robertito. Vera had been in Pittsburgh with him for part of the season, making their first Stateside home on the roomy second floor of Mrs. Harris's house on Apple Street. It was a vastly different culture for her, but she started to learn the language and adjust to her husband's idiosyncrasies. "He would have a late breakfast and stay in the room and sleep" on game mornings when the team was home, she recalled. "He closed the shades, the drapes, and put plastic over the drapes to make them darker. He tried to sleep. He would stay there until he was ready to go to the game. I used to take him, and on the way from the apartment to the stadium he didn't talk much. I believe he was thinking, tonight so-and-so will be the pitcher, and how Pittsburgh could win. He was always thinking. Then I would go back to the apartment and get ready to go back when the game started." In that lonesome world, it made sense for Vera to return to San Juan late in her pregnancy, and to have the baby born there, where mother and infant could be attended to by friends and family. But even beyond the practical, the place of birth was a matter of pride and emotion. Roberto Clemente wanted all of his children born in Puerto Rico. *Land, blood, name, and race.*

There were no hard feelings now with Harry the Hat. Player and manager talked hitting, something they both loved. The Pirates finished eighteen games above .500, a vast improvement from the previous year, but not enough to challenge for the pennant. What they had, most of all, was Clemente, and that was something special in itself.

During a home stand late in September, the team brought in a group of youngsters from the farm clubs. These were the best prospects, not ready for roster spots but talented enough that the club thought they should get a feel for what it looked like in the big leagues. They took part in practice before games, then dressed in street clothes and sat behind home plate. One of them was a pitcher named Henry (Gene) Garber, who later would pitch nineteen seasons in the majors. Garber, then only seventeen, had already been traumatized once in his young career, being forced to sit shotgun in the front seat of a beat-up old Cadillac as the brilliant madman scout, Howie Haak, drove him and two other prospects north from Salem, Virginia, to Rochester, New York, splashing tobacco into a mildewed spittoon and swearing a blue streak the entire way. Now came something worse. The Pirates asked Garber to pitch batting practice, without a screen to shield him. According to the pitching instructors, a screen would only encourage bad habits.

Garber had never worn a protective cup in his young life, and here came Roberto Clemente. As part of his routine, Clemente started batting practice the same way every day—trying to line every ball back through the box. "He's hitting shots right past me, line drives and hard ground balls right up the middle," Garber recalled decades later, the terror of that first moment on a big league mound carved permanently into memory. He went downtown the next morning and bought two cups, one plastic, one metal, and wore the metal cup that afternoon when he threw to Clemente again and for the rest of his long career.

When the season ended a few days later, big brother Andres was proven wrong. Momen finished with a league-leading .329 average and returned home to Puerto Rico with his third Silver Bat. He joined four all-time greats, Honus Wagner, Rogers Hornsby, Paul Waner, and Stan Musial, as the only National Leaguers with three or more batting titles. His back pockets, he would joke, were wide apart, and bulging.

Home now was a funky modernist house nestled into the top of a hill in Río Piedras. Vera had found it the previous spring when she and her father-in-law, Don Melchor, had been driving around the hills scouting lots. When pictures of the already-built house, designed by the engineer Libertario Avilés, were sent north to Roberto, he immediately agreed to buy it for $65,000, falling in love with its openness and curiosities—the Aztec symbols on the bricks, the bridged front walkway leading from the street over shallow moatlike ponds to the front door, wide spaces for plants everywhere, the panoramic view down the hill and off toward San Juan and the Atlantic. It had only three bedrooms, and the Clementes had plans for a large family (a second child was already on the way), but the rooms were spacious and could be subdivided if necessary. The neighbors were doctors and engineers. It was an easy ten-minute drive to see the rest of the Clementes and Zabalas in Carolina.

Once again that winter, Momen played almost no winter league baseball. The Pirates begged him not to sap his strength, and paid him extra to serve as their scout. He was in no mood to travel anyway, and preferred fiddling around the house with his pregnant wife and baby son to riding the bus to Ponce, Arecibo, or Mayagüez. He bought a Hammond organ and taught himself how to play it; he did not read music, but could listen to a tune on the radio and hammer out the melody within five minutes. His nights were filled with banquets and appearances, and during the day he spent more time thinking about his dream of building a sports city for poor Puerto Rican kids. He started looking for land and talking to businessmen and politicians about how to make it happen. The house was always open, a steady stream of relatives and visitors from the mainland coming in and out. One visitor that winter was Myron Cope, a gifted writer who had worked for the *Post-Gazette* in the fifties before moving on to freelance for the *Saturday Evening Post* and *Sports Illustrated.* Clemente long had felt that he did not receive the national recognition he deserved—now here came Cope to tell his story to a vast sporting audience.

The visit was later described in Cope's delicious lead paragraph. "The batting champion of the major leagues lowered himself to the pea-green carpet of his forty-eight-foot living room and sprawled on his right side, flinging his left leg over his right leg," the story began . . .

> He wore gold Oriental pajama tops, tan slacks, battered bedroom slippers—and, for purposes of the demonstration he was conducting—a tortured grimace. "Like dis!" he cried, and then dug his fingers into his flesh, just above the upraised left hip. Roberto Clemente, the Pittsburgh Pirates marvelous right fielder and their steadiest customer of the medical profession, was showing how he must greet each new day in his life. He has a disk in his back that insists on wandering, so when he awakens he must cross those legs, dig at that flesh and listen for the sound of the disk popping back where it belongs.

The story line followed from there, forty-four evocative paragraphs, most of them devoted to some peculiar aspect of Clemente's health. Interpretations of the article were in the eye of the reader; to many he came across as somewhere between lovable and a nutcase, which to Cope amounted to one and the same. Cope had dropped his contract with the *Saturday Evening Post* precisely because he was tired of writing stories about boring superstars. His preference for colorful subjects was so strong that Ray Cave, who started editing him at *Sports Illustrated,* took to calling him "The Nut Specialist." In Clemente, Cope believed, he had the best of all writing possibilities—"a superstar and a nut." Cope never doubted Clemente's sincerity, yet the player's phobias were such easy targets. "Opera companies have performed *Parsifal* in scarcely more time than it takes Roberto to get ready for bed," he wrote, going on to describe how Clemente memorized everything in his hotel room to make sure where things were in case he walked in his sleep or needed to escape. All in good fun, but in the end none of Cope's thousands of words left an impression stronger than a single illustration that accompanied the article, a graphic that Cope himself did not see until he got his own copy of the magazine at the newsstand. It was a picture of No. 21 standing in his Pirates uniform, with an anatomical map of his ailments, real and imagined, from head to toe. It started with tension headaches, then: wayward disk in neck, six stitches in chin, tonsillectomy, pulled muscle in shoulder, serious chest cold, stomach disorders, bone chips in elbow, curved spine, wayward disk in lower back, meatoma in thigh, legs that don't weigh the same, and pulled muscle in calf. In the caption below, it noted "Unchartable part of Clemente medical history includes tired blood, malaria, insomnia and fear of nightmares [which he does not have but is afraid he might have]." In fact, Clemente did have nightmares, but he didn't tell Cope about them.

Before submitting the article to his editors in New York, Cope showed it to Roy McHugh of the *Pittsburgh Press,* his close friend. "This is Clemente to the life, but he's going to hate it," McHugh said. "I know it," Cope agreed. As it turned out, they were right; Clemente did not speak to Cope for a year afterward. The *Sports Illustrated* spread certainly gave him the wider exposure he had been seeking, though not in the way he wanted. Now not only Pittsburgh and San Juan but the entire sporting nation could consider his physiology and psyche and join the debate over whether he was a hypochondriac. But the final words in Cope's story, overwhelmed by the pained-man motif, had nothing to do with Clemente's body or mind, but were about his heart and passion. Clemente had driven Cope out into the countryside and showed him a piece of land where he hoped to start his sports city for Puerto Rican children. "I like to work with kids," he said, in words that took on more resonance in retrospect. "I'd like to work with kids all the time. If I live long enough."

*   *   *

Cope did not get out of Puerto Rico without one touch of poetic justice. Lounging at his hotel pool one hot afternoon, he took a misstep on the deck and cut his toes so badly that a rich matron, tanning herself nearby, snapped at him, "Do something about that foot, it's attracting flies!" The chronicler of the chronic complainer took home a souvenir pain of his own, and it felt authentic enough to him.

A few days after Cope left, Clemente received a letter from Joe L. Brown on Pittsburgh Athletic Company, Inc., stationery, copies of which were also sent to the other Latin players on the Pirates—Matty Alou, Al McBean, Manny Mota, José Pagan, Andre Rodgers, and Manny Sanguillen. Five seasons after the glory of the World Series, Brown was desperately trying to turn things around, and his effort now included this no-more-Mr.-Nice-guy edict to all his Caribbean players. "In the recent past, it was the practice of a number of our players from the Caribbean area who train with the Pittsburgh club to report to Fort Myers several days after the date set for their arrival," Brown wrote. "In the majority of cases, the lateness of their arrival was due either to carelessness or complete indifference. This will not be permitted in 1966 or in the future. If you are not in uniform in Fort Myers prepared to work out at the time and date on which you were requested to report, you will be fined One Hundred Dollars (100.00) for each day that you are late, and this money will not be given back to you at a later date." For pitchers and catchers, Brown repeated, the arrival date was February 23, for infielders and outfielders, February 27. "If you have not already done so, it is recommended that you make arrangements immediately for your plane reservations, visa or passport (if required) and anything else that will require advance preparations . . . 1966 can be a wonderful year for everyone with the Pirates and it is important that all of our players report on time. Your attention to this letter is IMPERATIVE, both for you and the club."

It was a perennial lament, the late arrival of Latin players. What interested Clemente and the others most about Brown's latest missive was the line that said *any fines will not be given back to you at a later date.* Maybe, this time, he was serious. But the letter did not please the proud Clemente. He saw it as a reiteration of the stereotypes he was trying to overcome, that Latins were lazy and irresponsible. And as the letter related to his own situation, it was true that he was a few weeks late reporting to spring training the year before, but was Brown insinuating that his malaria was a matter of complete indifference?

Clemente reported on time, leaving Vera in Río Piedras, where she not only took care of the infant Robertito but also made all the other arrangements for Pittsburgh. A week after her husband left, she wrote a note to Phil Dorsey, their friend and aide in the States. 'I'm fine but the baby has a cold now," she began. After a few more pleasantries, she got down to business.

> Phil, I sent the car this week by the Transamerican Steamship Corp. and will arrive in Newark, New Jersey on Tuesday or Wednesday [March 16]. I paid the expenses here. Enclosed are the key, the paper you have to present there and the car license. You can call the following person to ask if the car arrived. Mr. Ernie Caballero. Shed 152. Berth 20. Telephone BD 9-1700 (office). Newark, New Jersey. I sent some clothes and other things in the car, including one package of Mrs. Mota [wife of Clemente's teammate]. I hope you don't have trouble receiving the car. My best regards to Carole and kids and say them that I will see them on April. Please, excuse my bad English.
>
> Sincerely, Vera.

Three years earlier, Clemente had begun shipping his car to the States for use during the season. Dorsey would pick it up at the port of Newark and drive it back to Pittsburgh. The bill of lading showed that it cost Clemente $203.76 to send his ton-and-a-half white Cadillac by freighter. It was part of the seasonal routine now, the Caddy following Momen on his migrations between island and mainland. In many ways, this new season marked a turning point for Clemente, a time when he was approaching the fullness of his life and career, but his days still were not without some rough spots.

The sixth of May rarely found Clemente at his best. In 1965, that was the day of reaction to his "trade me!" outburst. In 1966 his explosion was not verbal but physical. In the ledger of his life, here was a day for the case against sainthood. Not everything about him could be resolved with the explanation that he was misunderstood. The truth was he had a temper and occasionally did stupid things. This was one such time. The Pirates were on the road, playing the Phillies in Philadelphia. They had begun the season solidly, with thirteen wins in the first nineteen games, good enough for first place. But on this Friday night, after tying the game in the late innings and taking a four-run lead in the eleventh, the Pirates fell apart, their loose play allowing the Phils to come back with five in the bottom of the frame to win, eight to seven. A key error in the sloppy rally came when Clemente fired a strike toward home after a bloop single to right and the ball caromed off the leg of cut-off man Donn Clendenon, the first baseman. After the loss, the visitors' locker room at Connie Mack Stadium was a trough of grumpy, foul-mouthed men.

A half hour later, as the Pirates were boarding the team bus at Lehigh Avenue near Twenty-first Street to return to the Warwick Hotel, Clemente was surrounded by several young fans. Among them was Bernie Heller, a nineteen-year-old from the village of Mary D, who was studying sheet metal work at Theodore Stevens Trade School in Lancaster. As Heller later described the scene, he and two friends had been walking to their car when "we seen where the players were coming out, and they happened to be giving autographs." Heller got in line and waited, holding a ball he wanted signed. Clemente was doing most of the signing, a task that he did day after day, often joyously, usually without complaint. Now there was some movement in the crowd, people pushing for position, and Clemente, with one foot on the pavement and another on the bottom step of the bus, ready to board, suddenly wheeled around and clocked young Heller with a swift fist. "All I seen is his right hand. He got me right in the mouth. All I seen is a big white star." Heller recalled forty years later. In his memory, Heller thinks he was knocked unconscious. According to police reports at the time, he told authorities that the blow buckled his knees and he fell to the cement, but got up and walked away, only then realizing that three of his teeth had been jarred loose. His friends escorted him to the stadium first-aid room, and from there he was taken to Women's Medical College Hospital, where he was kept overnight for observation and X rays.

By the accounts of other witnesses, Clemente seemed unperturbed by the incident, almost as though he didn't realize what had happened. After Heller fell to the ground, Clemente continued signing a ball for a young girl, then boarded the bus, and signed more scorecards and papers that were handed to him through an open window. The next morning, accompanied by Harry Walker and the traveling secretary, Bob Rice, he went down to police headquarters to be interviewed by Detective James Coyle. According to Coyle, Clemente told him that he didn't know who he hit or where he hit him, but that there was a scuffle near the bus and that he "might have hit somebody as he was getting on." Later, Clemente admitted directly that he threw the punch. He said that someone grabbed him and spun him around as he was boarding the bus. He then saw Heller with his hands up. "I took a punch at him," Clemente said. "Not a real punch, just more to stay away from him." What was Clemente's concept of a real punch? By any definition his was strong enough. According to Detective Coyle, Heller's teeth "were so loose they practically were falling out of his mouth." John Heller, Bernie's older brother, visited Bernie in the hospital in the middle of the night and said he looked "like a dog who had just had a fight with a skunk."

There was talk of a lawsuit, and the Hellers hired a lawyer, but before matters went further Clemente apologized. "I'm very sorry it happened," he said. "I hear [Heller's] a nice fellow." Harry Walker paid a visit to the hospital and brought along one of Clemente's gloves and a bat, a 36-inch Frenchy Uhalt model Louisville Slugger that flared without a knob at the end and had No. 21 etched into the bottom. An out-of-court settlement of a few thousand dollars paid for Bernie Heller's hospital bill; there were also free tickets for the family whenever the Pirates were in Philadelphia. Forty years later, Heller, who worked as the postmaster in St. Clair, Pennsylvania, still had the bat and glove, but not the ball that he brought to Connie Mack Stadium that long ago afternoon. "I took the ball with me from home to get autographs, but . . . I think the ball and everything went flying. I don't have the ball anymore. Like I said, when he hit me the only thing I seen, it looked like a big white meteor . . . Nobody could understand why he did it."

Much later, when reports of the incident filtered back to Puerto Rico, an embarrassed Clemente would concoct a version of the story that had centered on someone calling him names in the right-field bleachers during the game and then continuing the harassment afterward. But that story had nothing to do with the reality of his encounter with Bernie Heller. The punch seemed more instinctive, and part of a pattern. Clemente had reacted similarly in 1964 outside Forbes Field, pushing two fans who were jostling too close to him, though no one had his teeth knocked loose that time. And in May 1963 he had been suspended for five days and fined $250 for accosting umpire Bill Jackowski during a home game against the Phillies. After being called out at first on a double-play grounder, he flew into a five-minute rage, twice bumping against Jackowski. In the clubhouse later, he defended his behavior by saying that he and the Pirates never got any breaks. "Other teams argue and get close decisions. Dodgers get every close play. Why? We don't argue and we don't get them." Bad calls, he added, were costing him fifteen to twenty points a year on his batting average. "I seldom argue unless I feel the umpire is wrong," he said. "I have a good record in the league office, but this is the worst year for umpiring I have ever seen." Warren Giles, the National League president, sent a telegram to Clemente announcing his suspension and calling his actions "the most serious reported to our office in several years."

The supposed ineptitude of major league umpires could not explain a winter league incident back home in Puerto Rico, when Clemente had been suspended for a playing field dispute during which he kicked an umpire and broke a rib. His pal Vic Power kept a photograph of that incident to remind himself and the world that not even the revered Roberto Clemente was beyond human lapses of self-control. "He fought, yeah, he got mad like every human being," Power recalled in his blunt yet good-natured fashion. "The Puerto Rican people, I think 99 percent have bad tempers. They get bad temper, ohhh, baby." It was not for nothing that Carolina became known as the town of those who cut off arms. Within the world of baseball, there was that glint of unpredictability to Clemente. If one examines videotapes of the most famous moment in Pirate history, Maz bounding toward the plate after

clouting the homer that beat the mighty Yanks in the bottom of the
ninth of the seventh game of the 1960 World Series, there is Clemente
greeting him near the plate, and some fans rush close, and No. 21 jerks
around—was he threatened by the approaching shadows?—and it
seems as though he is about to deck a fan who is getting too close. He
doesn't, the threat passes in a split-second, and the celebration
resumes all the way to the dugout, but in that moment there is a surprising intimation of unpremeditated violence.

Clemente's edginess seemed confined to his profession. He was
gentle at home, no sudden explosions. In later years, when he had
three sons, he never spanked them, but could quiet them with a
solemn look. In his life away from the game, he did not appear driven
to affirm his manhood through the social rituals of machismo.

Random physics, an unpremeditated moment, and for better or
worse a life changes forever. Bernie Heller never forgot Clemente's
blow; Carol Brezovec would only see his kindness. The trajectory of
their stories arced in opposite directions, yet both started in precisely
the same spot—on the concourse outside old Connie Mack Stadium in
Philadelphia.

Six weeks after the Heller incident, the Pirates were back in
Philadelphia for another series, and among the fans attending the Sunday afternoon game were Carol and her dad, John Brezovec. They
both loved baseball, and the tickets to the game were a Father's Day
present from Carol, who was then seventeen. Her parents were
divorced. John, a barber and musician, lived in Bethlehem; Carol and
her younger sister, Sharon, lived with their mother, Carolyn, in Allentown. They all were regulars at the stadium, known to ushers and
many Phillies players. John was around so much he became virtually
part of the team, able to come and go in the home clubhouse. Carol
would draw sketches of her favorite players and gather with autograph
hounds outside the players gate after games, but she was so shy that
she often came home without any signatures. She was out there trying
for autographs after the Sunday game on June 26, which the Pirates
won, 2–0, when she noticed a crowd gathering around a Pittsburgh
player. For some reason, the Brezovecs had never seen the Pirates
before, so Carol was unfamiliar with the faces, if not the names. She

stayed in the background until the circle around the player dissolved, then approached and asked quietly, "May I please have your autograph?" He signed his name, Roberto Clemente. Carol had just started studying Spanish in high school. She thanked him by saying, *"Muchas gracias."*

Clemente began talking to her in Spanish. Feeling embarrassed, she had to confess that she didn't have a clue what he said. In English, Clemente asked her where she was from and why she was studying Spanish. His teammate Andre Rodgers, a shortstop from the Bahamas who had come over to the Pirates from the Cubs the previous year, was standing nearby, listening. There was something about Clemente's warmth and directness that helped Carol overcome her shyness, and they talked easily about language, home, and family. Why are you here alone? Clemente asked. Carol said she was with her father, who was over in the Phillies clubhouse. They talked on, losing track of time, until a security guard came by and announced that the Pirates' bus to the airport had departed, leaving Clemente and Rodgers behind. Carol was red-faced again. "Oh, my God. I'm so sorry!" she said. "Wait here and I'll go get my dad and we'll drive you to the airport." She ran to the Phillies clubhouse, found her father, and explained that they had to leave immediately for the airport because of an emergency.

As the odd quartet—father and daughter Phillies fans in front, visiting team right fielder and shortstop in back—pulled out of stadium traffic, John Brezovec turned to Carol and asked, in his blunt way, "Can you tell me what the fuck is going on? Who are these people?" Carol had not bothered to tell him who the passengers were. "Let me introduce you," she said. "This is Roberto Clemente and Andre Rodgers." He was stunned. How did this happen? She said she would explain it all on the way. Clemente appeared unfazed by his predicament and perfectly content in the backseat. From his traveling bag, he pulled out a battery-powered portable record player and a selection of albums, and the sweet lyricism of Roberto Ledesma's island ballads started filling the car. John Brezovec, who wrote his own polkas and waltzes, loved the music, and he and Clemente struck up a conversation about their favorite songs as the music played in the background. They discovered that they had other things in common, and the foursome talked animatedly all the way to the airport. Instead of dropping Clemente and Rodgers off at the departure curb, Brezovec parked the car and he and his daughter escorted the ball players to the Pirates' airline gate. The plane, as it turned out, had not left yet.

Clemente was still in no hurry. He seemed less interested in the flight than in his newfound friends. "This is incredible," he told Carol. "It feels like I've known you my whole life." He said he wanted them to meet his wife, Vera, and his family back in Puerto Rico. The Pirates wouldn't return to Philadelphia until late September, but he hoped to see them again before then. Would they like to come to New York the following week and see the Pirates play at Shea Stadium? He asked for a telephone number and said that he would call and make arrangements. Then, before boarding the plane, he autographed his Roberto Ledesma album and handed it to Carol.

All the way home, the Brezovecs kept saying to each other, no one will believe this. A half hour after Carol got back to her house in Allentown, the phone rang. Her mother answered. "Is this Carolina?" the voice on the other end asked, in a soft Spanish accent.

Close enough. Yes.

"This is Roberto Clemente. I met your daughter tonight and wanted to be sure she is home. Did she get home safely?" Carolyn said yes and asked whether he wanted to talk to her. No, he said, just wanted to make sure. Then he asked, "Do you like baseball?"

Love baseball, she said, adding that she usually went to the games with Carol, but her father took her tonight. Good, Clemente said. If they would come to New York next week, he would get tickets for them to see him play at Shea Stadium. That would be fun, Carolyn said. But where should they stay? Don't worry about any of that, Clemente said. Just come. His friend Phil Dorsey would take care of everything. The tickets would be waiting. And he had family in New York who would look after them, too. A day later, Dorsey called and said a room had been reserved for them at the Hotel Commodore at Forty-second and Lexington, where the Pirates stayed, and there would be tickets for the games on Saturday July 2 and Sunday July 3 waiting for them at the players' window at the stadium.

As Carol and Carolyn took their seats behind the visitors' dugout at

Shea for the Saturday game, they looked out to right field. "Carol, there's Roberto," Carolyn said to her daughter. "I can't believe this . . . he's waving at us." Before the game, Clemente sent a note up with a batboy asking them to wait for him afterward. The Pirates were hot, having won six straight, with Clemente, Stargell, Clendenon, Manny Mota, and Matty Alou all hitting over .300. In the series opener on Friday night, a young lefthander named Woody Fryman had given up a leadoff hit to Mets second baseman Ron Hunt in the first inning and then retired the next twenty-seven Mets in order, a one-hitter and near perfect game. On Saturday, Clemente's new friends from Allentown watched him stroke a home run, his twelfth of the year, but it was not his best game. Twice in the late innings he made an out with the bases loaded, and the Pirates lost 4–3. When the game ended, Clemente met his guests outside the visitors' clubhouse and announced that he was taking them out to eat at an elegant Spanish restaurant in midtown Manhattan. Clemente's friends Carlos and Carmen Llanos—he called them cousins, though they were not related—were there, along with José Pagan and Andre Rodgers and a few other Latin players. Carol ate paella for the first time, and was starstruck, and quickly agreed to come along after dinner when Clemente said they were heading up to a party at the Llanoses apartment. Her mother politely declined, saying she was tired. A half hour later, Clemente sent back an emissary to assure her that Carol was in safe company.

Later that night, back at the Commodore, Clemente was sleepless as usual, and called Carolyn's room and asked if she wanted to talk. She agreed, and they stayed up until three, sharing the stories of their lives. Clemente asked her whether she knew the name of the town where he was born. No, she said. "The name is Carolina," he said. "And that is what I'm going to call you. You are my Carolina. You're going to be my sister. You are going to be my family from now on." Clemente was warm but unthreatening; there were no sexual overtones in his dealings with either the mother or daughter. He was a man of many sides, and he kept that side from them. Women were constantly flattering him, flirting with him, throwing themselves at him, calling his room at every road hotel. His friend Phil Dorsey, if he was around, screened the calls for Clemente. Other friends filled the same role when Dorsey was not there. For all his love of Vera, Roberto was not above temptation. But with Carolyn and Carol his passion was about family. He had lost his only sister, Anairis, before he was old enough to know her, but had always felt her presence. Now he would have two American sisters, Carolina and Carolina. From now on, he would visit them whenever he came to Philadelphia, and they would come see him play in New York and make visits to Pittsburgh. And, he said again, they must come visit him in Puerto Rico.

When he first saw Forbes Field in 1955, Clemente told himself to forget about hitting home runs. The outfield was among the most spacious in baseball: 365 feet to the left-field fence, 442 to dead center, 416 to right-center, and right field was topped by an eighteen-foot-high wire screen. "I was strong, but nobody was that strong," Clemente said. The implication was that he could hit home runs if he wanted to, but smartly adapted his game to the surroundings. There is undoubtedly some truth to that, but it is also true that the arc of his swing simply did not produce home runs in the way that those of Henry Aaron and Frank Robinson did, to name the two other great all-around right fielders of his era. The issue was not raw power—at times, Clemente could clout the ball monstrous distances, as far as Mickey Mantle, Frank Howard, Willie Stargell, or any of the prodigious sluggers, a fact that he constantly reiterated to sportswriters and teammates. But when he stepped to the plate, he thought about getting a base hit and keeping his average above .300 and helping his team win, but never visualized hitting one over the fence. Never, that is, except in 1966, after he and Harry Walker patched up their differences. It was then that Walker told Clemente that the Pirates needed more power from him if they were to contend for a pennant, and that providing more power was part of what he had to do as the team leader, and that if he hit more home runs and the team won he might finally get the prize that had eluded him and bothered him for so many years, the MVP award.

"So the story goes, Harry said, 'I need more power from you,' and so Clemente goes out and hits twenty-nine home runs and drives in

119 runs," said the pitcher Steve Blass. "Now that's scary." Those were
Clemente's power numbers for 1966, the best of his career, and though
he said he was afraid his batting average would fall dramatically if he
went for home runs, the drop was minor, down to .317. The tradeoff
seemed worth it. And there was no padding in Clemente's statistics.
Day after day, his hits came when they were needed, not at the end of
a lopsided game. His play in right field was as thrilling as ever. He led
the league in outfield assists, with seventeen, and it was difficult to calculate all the ways that his arm made a difference. Gaylord Perry, the
crafty spitballer who won twenty-one games for San Francisco that
year, would never forget a game when the score was tied in the late
innings and Willie Mays was on second and there was a hit to right—
"and Mays rounds third and screeches to a halt" because Clemente
was in right. "When you have the world's best base runner put on the
brakes on a hit to right, you know it's because the world's best arm is in
right," said Perry later, shaking his head. "And it was a close game. We
needed that run."

As the year went on, his teammates noticed that Clemente's power,
perfectly rounding out his game, was accompanied by a more assertive
attitude. He seemed less preoccupied with himself and more obsessed
with winning. He had always played hard, every play of every game he
was in, but now he talked about it more in the clubhouse, urging his
fellow Pirates to put out more every day, saying they owed it to the city
and its fans. Only four players remained from the World Series champions, Law and Face on the mound and Clemente and Mazeroski on
the field, and this was now becoming Clemente's team. The twenty-
five-man squad included nine blacks and Latins, often five in the starting lineup, with Bob Veale emerging as their best pitcher. And it was
an increasingly loose bunch. "We haven't got a sane guy on this ball
club," declared catcher Jim Pagliaroni, who could be seen wearing an
old leather pilot's helmet and goggles. Clemente's countryman, José
Pagan of Barceloneta, Puerto Rico, was now playing third base and he
and his wife, Delia, lived in the other apartment on the second floor of
Mrs. Harris's house, making it feel more like home for Roberto and
Vera when she was in town. After a game, the smell of bacalaitos filled
the house, as Vera fried his favorite cod-cake fritters. All of this made

Clemente more comfortable, and the more at ease he was the more he asserted his will on his teammates.

It was not a complete transformation; there were still times when he appeared agitated and oversensitive. In the heat of the pennant race, when the Pirates visited Los Angeles in mid-September to play the streaking Dodgers, he grew angry after a crucial loss in which he had gone hitless in four at-bats against Sandy Koufax. He had read and heard that Koufax was complaining about an arthritic elbow yet pitching one superb game after another. "Sore arm, my foot! He couldn't pitch like that if it hurt very bad," Clemente told the press afterward, straight-faced, failing to see the irony of that particular statement coming from a player known for playing his best when he had some physical complaint.

But was Clemente really angry about Koufax or once again expressing the hurt he felt over being misunderstood? As he continued talking in the clubhouse, the latter seemed to be the case. "When my back hurts they call me goldbrick," he said. "But when Koufax says his elbow hurts, they call him a hero." It was as though he were beseeching the world: When will people start calling Roberto Clemente a hero?

The Pirates finished twenty-two games over .500, at 92–70, good but not quite good enough, three games behind the pennant-winning Dodgers. But for so many Pirates, led by Clemente, 1966 was a most productive year. The middle infield combination of young Gene Alley at shortstop and veteran Mazeroski was perhaps the best in the league in the field and at the plate. Stargell, the big lefty slugger, had the highest power numbers of his young career, hitting thirty-three home runs and driving in 102. Matty Alou, his hitting style revamped, largely by Clemente in daily tutoring sessions, transformed himself from a weak lefty pull hitter into a dangerous all-fields slap hitter and led the league with a .342 average. The team as a whole had the highest cumulative batting average in the league at .279. And all of this was accomplished during a season when National League pitching was dominant, led by the big three of Koufax, Marichal, and Gibson. Clemente was wrong about Koufax—the pain in his arm was not a ruse but enough to make him retire; 1966 would be the final brilliant season of his too-brief career. Juan Marichal of the Giants was still in the middle of his nearly decade-long string of great seasons. And Bob Gibson of the Cardinals had become virtually unhittable. Koufax, Marichal, Gibson—their numbers that year were golden. Gibson had twenty-one wins, twenty complete games, 225 strikeouts, and an earned-run average of 2.44. Not as good as Marichal, who won twenty-five games, had twenty-five complete games, 222 strikeouts, and an earned-run average of 2.23. Which was not as good as Koufax, who finished the season with twenty-seven wins, twenty-seven complete games, 317 strikeouts, and an earned-run average of 1.73.

Manager Harry Walker attended the World Series that year as a fan, watching the Dodgers lose to the young Baltimore Orioles. All he wanted to do was talk about his team, and especially about his team leader. In Walker's own peculiar way, knocking someone down and then building him up higher, he promoted Clemente as the most valuable player in the league. "Clemente has his critics," he said. "He's such a hypochondriac that some people also think he's a malingerer. But no man ever gave more of himself or worked more unselfishly for the good of the team than Roberto. I know the votes are already in for most valuable player. I'm convinced that Clemente deserves it. Whether he gets it or not, he's most valuable in my book."

When the MVP votes were counted, it turned out to be a two-man contest between Koufax and Clemente. In his darkest visions, Clemente thought there was no way he could win this contest—the darling of L.A. and New York versus the forgotten man of Pittsburgh and Carolina—the American hero, pitching through pain, versus the Puerto Rican hypochondriac and goldbricker. But now, six years after he had spiraled into bitterness over finishing eighth in the 1960 balloting, a lingering hurt that was so deep he refused thereafter to wear his 1960 World Series ring, here was redemption. Koufax received 208 votes, Clemente 218. At last, he was recognized by the North American sportswriters as the Most Valuable Player in the National League.

You have to visit me in Puerto Rico after the season, Clemente had told his American sisters, Carolyn and Carol, or Carolina the mother and

Carolina the daughter. The mother could not get free from her job with the regional office of HUD, the federal housing agency where she worked, and was spending time with her new boyfriend, Nevin Rauch, who would soon become her husband. They decided that the daughter should go. Carol, in her senior year of high school, arrived in San Juan in mid-December 1966, during the long and joyous Christmas season, and stayed with the Clementes in the guest room at their house on the hill. She was treated like part of the family. There were two little sons now, Robertito and Luisito. The house was warm, always busy, with visitors popping in day and night. Roberto's status on the island was higher than ever now that the mainland had recognized him as the very best, and he was constantly in demand. "He explained to me that he would be very busy, he was into so many things in the community and business," Carol recalled. She spent most of her days with Vera, whose knowledge of English was about as limited as Carol's rudimentary Spanish. She carried a little dictionary at her side. They spent hours in the kitchen during the day. Vera was a superb cook, but had to limit some of her recipes for her husband, who was on a protein kick. That winter he was into liver and eggs. At night, Carol and Vera would sit on a big bed in the bedroom with the two little boys and play cards and sing songs in English and Spanish.

Carol felt as though she had been reincarnated with a Spanish soul. Clemente was always talking about how much his back hurt. He would try to teach her new words in Spanish, and learn English from her, and she would want to laugh at his English because his pronunciation was awful. "But I had to be real careful because he was real sensitive to criticism. I would say, 'Well, you're getting there.'" He was always getting somewhere, she thought. When he had free time, Roberto piled the family and Carol into his Cadillac and drove around the island, treating it like a Jeep. They went to the beach near the bay of crabs, where he loved to collect driftwood. Then they drove to *la finca*—the farm he owned outside the village of El Verde near the exotic rainforest, El Yunque. Clemente seemed like a different person at *la finca*, totally at ease among his pigs, horses, and goats, and walking through his fields of plantain and coffee. He proudly showed Carol how he had built the farmhouse himself and had decorated the interior with bamboo. Wherever they went, Roberto had a presence about him that amazed her, but she could see it most strongly out here in the countryside hills, the heart of his homeland. "I came back being in awe of what a humble man he was. What a regular man he was. But just so connected to the people. If children recognized him, or the most humble-looking person somewhere on a mountain hill where we were driving approached him, wherever we were, it ended in a long conversation. I never remember a moment when Roberto didn't take the time to talk to somebody who came up to him. There never was a time when he didn't stop. I never remember him walking away or cutting someone off. And especially if it was someone young." Clemente among the people was an image that burned into her mind. In that setting, far from the major league stadiums, she said, "you could see him like a prophet."

What burned in the eyes of Roberto Clemente was the fire of dignity.

While still in high school, Clemente signed with the Santurce Cangrejeros, where he became teammates with many major leaguers, including Junior Gilliam of the Dodgers (left), known in Puerto Rico as "the Black Sea." Later, Clemente played in the same outfield as Willie Mays.

Clemente's early baseball patron was Pedrin Zorrilla, owner of the Cangrejeros, whose nickname was the Big Crab. Zorrilla was the son of the Puerto Rican poet Enrique Zorrilla, whose most famous poem was "Dream of Deeds."

When Clemente ran, it seemed not so much that he was trying to reach a base as to escape from some unspeakable terror. He had an unusual ability to stop on a dime after racing full speed to first.

The 1960 Pittsburgh Pirates, with Clemente (bottom row, second from left) starring in right field, defeated the New York Yankees in seven games to win the World Series. It was a bold and extraordinary upset (they won despite losing three games by the scores of 16–3, 11–0, and 10–0), an act of rebellion at the dawn of the sixties' decade.

Wedding Day, November 14, 1964. All through the slow, sweet Saturday afternoon, the people of Carolina, Puerto Rico, celebrated as if it were the festival for a local saint. Clemente looked as princely in his black tuxedo as he did in the cool white and black of his Pittsburgh uniform.

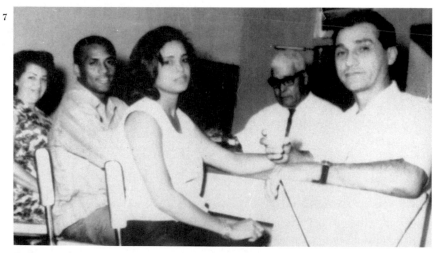

Roberto and Vera on their honeymoon in Curaçao. "I can walk down to the corner and probably get ten girls," Clemente had told Vera's father, Flor Zabala, while he was courting her. "But I don't care. The one I love is here."

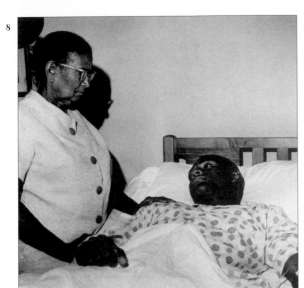

Clemente spent his career alternately worrying about his health and complaining about being called a hypochondriac. Before leaving home for spring training in 1965, he was hospitalized with malaria and lost nearly twenty-five pounds. Here he is visited by his mother, Luisa.

Vera visited Roberto at spring training, but never spent an entire preseason with him. Nothing in Puerto Rico was as overtly racist as the Jim Crow segregation Clemente experienced during his early years with the Pirates in Fort Myers.

Clemente in the living room of his modernist home atop the hill in Río Piedras. He had just won his third batting title, but still felt overlooked, misunderstood, and underappreciated. Any conversation with a sports reporter was likely to open with a loud complaint.

Roberto and Vera cross the sidewalk bridge out the front door of their house with Robertito and Luisito. Clemente insisted that Vera come home to Puerto Rico for the births of their sons.

Clemente ran out every ground ball, hustled on the bases, and thought he could catch any ball hit to the out-field and throw out any runner on the bases. His batting prowess, with 3,000 hits and four batting titles, was equaled by his skill in the field. He had one of the most fearsome throw-ing arms in baseball history and won twelve Gold Gloves. Critics noticed his less than sterling on-base per-centage and home run totals; his fans said his game could not be reduced to statistics.

Victor Pellot (left), known in the majors as Vic
Power, came up before Clemente and helped
pave the way for him as one of the Three
Kings, along with Hiram Bithorn and Luis
Olmo. Power and Clemente were close friends
off the field and were together in Nicaragua
coaching an amateur baseball team shortly
before Clemente's death.

In the late 1960s, Clemente wore the uniform
of the San Juan Senadores, the favorite team of
his childhood. Writers in Pittsburgh often
questioned why Clemente would tire himself
by playing winter ball, but he felt an obligation
to his homeland and connected his personal
history to the struggle of his people.

Clemente was like a big brother to dozens of Latino players who followed him
to the majors, including Orlando Cepeda (left), the slugging first baseman from
Puerto Rico. Here they pose with fans during the 1967 season, when Cepeda
was the National League MVP. Clemente had won the honor a year earlier.

Planeloads of Puerto Ricans flew to Pittsburgh for Roberto Clemente night on July 24, 1970. Clemente choked with emotion as he began to speak. At a moment like that, he said afterward, "You can see a lot of years in a few minutes. You can see everything firm and you can see everything clear."

The entire family came to Pittsburgh when Clemente was honored, including his father, Melchor (far left), who had never left Puerto Rico before and needed help to overcome his fear of flying. "I have achieved this honor for us the Latinos," Clemente said.

Clemente routinely visited sick children in National League cities. The hospital visits were rarely publicized, but ailing kids seemed to know about them everywhere. Before each road trip Clemente sorted out his large pile of mail in the clubhouse and made a special stack for children in cities where the Pirates were headed next.

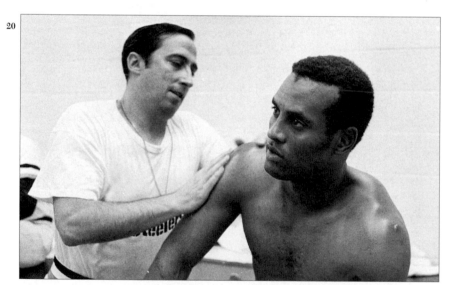

The Pirates trainer, Tony Bartirome (left), thought Roberto Clemente was a lot like his wife. Ask Clemente how he felt and he would tell you, "Well, I've got this thing with my neck." A pregame stop at the training table was a daily appointment, another of his rituals, like not sleeping at night and complaining about sportswriters.

At age thirty-eight, Clemente's body still evoked that of a world-class ballet dancer, with muscled shoulders rippling down to a narrow waist, thirty inches—the same measurement he had as a teenager— and powerful wrists, and hands so magical they were said to have eyes at their fingertips.

As the outstanding player of the 1971 World Series, Clemente was awarded a new car by *Sport* magazine. One of the guests at the award ceremony at Mamma Leone's restaurant said that Roberto and Vera "seemed to be unreal people, sculptured out of bronze instead of ordinary flesh and blood like those surrounding them." Clemente told the crowd that the World Series allowed him to talk to millions of people about issues that meant the most to him.

Bob Prince (center), the Pirates' colorful announcer, had a nickname for everyone, and shouted *¡Arriba!* whenever Clemente strolled to the plate. Roberto felt that Prince treated him fairly, and during an offseason he decided to honor "the Gunner" at a ceremony in San Juan. Along with a carved trophy, he gave Prince the Silver Bat he had won for his first batting title.

September 30, 1972, Three Rivers Stadium, Pirates vs. Mets. New York lefty Jon Matlack on the mound. It was an outside curve going just where Matlack wanted it to go until Clemente thwacked it against the left field wall for his three-thousandth hit.

When the inning was over, Clemente walked slowly out to his position in right and tipped his cap to the fans. *El Nuevo Día* photographer Luis Ramos followed him step by step and caught the moment forever.

On December 2, 1972, the lightning-striped DC-7 that would carry Clemente
to his death a few weeks later was taxied into a ditch at San Juan International
Airport by its owner, Arthur Rivera. Clemente knew nothing about the plane's
troubled history when he boarded the plane, overloaded with humanitarian
aid, on New Year's Eve.

Despite a massive effort to assist the people of Nicaragua after the devastating
earthquake that leveled Managua and killed thousands of residents two days
before Christmas, 1972, much of the aid was not getting to the people. In the
aftermath of the quake, the greed of Nicaraguan military leader Anastasio
Somoza became apparent. Clemente decided to go to Managua to make sure
that food and medical supplies from Puerto Rico reached the people who
needed help.

Eleven weeks after his death, Roberto Clemente was voted into the Hall of Fame. He and Lou Gehrig, the Yankees first baseman who also died a tragic early death, are the only players in major league history to be enshrined without waiting the normal five-year period after the end of their playing days. Vera represented the family at the ceremony.

Memory and myth are entwined in the Clemente story. "That night on which Roberto Clemente left us physically, his immortality began," the Puerto Rican writer Elliott Castro later observed. Clemente's three sons, including Roberto Jr., here kissing his picture, lost a father, and all of Latin America lost "one of their glories."

From beginning to end, there was a bond between Clemente and baseball fans, especially children. Clemente among the people was an image that burned in the memories of many of his friends. In some sense, they saw him as a prophet.

10
A Circular Stage

THE PIRATES TRAINER, TONY BARTIROME, THOUGHT
Roberto Clemente was a lot like his wife. Ask him how he felt and he
would tell you. *Well, I've got this thing with my neck.* Clemente would
not dismiss the question with an evasive *fine.* He took his body seriously, and regarded questions about it with earnestness. A pregame
stop at the training table was a daily appointment, another of his rituals,
like not sleeping at night and complaining about sportswriters. It was
his way to relax, or to avoid people he didn't want to see, but there was
always fine-tuning to be done. This mostly involved rubbing. Bartirome
would massage his neck for five or six minutes, kneading out the kinks.
X rays showed that some stiffness in his neck was arthritis, brought on
by the injuries from the auto accident in Caguas when he was driving
home to see his dying brother in 1954. After the neck work, Clemente
would flip onto his stomach and have his right Achilles tendon pulled
for a few minutes, then attention turned to his lower back. Often he
would relax to the point of almost falling asleep on the table, then
emerge from semiconsciousness calling out, "Where's Bob? Bob?"

That would be Bob Veale, the colossal six-foot-six left-handed
pitcher. Veale made the mistake of rubbing Clemente's shoulder one
afternoon, a friendly act that was followed by a good day at the plate.
"From then on I had a lifetime job," Veale remembered. "Every game
I had to touch him. I had to rub his shoulder for good-luck purposes.
He felt he could only have a great day if I rubbed him, and he had
quite a few of those. If he said, 'Rub hard,' I would rub hard." Like
many ball players, Clemente had his superstitions. Some actions or
totems brought good luck, some bad. He might have been wrong in

the end, but during the magical 1960 season he had insisted that the team's Dixieland band was a jinx, especially when it followed the Pirates on the road, and he didn't want it anywhere near him. He had lucky shirts that he would wear until the Pirates lost. And now the big hands of Bob Veale were a force for the good.

The training room was an inner sanctum for the players, but mostly it was Clemente's lair. As much as he loved baseball, he was obsessed with the healing arts. He thought of himself as an adjunct trainer, and knew more about massage than Bartirome, a former first baseman who learned how to be a proficient trainer so that he could stay around a major league club. Whenever a teammate, coach, or friend complained of a bad back or sore joint, Clemente offered his services. In many ways, he was ahead of his time, a New Age experimentalist searching for noninvasive methods to ease pain. With his long, sensitive hands, he was especially adept at deep massages. "It was something . . . supernatural," said his wife, Vera. "He would put pressure and say you have this or that and find the problems. He could see with his fingertips." When Harding Peterson, a former catcher who became director of scouting, complained of a sore lower back one night at training camp, Clemente, though nattily dressed for dinner, retrieved oils from his room, took off his suit coat, rolled up his sleeves, and went to work, rubbing Peterson down for twenty minutes. He often carried liniments in his duffel bag for just such emergencies.

Another tool of his trade seemed straight out of science fiction, an ultrashock device that reportedly went haywire and burned a red welt into coach Clyde King's rear end. "It looked like some kind of cross between a cattle prod and flyswatter with goddamn sparks flying all over the place," recalled pitcher Steve Blass. But Clemente could also use something as simple as his bat, which he employed to beneficial effect on Les Banos, the team photographer. Banos once complained of a stiff lower back before a game in Montreal after he had endured two cross-country flights within twenty-four hours, and Clemente eased the pain by adeptly manipulating his Frenchy Uhalt model Louisville Slugger into the little Hungarian photographer's pressure points, lending new meaning to the description of him as a magician with a bat in his hands.

Over the years, as Clemente sought help for chronic pain in his back and spine, he became a devotee of chiropractics. His interest in the practice went back to 1957, his third season in the majors, when his pain was so bad that he considered retiring. During a road trip to St. Louis, he visited the Logan College of Chiropractics, where the founder Vinton Logan took X rays showing the arthritic condition in Clemente's neck and relieved the pain. From then on, Clemente stopped in for treatment whenever the Pirates were in St. Louis, and began looking for chiropractors in San Juan and Pittsburgh as well. He learned their techniques so thoroughly that he started to think of himself as a member of their profession. Vera recalled that he had shelves of books on chiropractics. "He was a chiropractor without a license," she said. "He worked on many patients who would have gone to surgeons." As he began to consider his future after baseball, he often talked of two parallel dreams: One was to run a free sports city for the children of Puerto Rico; the other was to set up a lucrative chiropractic vacation spa on the ocean outside San Juan.

When he thought sportswriters mistook his health obsession for hypochondria, Clemente would explode. But inside the clubhouse, he learned to go with it. Early in the 1967 season, his teammates noticed a subtle change; he could rib and be ribbed with no hard feelings. Year by year after that, he eased more to the center of the locker room fun. His nickname for Bartirome was Dago. "I'm a dago, too," he would insist, pointing out that Clemente was also an Italian surname. "I don't know whether it was the personalities on the team or that he had matured and felt it was all right to put his guard down and enjoy it and be silly with us, but he seemed to loosen up," Blass observed. It was likely some of both, and also the fact that with the MVP award in 1966 he felt some measure of deserved recognition. In any case, it was a sign that he finally felt comfortable with the role of team leader.

Bartirome once heard Clemente tell a reporter that he stayed in shape by lifting weights and working out at the gym three hours a day during the off-season. It was Roberto's way of joking; not a word of it was true. His physique was a wonder of genetics, not an artificial creation. He was careful about what he ate. He loaded up on vegetables, was always looking for a new fruit shake concoction, and took great pride in knowing when to push away from the table. He never lifted weights and his workouts during the off-season amounted to little more than walking the beach in search of driftwood, playing some more baseball, shampooing the rugs, and mowing the lawn. Yet his body changed imperceptibly from the time he was eighteen. At five-foot-eleven, his weight barely fluctuated between 182 and 185 pounds. His biceps and calves had sinewy muscularity yet he was not muscle-bound. "He was a sculpture. He could have posed for Greek statues," said photographer Banos. "What you saw with him was archaeology. He was a perfect model. Not an ounce of extra fat. All the right muscle. A perfect figure for a man of any age."

Because of his persistent aches and occasional injuries, misconceptions surrounded Clemente. Some thought he had the sort of tightly wound body that was perpetually on the verge of breaking down from a pulled hamstring. Nothing was further from reality. Clemente had the ability to go full speed without even warming up. He was notorious for lingering in the locker room until the last moment. If a game started at eight, he would scuttle out of the clubhouse at 7:58:30, and go right to work. "Twenty seconds before the game he would go out to the field," Bartirome said. "He never did any sprints; no warming up. And there was something about him, that he did, that I could not believe any man could do without hurting himself seriously. In the first inning, he [might] chop a ball off the plate and run to first full blast and then five feet beyond first he would stop—completely. A dead stop. I never saw a ballplayer do that. He would not gradually stop. It was amazing."

For Clemente, 1968 started out troubled and deteriorated. In February, after winning his fourth batting championship the previous season, he was trying to climb between two patios built into the hillside of his home in Río Piedras when a steel railing collapsed and he fell, injuring his shoulder. He reported to spring training late and hurting, without telling Pirates officials what had happened. A doctor in Puerto Rico had suggested that he rest the shoulder for several months, he told friends, but he felt compelled to play, if only to prove to doubters that he was not jaking it. "I shouldn't have been playing in spring training," he said later. "I should have taken care of my shoulder."

The injury haunted him all year, and he was also slowed by a bout with the flu, and the result was his worst season of the decade, which in his case meant that he batted *only* .291. Following seasons of .314, .351, .312, .320, .339, .329, .317, and .357—with four batting titles and an MVP award in the mix—an average of .291 was deemed a miserable slump. But not only was Clemente subpar physically, he was struggling during a season that became known as the Year of the Pitcher, when all hitters were having difficulty. Only five National League players batted over .300 in 1968, and Clemente's average actually ranked as tenth best in the league. The twenty-fifth best hitter in the league was Richie Allen at .263. Meanwhile, the composite earned-run average for National League pitchers was a record low 2.98. Bob Gibson, only a year after having his lower right leg broken by a vicious Clemente line drive, pitched the most unhittable year in baseball history, finishing with an inhuman 1.12 earned-run average. Juan Marichal threw thirty complete games that season, and Don Drysdale pitched 58.2 consecutive scoreless innings.

That Clemente would have an off-year in those circumstances was understandable. In every respect, with the Pirates regressing to a losing record, 80–82, it was a season he wished to forget. In conversations with Vera, for the first time he broached the idea of retiring, though he always added "in a year or two." One nagging concern was the amount of flying a major league baseball player endured. During the long season, the airplane becomes a second home, but it was never a comfortable one for Clemente. In 1968 alone, the Pirates flew from Pittsburgh to Houston to San Francisco to Los Angeles to Pittsburgh to St. Louis to Pittsburgh to Philadelphia to Atlanta to Pittsburgh to New York to Chicago to Cincinnati to Pittsburgh to Los Angeles to Houston to San Francisco to Pittsburgh to St. Louis to Philadelphia to New York to Chicago to Pittsburgh to Atlanta to Pittsburgh to Cincinnati to San Francisco to Los Angeles to Houston to Pittsburgh to Cincinnati to St. Louis to Atlanta to Pittsburgh to New York to Philadelphia to Pittsburgh to Chicago and back to Pittsburgh. They were in the air for more than ninety hours covering 35,080 miles.

The Pirates had a congregation of nervous flyers during that era, including Donn Clendenon, Willie Stargell, Juan Pizarro, and Clemente. Stargell would shout prayers every time their plane flew over the Grand Canyon and encountered any turbulence. Clemente and Clendenon were so shaken during one flight through a Midwestern thunderstorm that they bailed out at a stop in Cincinnati and rode a bus back to Pittsburgh. Pizarro, while playing for the Indians, once got fined by manager Alvin Dark for refusing to fly from Detroit to Cleveland. Clemente usually was too proud to show fear to strangers, but he talked about the perils of flying with his friends. "He used to tell me that he was going to die in a plane crash," José Pagan remembered. After coming to the Pirates from the Giants in 1965, Pagan often sat next to Clemente on the team plane, and he noticed that Roberto would never sleep when they were in the air, even during a cross-country flight in the middle of the night. "Then, on one late-night flight to Los Angeles, Clemente somehow fell asleep. "When he was sleeping, he jumped, and I said, 'What is happening to you? What are you jumping for?'" Pagan recalled. " 'What happened, did you eat a rabbit or something like that?' And he said, 'You know what happen, José, you know I seldom sleep on airplanes. I went to sleep and I was dreaming that the plane we were traveling on crashed, and the only one that got killed was me.'"

When Juan Pizarro heard that story, in his dry style he said to Clemente, "Well, die when I'm not on the plane, okay?" Pagan took Clemente more seriously and tried to persuade him that dreams were not to be taken literally. "I would say, Clemente, you cannot think about that. That is only a dream. I dream sometimes that I am rich. That does not mean that I will be rich . . . unfortunately."

Vera dealt the most with Clemente's fatalism, though she hated to hear him talk that way. From the time they got married, he had told her that he did not expect to be around too long. "He always had the idea that he would die young," she remembered. "He would say, 'I know that I will die young and never get old, and you will probably remarry.' I would say, 'Don't talk about that. First, don't talk about sad things. Second, God forbid, if something happens to you, I will never marry again.' He was always talking about that. He measured his time."

At the end of the 1968 season, after the final game in Chicago against the Cubs, he and Vera flew to New York and stayed with their friends Carlos and Carmen Llanos in the Bronx before starting a long European vacation. He did not fear flying with Vera because in his premonitions she would live beyond him. While in New York, they went shopping for furniture to ship down to Puerto Rico. Roberto enjoyed shopping, and was particular in his tastes. He bought his cologne from a little shop in Montreal across the street from the Queen Elizabeth Hotel, where he could mix his own perfume (a blend of Royal Copenhagen) and keep the ingredients on file. For suits he preferred Clothes of Distinction at the Disco Mart in Chicago (size 38R). His clothes were refined but modish, the collars growing larger and stripes wider with the fashion trends of the era. Much of the furniture in the Río Piedras house was bought in Pittsburgh, known for its elegant department stores, but he thought they might find some more in New York. What started as a search for furniture ended up as a lesson in sociology that became part of the lore of his life.

The name of the store has been lost to history; Roberto never mentioned the name, nor did Carlos Llanos, who accompanied them, and Vera cannot remember. The rest of the story was unforgettable for them all. Vera was pregnant with their third son, Roberto Enrique, who would be called Ricky. In his wallet, Clemente carried a thick wad of hundred-dollar bills and traveler's checks, all totaling about $5,000. When a sales clerk met them at the door, Roberto said they intended to look through the showroom on the main floor. The clerk asked him to wait until a salesman was found who could take them to another floor of inexpensive furniture. "So they took us to a place where they showed me furniture that wasn't the furniture in the showroom," Clemente said years later in an interview with broadcaster Sam Nover. "And I said, 'We would like to see the furniture downstairs that we saw in the showroom.' And they said, 'Well, you don't have enough money to buy that . . . that's very expensive.' And I said, 'Well, I would like to see it because I have the right to see it as a human being, as the public that buys from you.'"

At Clemente's insistence, they returned to the classiest showroom. Clemente took out his wallet, nodded toward a furniture set he liked, and snapped, "Do you think this could buy it?" Vera noticed that another clerk was staring at them, puzzled. "I know who you are," he said finally, but couldn't bring up the name. When Clemente reluctantly identified himself, the store clerk's attitude changed. Now he was solicitous, taking the arm of the pregnant Vera as he showed them around. As Clemente remembered the scene later: "When they found out who I was they said they had seven floors of furniture and we'll show it to you and don't worry about, you know, when you walked in we thought you were like another Puerto Rican."

Nothing could have more infuriated Clemente, who carried his intense pride for his people, especially the poor of Puerto Rico, with him everywhere. "I said, 'Look, your business is to sell to anybody. I don't care if I'm Puerto Rican or Jewish or whatever you want to call me. But you see this is really what gets me mad—because I am Puerto Rican you treat me different from other people. I have the same American money that you ask people for, but I have a different treatment. Right now you are giving my wife different treatment, and my friend, because we are Puerto Rican. And I don't want to buy your furniture!' So I walked out."

Since coming to work in the United States in 1954, at the dawn of the civil rights era, Clemente had grown more assertive on questions of racial equality. Martin Luther King Jr. was at the top of the list of people he admired. They had met several times, and King once spent part of a day talking with Clemente at his farm in Puerto Rico. When King was assassinated in April 1968, Clemente led the way in insisting that the Pirates and Astros delay opening the season in Houston until after the slain civil rights leader's funeral. The schedule called for games in Houston on April 8 and 9. King was buried April 9. The Pirates and Astros, at the players' insistence, held off playing until April 10. Al Oliver, a black teammate who considered himself one of Clemente's disciples, said Clemente would draw him into long discussions, more about life than baseball. "Our conversations always stemmed around people from all walks of life being able to get along well, no excuse why it shouldn't be . . . He had a problem with people who treated you differently because of where you were from, your nationality, your color, also poor people, how they were treated . . .

that's the thing I really respected about him most, was his character, the things he believed in."

What Clemente admired most about King was not his philosophy of nonviolence, but his ability to give voice to the voiceless. "When Martin Luther King started doing what he did, he changed the whole system of the American style," Clemente said. "He put the people, the ghetto people, the people who didn't have nothing to say in those days, they started saying what they would have liked to say for many years that nobody listened to. Now with this man, these people come down to the place where they were supposed to be but people didn't want them, and sit down there as if they were white and call attention to the whole world. Now that wasn't only the black people, but the minority people. The people who didn't have anything, and they had nothing to say in those days because they didn't have any power, they started saying things and they started picketing, and that's the reason I say he changed the whole world . . ."

The Clementes spent twenty-two days in Europe. Roberto loved Spain and Italy. Every day, he went off through the streets, talking to strangers, listening to their life stories. In Rome, renewing his boast that all Clementes were part Italian, he ordered boldly from the menu without knowing the language, realizing only when his meal came what he had done. "When they brought that piece of raw meat . . . hah! We were laughing. You're not so Italian! Raw steak," Vera remembered. Before the trip, Clemente had talked several times with his friend Les Banos, the Pittsburgh photographer, about what it would be like. "Clemente wanted to know how people were treated in Europe," Banos said later. "Whether there was prejudice in Europe." Banos, who spoke with a thick Hungarian accent, had worked as a spy during World War II, infiltrating the Hungarian SS and secretly helping Jews escape. It was after listening to Banos and visiting Germany that Clemente began having nightmares about hiding under a house as the boots of a German soldier marched back and forth. At the airport arrival gate in Berlin, he and Vera were stopped and questioned by five men who did not identify themselves and vanished once the tour guide approached and said, "Mr. Clemente?" They must have been looking for someone else. When his tour group passed Checkpoint Charlie,

Clemente told Vera he was afraid they would be detained. "There was a Mexican on our tour, and when we stopped to get some sodas he was asking questions of the communist guide and the guide was getting nervous," Vera remembered. "The Mexican started shouting, 'Viva Mexico, Libre!' . . . and Roberto said, 'He better stop or I will punch the Mexican!'"

Throughout his career, Clemente was known for making good first impressions on the field. At the start of the 1960 championship season, he drove in five runs in the first home game. In his first at-bat in the World Series, he singled in a run and knocked the starting pitcher out of the game. Even during his first year of organized baseball, when the Dodgers were trying to hide him in Montreal, he hit an inside-the-park home run in his first spring training game. All during that time, he also luxuriated in the warm embrace of the fans. The occasional volatility of his dealings with sportswriters seemed to have little effect on the people in the stands. That changed, if briefly, on the Sunday afternoon of April 13, 1969. The lost year of 1968 was behind him, but now in the first week of a new season, he was making a bad first impression, and it was not going over well with the fans. The Pirates had won their first three games on the road against the Cardinals, and then came home for a series against the Phillies. Earlier that spring, Clemente had been criticized in the press for bailing out of spring training for several days to have his sore back worked on by Arturo Garcia, a masseur in San Juan. Joe Finegold, the team doctor, had suggested in private conversations with baseball writers that this was medically unsound and one step above sorcery, an assessment that only lent more weight to the notion that Clemente, for all his skills, was an individualist rather than team player and borderline nutcase on health issues. Now, in two uncharacteristic games, Clemente hit into three double plays and misplayed a ball hit to right into a two-base error. Roy McHugh, then sports editor of the *Pittsburgh Press*, watched the games from the press box, and heard something he had never heard before—the fans greeting the great Clemente with a shower of boos.

"Love and hate, goes a folk saying, are the opposite sides of the same coin," McHugh wrote in his column the following day. "It explains, if nothing else, the passionate booing of Roberto Clemente at Forbes Field Sunday afternoon." Under the headline FICKLENESS IS A VERY NORMAL THING, McHugh placed Clemente in the company of other great players booed at home: Ted Williams at Fenway, Mickey Mantle in New York, even Joe DiMaggio, jeered early in his career for diffidently refusing to tip his cap. But Williams, Mantle, and DiMaggio, McHugh wrote, all became "deities in their declining years. Clemente, instead of achieving grace slowly, fell from it all at once."

McHugh was a sharp, subtle writer, a professional in every respect. His observation about the booing was accurate, yet there was something deeper to Clemente's story. Clemente, at age thirty-four, was booed for a day, but in fact he was that rare athlete who was slowly achieving grace, not just as a ballplayer but as a human being. The reality of many athletes, even those who become hailed as deities, is that they diminish with time; Clemente was the opposite, becoming more sure of himself and his larger role in life. As a keen observer, McHugh picked up on some signs of this. He noted that Clemente was now able to poke fun at himself and his reputation for complaining about his aches and pains. That same week that he heard his first boos, Clemente showed up at the batting cage displaying a "horribly swollen finger" that turned out to be a slip-on practical joke. And his response to the boos also showed maturity. Rather than making any obscene gestures, like Ted Williams, or complaining about being misunderstood, Clemente waved his batting helmet, as if to say thank you. In the trainer's room after the game, Tony Bartirome came to Clemente's defense. "Those dirty bastards, booing you like that," Bartirome said. "I deserved to be booed," Clemente responded. "I stunk out there."

Later, talking to Bill Mazeroski, his oldest teammate, Clemente confided that it hurt him to think the fans would boo him "after all this time." But he would not criticize them in public. They had given him a lift so many times in his career. They were like his parents, always there for him. They were only judging his actions on the field, and hitting into three double plays and making an error were deeds that deserved boos. He would never play for any other fans, he said.

There was a distinction in any case between rooting for Pittsburgh and being a Clemente fan. The real Clemente fans, many of them young people, never booed him. One such fan was Juliet Schor, a tenth-grade student at Winchester Thurston School in the Shadyside neighborhood, who described herself as such "an obsessive Roberto Clemente idolizer" that she took pictures of him on television and clipped every mention of him in the Pittsburgh papers. Schor also possessed a baseball that a friend of her father's brought back from spring training and delivered to her at Children's Hospital when she was undergoing preoperative treatments for scoliosis. It was a Wilson ball, Pony League, horsehide cover, signed in blue ink: "To Juley, I hope that when you get this you are feeling much better. I hope to see you when I get to Pittsburgh. Love, Roberto."

Schor's attachment to Clemente eventually became so overwhelming that she rode a city bus across town early one morning just to stand in the parking lot of his apartment complex in hopes of seeing him. As luck would have it, he came out to his car carrying a basket of laundry. She worked up the nerve to approach him and blurted out exactly how she felt. *"I am more in love with you than any person in the world!"* Clemente smiled. She thought he must have heard this a million times. He said that he was going to the laundry. Did she want to come along? "I was totally undone by this, that I could just . . . go to the laundry with him," she recalled. "What a mensch. He was so unbelievably sweet and kind and nice to me. And so matter of fact, too. He was talking to me like any other person . . . When it came down to it, it was too overwhelming and I said, 'Oh no.' And he left. He drove off to the laundry." Schor never saw her hero again. She grew up to become a professor of sociology at Boston College. Among the clippings in her Clemente scrapbook was a story about people booing him that long ago April Sunday at Forbes Field. "I remember cutting out an article from the *Post-Gazette*," she said later. "Clemente booed! I kept it for a long time, it was so upsetting to me that it happened."

Aside from that early double-play-and-error skein, Clemente gave fans little reason to boo the rest of 1969. The previous season's .291 average was an aberration, not the typical slide of an aging ballplayer. Clemente began rapping the ball with his trademark ferocity again. No National League pitcher wanted to face him. Ferguson Jenkins, the ace of the Cubs, said that it seemed every time he looked over "there was No. 21 in the on-deck circle, scaring the hell out of me. I never liked seeing him there. Didn't I just pitch to him? The lineup always seemed to come around to him too quickly." The only way to pitch Clemente, Jenkins decided, was "right down the middle"—he could reach anything outside, even as far off the plate as he stood. That had been the shared wisdom of most National Leaguers throughout the sixties decade. When Larry Jackson pitched for the Phillies, he once became so frustrated trying to get Clemente out that in exasperation he decided to knock him down. Clemente got up and smacked the next pitch over the center-field fence. That is when Gene Mauch, then manager of the Phillies, established the Clemente rule. As second baseman Tony Taylor remembered: "Mauch would say, 'Let him sleep. Don't wake him up. Don't pitch him inside, he'll kill you. Just throw it right down the middle of the plate and let him hit it.'" But there was no way to get Clemente out, according to Taylor. "I would watch him hit and hit and hit. He was the best I'd ever seen at setting pitchers up. He'd look bad one at-bat and then kill them with the same pitch the next."

Don Drysdale, the fearsome Dodgers right-hander, acknowledged that his fear of a screaming line drive off Clemente's bat helped drive him from the game. In a reflective conversation about retirement with Bill Curry, the former Green Bay Packers center, Drysdale said that he could not see Clemente making that slow walk to the plate without "thinking of that terrible thing that had happened to Herb Score, the Indians' pitcher, when Gil McDougald hit the ball back into his face and almost blinded him." Big D would "stand on the mound and look down at Clemente and the Score thing would pop into his mind and he'd give an involuntary shudder," Curry remembered Drysdale telling him. "It got so bad . . . that when he delivered the ball, he flinched at his follow-through and tucked his head down a bit."

The moment that finished Drysdale's career came on August 5, a Tuesday night in the dog days of the summer of 1969. He was on the mound at home at Chavez Ravine. Clemente came to the plate and smacked a line drive to center, the ball leaving the bat with such velocity that Drysdale could hear it buzz past him. As Curry described the scene later, Drysdale then "had the sensation of a bug crawling on his neck; he reached and flicked at it. Leaning down for the resin bag, he noticed a runny substance on his finger, and still feeling the irritation, he reached up and discovered his ear was bleeding. The ball had actually taken the skin off the top of his ear on its way out to center field." He stayed in to pitch to one more batter, the young catcher, Manny Sanguillen, who was a Clemente disciple. The gopher ball that Drysdale threw to Sanguillen was his last pitch in the major leagues.

On that same West Coast trip, Clemente had another of his occasional power surges, rapping home runs in three consecutive at-bats against the Giants in San Francisco. (That game, which the Pirates won 10–5, marked the second three-home-run game of his career, the first coming in May 1967 against the Reds when he drove in seven runs but the Pirates still lost, 8–7.) Clemente ended the 1969 season with a .345 average, nineteen home runs, twelve triples (his eighth season of ten or more of those rare but beautiful hits), and ninety-one runs batted in. He lost another Silver Bat on the final day of the season to Pete Rose, who bunted for a base hit in his final at-bat to overtake Clemente for the batting title. At the end of the 1960s, a brilliant era of National League baseball illuminated by Mays, Aaron, Frank Robinson, Banks, Cepeda, McCovey, Koufax, Drysdale, Marichal, and Gibson, Clemente finished at the top of the game, with the highest batting average of any player over the entire decade. His Pirates, who started the sixties as champions, spent the decade futilely trying to return to those heights, but appeared at least to be on a winning track again. With a crew of young players including Sanguillen, Richie Hebner, Dave Cash, Bob Robertson, Gene Alley, and Al Oliver supplementing steady old Mazeroski and the hitting machine trio of Clemente, Matty Alou (231 hits), and slugger Willie Stargell, the Pirates finished 1969 fourteen games over .500, in third place of the newly created NL East behind the Mets and Cubs.

One other event that season was kept quiet at the time but eventually became part of Clemente lore. Aside from a crew of brutes who for obvious reasons never came forward to talk about it, he was the sole witness to the incident, so history has only his version, as passed down to Vera, José Pagan, *Post-Gazette* writer Bill Christine, and eventually the San Diego police. It happened during a West Coast road trip after a game in San Diego. As Clemente told the story, he saw Willie Stargell coming back to the Town and Country Motel with a box of take-out chicken, and asked him where he got it. Stargell directed him to a nearby restaurant on the other side of an eight-lane highway. A short time later, as Clemente was walking home with his dinner, he noticed a man walking toward him. A car suddenly swerved onto the sidewalk, a door opened, and the man rushed toward Clemente and pushed him inside. He had been kidnapped by four men: two Mexican nationals and two Mexican-Americans. One was driving, one put a gun to Clemente's mouth, a third held a knife at his back, and a fourth sat on his legs so that he couldn't move. According to Vera's account, which correlates with what Clemente later told Christine, the kidnappers drove Clemente to an isolated park above Mission Valley and ordered him to take off his clothes.

"Once they arrived at the park, they took his wallet and divided up the money," Vera recounted. "They took his clothing, his tie, and he was only left with his pants and one shoe. Roberto was silent at first . . . anesthetized by fear. But he thought he ought to do something. When he said, 'I am Roberto Clemente and if you kill me the FBI will find you,' they didn't believe him." Clemente told a slightly different version to Christine, saying that he informed the men that he played for the San Diego Padres (figuring they had never heard of the Pirates). In both versions, he urged them to look at the ring they had taken from his finger. It was from an All-Star game and had his name on it. And look at the cards in his wallet, he said. When the robbers realized that they had in fact chosen the famous baseball player as their prey, everything changed. "They returned everything to him," Vera remembered him telling her. "They put together the money they had divvied up and put it in his wallet, which they gave to him. They gave him back his shirt . . . and told him to put on his tie so that he would look normal. They took him back to the place where they had swiped him from . . . and his heart jumped again when he saw they were returning. One of the thieves told him, 'Here, you left your food.'"

It would not be unusual if this story, like many stories, became more dramatic with every retelling. Whatever the hidden reality, it fit perfectly into the mythology of Roberto Clemente as a man of the people, respected even by urban desperados.

Nineteen sixty-nine is remembered in baseball as the year of the Miracle Mets. In their eighth season, the Mets overtook the Cubs in August, defeated the Braves in the divisional playoffs, and then shocked the favored Baltimore Orioles to win the World Series. Their championship was a perfect bookend to the upset victory of the Pirates in 1960, two scrappy underdog teams beating the establishment. From a long-term perspective, the Mets accomplished something even more unlikely than the Pirates did in defeating the Yankees. The expansion Mets became the best club in baseball in 1969 following seven straight sad-sack seasons during which they lost 737 games—an average of more than one hundred defeats a year—and won only 394. Their stunning rise has taken its justifiable place among the great stories of modern baseball. Yet one could argue that in terms of baseball history it was the second most important story of the year. The most significant event in baseball in 1969, and perhaps of the entire decade, might have taken place after the season, on December 13 and 14, inside a conference room at the Sheraton Hotel in San Juan, Puerto Rico, where the Executive Board of the Major League Baseball Players Association held its annual winter meeting. There professional athletes took the first step toward freedom.

At ten on the morning of the thirteenth, Marvin Miller, executive director of the players association, called the meeting to order. Seated next to him was Richard Moss, a Pittsburgh native who served as legal counsel. Miller, an economist, and Moss, a lawyer, were skilled organizers who had come to the players association from the steelworkers union in 1966. At the table around them were representatives from each team: Bernie Allen of the Senators, Max Alvis of the Indians, and Ron Brand of the new Montreal Expos; Moe Drabowsky of the Royals, Eddie Fisher of the Angels, and Reggie Jackson (sitting in for Catfish Hunter) of the Athletics; Ed Kranepool of the Mets, Denny Lemaster of the Astros, and Bob Locker of the new Seattle Pilots (about to become the Milwaukee Brewers); Jim Lonborg of the Red Sox, Dal Maxvill of the Cardinals, and Tim McCarver of the Phillies; Mike McCormick of the Giants, Milt Pappas of the Braves, and Jim Perry of the Twins; Gary Peters of the White Sox, Phil Regan of the Cubs, and Brooks Robinson of the Orioles; Tom Sisk of the Padres, Joe Torre of the Cardinals, and Woody Woodward of the Reds; Tom Haller for the National League, Steve Hamilton for the American League, and Jim Bunning for the Pension Committee. And representing the Pittsburgh Pirates, Roberto Clemente. Bunning and Clemente, Pirates teammates at the time and two future Hall of Fame players, had the most seniority among the players, fifteen years apiece, each making the majors in 1955. Clemente, who had replaced Donn Clendenon as player representative after Clendenon was traded, was the first Latin on the board.

Three years into Miller's leadership of the union, the players had started to assert themselves. In 1968, they had reached the first collective bargaining agreement with the owners, which among other things raised the minimum salary to $10,000. Now they were negotiating a new contract, and Miller spent the first part of the meeting assessing the latest management offer. The players wanted to cut the number of regular season games from 162 to 154, but the owners rejected any reduction. The owners also refused to discuss all proposals that would allow players freedom in moving from one team to another, and would not consider the concept of submitting salary disputes to arbitration. They agreed "in principle" to allow players to bring agents into contract negotiations, but refused to include that language in the basic agreement. Their proposal would raise the minimum salary by $500 for each of the next three seasons to an eventual $11,500. They would increase the daily meal money by 50 cents a year to $16.50. By unanimous vote, according to minutes of the meeting, the players rejected the offer but urged the negotiating committee to continue bargaining with the owners.

The players then returned to the central issue of the negotiations, the restrictions on player movement imposed by what was known as the reserve clause, which allowed teams to maintain the rights to players beyond the length of a contract, in effect binding them to a single team unless they were traded or released. For generations of ballplayers, the reserve system had been an accepted part of major league life; all control rested with the owners. Now, slowly, the imbalance of power was being challenged. Miller noted that in the 1968 Basic Agreement the owners had promised to participate in a joint study of "possible alternatives to the reserve clause as presently constituted"— but since signing the agreement had "not advanced one single idea of their own for reform." Player representatives agreed that the reserve clause was the most serious issue they faced and had to be resolved in future negotiations. Then Miller introduced an invited guest, Curt Flood, the veteran center fielder who had played twelve seasons for the St. Louis Cardinals. In a blockbuster deal at the end of the 1969 season, Flood had been traded by the Cardinals along with Tim McCarver, outfielder Byron Browne, and pitcher Joe Hoerner to Philadelphia for first baseman Richie Allen, infielder Cookie Rojas, and pitcher Jerry Johnson. The trade infuriated Flood. He did not want to play for the Phillies and started thinking about challenging the system.

As he was introducing Flood, Miller recalled a conversation they had had shortly after the October trade. Miller said he gave Flood "the third degree" to test his convictions. The stakes for an individual ballplayer challenging the system, Miller said, were so great that he was "concerned that any player doing this understand all the consequences—personal and otherwise."

Flood then presented his case. Regardless of what the players association decided to do, he said, he would go ahead with his challenge. He had not yet made public his decision, but was about to announce that he was taking the owners to court to contest the legality of the reserve clause. He said that he was no longer willing to be bought and sold as a piece of property. All players were being treated like slaves, he said. "We are all under the same yoke." Someone had to challenge the system, he added. "I feel I'm qualified and capable of doing it."

According to official notes of the meeting, along with more detailed handwritten notes taken by a participant, Miller offered two reasons why the players should support Flood. First, when a member of the union undertook a fight of concern to all players "the players association should give assistance to its full ability." More important, he argued, they should join Flood to ensure that the case was argued effectively and did not result in bad law.

Jim Bunning asked Flood whether he would be taking action if he had not been traded.

Flood responded that his feelings were "brought to a head by the trade." It made him feel like he was being "treated like chattel."

Tom Haller asked whether being black was one of Flood's motivations, given the social situation in the United States.

"I am a black man and we have been denied rights," Flood said. "But in this situation, race should not make the difference. We're ballplayers, all with the same problem."

Tim McCarver, who had been moved from St. Louis in the same trade, asked what might happen if Flood won the case.

The courts would only determine whether the system was legal or not, Marvin Miller answered. It may also award damages, but the real solution had to come from collective bargaining with the owners.

Bob Locker asked what dangers might arise if Flood won.

No danger, Miller said, "so long as all of us understand that our aim is not to wipe it [the reserve clause] out, but to make appropriate revisions."

Milt Pappas asked whether chaos would ensue if Flood won and twenty other players decided to follow him to court.

Clemente spoke up in Flood's defense, pointing out that to that point he was the only player with the courage to take action. "So far," Clemente said, "no one is doing anything."

If they supported Flood, Bunning said, picking up Pappas's train of thought, what would they tell the next player who wanted their support for a similar case?

"We must say to the second player that it is not in the interest of the players association to have multiple cases," Miller said. "We're supporting a test case."

"What other thing can we do?" asked McCarver, making his position clear. "I think there is no choice [but to support Flood]."

"I agree," said Miller. "It is the cleanest way to establish a position."

Clemente then returned to the emotional heart of Flood's case, the imbalance of power that allowed owners to control a player's fate. He told the story of how he was signed by the Brooklyn Dodgers fifteen years earlier because he wanted to play in New York, even though the Milwaukee Braves offered him three times more money. But the Dodgers decided not to protect him on their major league roster and tried to hide him on the bench with the Montreal Royals. Clemente had no say in this, and was helpless when the Pittsburgh Pirates took him away from Brooklyn in the supplemental draft. With the owners having all the power, he told his fellow player reps, his initial decision to choose location over money was rendered meaningless. It cost the Pirates only $5,000 to draft him, Clemente said, and for that meager sum, as he said of general manager Joe L. Brown, "He had me." Over fifteen years, by Clemente's conservative estimate, if the Pirates made an extra $300,000 by having him on their team, their profit was $295,000.

Dick Moss, the counsel, said later that when Clemente spoke everyone listened. Even though he was relating his own story, the point Clemente was making was not the complaint of a wealthy superstar—among the few players in the room then making more than $100,000 a year—but a statement of solidarity for younger players. "Roberto was respected by everyone," Moss said. "He was very important to us."

After Clemente's story, the players returned to the specifics of taking up Flood's case. Max Alvis wanted to know how quickly it would get into court. Reggie Jackson asked whether the situation would have been different had St. Louis consulted Flood about a trade. "Basically, yes," Flood said. Jim Bunning asked how Flood and the players association would split the court costs. Haller said there was no problem with the union's finances. Joe Torre said that as long as Curt Flood was serious, and he seemed to be, they had to back him.

The discussion had gone on for more than an hour when Flood was excused from the room. "Are there people here who feel we should not assist?" Miller asked.

There were none. Brand made the motion to support Flood. McCarver seconded. Clemente, Bunning, and all their younger colleagues voted aye—unanimous, 25–0. In the minutes of the meeting, the Executive Board made a point of emphasizing that it was not seeking radical change. "The Board reiterated the position of the Association that our goal is not to do away with the entire reserve system and substitute nothing in its place—rather, we seek to make appropriate revisions which will enhance the players' position but which, at the same time, will not endanger the integrity and appeal of the game and will not affect the value of the franchises." It was the modest first step into a new world, though none of those players could then realize how long the journey would take or how different that new world would be. How could Cardinals player representative Joe Torre, in the prime of his playing days, imagine that three-and-a-half decades later he would be managing a $220 million payroll of mercenary Yankees, many of whom made more in a year than he would earn his entire career?

Clemente had intended to take a break from winter baseball in 1969, just as he had the previous year. But he received a call in early December from his old friend and first professional boss, Pedrin Zorrilla, the original owner of the Santurce Cangrejeros, who had returned to the winter leagues as general manager of San Juan. "Would you consider playing here?" Zorrilla asked, knowing that Clemente's contract with the Pirates provided a bonus if he did not play winter ball. "Don Pedro, whatever you say, I will play," Clemente answered. His respect for Zorrilla was so deep that he signed a contract without looking at the salary—different culture, different history, different circumstances from the major leagues and his disdain for the dominance of owners.

The San Juan Senadores had several top major leaguers, including Indians outfielder José Cardenal, Reds first baseman Lee May, and Orioles pitcher Miguel Cuellar, but even with Clemente in the lineup they struggled as a middling .500 team, far behind the Santurce Cangrejeros, who were managed that season by another of baseball's great right fielders, Frank Robinson. At lunch one day during a weekend road trip to Mayagüez on Puerto Rico's west coast, Clemente was talking with Zorrilla about the team's troubles and how they could improve things. Listening in on the conversation, Zorrilla's young son

Enrique, named for his grandfather, the nationalist poet Enrique Zorrilla, blurted out to Clemente, "Well, that's what we have you there
for!" The father gave his son a stern look, and Enrique felt embarrassed for talking without thinking and saying something so embar-
rassing.

At the stadium that night, before the game, Clemente found
Enrique and said softly, "Come with me." Enrique was anxious, still
ashamed of what he had said. Clemente led him into the clubhouse
and started to change into his uniform as he talked about what it took
to be a great baseball player. Enrique was thirteen, standing in front of
the great Clemente, who was in his underwear. "You know," Clemente
said, "everybody thinks it's easy to go out there and hit and run. But
you have to be in good physical condition, because you have to play
this game well, especially if you love this game. And if you want to do
what you love most in life, you have to be prepared for it. And also, you
are playing for people who pay to see you. You are giving entertainment to people. So you have to be the best. So that's why I keep in
shape."

Clemente then stretched and asked Enrique to feel his calf. It was
rock hard. "A baseball player is just legs. Strong legs. You have to run
every day." Clemente had now changed into his San Juan uniform.
"Come with me," he said again, and Enrique followed him into the
dugout and sat next to him the entire game.

"I had felt so bad for my comment," Enrique Zorrilla said decades
later, the memory still fresh in his mind. "And I know that my father
must have told him, 'My son feels so bad, so ashamed.' And for at least
two or three hours Roberto Clemente dedicated his time to give me
some peace of mind. And he gave me the best day of my life, because I
will never forget that. It was so heartfelt."

This was typical Clemente. In his world, kids and sportswriters
were at opposite poles. Sportswriters rarely understood him, he
thought. When they were nearby his tendency was often to retreat to
the trainer's room or berate them for a few minutes to release his frustrations. But he sensed that young people understood him intuitively,
and he wanted to be around them. Over the Christmas holidays that
winter, the Clementes invited another thirteen-year-old to their home

in Río Piedras. It was Nancy Golding, who lived on Fair Oaks Street in Pittsburgh's Squirrel Hill neighborhood. A few months earlier, Clemente had visited his accountant, Henry Kantrowitz, who lived a few houses down from the Goldings. Kantrowitz's wife, Pearl, adored Roberto and often invited him over for meals. On one of his visits, Nancy had been urged to stop by and play catch with him in the driveway. That experience was unbelievable enough, but then seemingly out of nowhere came a letter from Vera Clemente saying that they would love for her to visit them in Puerto Rico. Nancy's parents agreed, and she found herself flying alone to San Juan at the Christmas break.

"I don't know why they invited me," Golding said decades later. "I wasn't a peer. Not a babysitter. I didn't bring with me anything special to them. I hardly knew them, and they invited me." These are her memories: They were extremely nice to her. She had her own bedroom. One room in the house was just for his trophies. Four silver bats and all those gold gloves: 1961, 1962, 1963, 1964, 1965, 1966, 1967, 1968. Always visitors at the house in Río Piedras. Lots of parties. Commotion, laughing, late into the night. Everything gracious and warm. Clemente busy playing baseball. He took her to Hiram Bithorn Stadium and showed her where he played. She knew little Spanish. Vera spoke a little English with a thick accent. But there was no trouble communicating. She had never before seen someone so revered as Clemente. He was stunningly handsome, extremely soft-spoken, charismatic. You got the sense that he was the king. It awakened her to the realization that there were special people in this world and things happened around them. When she was trying to fly home, Pittsburgh was buried in a snowstorm and she was having a hard time arranging a flight back to the States. Clemente came with her to the ticket counter and in a flash she was on a plane. From then on, Nancy Golding's favorite number was 21. Later in life, she even used it for her garage code.

When Danny Murtaugh made his first comeback as manager of the Pirates, replacing Harry Walker in the middle of the 1967 season,

Clemente was so distraught that he closed the door to the trainer's room and asked Tony Bartirome for advice. "I'm in trouble, Dago, what should I do?" he asked. Bartirome told him to forget the past. In the old days, Clemente had felt hurt that Murtaugh considered him a malingerer. The second managing go-round didn't last long; Murtaugh finished out the season and then retired again. A few years later, when the Pirates looked for a manager again before the 1970 season, many people thought the choice would be Don Hoak, the fiery third base-man from the 1960 championship team. Hoak had been campaigning for the job, and that would have been fine with Clemente, but instead, Joe L. Brown turned a third time to his old reliable, Murtaugh. On the very day that Murtaugh was chosen, Tiger Hoak died of a heart attack on the streets of Pittsburgh, chasing after a thief who had stolen his brother-in-law's car. And so—Murtaugh and Clemente, again. Would it be more of the same for the manager and his star player? Both said no. "As a man and a player, we didn't communicate," Clemente said of their previous relationship. "But as a person I think I'm different now and as a manager I think he's different." Murtaugh, in his own way, agreed. "Clemente's Clemente," he told the press. "He's the best player I've ever seen."

Clemente was thirty-five now and had some physical and psycho-logical bumps during the season. In early May, he bruised his left heel when he caught it on the back of first base rounding the bag in a game against the Atlanta Braves. That injury kept him sidelined for a week. He also suffered from a sore neck, and was in and out of the lineup, but Murtaugh appreciated it when he played and told him to sit—no hard feelings—when his body was overwhelmed. In early July, when he was not elected to the starting All-Star team, but named as the fourth outfielder (behind the Giants' Willie Mays and Hank Aaron and Rico Carty of the Braves), he made the mistake of saying publicly that he would rather take the three days off to rest his shoulder. One reporter quoted him as saying, "To hell with the All-Star game." This was not a misquote—Clemente could sound profane and petulant—but he said it as a means of emphasizing that he cared more about the Pirates and the pennant race than about an exhibition game. He said it the wrong way in the wrong year. This was the first year in decades that the starters were chosen by popular vote, making his remarks seem directed at the fans, the very people he courted assiduously. In the end, Clemente did participate in the All-Star contest in Cincinnati, and helped the National League prevail again. In a legendary game that ended 5–4 in the bottom of the twelfth with Pete Rose, the hell-bent hometown hero, barreling over Indians catcher Ray Fosse for the winning run, Clemente set the stage by driving in the tying run in the bottom of the ninth.

In Pittsburgh two days later, a new era began with the opening of Three Rivers Stadium. Forbes Field, with its ivy-covered wall in left, and stylish fourteen-foot Longines clock above the scoreboard, and center field so vast they stored the batting cage out there . . . Forbes Field, with its high screen at the flagpole in right, and cement-hard infield, and obstructed seats, and dingy and dank locker rooms, and tunnel rats, and Forbes Avenue trolleys, and hucksters and peanut men on Bouquet—old Forbes was obsolete. Now, near where the Monongahela and Allegheny converge to form the Ohio, here rose Three Rivers, a sleek concrete bowl with a record sixty-one turnstiles and sophisticated scoreboard and synthetic playing field and synthetic, zipperless, buttonless lightweight stretch uniforms to match—all the latest in modern artificiality. Forbes Field served the city well for more than sixty years, noted the *Pittsburgh Press.* "Here's to the next 60 at Three Rivers Stadium." (But they didn't build them the way they used to—only thirty years and Three Rivers was gone.)

The Pirates were in a pennant race that July, leading the Mets and Cubs in the NL Eastern Division, but even with a solid team and a new stadium they were not attracting big crowds. On July 23 against the Atlanta Braves, they drew only 14,327 fans. One night later, the stadium was packed, 43,290 in attendance. It was not the game that brought them, but the man being honored. July 24 was Roberto Clemente night at Three Rivers Stadium. In the crowd were several planeloads of Puerto Ricans who had been flown up for the event, many of them wearing pavas, the traditional straw hats of *Jíbaros,* the island's rural peasants. Ramiro Martínez, the Cuban-born announcer and jack-of-all-trades who had moved to San Juan in the early 1960s, and had first met Clemente when the Montreal Royals played the

Havana Sugar Kings in 1954, helped organize the ceremonies, which were bicultural in every respect, half conducted in Spanish, half in English.

There were tables of plaques and gifts, but at Clemente's request fans who wanted to show their appreciation were asked to donate money to Children's Hospital. Juliet Schor, his devoted young fan, wearing a body cast from her back operation, was one of the youths who took the field to receive the charitable check for the hospital. Vera and the three little boys, all wearing suits, were there, along with Doña Luisa and Don Melchor, who had turned to a psychiatrist to help him overcome his fear of flying so that he could visit Pittsburgh for the first time at age eighty-seven. His friends Carol and Carolyn came over from Kutztown, along with Carolyn's new husband, Nevin Rauch, and sat with Stanley and Mamie Garland, Phil Dorsey, and Henry and Pearl Kantrowitz, his American extended family.

The Puerto Rican side of the ceremony began more than an hour before game time, as the park was still filling with fans. The snug, new Pirates uniforms did not flatter all who wore them, but Clemente came out looking perfect, even in their new tight-fitting synthetic clothes. His family sat on folding chairs behind him on the side of the field as Ramiro Martínez took the microphone and began the proceedings, which were being broadcast on radio and television back to Puerto Rico. He introduced the entire family. Melchor said he was very proud. Luisa said it was an honor to be in Pittsburgh with all the Puerto Ricans who came to honor Roberto. Vera said she was very touched and grateful. Robertito said his daddy was the best baseball player in the world. One by one, the Latin players, José Antonio Pagan, Orlando Peña, Manny Sanguillen, and Matty Alou, came out and embraced their friend. Then Martínez invited Clemente to speak. Clemente stood silent, hands on hips, his hat off, looking down. "Oh, Ramiro, before we get started, I'd like to send a big hug to my brothers . . ." His voice was soft, surprisingly sweet and lyrical to those who had not heard it before. He tried to continue, but choked up. Martínez, a showman never at a loss for words, filled the silence.

"That's okay. We understand the emotion," Martínez said. "Roberto is reliving the last forty-eight hours. He has been nervous [with] doubts, emotions, as this moment has been approaching. This is the greatest moment of his existence. We'd like for him to say some words for us. Some words that are surrounded by tears. Men cry, but when men cry it is because their hearts are turning in happiness. And this evening, Roberto Clemente's words for you . . ."

Little Ricky, his youngest son, had escaped from an adult's grasp and toddled toward first base. Robertito, the oldest son, mistook his father's tears for sadness and wondered what had gone wrong. Clemente continued, slowly.

"Ramiro, I would like to dedicate this honor to all the Puerto Rican mothers. I don't have words to express this thankfulness. I only ask those who are watching this program and are close to their parents, ask for their blessing, and that they have each other. As those friends who are watching this program or listening to it on the radio shake each other's hands as a sign of friendship that unites all of us Puerto Ricans. I've sacrificed these sixteen years, maybe I've lost many friendships due to the effort it takes for someone to try to do the maximum in sports and especially the work it takes for us, the Puerto Ricans, especially for the Latinos, to triumph in the big leagues. I have achieved this triumph for us the Latinos. I believe that it is a matter of pride for all of us, the Puerto Ricans as well as for all of those in the Caribbean, because we are all brothers. And I'd like to dedicate this triumph to all Puerto Rican mothers . . . and Ramiro . . . as I've said, for all those Puerto Rican athletes, for all of those who have triumphed and those who have not been able to. And that is why I don't have words to express this thankfulness. And especially to see my parents, who are already old. The emotion that it gives them. And I want to send a hug to my brothers, Osvaldo, Andres, and Matino, Fafa [his niece, Rafaela], and all my friends in Puerto Rico, thank you."

For the Pittsburgh-oriented half of the ceremony, there were more gifts, an entire yellow pickup truck full of them, and heroic words from his pal the Gunner, Bob Prince, voice of the Pirates. *¡Arriba! ¡Arriba!* And when it was over everyone rose and thunderous applause waved across the new stadium and Clemente tipped his cap in recognition. He thanked the fans again during the ball game by the way he played, cracking two hits and making two of his trademark sliding catches, before Murtaugh took him out for another standing ovation in the eighth inning.

In the locker room afterward, reporters jostled around him as Bartirome worked on a cut on his knee. *What was going through your mind as you stood out there during the ceremonies?* he was asked. Sometimes, the honest answer is, nothing. This time, for Clemente, the heartfelt answer was, everything.

His whole life raced through his mind, he said, going back to the old house in Carolina on Road 887 and his first baseballs made of socks and bottle caps, and taking the bus to Sixto Escobar to watch Monte Irvin play, and how Roberto Marín believed in him when no one else did, and how Pancho Coimbre and other great Puerto Ricans never got the chance, and how hard he had fought over the years to be understood and recognized for who and what he was, a proud Puerto Rican. Maybe he cried, he was not ashamed to cry, he said. He was not crying from pain or disappointment. But if you knew the history of his island, the way he was brought up, the Puerto Ricans were a sentimental people, and his feelings now were about his island and all of Latin America, and how proud he felt when he stepped on the field knowing that so many people were behind him, and how lucky he was to be born twice, in a way, once in Carolina in 1934 and again in Pittsburgh when he arrived in 1955. "In a moment like this, your mind is a circular stage," he said. "You can see a lot of years in a few minutes. You can see everything firm and you can see everything clear."

11
El Día Más Grande

IN BALTIMORE ON THE EVE OF THE 1971 WORLD SERIES, Vera Clemente was deeply concerned about her husband. She had seen Roberto this sick only once before, when he was bedridden, delirious, and losing weight in the spring of 1965. Then it had taken his doctors in Puerto Rico several days to determine that he had malaria. Now the cause was obvious: food poisoning. Earlier that night, Vera, Roberto, and two of his teammates, José Antonio Pagan and Vic Davalillo, had joined a festive party of family and friends for dinner at a restaurant in nearby Fort Meade, where Vera's brother, U.S. Army Captain Orlando Zabala, was stationed. Roberto had ordered clams, and by the time they returned downtown to the Lord Baltimore Hotel he was so sick the team doctor had the dehydrated star hooked up to an IV at his hotel bed. "I was so worried," Vera said later. "Tomorrow is the first game of the World Series. He was so weak. I said, 'Oh, my God, maybe he cannot play.'"

The next morning, after a troubled night, the thirty-seven-year-old Clemente was still weak but determined to play. Only his wife and a few others knew of his illness. The press was preoccupied with the latest discomforts of another Pirate, Dock Ellis, a nineteen-game winner with a sore arm but indefatigable mouth who was scheduled to start the series opener.

During the National League playoffs against the Giants, Ellis had reaffirmed his freewheeling reputation by carping about his hotel bed in San Francisco. Now, before throwing his first pitch in Baltimore, he had switched rooms three times and made headlines by saying whatever entered his mind. He had always been a free-talker, Ellis said, it was just that no one listened until he started winning. "I'm never sorry for anything I say," he explained. "If you don't say what you want in so-called America, I might as well go to Russia." This riff was tame for Ellis, whose eccentricity was amplified by his counterculture predilections for Jimi Hendrix, greenies, dope, and acid, which he once dropped before pitching a no-hitter against San Diego. (The ball appeared to have comet tailings as it soared toward the plate, he said.) None of his beefs about hotel rooms compared with his declaration at mid-season, after he was named to the All-Star team, that he would not be chosen to start because another black pitcher, Vida Blue, was starting for the other league. (In fact, Ellis did start, and was on the mound when Oakland's Reggie Jackson cracked a memorable early career home run off the right-field light tower at Tiger Stadium.) But in the so-called America of 1971, Dock Ellis was a kaleidoscope of color in what many thought would be a monochromatic World Series.

Pittsburgh and Baltimore were solid baseball towns, but there were no teams from New York or Los Angeles for the media machines to hype, and baseball seemed on a downward trend in any case. A Louis Harris survey released that week showed that among the major American sports, football and basketball were rising in popularity while only baseball had declined from the previous year. Baseball games took too long, people complained, and there was not enough action. The consensus in the sporting press was that Orioles versus Pirates was a one-sided matchup that would do nothing to reverse the trend. The O's came into the series as defending champions, winners of 101 games, riding a fourteen-game winning streak that included four shutouts in the waning days of the regular season and a sweep of Oakland for the American League pennant. The Pirates, after losing to Cincinnati in the playoffs a year earlier, had finally captured the National League pennant this time by defeating the Giants, and had run up a respectable ninety-seven wins during the regular season, yet few gave them a chance against Baltimore. In place of the Murderers' Row that the Pirates had faced in their last World Series against the slugging Yankees in 1960, this time they were going up against a fearsome quartet on the mound. Good pitching beats good hitting is the first truism of baseball, and Baltimore had superlative pitching, with four twenty-game winners: Dave McNally, Jim Palmer, Mike Cuellar, and Pat Dobson.

"Now they'll learn about agony," a San Francisco writer, reflecting the common wisdom, said of the Pirates after they had defeated the Giants. "Now they have to play the reigning champions of the Universe and the light and dark sides of the moon."

Clemente entered the World Series overshadowed again. His magnificent talents as a hitter and fielder were duly acknowledged (*Right Field: Roberto is there, and what do you say about a player who can do it all?* read a position report in the *Baltimore Sun*), yet he was not at the center of the discussion. While writers quoted Dock Ellis, many Orioles talked about how much they feared Willie Stargell, who was coming off a career year of forty-eight home runs and 125 runs batted in. That Stargell had gone hitless in the playoffs against the Giants only made Baltimore fear him more. "Willie scares the hell out of me," said catcher Elrod Hendricks. "Hitters like him don't stay in a slump very long." Brooks Robinson, the Baltimore third baseman who had made a lifetime's worth of spectacular plays against Cincinnati in the last World Series, said he had watched the Pirates on television several times and was impressed by the power of Bob Robertson. He would "cheat a little," Robinson said, and move a step or two closer to the line when the strapping young infielder came to the plate, since he tended to pull everything.

This lack of attention was exactly what Clemente needed to prepare himself for the occasion. Phil Musick, a Pittsburgh writer who had endured Clemente's wrath and come out on the other side, respecting him, considered him "headstrong and prouder than a lion," and always thought that his enemies "real or imagined, weren't worth the passion he invested in them." Perhaps they weren't, but the key phrase was "real or imagined." The truth is they were mostly imagined, and they were imagined for the very purpose of stirring passion. Roy McHugh, the *Pittsburgh Press* columnist, had studied Clemente for years and struggled to understand him, and concluded that he used every perceived slight to his psychological advantage. "Anger, for Roberto Clemente, is the fuel that makes the wheels turn in his never-ending pursuit of excellence," he reasoned. "When the supply runs low, Clemente manufactures some more." And so, offered another chance to show his genius to the world, here came Clemente, at age thirty-seven the oldest player in the World Series, fueling himself with the anger of an underappreciated artist. Hours before the first game, even as he recovered from food poisoning, he told some teammates not to worry, this was his moment, and he was ready for it, and he would not let them down. José Pagan heard him recite precisely what he would do to win the championship for Pittsburgh.

In the final days of the season, Orioles scouts Jim Russo and Walter Youse tailed the Pirates. They traveled on the National League club's plane and stayed at the same hotel. If an opposing player were caught stealing signs from second base, or a team hid someone behind a center-field scoreboard hole for the same purpose, all hell could break loose. But scouts were allowed to infiltrate the very bloodstream of another team. It was part of the code of baseball. The Orioles gave the same courteous treatment to Howie Haak and Harding Peterson of the Pirates organization.

Russo and Youse returned from their scouting mission with several tips for Orioles manager Earl Weaver and his staff. One strong recommendation was that the Orioles throw lefties at the Pirates, even though Pittsburgh had a 29–19 record against left-handed pitchers during the regular season. They felt that lefthanders might handcuff Stargell and encourage Danny Murtaugh to keep two tough young Pirates hitters, Richie Hebner and Al Oliver, on the bench. And no NL team had a pair of southpaws the quality of Dave McNally and Mike Cuellar. Weaver tabbed McNally to start games 1 and 4 or 5, and Cuellar to pitch Game 3 and be ready if necessary to pitch Game 7. Among the Orioles aces, young Jim Palmer, who would pitch games 2 and 6, had the most flash and brilliance, but McNally indisputably was the leader of the staff. Over the past four years he had been the best left-hander in baseball, winning nearly three of every four decisions. He had won twenty or more games each of those years; this year, a McNally classic, he had finished with twenty-one wins and only five losses.

Game 1, on the Saturday afternoon of October 9, followed predictable form. Clemente doubled in the first off McNally—had he recovered fully from the food poisoning or was he just once again reinforcing the belief that he played best when sick? In either case, Stargell stranded him by striking out, and the Pirates were able to scratch out only two more hits off McNally all day, another by Clemente and a run-scoring single from Dave Cash, the young second baseman whose stellar play had relegated Maz to the bench. Stargell was now 0–17 in the postseason; Clemente had extended his World Series hitting streak to eight games. Aside from a few uncharacteristic blunders in the second inning that allowed the Pirates to score three runs, the Orioles looked smart and dominant. Ellis, his arm as zipless as the double-knit uniforms, failed to survive the third, giving up two home runs and four runs before being yanked. Fans at Memorial Stadium, remembering his insults of their town's hotels, showered him with boos, which Ellis said was nothing because he had once played winter ball in the Dominican Republic.

The key hit came in the third with Orioles shortstop Mark Belanger on second, left fielder Don Buford on first, and center fielder Merv Rettenmund at the plate. At breakfast that morning, kidding around with his nervous father, who supervised a body shop in Flint, Michigan, Rettenmund had boasted that he would hit a home run. Steady rains and football games had made such a mess of the stadium recently that groundskeeper Pat Santarone resorted to dyeing barren spots in the outfield. Now, as Buford led off first and studied Ellis on the mound, he detected a wide splotch of dark green on the baseball and shouted down to the plate urging Rettenmund to ask for a new ball. Rettenmund did, and the bright white replacement never touched dyed ground, flying from Ellis's right hand to Rettenmund's bat and over the fence for a three-run homer.

Solo homers by Buford and Frank Robinson, the great Orioles right fielder, made the final score 5–3. Ellis, the loser, was out for the rest of the series, his sore arm beyond the help of the finest bed in Baltimore. The star was McNally, with his three-hit complete game. Only three days earlier, his eight-year-old son Jeff had been injured in a bike accident near their home in Lutherville. Once McNally was assured that his son had not suffered brain damage, he had been able to focus on the Pirates, his powers of concentration aided on this day by the best fastball he had shown all year.

In the locker room after the game, reporters asked Clemente whether he had ever faced such a pitcher as McNally. Given his competitive nature, his determination to show the world his greatness once and for all, this was not a question he wanted to hear. His answer sounded ungracious if not egotistical, with a touch of Muhammad Ali or Dock Ellis to it. It was not so much a boast as an assertion of will. "I faced lots of good pitchers," he said. "Another good one don't mean anything to me. Ask him what he thought about me. I got two hits off him so I say we're even."

Eleven years earlier, before the second game of the 1960 World Series, it had rained all night and kept raining until an hour before the first pitch, but the bad weather system rumbled past Pittsburgh just in time and the game was played as scheduled. Pittsburgh surely would have preferred a rainout—the Pirates got clobbered by the Yankees that day, 16–3. Now, for the second game of the 1971 series in Baltimore on Sunday, October 10, the rains would not stop and the game was postponed for a day. Orioles ownership urged Bowie Kuhn, the commissioner, to reschedule the second game for 7 Monday night, so that ticket-holders from the rainout would have a better chance of attending, but Kuhn rejected that request and made it a Monday day game. Night baseball was coming to the World Series all too soon, but Kuhn wanted to hold fast to his plan to hold the historic first night game in Pittsburgh a few days later.

After the Sunday game was called, the Clementes returned to Fort Meade to have dinner again with Orlando Zabala and his wife, Norma. No bad clams at the restaurant this time. They ate at home and Roberto invited more teammates and friends to join them. Carol Brezovec's mother, Carolyn, now married to Nevin Rauch, came down from Kutztown, Pennsylvania, and brought several blueberry cheese pies, Roberto's favorite. After dinner, the men played cards and little children ran around and Nevin Rauch taught Clemente how to play his Horner harmonicas. "It was wonderful, just wonderful," Carolyn Rauch remembered.

But it was of no help to the Pirates. The next day, in keeping with second game tradition, they got slaughtered again, losing 11–3. First Lady Pat Nixon threw out the first ball and had as much stuff as the six Pirate pitchers who followed in pathetic procession, from Johnson to Kison to Moose to Veale to Miller to Giusti. Veale replacing Moose at least provided the press box material for carnivore jokes. Instead of the monstrous Mickey Mantle home runs that destroyed them in 1960, this time the Pirates were done in by fourteen well-placed singles. The M and M boys of Mantle and Mays were replaced by the R and R boys of Brooks Robinson and Frank Robinson. Frank Robinson led off three innings with hits and left the game in the eighth to a standing ovation. Jim Palmer continued the O's pitching mastery, holding the Pirates scoreless until he tired in the eighth and gave up a three-run homer to Hebner. The loss showed how difficult it is for a lone outfielder to control a game, yet it also revealed Clemente's transcendence.

In the midst of the carnage, he got two more hits and made a throw from right that did nothing overtly to change the course of that particular game, and indeed did not even result in an out, yet became the most remembered play of the entire series. In the fifth inning, as the Orioles were pounding out six runs, Rettenmund was on second when Frank Robinson looped a ball deep down the right-field line into the swirling winds. Clemente raced over and grabbed it with one hand. Rettenmund tagged and advanced to third, certain that no human, not even Clemente, could make this a close play. But Clemente caught the ball, swirled, and fired toward third and—*¡Arriba!*—the ball arrived on a perfect line at the same time as Rettenmund. Decades later, Hebner could still see the play unfold in front of him, and remain amazed by it. "He was in another zip code in right field," Hebner said. "He turned around and this ball got to me pretty damn quick. Usually a ball would take three or four hops from that spot in the outfield. He threw an absolute cannon. Rettenmund tagging up on a ball like that was probably saying, 'This is a piece of cake.' I had the ball and he was sliding. I said, 'Wow, this is close!' When I look at it now—I see the 1971 Series on TV a lot—I think he was probably safe. At the time, I thought he was out. Of course [Clemente] had the same uniform on. But to make a play that good . . . if I'm an umpire and somebody throws it that good from that far, I might bang him out. After the play was over, I was like, wow, If somebody got my ass at third base like that I would have been embarrassed. The ball got there like it had some hair on it when it came in. And he was like thirty-seven when he did it!"

Andy Etchebarren, watching from the Orioles dugout, said it was the best throw he had ever seen. Danny Murtaugh, in the Pirates dugout, had witnessed too many impossible deeds by Clemente over seventeen seasons to go that far. He and other Pirates had their own collection of greatest-ever Clemente throws, most involving some variation of the time he let loose a bullet from the deepest corner of old Forbes Field and the ball zipped just over the heads of relief pitchers in the bullpen down the right-field line and stayed no more than seven feet off the ground—easy to cut off, but what infielder would dare?— all the way until it smacked into the catcher's mitt at home plate knee-high, without a bounce. Clemente, when asked about the Rettenmund throw, did not feign modesty. "Ask the other players," he said. "They remember a few years ago when my arm was really strong. No one can compare with my arm when it feels right. I'm not bragging. That is a fact." Dick Young, the columnist for the *New York Daily News,* had become a great admirer of Clemente, yet chose to quote him in pho-netic English on the same subject: "Eef I have my good arm thee ball gets there a leetle quicker than he gets there."

The 1971 Pirates were a boisterous lot: Blass, Dave Giusti, San-guillen, Veale, Nellie Briles, Stargell—Dock Ellis wasn't the only one who said what he wanted to say. But after Game 2 no one was saying much of anything. Clemente looked around the locker room and saw all the heads hanging low. Not good, he thought, and he decided to speak. "I just say some things in the clubhouse when they have their heads down," he explained later. "I tell them not to worry about it. We're going to Pittsburgh and that's our ballpark. When fellows have their heads down, you have to pep them up. If I put my head down they'll say, 'Why try?' A man they trust, if he quits, everyone quits . . . I said, 'Hold on, we're gonna do it.'"

At the same time, in the press box, the baseball writers had all quit, or were urging the Pirates to quit, hauling out their bag of death-knell clichés for Clemente's club. It was always this way with the reporting tribe. They had done the same thing to the Pirates in 1960. Arthur Daley of *The New York Times,* who had declared Pittsburgh dead after three games in 1960, needed only two games this time to call for an executioner "to put the poor devils out of their misery." David Condon, in his "In the Wake of the News" column for the *Chicago Tribune,* relied on his repartee with Earl Weaver to make the same point. He was just about to ask the Orioles manager whether there was even much sense in continuing the series, Condon wrote, when he heard Weaver say that he took Palmer out of the game near the end because he might need to use him again. "That's what the Baltimore man said. Honest. Honest. Honest. After slaughtering the Pirates twice to take a 2 game to 0 lead. Weaver says he might need Palmer again. The laugh that greeted his remark was the loudest heard in Baltimore since H. L. Mencken used to rip off some rib-splitters. There was a report that Weaver's jest, when repeated, even drew some grins in the Pirate locker room, which was no more lively than a funeral parlor."

At the head of the pack was Jim Murray of the *Los Angeles Times.* With Murray at least, it was as much about the way he made his points as the points he made. Murray was not one for understatement; his style was all metaphor all the time. "This World Series is no longer a contest," he began. "It's an atrocity. It's the Germans marching through Belgium, the interrogation room of the Gestapo. It's as one-sided as a Russian trial . . . The Pirates should ask where they go to surrender. It should rank with such other great contests of history as the St. Valentine's Day Massacre, the yellow fever epidemic, and the bombing of Rotterdam. To enjoy it, you'd have to be the kind of person who goes to orphanage fires or sits at washed-out railroad bridges with a camera . . . They're taking the execution to Pittsburgh today. Unless the Red Cross intervenes."

At home in Pittsburgh on the night before Game 3, Clemente could not sleep. Vera stayed up with him until dawn, and they talked about everything but baseball. Then she made him breakfast: pork chops, three eggs, always sunny side up, fruit shake; it seemed like his breakfast feast would fill the entire table. After eating, he retreated again to the bedroom where they darkened the room by pinning the drapes to the walls with black rubber tape, and finally he got a few hours' rest.

Steve Blass, slated to pitch that day for the Pirates, had also stayed up all night, anxious about the game. He lay in bed thinking about the Orioles hitters, and what he would say to the press if he won, or what he would say if he lost. In Baltimore during the first two games, he had slipped into the clubhouse to study the Orioles batters on the television monitor and had taken copious notes, but left them in the hotel room so they were of no use to him now. He went out for breakfast with his father and thought he was starving but when the food came he couldn't touch it. All he had was some "toast and a few pulmonary wheezes."

Before the game, as usual, Blass and Clemente met in the trainer's room at Three Rivers Stadium. Clemente was getting his neck massaged by Tony Bartirome. Blass sat nearby, trying to settle his nerves. Those two hours before walking out to the mound were the worst part of the day for him. He tried to take his mind off the game by leafing through *Penthouse*, a skin magazine. Bartirome looked over at Blass as he gazed at the photographs of nude women then turned to Clemente and said, "Well, Robby, look what we got our fuckin' money on today, this pervert!" As for Blass, just being in the vicinity of Clemente was reassuring. Every time his turn came in the rotation, he'd look at the lineup, see the name Clemente, and say to himself, "Robby's playing and there's peace in right field."

It was Blass against Cuellar on the afternoon of October 12 as a sellout crowd of 50,403 filled Three Rivers. The Red Cross did not intervene, but Blass and Clemente did. In the first inning, Clemente knocked in a run to give the Pirates a lead they never relinquished. In the fifth, he singled to extend his World Series hitting streak to ten games. In the bottom of the seventh, with the Pirates leading 2–1 in a tight pitching duel, he took a fierce cut at a Cuellar screwball but failed to hit it squarely, chopping a high bouncer back toward the mound. Cuellar casually waited for it to come down, and when he turned to throw to first there was Clemente busting down the line as though he had a chance to beat it out. Cuellar hurried his throw and pulled Boog Powell off the bag, allowing Clemente to reach safely on the error. Of all the plays before and after, this is the one that would haunt Orioles manager Earl Weaver—not a home run or great catch or throw, but the sight of thirty-seven-year-old Roberto Clemente making a mad dash to first on a routine ground ball back to the pitcher. "The most memorable play of the series," Weaver said decades later. "The one that I think turned it around, the key to the series, when [Clemente] ran hard after tapping the ball back to Cuellar on the mound. Cuellar took his time, looked up, and Clemente was charging to first, and it surprised him and he threw it off target . . ." As it turned out, this was the equivalent of the little dribbler Clemente had hit in the seventh game of the 1960 World Series off Jim Coates in the bottom of the eighth, the ball that Skowron had fielded down the first-base line but could not make a play on, setting the stage for Hal Smith's dramatic three-run home run.

Cuellar, flustered, now walked Willie Stargell on four pitches, bringing up first baseman Bob Robertson with runners on first and second. Robertson to that point was hitless in the series and had lined out and struck out twice in three previous at-bats against Cuellar. He took the first pitch for a ball, then fouled off the next. From the Pirates dugout, Danny Murtaugh noticed that Brooks Robinson was cheating by two or three steps, as he had said he would against the big right-handed pull hitter, playing deep and close to the line. Murtaugh gestured to third-base coach Frank Oceak, who flashed a sign down to the plate. Robertson gave no recognition that he received the sign, so Oceak went through the motions again. From second base, Clemente sensed the confusion and raised his hands over his head, attempting to call time. But it was too late; Cuellar was in his windup. In came a screwball, a few inches outside, and out it went, soaring into the seats in right center. Only as Robertson touched home plate and Stargell congratulated him with the words "That's the way to bunt the ball!" did he realize what he had done. "Guess I missed a sign," he said sheepishly when he reached the dugout. "Possibly," responded Murtaugh, smiling.

That was the game, the Pirates winning 5–1. Blass went the distance and gave up only three hits, including a solo home run to Frank Robinson. He said it was the best game he had ever pitched.

Few spans in American history involved more cultural change than the eleven years between the Pirates' World Series appearances of 1960

and 1971. The social revolutions of the 1960s were trivial and profound, obvious and complex, in baseball as in society at large. It is a
long way from Deacon Law to Dock Ellis. The Pirates club of 1960
was still rooted in the old school. Ten players on that roster had been
born in the 1920s and a few were veterans of World War II. They were
crew-cut white guys, mostly, with nicknames like Tiger and Rocky and
Vinegar Bend and Smoky. From that squad, only two players were still
around when the Pirates returned to baseball glory in 1971—Bill
Mazeroski, hero of the 1960 series with his dramatic bottom-of-the-
ninth seventh-game home run, and Roberto Clemente. Maz, now
thirty-five and approaching retirement, was cut from the old school
mold, with his square jaw and West Virginia coal miner heritage, but
he had adjusted comfortably to the new. He sat on the bench, mostly,
and tutored young Dave Cash and Rennie Stennett, and joked with
the youngsters about Clemente and the old days. When the proud
Clemente, sensitive about his modest home run totals, tried to tell the
kids about one of his old tape-measure shots, Maz responded, "Nah,
he didn't hit that one very good"—sending Clemente into a playful
funk about the "dumb Polack." Manny Sanguillen, the ebullient Panamanian catcher, worshipped Clemente, but turned to him in the clubhouse once and announced that Maz was his hero. "Okay, Polack,"
Clemente responded.

There were many reasons why Clemente felt more at ease with the
1971 Pirates than the earlier team. Much of it was him—he was older,
wiser, more established and secure. But much of it was the composition of the team. On the 1960 roster, there were only four players of
color during the season—Clemente, Gene Baker, Joe Christopher, and
Roman Mejias, and only Clemente got much playing time. The 1971
squad was dominated by blacks and Latins: Dave Cash, Roberto
Clemente, Gene Clines, Vic Davalillo, Dock Ellis, Mudcat Grant,
Jackie Hernández, Al Oliver, José Pagan, Manny Sanguillen, Willie
Stargell, Rennie Stennett, and Bob Veale. Late in the season, in a September 1 game against the Phillies, without fanfare and little notice
beyond the clubhouse, the Pirates in fact had fielded the first all-black
and Latin lineup in major league history—Stennett at second, Clines
in center, Clemente in right, Stargell in left, Sanguillen catching, Cash

at third, Oliver at first, Hernández at short, and Ellis on the mound. Hebner, the normal third baseman, was out with a minor injury, and Bob Robertson, who usually played first against lefties (southpaw Woody Fryman was on the mound for the Phillies), was being rested by Danny Murtaugh.

It only lasted an inning—the Phils knocked Ellis out in the second by scoring four runs—but it was another marker in the long road traveled since Jackie Robinson came up with the Dodgers in 1947, and Curt Roberts broke the color line with the Pirates in 1954, and Clemente played as the team's lone black starter through the remainder of the 1950s. Just as sports were a step ahead of society on civil rights matters, the racial transformation of the Pirates moved more quickly than the attitudes of Pittsburgh fans. The correlation was anecdotal, not methodologically established, but fan fervor in Pittsburgh, a predominantly white blue-collar city, seemed to decline as the team's racial composition changed. Bruce Laurie, who attended graduate school in Pittsburgh during that era, lived in an apartment on North Dithridge Street and often encountered "a beefy big-boned guy named Jim" on the first floor, who would "sit on a beach chair at night in the warm months with a couple of quarts of Iron City beer and a radio"—but never listened to a ball game. As Laurie, who became a history professor at the University of Massachusetts-Amherst, later recounted the scene, whenever Jim was asked the score of a Pirates game, he would never answer—"until one day when I asked him why he didn't follow the Pirates. 'Too dark,' he snorted. 'Too many niggers.' I think the feeling was widely shared."

On Wednesday, October 13, Game 4 of the 1971 series made baseball history for a more prosaic but nonetheless sport-changing reason. There had been 397 World Series games staged over nearly seventy years, and this was the first one held at night. The dominance of black and Latin players made the Pirates no less popular on this night. The prime-time weekday game drew the largest crowd in Pittsburgh history—51,378, and the largest national television audience in history, more than 61 million. The hurler-rich Orioles brought out their fourth-best pitcher for the occasion, Pat Dobson, who sported a mere 20–8 record with eighteen complete games and a 2.90 earned-run average, all of which would have made him the ace of the Pittsburgh staff. The Pirates countered with Luke Walker, who won ten games that year on his way to a 45–47 career. A pitcher turned out to be the story of the game, but it was neither Dobson nor Walker, but Bruce Kison, a twenty-one-year-old sidearmer for the Pirates who entered with two outs in the first inning and threw six and a third innings of shutout ball, giving up only one hit and walking none, though it would be hard to say he had pinpoint control, since he hit three batters. He seemed less nervous about facing the veteran Orioles hitters than he was about getting married at the end of the week. After jumping to a 3–0 lead in the first off Walker, the Orioles never threatened again and lost the lead for good in the bottom of the seventh on a game-winning pinch-hit single by another kiddie corps Pirate, twenty-one-year-old catcher Milt May.

Clemente shone again, rapping out three hits. He was so hot that the Three Rivers organist played "Jesus Christ Superstar" every time he strolled to the plate. The Baltimore scouts, in going over Pirates hitters before the series, had no clue how to pitch to Clemente. Try low and away, they said, and if that doesn't work try something else. "How to pitch Clemente? There was no way," Earl Weaver observed later. "But we tried to pitch him inside. Jam him. But he'd hit anything. We couldn't get him out." The best play against Clemente on this night was made by the umpire down the right-field line, John Rice. In the third inning, with the Pirates still trailing 3–2, Dobson tried to pitch Clemente outside, but Clemente went with the pitch, slashing the ball straight down the right-field line. It cleared the ten-foot fence at the corner, but the question was whether it was fair or foul. Rice called it foul. Don Leppert, the first base coach, insisted that it was fair, and raced out toward Rice to argue, joined quickly by a furious Clemente. From most vantage points it looked like a fair ball, a home run. Leppert insisted then and decades later that he saw the ball hit fair. The problem was that there was a gap between the fence and the stands of about twenty inches, and that gap made it difficult to follow the white stripe that was painted below the foul pole to serve as the demarcation between fair and foul. According to a few Pirates relief pitchers who had a fairly close perspective on the ball, it was indeed foul by no more than an inch or two.

After the argument, Clemente strolled back to the plate and thwacked another hit, a single. Kison was the main story, but the rumble in the press box was starting to grow louder about the wonders of the oldest man on the field. Not only was he hitting everything the Orioles threw at him, and making great throws from right, but he also was running superbly on the base paths, taking an extra base that night on Paul Blair, just as the day before he had raced down the line to beat a double-play throw, along with the hustle he showed on the dribbler that flustered Cuellar. "The best damn ballplayer in the World Series, maybe in the whole world, is Roberto Clemente," wrote Dick Young. "And as far as I'm concerned they can give him the automobile [as the outstanding player] right now."

In Game 5, the Orioles returned to Dave McNally, but the Pirates sent out their fifth different starter in five games. This time it was Nelson Briles, who was the 1971 team's version of Vinegar Bend Mizell— a veteran who came over from the St. Louis Cardinals to stabilize the rotation. Briles had pitched six seasons for the Cards, and had won nineteen games in 1968, his best season. Then major league officials, reacting to the utter dominance of pitching that year and the resultant lack of scoring, lowered the pitching mound. Briles suffered more than most from the change, until he altered his pitching motion in an effort to replicate the action of his old overhand curveball. His new motion left him off-balance, tumbling from the mound. In one game he fell down eleven times. Against the Orioles on Thursday, October 14, he fell down three times—which was one more than the number of hits he gave up to Baltimore's hitters. Briles was virtually unhittable. He allowed only singles to Brooks Robinson in the second and Boog Powell in the seventh, and left only two runners on base in pitching a 4–0 shutout. When he came to bat in the eighth, Pittsburgh fans rose for a thunderous ovation and Briles was overcome by emotion. Among his many talents, Briles was an actor who could draw on his emotions to appreciate a scene. In college at Chico State in California, he had even played the lead character, Joe Hardy, in *Damn Yankees*, and now, though not selling his soul, he was living out his own Joe Hardy moment. The fans could not see it, but Briles was crying as he stood at the plate and thought about the struggles of the last two years and all the people who had helped him reach this point, back to his high school coach.

Clemente singled up the middle in the fifth, driving in a key run and extending his World Series hitting streak to twelve straight games. "He's showing the others how to play the game, isn't he?" longtime baseball executive Lee McPhail said in the press box after the game. There was something about Clemente that surpassed statistics, then and always. Some baseball mavens love the sport precisely because of its numbers. They can take the mathematics of a box score and of a year's worth of statistics and calculate the case for players they consider underrated or overrated and declare who has the most real value to a team. To some skilled practitioners of this science, Clemente comes out very good but not the greatest; he walks too seldom, has too few home runs, steals too few bases. Their perspective is legitimate, but to people who appreciate Clemente this is like chemists trying to explain Van Gogh by analyzing the ingredients of his paint. Clemente was art, not science. Every time he strolled slowly to the batter's box or trotted out to right field, he seized the scene like a great actor. It was hard to take one's eyes off him, because he could do anything on a baseball field and carried himself with such nobility. "The rest of us were just players," Steve Blass would say. "Clemente was a prince."

The prince was a pip in the locker room after the game, with the Pirates now holding a three games to two lead in the series. "I've always felt I've been left behind," Clemente told the national press corps gathered around him. And then came his long lament—how he was tired of reading that he was second best, and hearing that he had one of the best arms, instead of the best arm; and that he was a hypochondriac, when in truth he would soon pass Honus Wagner for most games played in a Pirates uniform; how some players would only dive headfirst for a ball in the World Series but he always played that way, the Clemente you saw in this series was the Clemente who played every day; how he never got enough endorsement offers because he was black and Puerto Rican; and how he is really a happy person, not some sourpuss, but only smiles when the occasion calls for smiling. Roy McHugh took it all in with some bemusement. He had heard this many times before. McHugh thought the Pittsburgh press gave Clemente a better accounting than it got credit for, and that it was disingenuous of big-city writers to swoop in and pretend they understood him in a way the locals did not—but it was all part of the sportswriting dodge. And Clemente knew precisely what he was doing. His passion play had become an act, a ritual, part of what it meant to be Clemente. "When he was younger, Clemente reached passionate heights of eloquence on the subject" of his being misunderstood, McHugh thought. "Dark eyes ablaze, his voice would rise to a shout. Now he is just a trooper going through a performance, dressing it up with subtle touches of humor and not unaware of the effect he is having on his audience."

The main effect Clemente had on his audience was to increase the talk about his prowess at the end of a long career played in the relative obscurity of Pittsburgh. Had he spent his baseball days in New York, Boston, Chicago, or Los Angeles, he would have been a national icon already, a living legend, and now was his chance to make up for lost time. When a visiting writer asked a Pittsburgh man in the press box whether Clemente had ever run and thrown and hit like this before, the simple response was, yes, every day. But the out-of-town sportswriters had not seen him play every day, until now. "He wants to be appreciated," wrote Steve Jacobson of *Newsday*. "That's why he plays the game so hard, making his old, spraddle-legged mad dash on the bases, burning in his throws from right field, and generally behaving as if his reputation were on the line every day." The way Clemente was going, wrote Bob Maisel of the *Sun*, he could extend his World Series hitting streak until he was a hundred. "Put it altogether and you have about as good a player as there is in the game. He has a license to hurt you." Jim Murray praised Clemente after doing his version of Carl Sandburg on Pittsburgh: "This is where they poured the steel that forged the cannon, that laid the track. Toughtown, U.S.A. America's glare in the sky. One million guys in bowling shirts with Tick Tock Lounge stenciled on the back. A town that needed a shave twice a day. Hard coal and molten iron. The sinew of America. It was all power, and guys who dunked doughnuts in hot coffee, and worked the mills till the sweat ran black across their backs and down their eyes . . . But the greatest player this town will ever see came not out of the crucibles or the mine shafts or the ore boats, but out of the canebrakes of the Caribbean." It was common for the World Series to produce an unlikely hero while the big names flopped, Murray added. "It's nice to see a great player living up to his greatness. It's about time 60 million people got in on a legend and not just Toughtown, U.S.A. It's nice to see a great artist giving people goose pimples instead of just goose eggs."

There were two outstanding right fielders in the 1971 series, and by the time the teams returned to Baltimore for Game 6 the contest in some ways had become a test of wills between Roberto Clemente and Frank Robinson, on and off the field. Since the first practice in Baltimore before Game 1, Clemente had complained about Memorial Stadium, saying the outfield was the worst in the major leagues, full of holes and ditches that made it hard to charge the ball, and with lights positioned so that it was hard to see the ball in the air. The reporters dutifully reported the criticisms to Robinson, who said he appreciated Clemente and did not want to start a feud, and then in essence started one by adding: "Why, until the middle of last year Roberto played in a coal hole himself [Forbes Field]. Sure, there are shadows in our park. He's supposed to be a great outfielder, though. He should adjust. If he has any trouble . . . just tell him to watch me in the outfield and stand where I stand."

Robinson, a year younger than Clemente, had come up with the Reds in 1956, a year after Clemente began with the Pirates, and for the next ten seasons their careers had run along parallel tracks as two of the finest five-tool right fielders the game had ever seen. But both played in the shadows of Mays and Mantle, and in those early years, before F Robby was traded to Baltimore in 1966, they had to compete not only with each other but with Henry Aaron just to land a starting berth on the National League All-Star team. Robinson lacked Clemente's flair, but always got the job done, and burned with the same aggressive fire. Each had matured into the undisputed leader of his team, the player their teammates relied on physically and emotionally. They both had surprisingly soft, second-tenor voices, yet spoke with confidence and authority. Their leadership skills were readily apparent, and had been tested during the winter league in Puerto Rico the previous winter, when Robinson managed the Santurce Cangrejeros, Clemente's original team, and Clemente managed the San Juan Senadores. The major league establishment was not yet considering the possibility of a black Latin manager, but the idea of a black American manager was now within the realm of discussion, and the man most often talked about was Frank Robinson. During the series, in fact, Robinson had made news one day by saying that he had changed his mind and thought now that he didn't want to "go through the strain, the agonies, the frustrations of managing" in the big leagues. "Managing is out for me—period!" he announced. (Never say period: Four years later, Robinson became the first black manager in the majors, taking over the Cleveland Indians, and a full three decades after *that* he would still be receiving notice as the skilled manager of the overachieving Washington Nationals.)

In their Game 6 showcase, Clemente could not have performed better, yet Robinson did what he had to do. While the Pirates brought out Bob Moose, their sixth starter in six games, Baltimore's rotation came around again to Jim Palmer, who went nine strong innings, leaving with the score tied 2–2 as it entered extra innings. Clemente opened the game with a booming first-inning triple. Bust him inside, the Orioles had finally decided, after failing utterly with their low-and-away theory, so Palmer came in and Roberto pulled the ball down the left-field line for three bases, but he was stranded at third when Willie Stargell struck out. In the third inning, he strode to the plate for the second time. "And now here comes Bobby Clemente," announced Bob Prince on the radio. "If there's ever been a vendetta, this might be it. Pitch to him from Palmer . . . And there's a ball hit very deep to right field. And going back for it is Frank Robinson. He's at the wall. He can't get it. It's gone for a home run. Bobby Clemente continues to totally annihilate Baltimore pitching."

That gave the Pirates a 2–0 lead. Moose pitched well, shutting out the Orioles for five innings, but left in the sixth, grousing about the balls and strikes calls of home plate umpire John Kibler. He had the support of his manager, Murtaugh, who was "getting really pissed about the umpiring behind the plate," according to Tony Bartirome, who was sitting next to him in the dugout. It was actually a strike call that hurt Moose most, ironically. Baltimore's Don Buford, trying to coax a walk, threw his bat away and started trotting to first base after a three-and-one pitch, but Kibler called it a strike, so Buford returned to the plate and promptly hit the next pitch far over Clemente's head in right for a home run, starting the O's comeback. In the top of the ninth, with Belanger on first, Buford doubled to right—but Clemente was out there, and a perfect throw kept Belanger from scoring.

To relieve Palmer in the tenth, Baltimore turned to two of its twenty-game winners, Dobson and McNally. Dobson gave up a single to Dave Cash, who stole second, placing the lead run in scoring position. In most situations such a steal would be beneficial, but here it had the same boomerang effect as the strike call on Buford in the sixth. With first base open and two out, the Orioles intentionally walked the hitter they least wanted to face—Clemente. Weaver brought in McNally to pitch to Stargell, who also walked, but Al Oliver flied out to end the inning. Frank Robinson was first up for the Orioles in the bottom of the tenth. He had gone hitless in four at-bats, but now drew a walk, then raced to third on a single by Rettenmund, and was ninety feet from home when Brooks Robinson lofted a soft fly ball to center field.

The ball was so shallow that Brooks Robinson felt disappointed as he ran to first, thinking his teammate might not be able to tag up and score. If the ball had been hit to Clemente in right, there would have been no debate: stay put. But Billy Hunter, the third base coach, figured this might be their only shot. In center field now was Vic Davalillo, who had entered the game as a pinch hitter in the ninth. They could challenge his arm, even though he had almost nailed the runner at third on Rettenmund's single. Frank Robinson had barely avoided Richie Hebner's tag with a daring headfirst slide. Now Hunter turned to him and said, "You're going!" Robinson had already decided that he was going in any case. Davalillo, from the corner of his eye, saw the runner tag as he made the catch. He decided it was too far to reach the plate on a fly, so he fired a one-hopper toward the plate. Hunter, following the throw from near the third base box, thought F Robby was dead at home if the ball took a true bounce to Sanguillen, the catcher. Sanguillen, his attention divided between the ball and the shadow of the runner barreling toward him, also thought he had time to make the play. But the ball hit the grass in front of the plate and took a high, slow bounce, forcing Sanguillen to jump up and then lean back to try to make the tag. F Robby, churning down the line with his spindly thirty-six-year-old legs, slid in safely—game over. The series was now tied three games apiece.

In the visitors' locker room before the start of Game 7 on Sunday, October 17, Clemente moved from one teammate to the next, reassuring them. "Don't worry," he said, again and again. "We are gonna win this game. No problem."

Two of his best friends on the team, Pagan and Hernández, who would comprise the left side of the infield, felt lucky just to be there. Pagan, knowing that he would start at third against the left-handed Cuellar, was so anxious at the hotel before the game that he decided to take an early cab instead of waiting for the team bus. Hernández came with him. As the taxi hurtled north and then east from downtown to Memorial Stadium, a little too fast for Pagan's comfort, a Volkswagen bug ran a stop sign, forcing the cabbie to swerve and slam on the breaks, spinning the vehicle in three full circles before it came to a stop. So close—and yet as it turned out the carnival-like taxi ride might have been just the shakeup José Antonio Pagan and Jacinto Zubeta Hernández needed to excel in the most important game of their lives.

The capacity crowd of 47,291 started a clamor before the opening pitch and maintained a steady roar throughout. It was Cuellar and Blass again, and both pitchers were in command. Cuellar retired the first eleven Pirates in order until Clemente, neck rotating, made his regal stroll to the plate with two outs in the fourth inning. This was a grudge match, Clemente v. Cuellar. Over the winter in Puerto Rico, Clemente had managed Cuellar on the Senadores, and it had not gone well. Cuellar thought Clemente was unreasonably demanding, and said so. The rub of their relationship was only aggravated by that dinky little play in Game 3, when Clemente discombobulated the pitcher with his mad dash to first base. Now the Orioles were still following their revised game plan to pitch Clemente inside. When Cuellar came in, Clemente turned on the ball and pulled it 390 feet over the left-field wall, putting the Pirates ahead, 1–0. With the crack of the bat, something like an electric jolt zapped through the Pittsburgh dugout. Clemente had said all along that he would win this thing. Murtaugh looked around and realized that the home run had "set off a chain reaction" among his players. Now they believed him.

Cuellar, unruffled this time, remained virtually unhittable, setting down ten of the next eleven batters until Stargell singled in the eighth. Up came Pagan, Clemente's Puerto Rican pal, the thirteen-year veteran who had recovered from a broken arm in August to share time at third with Hebner. Murtaugh flashed the hit-and-run sign to Oceak, who relayed it to Pagan. Stargell, taking off with the release of the pitch, was around second when Pagan's liner fell beyond Rettenmund's reach in deep left center, and came all the way home when the outfielder had trouble getting the ball out of his glove. The score was 2–0 Pirates going into the bottom of the eighth.

Blass was even more effective than Cuellar, working with an urgency that Jim Murray said made it look like "he was pitching out of a swarm of bees." Weaver had tried to distract him in the first inning, coming out of the dugout to complain that Blass was not touching the rubber on his delivery. Weaver was right, Blass would later confess. He had fallen into the habit of slipping his right foot off the rubber before releasing the ball, and for the rest of the game had to keep reminding himself not to do it. But Blass was in his own world again, at once a bundle of nerves and utterly unstoppable, shutting out the Orioles through the first seven innings. "I could hardly stand still," he said later. "I kept coming back to the clubhouse between innings and I must have opened seven Cokes, but I didn't drink any." In the bottom of the eighth, catcher Elrod Hendricks got a leadoff single, and Belanger followed with a soft single to center. Cuellar, up third, hit a bouncer back to the mound, and Blass, ignoring Sanguillen's shouts to go for the force at third, took the sure out at first instead. Runners on second and third, one out. Buford bounced to Robertson at first, who stepped on the bag for the second out, allowing Hendricks to score.

Blass now led 2–1, a runner on third, two outs. He was so nervous he could barely stand still, and paced a full 360 around the mound before approaching the rubber to face Davey Johnson. Jackie Hernández, at short, remembered from Howie Haak's scouting reports that Johnson pulled the ball, so he moved a few feet toward third. Earlier in the year, after making a game-losing error, Hernández had been inconsolable in the locker room. "I'm nothing!" he had said, head bowed. It was Clemente who sought him out and reassured him that he was an important member of the team and that everyone makes mistakes. All anyone could ask was that he give it everything he could. When Earl Weaver questioned how the Pirates could win with Hernández at short, Clemente stood up for him again. Now, with a runner on third and the series in the balance, Hernández was so confident that he *wanted* the ball hit to him. And it was—Johnson slashed one deep into the hole, and Hernández moved expertly to his right to field the ball and make the long throw for the third out. One inning to go.

In the top of the ninth, Blass was so nervous he couldn't watch his team bat. He came into the clubhouse and threw up and was so psyched he couldn't stand still. When the Pirates were retired, he was "scared to death." He had to force himself up the steps and out of the dugout to the mound. O's fans were roaring. They had Boog Powell, Frank Robinson, and Rettenmund coming up, with Brooks Robinson waiting if anyone got on base. It had been cloudy all afternoon, but suddenly the sun came out. Blass figured he would throw strikes and hope for the best. They couldn't all hit home runs off him, he joked to himself, because after the first homer Murtaugh would yank him. There were no homers, no hits, just Blass, one last time, setting down the heart of the order, and with the final out he jumped and bounded and leaped until he landed in the arms of Manny Sanguillen. Clemente sprinted in from right field and bounced down the steps and into the delirious locker room, where Bob Prince, the Gunner, was rounding up interviews.

"I can't believe it. I don't know what to say," Blass told Prince. "The biggest thrill that could ever happen. A skinny kid from Connecticut . . ."

"Any moments when you were really worried?" Prince asked.

"There were several. One was a hanging slider to Davey Johnson, but he missed the pitch. I can't believe it! How many people have this kind of opportunity."

Blass, drenched in champagne, headed off to hold court with the rest of the press horde. At one point he picked up the ringing telephone and answered, "Wally's Delicatessen," then, going into a Bob Newhart–style routine, he continued . . . "What? You want to talk to Clemente? Spell that please. Clemente who?"

Willie Stargell came in arm-in-arm with Jackie Hernández. Clemente stood nearby. He had just been named the outstanding player in the series, finishing with a .414 average, hits in every game, extending his World Series streak to fourteen, two doubles, a triple, and two home runs, along with his stellar base running, fielding, and throwing. Roger Angell, the pitch-perfect baseball writer for the *New Yorker*, described Clemente's performance over the seven games as "something close to the level of absolute perfection"—and no one disagreed. Prince turned to Clemente in the locker room. "And here with me now, the greatest right fielder in the game of baseball. Bobby, congratulations on a great World Series . . ."

"Thank you, Bob," Clemente said to Prince. "And before I say anything in English, I'd like to say something in Spanish to my mother and father in Puerto Rico . . ."

An ebullient Blass stepped in and blurted out, "Mr. and Mrs. Clemente, we love him, too!" It was spontaneous and joyful, but Blass would later wince whenever he thought about his interruption.

After seventeen seasons in the major leagues, this was Clemente's time, with the world listening and watching at last, having seen him perform at his best, carrying his team for seven games—and he made a conscious decision to speak first in Spanish. It was one of the most memorable acts of his life, a simple moment that touched the souls of millions of people in the Spanish-speaking world. *"En el día más grande de mi vida, para los nenes la bendición mia y que mis padres me echen la bendición.* [In the most important day of my life, I give blessings to my boys and ask that my parents give their blessing] . . ."

Later, when the television cameras were off, Clemente stood on a bench in the dressing room, surrounded by reporters, and let it out one more time, a stream-of-consciousness monologue that fluctuated between pride and fury and grace. "Now people in the whole world know the way I play," he began. "Mentally, for me, I will be a completely different person. For the first time, I have no regrets." Completely different? The words were the same, still evoking his underappreciated past, but there was a barely repressed smile as he continued. He wanted people to know, again, that he played this way all the time, all season, every season. And that he wasn't a hypochondriac. And that he could pull the ball when he wanted to. And that he was tired of writers adding some qualifying "but" to their comments about him. He didn't play for himself, he said. He was happy the Pirates won because it was a team effort all year and it was great for the Pittsburgh fans. This win was more satisfying than 1960. George Hanson of the *Montreal Star* was on the edge of the crowd, not far from Manny Sanguillen.

"He's going pretty good, eh?" Sanguillen said. "Everything he is saying is true, you know. It's strange that he would have to remind people. Everyone should know it."

At the White House, President Nixon placed a call to Danny Murtaugh, the winning manager, and said he thought it was a team victory even though Roberto Clemente and Steve Blass were so outstanding. In a classic Nixon-the-sports-expert moment, he also said he was impressed with how the Pirates second baseman, Dave Cash, had played all year. Murtaugh thanked the President for taking time out from his serious duties to call. Nixon then phoned Earl Weaver in the other locker room. "Hey, Pop, I just spoke to your boss!" the Baltimore manager called out to his father, a retired parking meter collector and longtime rank-and-file Republican in St. Louis. Weaver was also visited by Secretary of State William P. Rogers, who attended the game. A short time later, Nixon and Rogers had a brief telephone conversation, recorded by the White House taping system.

NIXON: You saw a good game, didn't you?
ROGERS: Great game. I went into the locker room the way you
        did . . . we were so pleased you called . . .
NIXON: Two great teams and could have gone either way, but boy . . .
ROGERS: Well, I'm sort of glad to see Pittsburgh win because that
        Clemente is so great.
NIXON: Oh, my God. Unbelievable. Unbelievable. Really . . .

The Pirates by then were on the charter flight back to Pittsburgh. The pitching star, Blass, and his wife, Karen, were in seats near the wing. Clemente and Vera were seated farther back. Blass was staring out the window, still trying to process what had happened, when he heard a familiar voice. Clemente was standing in the aisle. "Blass, come out here," he said. "Let me embrace you."

That joyous hug, Blass said later, was his deepest validation.

Three days later, on the afternoon of October 20, Clemente was at Mamma Leone's restaurant in New York to accept the *Sport* magazine award as outstanding player of the series. The award was a new car, a Dodge Charger. Among the many guests and writers at the event inside the dimly lit restaurant was Stu Speiser, a plaintiffs attorney who specialized in airplane crashes. Viewing the Clementes for the first time, Speiser thought they "seemed to be unreal people, sculptured out of bronze instead of ordinary flesh and blood like those surrounding them." Even in a business suit, Clemente "conveyed power and intensity." He had a charisma that Speiser had seen only once before in an athlete, in Pelé, the great Brazilian soccer player. Like others in the crowd, Speiser was expecting very little beyond a few jokes and drinks and slaps on the back, all the normal sporting world pleasantries. But Clemente had a deeper purpose. He spoke with a "huge, bursting beautiful heart," recalled Roger Kahn, the sensitive chronicler of the Brooklyn Dodgers, who might have featured Clemente in his renowned book *The Boys of Summer* had the Dodgers not failed to protect the young player.

Over the past year, Clemente's speeches, even in his second language, had become sharper and more powerful. He had a specific goal, the creation of a sports city in Puerto Rico, but also a more urgent sensibility, one that he had first articulated at a speech in Houston back in February 1971, before the start of his championship season, when he received the Tris Speaker award. "If you have a chance to accomplish something that will make things better for people coming behind you, and you don't do that, you are wasting your time on this earth," he had said then, and the line had become his mantra. Now, at Mamma

Leone's, he said that he was gratified by the attention he had received because he could divert it to better use, turning his sports city idea into a reality.

"The World Series is the greatest thing that ever happened to me in baseball," he said. "Mentally it has done for me more than anything before. It give me a chance to talk to writers more than before. I don't want anything for myself, but through me I can help lots of people. They spend millions of dollars for dope control in Puerto Rico. But they attack the problem after the problem is there. Why don't they attack it before it starts? You try to get kids so they don't become addicts, and it would help to get them interested in sports and give them somewhere to learn to play them. I want to have three baseball fields, a swimming pool, basketball, tennis, a lake where fathers and sons can get together . . . one of the biggest problems we have today is the father doesn't have time for the kids and they lose control over the children . . ."

In the audience, Speiser noticed that Clemente was choking with tears as he talked about the poor kids of Puerto Rico and the need to treat all people with dignity. He did not intend to waste his time on this earth. "If I get the money to start this, if they tell me they'll give us the money this year and I have to be there, I'll quit right now," Clemente continued. "It's not enough to go to summer camp and have one or two instructors for a little time and then you go home and forget everything. You go to a sports city and have people like Mays and Mantle and Williams and kids would never forget it. I feel the United States should have something like this all over. If I was the President of the United States I would build a sports city and take in kids of all ways of life. What we want to do is exchange kids with every city in the United States and show all the kids how to live and play with other kids. I been going out to different towns, different neighborhoods. I get kids together and talk about the importance of sports, the importance of being a good citizen, the importance of respecting their mother and father. I like to get together with the fathers and sons and talk to them. Then we go to the ball field and I show them some techniques of playing baseball."

12
Tip of the Cap

WHEN CLEMENTE CAME HOME TO PUERTO RICO THAT winter, he sought comfort in the rituals of his island life. He drove the family out to *la finca*, their rural retreat in the shadows of the El Yunque rainforest, and on the way home after a long weekend stopped to buy crabs from his favorite roadside vendor, Don Palito. Momen was a fanatic about crabs, he seemed to have an insatiable appetite, and bought them by the dozens and dozens. The stop at Don Palito's was a great adventure for Robertito, Luisito, and Ricky. They stared with fascination as the vibrating jumble of live critters scrambled around in the big caged containers. But this time, once the family returned to the house on the hill, Roberto and Vera were distracted for a few minutes, the cage opened, and the soon-to-be-boiled crabs made a mass jail break, scuttling for freedom. Most of the escapees were rounded up by the hungry ballplayer, but for a week or more afterward the boys would suddenly come across a vagrant crab as they played in the far reaches of the house.

Everyone wanted to hang around the Clemente house that winter, crustacean and human alike. His place in Río Piedras became "like a museum," he said, with "people from town and even tourists" stopping by night and day, "walking through our rooms" or just stopping outside on the street until they sighted *El Magnífico*. The governor sent for him, the parks administrator wanted help, every civic club in San Juan had to honor him, every banquet hoped he would speak. The demands were so relentless that Clemente made it back to *la finca* only one more time. Finally, in late November, he and Vera escaped by embarking on a month-long tour of South America. They visited Caracas, Rio de Janeiro, São Paolo, Buenos Aires, Santiago, and arrived in Lima, Peru, on an Avianca flight on the morning of December 17. When they reached the front desk of the old Gran Bolívar Hotel downtown on the historic Plaza San Martin, there was a message to call the family in Puerto Rico. Word came that Don Melchor had collapsed and was in the hospital. Without unpacking their suitcases, the Clementes returned to the airport and caught the next flight home. In his moment of triumph after the World Series, Momen had asked for the blessings of his father, but now it seemed that the baseball triumph and all the celebrations that followed were a bit much for the old man, who was approaching his eighty-seventh birthday.

As soon as Clemente returned to San Juan, he visited his father at the hospital. Deep into old age, Melchor still seemed indestructible, his body toughened by decades in the canebrake and miles of walking the dusty country roads every day. His organs were weakening, but doctors said it was not life-threatening; all he needed was medication and bed rest. On one visit, Clemente started talking to the patient in the next bed who shared a room with Melchor. The man said he was in great pain and was in the hospital to undergo a back operation. The words back and pain caught Clemente's attention, and soon he had spread a blanket on the bathroom floor and was stretching the man's legs and kneading his back with his magical fingers as Vera guarded the door to make sure no doctors or nurses came by. The next day, the man reported that his pain was gone and that he felt like he was walking on air. "God bless you," he said to Clemente, and broke into tears.

The word about Roberto Clemente's healing powers had spread throughout the San Juan area. Sick and sore friends of friends would make pilgrimages to the house on the hill at all hours of the day and night seeking his magic, and if Clemente was available he would treat them. If only he could ease his own aches and troubles so effectively. He was sleepless again, staying up through the night, every night, until four or five in the morning. Robertito, now almost seven years old, also had insomnia, and sometimes slipped downstairs to find his dad playing pool. Vera was a sound sleeper, but she stayed up many nights keeping Roberto company as he worked on his decorative arts. He had two specialties now: tables and furniture pieces crafted from driftwood he collected on the Atlantic beach; and ceramic lamps, brightened by marbles that he heated in the oven until they exploded. But the hectic schedule and lack of sleep were taking a toll. He had lost ten pounds, down to 175, and his stomach was hurting. Vera developed sympathetic stomach pains. The requests kept coming, and Clemente had a hard time saying no.

"Since I've been back to Puerto Rico, I've been having my problems," Clemente said one night in January 1972 at a banquet of fathers and sons in San Juan. The speech was recorded by his friend, the broadcaster Ramiro Martínez, who tailed him wherever he went that winter.

"I think the World Series was too much for my father," Clemente continued. He spoke of his deep love for his parents—"the most wonderful mother and father who ever lived" as an introduction to the themes of sports, competition, country, teamwork, and parenthood. Though his extemporaneous speeches had the rhythm of stream-of-consciousness, they integrated the disparate threads of his life—as a Puerto Rican and an American citizen, as a ballplayer who loved his game, as a black and Latino, as a former Marine, as a believer in the underdog, and as someone who refused to be undervalued or dismissed. "All my life I have to thank God to make me a sports figure because I love competition and I think competition is part of the way that we are living today," he said. "I love competition because when we compete, we compete to be proud of our country. I see myself sometimes wondering why some people still have to fight for their rights. As you people know, I have been fighting for my rights all my life. I believe every human being is equal. At the same time, we also have problems because we are a great nation." For all of Clemente's struggles adjusting to the culture and language of his baseball life on the mainland, he felt very much a part of the United States. "I am from Puerto Rico, but I am also an American citizen," he continued. "We have an opportunity to travel. I just came from South America. I've been in Europe . . . I can tell you one thing, I won't trade this country for no one country. We, no matter what, we have the best country in the world and you can believe it."

The World Series victory was still on his mind. "I always say to myself that we athletes should pay the public to come and see us play. Because if you see what we saw in the World Series, what we see when we play ball, I guess I don't have any money to buy the feelings inside the clubhouse. This year to have the opportunity to see Willie Stargell have the greatest season I've ever seen a player have . . ." He meant this as a gesture of goodwill to his friend and teammate who had been overshadowed in the series after carrying the Pirates much of the year. He would never forget the sight of Stargell and Jackie Hernández bounding into the locker room arm-in-arm after the seventh game, a picture of solidarity.

Life is nothing. Life is fleeting. Only God makes man happy—so went his mother's favorite spiritual verse. But Clemente looked for the lasting meaning in fleeting life. "As you know, time goes so fast," he told the San Juan audience. "And we are living in a really fast life. You want to have the opportunity to have sons . . . We come home from work, sometimes our kids are in bed already. We go back to work, our kids are already in school. So sometimes we hear how bad our kids are, and how bad our American schools are. This is a big world and we are going to have our problems, but I think that we can help our difficult youth. We can give them the love and more attention to our home, our kids, our family, and our neighbors. We are brothers. And don't say, 'Well, I don't want to do it. Somebody else will.' Because you are somebody . . ." His closing message took on more urgency every time he said it. If you have a chance to help others, and don't, you are wasting your time on this earth.

In his eighteenth spring with the Pirates, after all he had accomplished, Clemente chose to live like a rookie. Many veterans rented houses on the beaches or golf courses around Bradenton, the Gulf Coast town that had been the team's Grapefruit League headquarters for four years, but Clemente stayed in Room 231 at the four-story dorm at Pirate City on Twenty-seventh Street East. In late afternoons after practice, he was surrounded by young players and hangers-on who wanted to soak up his advice. "A lot of us young guys would just sit there and listen to him," said Fernando González, a rookie infielder from Arecibo, Puerto Rico, who had admired Clemente since he was a ten-year-old collecting autographs when winter league teams stopped at El Gran Café in his hometown on bus trips between San Juan and Mayagüez. "Clemente would talk about the way that baseball was going to be . . . situations in games . . . almost everything."

Also hanging around was Roy Blount Jr., who came down to Bradenton to do a feature story on the hero of the 1971 World Series for the *New York Times Magazine*. Writing under the felicitous pseudonym C. R. Ways, which he later told Pittsburgh writers was the name of his dog, Blount took note of how Clemente "strolled the team's Pirate City complex in his long-collar tab shirts and brilliant slacks, as vivid a major leaguer as there is . . ." While dutifully visiting the stations of Clemente's cross—his maladies and complaints, his sore feelings going back to the 1960 MVP vote, his distaste for being quoted in broken English—Blount found a humorist's delight in Clemente's eccentric style, which he considered representative of Latin players who "in the 20 years since they began to enter American baseball in numbers from Cuba, Mexico and South America, have added more color and unexpected personal drama to the game than any other ethnic group." The headline on the piece was "NOBODY DOES ANYTHING BETTER THAN ME IN BASEBALL," SAYS ROBERTO CLEMENTE . . . WELL, HE'S RIGHT. Full recognition from New York, at last, just what Clemente had always wanted. The article had Blount's sweet touch and was mostly accurate, yet reflected an attitude that could upset Clemente. The quirks of his personality were irresistible, but Clemente more than anything else wanted to be treated seriously, not as a stereotype, even when the stereotypes were true.

There had been another changing of the guard with the Pirates. Murtaugh was gone, again, his career capped by a second championship, and Bill Virdon, who had prepped for the job in San Juan, was now Pittsburgh's manager. Perhaps the only situation as thankless as managing an abysmal team is taking over World Series winners. Virdon inherited a talented squad, yet had nowhere to go but down. His best player, Clemente, was nearly as old as he was and slowed that spring by stomach pains. "The other day I went out to buy an Osterizer [blender] when you called me," Clemente wrote Vera one early March evening. "It is the only time I've left here since I arrived. I've tried to control my nerves to see if that helps my stomach." Even if the accounting of his time sounded like an absent husband's fib, the stomach trouble was real.

Clemente's life was far more than baseball at that point in his career. In his letter to Vera he wrote about plans to open a chiropractic clinic. "God willing, we can move forward this clinic proposal," he said. He had already bought a one-story house at the bottom of his hill in Río Piedras to treat neighbors, a modest beginning to his larger idea of someday running a chiropractic resort. He was also preoccupied with his plans for a sports city for underprivileged youths in San Juan. And Jim Fanning, then the general manager of the Montreal Expos, said that Clemente called him four or five times that spring hoping to persuade the Expos to move their spring training headquarters to San Juan. Yet when it came to baseball, Clemente kept looking for new methods of enhancing his powers of concentration. Late one afternoon after practice, when the major and minor league players had retreated into the clubhouse, Harding Peterson, the farm and scouting director, walked out to the fields and was surprised to see a lone figure in the distance, near the batting cage. "It is Clemente, and there is no one there but him, and he is standing at home plate," Peterson remembered. "And he makes a stride but doesn't swing, then makes a stride and swings, and runs three quarters of the way to first. I don't want to bother him, but I go up to the batting cage and say, 'Hey, Roberto, don't want to interrupt, but what are you doing?' And he says, 'Well, I know we're opening against the Mets. I'm making believe I see the same pitches I see on opening day.'" In Clemente's mind, Peterson realized, Tom Seaver was on the mound, throwing sliders low and away.

The season was scheduled to open April 5, but there were no games that day, and none for the next nine days. On a vote of 663 to 10, the players had voted to strike until the owners agreed to improvements in the health and pension plans. It was the first full strike in major league history, and reflected the transformation of the players association in the more than five years since labor experts Marvin Miller and Richard Moss were hired. Earlier, the U.S. Supreme Court had once again upheld baseball's antitrust exemption, deciding the Curt Flood case against the player, but the struggle for player freedom was not over, and the court had directed organized baseball to resolve the issue on its own. Clemente strongly supported the strike, though he had passed along the job of Pirates' player representative to Dave Giusti, the relief pitcher. The strike ended abruptly in a victory for the players, and the Pirates opened the season in New York against Seaver and the Mets on April 15. Clemente's spring training pantomime proved of no help as he went hitless in four at-bats.

As loose as the 1971 Pirates were, the 1972 team was even looser. It was virtually the same squad, but more confident and comfortable after winning the championship, and the culture was becoming more informal year by year. From the perspective of the early twenty-first century, when goatees seemed to come with the issuance of a major league uniform on some teams, it is difficult to imagine that Reggie Jackson and his Oakland A's were breaking with more than a half-century of tradition that spring by daring to sport facial hair. The Pirates were still clean-shaven, but the irrepressible Dock Ellis had a vibrant Afro in the works, and the prevailing antiestablishment mood meant that everything was fair game in the clubhouse, including old man Clemente. Ellis and Sanguillen mimicked "Grandpa" by limping and moaning when they saw him heading to the trainer's room. Clemente had his own antics; he enjoyed holding his nose to mimic the nasal drone of the team physician, Dr. Finegold. (This routine was a surefire hit at home, where little Robertito would say "Do Dr. Finegold" and then fall on the floor laughing to the point of tears.) Giusti and Clemente were constantly yapping at one another. "The byplay between them became almost a ritual for us," recalled Steve Blass. "Any subject and suddenly they'd be hollering and insulting each other. Robby was our player rep before Dave and when something would come up, he'd say, 'When I was the player rep we never had these kinds of problems, but you give an Italian a little responsibility and look what happens!'"

His confidence boosted by his flawless World Series performances, Blass got off to a brilliant start in 1972 and remained strong all year, leading one of the deepest staffs in Pittsburgh history. There were no weak spots in the rotation: Blass would win nineteen games with a 2.49 earned-run average, followed by Ellis with fifteen wins and 2.70, Briles, fourteen and 3.08, Moose, thirteen and 2.91, and Kison, nine and 3.26. From the bullpen Virdon turned to an effective right-left duo of Giusti, who had twenty-two saves, and Ramon Hernández, who had fourteen. Clemente naturally thought he could pitch better than any of them. "Come here, Blass, I gonna tell you one fucking thing," he would say, warming up before a game. "Look at this fucking breaking ball"—and he would uncork what Blass regarded as a pathetic attempt at a curve. "Robby," Blass would say, "you couldn't get anybody out with that if your life depended on it."

Among the many characters in the clubhouse, third baseman Richie Hebner stood out because of his off-season job as a gravedigger in Massachusetts. When opposing players slid into third, Hebner would joke that he gave discounts to major leaguers. Clemente felt a bond with Hebner since they had both served in the Marines Corps, but he was spooked by his teammate's occupation. "He'd say, 'You dig graves?' I'd say, Yeah, somebody's got to dig them," Hebner remembered. Clemente, he said, seemed skeptical. "'You bury people?' he'd ask. I'd say, 'Come up in the middle of winter and you can dig one yourself, then you can tell me if I'm full of shit.'" One day, Clemente had been taking a nap in the trainer's room with a towel over his head and awoke to find Hebner hovering over him. "What are you doing?" Clemente asked. "I thought you were dead," Hebner said, deadpan. "I'm measuring you up to see what size casket I got to get you, buddy."

Although he went hitless the first two games, Clemente quickly came alive in the batter's box that season and began rapping out his usual rataplan of base hits. The better the pitcher, the better Clemente hit. Bob Gibson, homer; Don Sutton, homer; Ferguson Jenkins, triple. Through early July, he was playing five or six times a week, with Virdon resting him on day games after night games or part of a double-header. His stomach was still hurting, and he kept losing weight until finally a sore heel took him out of the lineup altogether. He missed twelve consecutive games until July 23, when he started and drove in two runs, but left in pain and was out again through the first half of August. He was selected to the July 25 All-Star game in Atlanta, which was held later than usual because of the April strike, but withdrew from the contest because of injuries.

With Stargell, Oliver, Hebner, Robertson, Sanguillen, Cash, Davalillo, Clines, and Stennett all clubbing the ball, the Pirates were so loaded that they kept winning without Clemente, and by August 20 they were thirty games over .500 with a 72–42 record. Clemente returned to the lineup during the final West Coast trip of the season and slowly got back into his hitting groove. Fernando González, the young Puerto Rican, had joined the team after a stint in the minors, and quickly became Manny Sanguillen's foil. "Hey, Roberto," Sanguillen called out in Spanish during a flight from Pittsburgh to Montreal in September. "Fernando says you are not a good ballplayer. He has been here watching you play and you are no good." González was terribly embarrassed. He had adored Clemente since he was a kid, and now here he was on the same plane with him, and it seemed that Clemente was taking Sanguillen seriously. "I know, I know," Clemente said. "I don't get the recognition I deserve!" The next day, in the visitors clubhouse, González approached Clemente and apologized. "I didn't say anything like that," he said of Sanguillen's claim. "Don't pay any attention to them," Clemente assured him. "They like to get on me,"

González would sit on the bench next to Clemente after that, trying to learn as much as he could. After Montreal, the Pirates reached Chicago on September 12, and by then no one could get Clemente out. He went three for four in the first game, then three for three with a homer and triple and game-winning home run against Ferguson Jenkins the next day. In an early inning, González watched Clemente take a strike on the right-hand corner of the plate. "I know you can hit that ball good," González said to him the next inning on the bench. "You'll see why I took it later in the game," Clemente said. In the seventh, he was up with a man on and Jenkins threw the same pitch to the same spot and Clemente knocked it over the fence in right-center. "When he came to the bench, he said, " 'That's why I gave him that pitch in the first at-bat,'" González recalled. "He was doing things by that time that I never saw anyone do and I haven't seen anyone do since. He was like a computer. He was set to play baseball. He always knew what he had to do."

What he had to do that year was collect 118 hits to reach three thousand, a mark reached then by only ten players in major league history: Ty Cobb, Stan Musial, Tris Speaker, Honus Wagner, Hank Aaron, Eddie Collins, Nap Lajoie, Willie Mays, Paul Waner, and Cap Anson. After going eight for twelve in Chicago, Clemente was within fourteen hits of the magic number. Four hits against the Cardinals, three against the Mets, one against Montreal, and he was down to six as the Pirates made their final visit of the year to Philadelphia. By then the team had clinched the National League's Eastern Division title on its way to a 96–59 record.

Before the series against the Phillies, Clemente had called his friends Carolyn and Nevin Rauch in Kutztown and asked them to meet him in Philadelphia. When they arrived at the Pirates' hotel, they realized that they had not made reservations, but Clemente insisted that they stay in his suite with him. "We stayed and we talked and talked and talked," Carolyn Rauch said later. "And then he stood up, and we were getting ready to go to the game, and he said, 'I want to talk to you, Carolina.' You never knew what to expect next. He said, 'I want you and your family to come to Puerto Rico for the [New Year's] holidays.' I thought, yeah, sure, we can make it. Plenty of time to make arrangements. And he said, 'But promise me right here, right now, that you will come and you will bring [daughters] Carol and Sharon.'"

Recalling the scene more than three decades later, Carolyn Rauch said she still got chills thinking about it. "I said, 'Okay, Roberto, we will gladly come.' He said, 'I'm telling you why. I'm not going to be there. Something's going to happen and I want you to be with my family.'"

At the ballpark that night, the Rauches asked themselves what he meant. Why did he want them to come to Puerto Rico if he wasn't going to be there? What did he mean something was going to happen to him? Did he already know about a trip? Did it have to do with baseball?

Against the Phillies, Clemente rapped out two hits on September 26, two on September 27, and one the next day, reaching 2,999 hits after two at-bats, when Virdon pulled him so that he could reach the milestone before the hometown fans in Pittsburgh. What did three thousand hits mean to Clemente? "To get three thousand hits means you've got to play a lot," he told reporters in Philadelphia. "To me it means more. I know how I am and what I've been through. I don't want to get three thousand hits to pound my chest and holler, 'Hey, I got it!' What it means is I didn't fail with the ability I had. I've seen lots of players come and leave. Some failed because they didn't have the ability. And some failed because they didn't have the desire."

For baseball games, a capacity crowd at Three Rivers Stadium was 47,971. Barely half that many people came to the stadium on the night of September 29 to see Clemente seek his three-thousandth hit against the Mets and Tom Seaver. Clemente versus Seaver was an even match of two talented, intelligent, strong-willed players. Seaver was in awe of Clemente's powerful hands and how he could stand there "far away from the plate, with that great big long bat, and those strong hands and control it like crazy, hitting pitches on the side of the plate." There was one spot, outside at the knees, where Seaver thought Clemente was vulnerable. If you hit that spot, he would just look at the pitch and walk away. But if you missed it, the ball would go screaming to right.

The drama this time almost came to a quick and unsatisfactory close. Clemente strode to the plate in the first inning, acknowledged a standing ovation from the crowd, and then took a mighty cut at a Seaver fast ball. He barely topped the ball. This had happened before in Clemente's career. Though this time the ball bounced a little higher and went a little further, the play was reminiscent of the dribbling hit between the mound and first in the eighth inning of game seven of the 1960 World Series, and the topper back to Mike Cuellar in the third game of the 1971 series. After the ball bounded high past Seaver, second baseman Ken Boswell moved over to make the play, but it skipped off his glove and Clemente reached first. The scoreboard light immediately flashed H for hit. A roar went up, and toilet paper streamers unfurled from the stands.

Would the quest for three thousand end with a meager infield hit? First baseman Ed Kranepool flipped the ball to the umpire, who handed it to first base coach Don Leppert, who patted Clemente on the rear. But in the press box, Luke Quay of the *McKeesport Daily*

News, the official scorer for the game, jumped up in alarm. The scoreboard had it wrong; he had not ruled it a hit. "Error, second baseman. Error, Boswell," Quay announced on the press box microphone. The lights went off the H on the scoreboard and the E lit up for error. More toilet paper, followed by a round of boos. This was no day for hitting in any case. Seaver and Nelson Briles locked up in a pitcher's duel, with Seaver prevailing 1–0, striking out thirteen and allowing only two hits, to Oliver and Hebner. Clemente had one other chance at a hit. Seaver came in with a slider low and away—the very pitch he had envisioned in his preseason pantomime—and Clemente sliced it deep down the line to right, but Rusty Staub had been playing him toward the line and made the play.

After the game, Clemente was at his most churlish, feeling wronged again. Even now, with another World Series championship ring and a milestone unavoidably within reach, anger could be the fuel that drove him, as Roy McHugh had earlier observed. But was he really peeved, or was it just a show? When Dick Young of the *New York Daily News* reached the Pirates locker room, Clemente was in the whirlpool, his neck sticking out of the water, a sardonic grin on his face. He said he was celebrating being robbed of his three-thousandth hit by "the assholes in the press box."

So you think it was a hit? someone asked.

"Think? I know it was a hit. Everybody knew it was a hit."

But Boswell himself said it was an error, Clemente was told.

"He's full of shit. Anyway, I'm glad they didn't call it a hit. They've been fucking me all my life, and this shows it."

Then it was pointed out to Clemente that Luke Quay was the official scorer. Clemente liked Quay immensely and thought he had always been fair to him. So much for the they're-out-to-get-me routine. Abruptly, Clemente's mood changed. This was something that all the sportswriters had known about Clemente for years. He would erupt, but his anger would pass, and if he was proved to be wrong, he would apologize. When the postgame show was over he got a baseball and wrote on it . . . *It was a hit. No it was an error. No it was superman Luke Quay. To my friend Luke with best wishes, Roberto Clemente.*

The next morning at eleven, fourteen-year-old Ann Ranalli and two friends from St. Bernard's parochial school in Mount Lebanon caught a streetcar into downtown Pittsburgh, got off near Grant Street, and walked over the bridge to Three Rivers Stadium. The girls carried brown paper bags of confetti they had created from strips of the *Pittsburgh Press* the night before. Ranalli loved baseball, and loved Clemente even more. There was something unusual about him, she thought. "He was quirky . . . He always seemed to be his own person, on and off the field." She wanted to be there cheering him on when he got his three-thousandth hit. On this misty, overcast day, they entered the stadium and went up to the right-field bleachers to find seats. No problem. Ranalli was disappointed when she looked around and saw such a measly crowd. Where is everybody? she thought. How could you not be out here for this? The official attendance was 13,117. Clemente's teammates were equally distraught to see the virtually empty stadium as they warmed up. But it was a college football Saturday. "Pittsburgh was such a football town, even with the good teams we had," recalled Richie Hebner. "It was a shitty, overcast day. Saturday afternoon. Only thirteen thousand in the stands. There should have been more. Here a guy who had played there eighteen seasons. [But] college football was on TV, money was tight, steel mills struggling . . ."

Those who were at the stadium that day, like Ranalli and her friends, were mostly die-hard Clemente fans, including a few dozen who had flown up from Puerto Rico. From the moment Roberto emerged from the dugout, he was hailed with shouts and greetings, and his every move was tracked by Luis Ramos, a photographer for the San Juan newspaper, *El Nuevo Día.* Ramos later estimated that he took twenty-five rolls of 300 millimeter film on his Nikon camera with a 4.5 lens. "I had to shoot from a distance of a hundred feet," he remembered. "Every time he picked up a bat, I shot. And I kept doing it when he was in the on-deck circle, in the dugout, when he was here, there, I didn't miss a single step." Up in the press box, along with the voice of Pittsburgh, Bob Prince, the game was being called for Puerto Rico by the Spanish-language broadcasters Felo Ramírez and Carlos DeJesus. It was Dock Ellis against the lefthander for the Mets, Jon Matlack, who after going 0–3 in a brief call-up the year before had blossomed in 1972 with fifteen wins. In the first inning, Chuck Goggin, just called up from the minors to play second for the Pirates, got his first major league hit. Doug Harvey, the second base umpire, stopped the game and gave him the ball. One down, two thousand nine hundred and ninety-nine to go to match the great Clemente, Goggin would say later. At the rate he was going it would take three thousand years. No more magic that inning; Clemente struck out.

Ramírez, the Vin Scully of Latin broadcasters, was at the microphone when Clemente stepped to the plate for the second time. "The audience is concentrated on the *boricua* behind home plate," Ramírez began. *Boricua* is how Puerto Ricans often identify themselves; it comes from the Taino Indian name for the island. "They are waiting for the pitch from Jon Matlack. The fourth inning, bottom of the fourth inning. And the windup and it's a fastball strike. The pitch was at the knees. Matlack ready again. Clemente ready at the plate . . . as always, very far away from the plate. And the windup, bye bye, he throws." Crack of the bat. Ramirez's voice rises and soars with the flight of the ball. "A double for Roberto Clemente against the wall! No-no-no! No-no-no! A double for Roberto Clemente! Completely clean double against the wall. On the pitch from Jon Matlack. Ladies and gentlemen, the fans are going crazy here in Three Rivers Stadium! Everyone is on their feet. Great emotion. They are giving Roberto Clemente the ball. He takes off his hat. He greets the public and receives the congratulations of the shortstop, Jim Fregosi. By his action, the shortstop is greeting him as the best. The fans are on their feet. The enthusiasm is huge here in Three Rivers. We are seeing a historic event, a historic event in baseball."

It was an outside curve going just where Matlack wanted it to go until Clemente thwacked it against the left-field wall. The umpires called time after the play to allow the scene to play out properly. In the excitement of the moment, Don Leppert, the first base coach, took out a package of Mail Pouch chewing tobacco and was about to stuff a wad into his mouth when Clemente came over and gave him the ball. Leppert stuck the piece of history in his back pocket for safekeeping. In the dugout, looking out at the regal Clemente standing on second base, Al Oliver was overcome by emotion. "It gave me a serious charge to see a guy who I know, who didn't get the credit he truly deserved, but to see him standing on second base, it meant a lot to me as a young player coming up. And I will never forget how it made me think, you know, here's a guy who's taking care of himself, and I said, that will be a good goal for me. I felt better about it than he did. He seemed nonchalant."

When the inning was over, Clemente walked slowly out to his position in right. Ramos followed him step by step with his zoom lens. In the right-field stands, Ann Ranalli was ecstatic. She had wanted her hero's three-thousandth hit to be more than a dribbler, more than a single, and she got what she wanted—a line shot into the gap in left-center. Now, as Clemente moved in his easy, athletic gait toward them in right, Ranalli and her friends rushed down to the rail and threw their confetti. Some of it landed on the field. Nearby, some fans from Puerto Rico were cheering loudly. Facing the bleachers, with his back to the plate, Clemente doffed his cap and raised it high. Luis Ramos caught the moment forever, in what became the most famous picture he ever shot. From the back, No. 21, tipping his cap. Ramos thought Clemente was raising his hat to God. The Puerto Rican fans thought he was acknowledging their cheers. And Ann Ranalli felt certain that he was tipping his cap to his three fans from the eighth-grade class at St. Bernard's. Over time it would seem that his gesture had a deeper meaning, that he was saying farewell.

Virdon sent in a replacement for Clemente the next inning and intended to rest him the final three games of the season, until the team's director of press relations, Bill Guilfoile, discovered that with one more appearance Clemente could break Honus Wagner's record for most games played by a Pirate. Clemente felt no urge to play; he wanted to rest for the divisional playoffs against the Cincinnati Reds, but in a late inning against the Cardinals on October 3, the second-to-last game of the season, Virdon sent Clemente out to right field for an inning, and the record was broken. He had played 2,433 games for the Pirates. Not bad for a hypochondriac, he would say.

All in all, it had been a rough year for Clemente. He had played only 102 games and hit .312, a figure that most players would envy but that was subpar for him. His fielding was superior, as usual, good enough for him to win his twelfth straight Gold Glove. But his final push for three-thousand hits left him with little energy for the playoffs, and it showed early on against the emergent Reds of Johnny Bench, Joe Morgan, Pete Rose, and Tony Perez. He went zero for seven in the first two games, which the teams split, then heated up in the next two, with a double and home run, but could do nothing to change the course of the five-game series. After Bench tied the decisive fifth game with a home run in the ninth, the Pirates ended up losing 4–3 on a wild pitch by Bob Moose. In the clubhouse later, everyone seemed down, except Clemente. He gave a spirited speech about next year, then found Moose alone in a corner, slumped in despair. "Don't worry about it anymore," Clemente told him. "It's gone. It's gone."

There had been talk when the playoffs ended that Clemente wanted to retire, but the surest evidence that he intended to keep playing came from Rex Bradley, the bat expert at Hillerich & Bradsby. Bradley made the trip from Louisville to Cincinnati during the playoffs just to talk to Clemente about his bats. "He wanted a new model made," Bradley recalled. It would be a refinement on the knobless Frenchy Uhalt bats Clemente had been using for years. The new model would be a C276, and Clemente wanted it heavier than ever, thirty-eight ounces. Bradley promised to make two bats right away and send them to Puerto Rico for testing during the winter. If Clemente liked them, he would order a few dozen.

The question of retirement was broached by Sam Nover of WIIC-TV, who recorded an hour-long conversation with Clemente on October 8, a wide-ranging interview that was perhaps the most revealing of his career. "Bobby, at thirty-eight years old, and eighteen years in the major leagues, and having accomplished everything you wanted to accomplish in baseball, I guess the thought enters your mind that one of these days it's going to be all over," Nover began. "Do you have any idea now when it will be over, and when it comes, what are you going to do with your life? What would you like to do?"

Offering no hints that he planned to retire, Clemente instead took the opportunity to delve into his philosophy of life and happiness. "People are always asking me, 'How much money do you have? Are you secure?' I don't worry about that. The only thing I worry about is being happy. If I can live. If I can for example have my health I can work. I don't care if I'm a janitor. I don't care if I drive a cab. As long as I have a decent job, I will work. I know these players that they've been rich and they lost everything they have and they kill themselves because of the money. To me, I can be a person like me—I make a lot of money, but at the same time I live the life of the common fellow. I am not a big shot. If you go outside the ball park you are never going to see me trying to put on a show or pull attention, because that's the way I am. I am a shy fellow and you see me with the same people all the time. If you want to be my friend you have to prove to me that you want to be my friend and you want to be aware that I need lots of time when I play baseball. Now in the wintertime we can be as slow as you want, but in the summertime we have to call it short. So I would say I don't worry about what I am going to do after I stop playing baseball. Probably I will stay in some capacity in baseball. But I don't worry one way or the other. I just worry that I be healthy and live long enough to educate my sons and make them respect people. And to me this is my biggest worry: to live for my kids to be people that people look at them and respect them and they respect other people."

Clemente had a busy winter ahead. He had been hired on a three-year contract by Eastern Airlines as a special sports consultant, which meant the company could use his name on promotions and call on him to speak at conventions and sales meetings. In return, Eastern would sponsor baseball clinics for underprivileged children in Puerto Rico, which Clemente viewed as a precursor to his larger dream for a sports city. The planning had already begun for clinics to be held in October and early November in Carolina, Ponce, Mayagüez, Arecibo, and Aguadilla. Clemente had also asked his friend Ramiro Martínez to help him organize a Bob Prince Day celebration for later in October. *¡Arriba!* Clemente believed that Prince had always treated him fairly, and he wanted to show his appreciation by honoring the Gunner in San Juan. (When the time came, Clemente showed how deeply he cared for Prince by presenting him with one of his most cherished possessions, the Silver Bat he was given for winning his first batting title in 1961.) And there was more: Osvaldo Gil, president of the Puerto

Rico amateur baseball federation, had asked him to manage the Puerto Rican team at the world championships in Nicaragua, a job that would take three weeks in November and early December.

On October 14, the night before he left the mainland for his off-season in Puerto Rico, Clemente joined several teammates for Al Oliver's twenty-sixth birthday party at his apartment in Pittsburgh's Greentree section. "Everybody's lips were moving," Oliver later said of the party. "That's one thing about the Pirates, all of us can talk. We enjoy talking and we really liked each other . . . Roberto I remember was bringing a sermon. He always did. He gave sermonettes. This time he was talking about life, people getting along, that's all he talked about, how he just can't understand why people can't get along. I was in his amen corner. He had a tendency to use his hands when he spoke, and he had a passion about what he believed in that was so obvious."

Late that night, before they scattered, Oliver asked his teammates to gather around him. "Okay, let's all take a picture," he said. "It might be the last time we'll be together."

13
Temblor

THREE DAYS BEFORE CHRISTMAS, AT FIVE-THIRTY ON A
Friday afternoon, President Richard Nixon drafted a congratulatory
note to his friend Howard Hughes. Nixon was in Florida, unwinding at
the Southern White House compound on Key Biscayne that he shared
with his loyal friend Charles (Bebe) Rebozo. Hughes, the billionaire

recluse, was in Managua, Nicaragua, holed up in a seventh-floor suite at the Hotel Inter-Continental, where he oversaw his business enterprises from a darkened room, dealing exclusively with male secretaries, security guards, and nurses, who at his insistence had to be Mormons. It was the same hotel that Roberto Clemente had left fourteen days earlier after managing Puerto Rico's team in the world amateur baseball championships.

Nixon and Hughes were longtime acquaintances, the knot of their connection tightened by power and money. Hughes had ingratiated himself with the Nixon family by once making a $205,000 loan to the politician's brother, Donald. He also had funneled a hundred thousand dollars in secret donations to Nixon's recently completed 1972 reelection campaign (though the existence of those donations would not be revealed publicly until Senate Watergate Committee hearings a year later). The campaign money arrived in briefcases full of hundred-dollar bills, and the person to whom a Hughes aide handed the cash was none other than Bebe Rebozo.

The President considered his friendship with Hughes so important that he wanted his message delivered in person by the U.S. ambassador to Nicaragua, Turner B. Shelton. A written note had become necessary because Nixon—even with one of the world's most sophisticated communications systems at his disposal—could not get a telephone call through to the obsessive-compulsive germ-freak who was hiding from the world up in his cave-like hotel suite. The occasion was the approach of Hughes's seventieth birthday, or so Nixon thought. There was mystery even to the inception of Howard Hughes: while his commonly stated birthday was December 24, 1905, court documents in Texas recorded another date, September 24. In either case, Nixon was wrong about the age. Hughes was sixty-seven.

"Threescore years and ten is a major milestone in any man's life, and you especially have much to look back on with pride and much to look forward to with pleasure from this vantage point," Nixon wrote. "I'm sorry that circumstances don't permit me to congratulate you by telephone on this important birthday, as I had wished to, but I trust that the warmth of my good wishes can be conveyed by this means as well. Not only have I greatly valued your support, but I also have enormous respect for the contributions you have made to the nation during the course of a long and brilliant career. Pat joins me in wishing you a very happy birthday, and many more to come. Cordially, Richard Nixon."

The birthday greeting was sent from Key Biscayne up to the White House and then conveyed by telex from the Situation Room down to the ambassador's residence in Managua. Shelton was to hand-carry it to the hotel the next morning. It never happened.

This was the start of a joyous weekend in Managua, the height of Christmas season. Colored lights festooned the shops along Avenida Centrál and glowed from the pyramid-shaped hotel up on the hill. Holiday revelers were out strolling along the narrow streets of the old city late into the night. For days, it had been hot and oddly still, following the worst drought of the century, but now, after midnight in the first minutes of December 23, a sudden wind blew in, cold and strong. The animals could tell. And Pedro Chamorro, with the alert instincts of an opposition newspaper editor on guard against danger, also noticed something. The leaves rustled as if in warning, he thought. Then came the first tremor and the earth shuddered side to side. Soon a second rumble, more up and down than horizontal, like some gargantuan creature bursting to the surface from deep underground. Later a third quake, again up and down, more violent than the second—and in a thunderous spasm the city collapsed on itself. The temblor, registering 6.5 on the Richter scale, flattened 350 square blocks in two horrific hours, pipes erupting, fires flashing, debris and soot choking the air, people running, staggering, screaming, ripping off their burning clothes, dazed, blood everywhere. The clock atop the Cathedral of the Immaculate Conception at the epicenter of the earthquake stopped at exactly twelve twenty-seven.

When the oscillating began, Ambassador Shelton was at his residence in the El Retiro section on a hill above town and had just tuned his radio to listen to the news. Chairs started flying, paintings, small tables, glassware, anything loose. The lights went out. He dashed upstairs to check on his wife, who was safe, then retreated to his study, where he had an emergency generator and radio. Within minutes, he learned that the American embassy had been in the vast destruction zone. His secretary, Rose Marie Orlich, had been trapped inside, one among the probable thousands of victims. Shelton sent a Morse code message that made its way to the State Department's relay station in suburban Washington. *Embassy destroyed. Will require help. More later.*

Nicaragua's military leader, Anastasio Somoza Debayle, was next door, inside his sprawling ranch house with his wife, Hope, and the three youngest of their five children. At the first tremor they ran from the house into an alley. The second and powerful third tremors bounced them around so much, Somoza later said, that "we thought we were pieces of ice in a cocktail shaker." When the rumbling ended, Somoza climbed into a car he used as supreme commander of the Armed Forces of Nicaragua and began working the radio, contacting police and guard headquarters. He learned that the guard building downtown had been destroyed, with massive casualties, and the national communications center, housed in the presidential palace, also had been knocked out of commission. He decided to set up emergency headquarters at his ranch house, which suffered only minor damage. Somoza was not the president of Nicaragua—he had relinquished that title temporarily to satisfy a constitutional requirement— but there was no doubt about who ran the country. Earlier in the month, in fact, the Nixon administration had given him the security protection of a head of state when he visited the Kennedy Space Center to watch the night launch of Apollo 17, the last manned flight to the moon. Now, with the earthquake crisis, Somoza dropped all pretensions and seized full control.

Over at the Inter-Continental, there was much commotion in the postquake darkness. With its squat base and pyramid shape, the building had not collapsed, though there were several cracks and the top floors listed slightly. The elevators were useless because of the power outage. Guests escaped down emergency stairwells, weaving their way past junked furniture that was being stored on the landings of several floors. Julie Sinkey, a Pan Am stewardess, scrambled down the steps and outside in her nightclothes. She had been asleep, and the rumbling split apart a wall so that when she rose from bed she could see the people in the room next door. Somehow, on the way out, she had remembered to bring along her ten-dollar camera, and from the hill-side she took pictures of the inferno raging below in the old center of town. Howard Hughes was said to have had a fear of dying in a natural disaster, but when this one struck he remained so unruffled that his staff had trouble persuading him to leave his protective suite. "He was cool, so cool," recalled aide John Eckersley. "Everyone was saying we must evacuate immediately, but he said no. He wanted to be sure it was absolutely necessary." His delay gave aides time to pack his clothes and medicines, which were scattered about the suite. He was so frail that they carried him down the darkened stairwell and placed him in a Mercedes-Benz limousine in the hotel parking lot. At dawn, they drove him to the nearby residence of Somoza, the man who ten months earlier had invited him to use Nicaragua as his hideaway when he had scooted from the Bahamas. The strongman general and phobic billionaire had a few things in common, foremost that they were both friends of the President of the United States.

The Clementes, at their house on the hill in Río Piedras, awoke on December 23 to news of the deadly quake. To them this was not some distant tragedy, but so close in time and memory that it felt like a family disaster. The old city, the shops where Roberto had bought fine clothes for Vera, all in ruins. What happened to the many people he had met during his more than three weeks in Nicaragua? The merchants, baseball fans, restaurateurs, the workers and farmers who reminded him so much of the poor in Carolina, the ones to whom he had given coins every morning. And the young boy at the hospital waiting for artificial legs to be fitted so that he could be the Puerto Rican amateur baseball team's batboy next year—what happened to him? "As soon as we heard about the earthquake early that morning we were very upset because we met some very nice people down there and felt like we lost someone—you know, a relative or someone. We felt very involved with this," Vera Clemente said later. Roberto wanted to know more than the San Juan media could tell him. Friends at a local radio station said they had no direct communications to Nicaragua.

Clemente eventually found a ham radio operator who was picking up detailed reports of the earthquake. A team of radio operators from San Juan to Chicago to Caracas to the State Department shortwave station in Washington had formed a link with a Managuan identifying himself as "Enrique," who was broadcasting in Spanish from a mobile unit inside a truck as he drove around the remains of the city. There were still minor tremors, Enrique reported. It looked like five or six thousand people were dead. Maybe a hundred thousand homeless. Two of the three major hospitals were destroyed, along with the presidential palace, the newspaper offices of *La Prensa* and *Novedades*, the U.S. embassy, and two of the three major hotels, the Balmoral and Gran. The main fire station had collapsed, trapping essential equipment and making it more difficult to fight the fires. Even a giant statue of Somoza's father had toppled from its pedestal. "People run through the streets like zombies, with terror. Big buildings are cracked," Enrique reported over his mobile radio. "There is blood on people's faces, legs, and arms as they leave their houses. We have never seen a catastrophe like this."

What did people need? Clemente asked. Everything, was the answer—food, clothing, medical supplies.

The disaster relief effort was underway. At seven-thirty that morning, a telex from Ambassador Shelton requesting immediate medical help had crossed the desk of Colonel Maurice Berbary at the United States Southern Command in the Panama Canal Zone. While larger tactical hospital units were readied to fly in from Fort Hood in Texas and MacDill Air Force Base in Tampa the following day, Berbary had the first forty-six-man medical team loaded inside a mammoth C-130 and on its way to Managua before noon. The Red Cross and other volunteer groups were traveling to the devastated capital from Mexico City, South America, the United States, and even Europe. Only a year earlier, in the wake of a humanitarian crisis in Biafra, a small group of French doctors had formed a new medical assistance organization called Doctors Without Borders, and upon hearing of the Managua earthquake they went into action for the first time.

It was right then, twelve hours after the temblor, when many were coming to Managua's rescue, that Howard Hughes made his escape.

Somoza had hoped that Hughes might somehow assist in the recovery. But as soon as the general passed word along to his guest that the runways at Las Mercedes International appeared undamaged, Hughes and his entourage left directly for the airport. When they got there, an aide asked a local rental car agent, who was also an amateur radio operator, to send a message to Florida. After some trouble with the equipment, a second ham radio operator was found, and the cryptic message he sent, as he recalled it later, went like this: *We're okay. Leaving on Lear jet. Destroy all records and x-ray. Proceed immediately to Miami. When arrive in Miami call 31 Los Angeles for ultimate destination.* And with that, Howard Hughes fled Managua at its time of greatest need. American soldiers arriving from the Canal Zone in the first C-130 remembered seeing the private jet take off just after they landed.

On that first long day of the Managua disaster, the attention of President Nixon at his compound in Key Biscayne and millions of sports fans around the United States was focused on something else: the first round of playoff games in the National Football League. Interest was especially intense in Pittsburgh, where the resurgent Steelers were hosting the Oakland Raiders at Three Rivers Stadium. The Steelers had been perennial losers, known for getting beat and beating the hell out of the other team at the same time, but now, for the first time since 1947, they were playing in the postseason. After calling Henry Kissinger in Washington, D.C., Nixon settled in to eat lunch and watch the game in the living room of his vacation house at 516 Bay Lane. It was a defensive struggle with little action until the end. With a minute and thirteen seconds remaining, the Oakland quarterback, Ken Stabler, ran thirty yards for a score to put the Raiders ahead 7–6. Then, with Pittsburgh's last gasp, came one of the most memorable plays in NFL history.

Fourth and ten, ball on the Steelers' forty, another sixty yards to score. Twenty-two seconds left. Art Rooney, Pittsburgh's owner, resigned to a loss, was taking the elevator from his box down to the clubhouse to deliver a consolation speech. Bill Nunn Jr., the former sports editor of the *Pittsburgh Courier,* now a personnel man for the Steelers, thought the game was over and sat in the team box cussing out the defense for the breakdown that allowed Stabler to score. Terry

Bradshaw, the third-year quarterback, called the play: 66 Option. *Bradshaw back and looking, looking for someone to throw to . . . fires it downfield . . . It's caught in the air . . .* The pass was intended for the halfback Frenchy Fuqua, but Oakland's fearsome safety, Jack Tatum, arrived with a wallop just as the pass got there, and the ball ricocheted back several yards and was snatched out of thin air at ankle level by rookie running back Franco Harris, who swept across the field and down the sideline for the winning score.

Myron Cope, the Pittsburgh sports figure who had written the seminal story on Clemente's aches and pains for *Sports Illustrated* in 1966, was now the color announcer for Steelers football. He had left the broadcast booth with two minutes to go and was on the field, standing behind the corner of the end zone as Franco thundered toward him. After conducting postgame interviews in the bedlam of the Steelers locker room, Cope went to dinner and then drove to the WTAE-TV studios to write a commentary for the eleven o'clock news. Pecking at his typewriter, he took a call from a woman named Sharon Levosky, who said she was celebrating with a group of delirious Steelers fans at the Interlude bar downtown. One of her friends at the bar, Michael Ord, had thought up a name for Franco's miracle catch—the Immaculate Reception—and told her to call Cope to spread the word. Cope thought it was a phrase well worth appropriating, so he wrote it into his commentary, and it caught on from there. Forever after, the Immaculate Reception meant only one thing to any pro football fan—perhaps the most stunning last play in pro football history.

If one were to point to the moment when pro football permanently surpassed baseball as the sporting passion of Pittsburgh, when the Steelers became a winning rather than losing tradition, that might be it. The Immaculate Reception transcended even Maz's home run in the bottom of the ninth in the seventh game of the 1960 World Series. It was the talk of western Pennsylvania all weekend and all week through Christmas and the days leading up to the next game against the Miami Dolphins on New Year's Eve. The disaster in the rubble surrounding the Cathedral of the Immaculate Conception in Managua seemed far, far away.

All day long Clemente had been tracking the ham radio reports from Managua and thinking about what he could do to help. He called his friend Osvaldo Gil, the amateur baseball president who had been at his side all those days in Nicaragua. "What should we do?" he asked. Before Gil could answer, Clemente added, "I don't know what you're going to do, but I'm going to do something about it." Luis Ferré, in his final week as governor of Puerto Rico, and Rafael Hernández Colón, the governor-elect, had both issued public expressions of sorrow and promised to help Nicaragua. That night, Roberto and Vera went to a nightclub he owned, El Carretero, in Carolina, then drove downtown to the San Jeronimo Hotel for a banquet at which he was to receive another award. He was tired, but felt an obligation to go. Vera wore the elegantly embroidered dress that Roberto had bought for her in Managua. Ruth Fernández, the singer and political activist who had just been elected to the Puerto Rican Senate, was there, along with Luis Vigoraux, a local television personality. They huddled with the Clementes to talk about the temblor, and Vigoraux suggested that as well-known figures in the community they should take prominent roles in the relief effort. Clemente, as a national hero, would lead the way. What came to be called the Comité Roberto Clemente Pro-Nicaragua was born.

The next morning, a Sunday, Christmas Eve, President Nixon took breakfast at eight forty-five in his Key Biscayne bungalow. The morning papers were full of reports about the devastation in Nicaragua. According to the daily diary kept by his secretaries, Nixon began making long-distance calls as soon as he finished breakfast. There were two people in Managua that he especially wanted to reach. First he tried General Somoza at his residence, but the call was not completed. Then, two minutes later, according to the diary, "the President telephoned long distance to Howard R. Hughes, President of the Hughes Tool and Manufacturing Company, in Managua, Nicaragua." That call, too, went unanswered, since Hughes by then was long gone. A half hour later, the President finally got through to Somoza. His concerns were personal and political. Nixon had first met Somoza in 1955 when he was Vice President and toured Central America. Sixteen years later, as President, he had hosted Somoza at a White House dinner. The general had arrived with six boxes of cigars for Nixon and a gold lapel pin for the First Lady. Nixon, in his toast, had congratulated Somoza for "a quarter-century of service to the cause of peace and freedom." Now, in his call to the disaster zone, Nixon was reassured to learn that Somoza and his family were safe. But he was worried that chaos in the aftermath of the natural disaster might lead to civil disturbances and give an opening to Somoza's opponents. His instinctive fear was that the tumult might lead to a Communist uprising.

Along with medical teams and combat engineers, Nixon would dispatch a battalion of paratroopers to keep order in the Nicaraguan capital.

At the White House, the President's military adviser on the National Security staff, General Alexander M. Haig Jr., was receiving hourly updates on Nicaragua. At five-fifteen that morning, the first of fourteen C-141s, departing in one-hour intervals, left MacDill Air Force Base with medical supplies, equipment for a field hospital, and emergency communications. The planes, Haig was informed, were to bring back "some one hundred dependents of American personnel and nonessential staff members as well as those nonofficial Americans who want to be evacuated." People everywhere were doing what they could to help. In Atlanta, workers at an Army depot spent the day filling more than four thousand five-gallon jugs with water. Fire stations in New Orleans became collection centers for food and supplies. The Associated Press noted that a church congregation in Mountainview, Ohio, "donated its entire Christmas Eve offering." The offices of Lanica, the Nicaraguan national airlines, served as Red Cross relief headquarters in Miami, whose large Latin population responded generously to the crisis, some people coming in with their Christmas turkeys and pigs.

In San Juan, Clemente and Ruth Fernández made a public plea for assistance on WAPA-TV, getting air time between telecasts of horse races at El Comandante Racetrack in Carolina. They announced that the parking lot of Hiram Bithorn Stadium, the winter league ballpark for San Juan and Santurce, would be used as the collection point for aid for the entire Christmas Day. By then, Clemente had developed a direct ham radio connection to a hospital in Masaya, thirteen miles from Managua, and was told how much they needed medicines and

X-ray equipment. Masaya itself had been hard hit. The size of the town, known for its handicrafts, had nearly doubled to more than sixty thousand because of the exodus from the capital. Many houses there had red flags hanging from windows indicating there were survivors inside. Conditions could not be more urgent. Clemente decided to lease a plane to get supplies to Nicaragua faster.

On Christmas morning, Pedro Chamorro circled Managua on his motorcycle, weaving his way through what he called the rubble zone. No one was thinking about the religious holiday, he noted. "However, on the sidewalks, patios and parks of the fallen city, those who were still together shared their things—and the earth stopped shaking." His city, the editor of *La Prensa* observed, seemed "crushed by a sort of incomprehensible peace." Nicaraguan troops were stationed at street corners in the downtown section, their concentrations most obvious outside banks and government buildings. The stench of death was overwhelming. On some blocks, hundreds of mutilated bodies still littered the streets and many more remained trapped under debris. "We are fighting against time," said Jorge Cogna, a Red Cross volunteer from Mexico City. Health officials were concerned about the spread of typhoid and other diseases if the dead were not recovered and buried soon. In contrast to the sharing that Chamorro saw, General Somoza thought the best policy was to instruct all service agencies to stop feeding the poor and hungry in the center of town; it was, he argued, a matter of public health, the only way to force people to obey his evacuation orders and leave the dangerous precincts. A six o'clock curfew was imposed, but late into the night the old city echoed with gunfire. Some looting had begun, people walking off with whatever they could find in the rubble. Somoza now issued another order. He directed his civil guardsmen to shoot looters on sight.

Dawn on the morning of December 26 "broke with the arrival of parachutists," Chamorro recalled. They were U.S. troops dropped in from Panama to supplement Somoza's guard. But the tension only increased. Chamorro, in his lyrical style, described "the thousands and thousands of hands extended toward emptiness, asking for the food, which was kept in the same place as the limousines . . . under custody of the government tanks. They didn't give out the food. They didn't give out the food." The paradox grew starker; more aid, less help. Chamorro was amazed at how the "boxes of medicine and food continued to arrive at the airport and the tent hospitals waved flags from all countries." Yet as aid was coming, residents were leaving. "Processions of people left the city from the three roads, barbed wire stretched around the most destroyed parts and the sounds of dynamite blasts could be heard smashing walls and sinking rooftops. Buses, trucks, small carts loaded with paintings, dressers, scissors, suitcases, trunks passed over the ashes and rocks looking for an exit." A massive white tent city was arising on the edge of town. At the general cemetery, they dug a mass grave and buried the first thousand bodies. Most of the old city had been declared a contaminated area. U.S. Army engineers, following a block by block grid system, began systematically clearing the ground in the hundred-degree heat. Demolition crews used bulldozers and dynamite to level anything that had managed to stand after the quake. Lime was spread over the rubble. For the first time, on that day after Christmas, vultures circled overhead, drawn by the odor of death.

Clemente spent the day at the parking lot of Hiram Bithorn Stadium in the Hato Rey section of San Juan, across from the Plaza Las Americas shopping center. From eight o'clock that morning, the action seemed to orbit around him, all the incessant noise and bustle of people coming and going, dropping off food and cash. Every so often, Clemente grabbed the microphone and instructed people on how to make donations. "Don't give money that you cannot afford," he said. "If you can give money, so there is no problem, make your checks out to the Roberto Clemente Relief Committee for Nicaragua, not to Roberto Clemente. Thank you very much." The mood was urgent, pulsing, always more to do, arrangements to be made for crates, boxes, trucks, medical supplies, and squads of fit young students who could unload here and load there. Enough had been collected already for more than one trip. The committee had reached an agreement with an air transport company based in Miami to lease a Lockheed Constellation known as the Super Snoopy for three round-trips between San Juan and Managua, each at a cost of $3,700.

At the end of the day, Clemente and Ruth Fernández drove to

Channel 4 to promote the relief effort again, this time on Luis Vigoraux's 8 P.M. television show. The program itself was a comic absurdity in contrast with the seriousness of events in Nicaragua. It was known as *Sube, Nene, Sube*—or *Up, Baby, Up.* Engaged couples would appear on the show, with the woman yelling words of encouragement—*Pa'arriba, Papi, Pa'arriba,* or Get There, Daddy, Get There—as her fiancé tried to climb a greased pole and retrieve a flag planted on the top. If he succeeded, they would win an all-expenses paid honeymoon. It was after that segment of the show that Vigoraux turned his attention to the Managua earthquake. He explained the magnitude of the disaster and said that all Latins were coming together to help their brothers and sisters in Nicaragua. Fernández spoke next. "I want to say to the people of Puerto Rico, the best way to serve God is to serve the other people," she said.

¡Arriba! ¡Arriba! For all those years, that had been Bob Prince's exuberant radio greeting whenever Roberto Clemente of the Pittsburgh Pirates rose from the on-deck circle and stepped toward the plate. Day after day, year after year for eighteen seasons, Clemente met the challenge. *¡Pa'arriba, Papi, Pa'arriba!* Fernández turned to Clemente to speak. He focused on what the disaster meant to young people and how they had responded. It was apparent that Roberto's dream of a sports city for Puerto Rican kids remained at the front of his mind. "I want to take this opportunity to thank the people of Puerto Rico," he said. "The teenagers have been very helpful in picking up the boxes and gathering everything for the planes. They are from twelve to sixteen years old and they have helped us a lot . . . The young people of Puerto Rico are the ones most worried about this."

Howard Hughes, after refueling stops in Florida, Newfoundland, and Ireland, had arrived at Gatwick Airport on the southern rim of London by then. Authorities detained him inside his ten-seat Lockheed Jetstar for more than a half hour as they sought to determine his identity. His American passport had expired. Through the intervention of his local sponsors, N. M. Rothschild & Sons, the London bankers, his entry was finally approved, and he was chauffeured in a fleet of four Rolls-Royce sedans to the Inn at the Park, overlooking Hyde Park, where he was put up in a $2,500-a-night suite. His wing of the hotel was sealed off, all the fire escapes in the hotel were blocked, and Roth-schild security guards patrolled the sidewalks below with walkie-talkies. A wealthy guest from Canada, quartered at the same nightly rate on the other side of Hughes's floor, was vexed to discover that overzealous guards had seized a brace of pheasants he had bagged in a weekend hunt and had hung proudly on the hotel balcony. But if Hughes was looking for seclusion, it was not to be had. Fleet Street reporters and television crews huddled outside, recording any scrap of news about him. At one point, apparently without irony, an aide came out and told the assembled press corps that his boss was hoping to "live more of a life, if people will let him."

The first step in living a more normal life, officials at the U.S. embassy suggested, might be for Hughes to fill out an application form and pay the $12 fee for arriving without a valid passport. In Managua, a reporter for the *New York Times* drove up to the Hotel Inter-Continental and thought about how the place had been abuzz ten months earlier when Hughes had arrived from the Bahamas, and now here it stood, overlooking the fallen city, "black and empty."

Volunteers in San Juan worked overnight to load the Super Snoopy with supplies donated to the relief effort. There was an X-ray machine and other medical equipment for the hospital in Masaya. The plane would leave the next morning at dawn. Raul Pelligrina, a major in the Puerto Rico National Guard and close friend of Osvaldo Gil, had agreed to accompany the crew and shepherd the delivery to Managua, along with Ana Salaman, a registered nurse from Carolina. The Clementes came to the airport to see them off in the dark, misty chill. Vera remembered looking over at her husband as the plane rolled down the runway and wondering whether that was a tear she saw in his eye.

Nicaragua is the largest country in Central America, about the size of Iowa, but the least populated. In 1972 it had about 2 million citizens, a quarter of them in metropolitan Managua. The people were known for their beauty, the nation for its poverty. More than half the populace was illiterate. Like other Central American countries, Nicaragua had its own difficult and peculiar history with the United States. It was long coveted by American interests as a pathway to the Pacific and the gold of California, and was the first proposed route of a canal that eventually was built in Panama. In 1855 an American freebooter from Tennessee, William Walker, invaded the country with the idea of transforming it into a slave-holding colony, and for a brief time, before he was driven out, he established English as the official language and called himself emperor. U.S. Marines arrived in Nicaragua in 1909 and were there much of the time until 1933. Three years after they left, the reign of the Somoza family began. Describing the singular hold the Somozas had over Nicaragua for nearly fifty years, University of Denver professor Tom J. Farer once wrote, "If El Salvador was the country of the fourteen families, Nicaragua was the country of only one." The first Anastasio Somoza ruled for twenty years until he was assassinated in 1956, but power was passed along to his sons.

Anastasio Somoza Debayle, who would be the last in the Somoza line, took power in 1967. He spoke fluent English, went to prep school on Long Island and in Washington, D.C., and was a member of the U.S. Military Academy class of 1946. He graduated 752nd out of 875 cadets but excelled in marksmanship and military tactics. At home in Nicaragua, Somoza also came to excel at using power for financial gain. By 1972 it was estimated that he and his family controlled 25 percent of the gross national product. The Somozas controlled cattle ranches, coffee and sugar plantations, sugar mills, distilleries, auto dealerships, textiles, hotels, airlines, and a newspaper, *Novedades*, while also owning vast stretches of real estate on the outskirts of Managua. Looking back on the years of Somoza's rule, a commission on Central America chaired by Henry A. Kissinger declared that the general's "galloping greed discouraged foreign investment, distorted the economy and progressively concentrated in his hands capital assets and investment opportunities." The Somoza family's selfishness, the commission report stated, reached its fulfillment in the person of Anastasio, "whose achievements gave new meaning to the term kleptocracy, that is government as theft."

By December 27, on the fifth day after the earthquake, the greed of Somoza and his cronies was becoming apparent. Red Cross volunteers wondered where all the aid was going. Money seemed to disappear.

Raul Pelligrina returned to San Juan that night after a round-trip to Managua with the first delivery from Puerto Rico. He went directly from the airport to the relief committee headquarters outside Hiram Bithorn and could barely contain his disappointment. It was awful, he told Clemente. The moment they landed, Somoza's soldiers surrounded the plane and tried to take everything. Nicaragua was in chaos. No one knew whether aid was getting to the right people. Pelligrina, calling the military's bluff, said that if they didn't let him through he would reload his aircraft and fly back to San Juan and tell the great Roberto Clemente what was happening. Finally, Somoza's son Tachido came to see who was giving his soldiers trouble. Upon hearing the invocation of Clemente's name, Tachido relented and let them go on to Masaya. But it was a hassle from beginning to end, and it seemed to Pelligrina that most supplies were being diverted. Osvaldo Gil stood nearby as Pelligrina told this story. Clemente was silent, but it was apparent how angry he was, Gil said. They could see it in his eyes. When Pelligrina finished, Clemente, his voice reaching a high pitch, said they had to do something to get the aid to the people who needed it. If he had to travel to Managua himself to make sure Somoza and his guards weren't stealing it, he said, then that is what he would do.

Special missions had been reaching Managua every day during that week between Christmas and New Year's Eve. On the same day that the Super Snoopy flew in from Puerto Rico with the first shipment from Clemente's relief committee, a small chartered plane arrived from Jamaica carrying Bianca Jagger, her husband, Mick Jagger, of the Rolling Stones, and some medical supplies. Bianca, then only twenty-two, had grown up in Managua and was worried about her divorced parents, neither of whom she had been able to reach since the earthquake struck. Her mother, Doris Macias, ran a shop in the old section of Managua, where everything was rubble. Mother and daughter shared a love of politics and an intense dislike of Somoza; during a student protest when she was a teenager, Bianca had been tear-gassed by Somoza's National Guard. What she saw as soon as they landed at the airport in the aftermath of the earthquake only intensified her feelings. Soldiers were everywhere, she recalled in an interview with journalist Kurt Jacobsen, but they were just seizing supplies and taking them to government warehouses. Nearby, on the other side of the fences, hungry people were shouting for food and water, their pleas ignored. With the help of a British journalist, the Jaggers roamed the city in search of Bianca's parents. As it turned out, her mother and father had made it out of Managua safely and were staying in Leon, where they were reunited two days later. But her experiences during those few days in her hometown affected Bianca Jagger so much that she persuaded her husband and the Rolling Stones to perform a benefit concert for the Nicaraguan people. She would never forget the arrogance of the Somoza regime, she said, nor the "stench of burned flesh" that overwhelmed her as they drove through the ruins.

From the North, arriving within hours of the Jaggers, came a thirty-three-member medical team organized by health officials in Rockland County, New York. At the end of a long flight, as the Pan Am jetliner was descending, Dr. Hart Achenbach noticed a jagged trench running parallel to the shores of Lake Managua that stretched for miles and was so deep he couldn't see the bottom. He was stunned to realize that earthquakes really did open the ground and swallow people and buildings into the great maw. Once the plane touched down, the doctors were met by one of Somoza's sons, who asked them whether they brought any barbed wire so he and his troops could put it around the cargo. This was the same demand that had been made of Major Pelligrina when the Clemente aid came in from Puerto Rico. The Americans ignored young Somoza and loaded four hundred cartons of a mobile hospital into trucks that they had arranged to have waiting for them.

Once they set up their hospital tents on the edge of downtown, the doctors were overcome by the stench. "The smell was incredible. There were lots of dead, though we didn't see them, we could smell them," Achenbach recalled. "It was sickening. We would take handkerchiefs and wet them and put them over our faces." His colleague, Dr. Frederick Zugibe, chief medical examiner for Rockland County, anticipated that the doctors and nurses would be overwhelmed with patients, but there were more dead than injured. They did treat 250 Managuans and deliver twenty-five babies, but what Zugibe remembered most was that some of his patients had been wounded by soldiers, not injured from falling debris. "I had more individuals that I treated who were shot," he recalled. "They were shot for looting. It was amazing. Young kids. I remember operating on young kids to remove bullets."

At about the time that Dr. Zugibe was removing bullets from a young patient on the afternoon of December 28, President Nixon placed a call to Maurice J. Williams at his holiday retreat in Martinsburg, West Virginia. Williams was the deputy administrator of the Agency for International Development, and the President had just picked him to be his representative at the earthquake scene. "I want you to go to Managua and take charge of the relief effort," Nixon said. "I'm concerned that the Communists may take over the country. Somoza is a personal friend of mine; I will have a letter for you to carry to him."

Williams caught a flight from Washington to Panama and then reached Managua by military helicopter. His first impressions were like all the others: desolation, smoldering rubble, ungodly stench. He visited the field hospitals and noticed that many casualties had resulted from gunshot wounds. Maybe, he thought, there had been an attempted revolt, as Nixon had feared. Then he went up the hill to visit Somoza, carrying with him the President's letter. The first thing he noticed was a platoon of U.S. infantry soldiers armed and camped on the site—there, he assumed, by order of President Nixon. "Quite a character," Williams said later of the Nicaraguan general. "Somoza impressed me as an entrepreneurial type. Certainly he had extensive business monopoly interests and apparently was milking the country economically." Williams tried to set up rigid accounting practices for the U.S. aid. "However, I found that relief supplies from other countries and private agencies were being received by Somoza's son, a young man in the uniform of an Army lieutenant, who stored them in a locked warehouse outside the city. One had a sense of inefficiency and corruption."

Clemente was determined that his own efforts would not fall victim to corruption. To several friends in those final few days of 1972, he made the same request: I'm going to Nicaragua. Come with me. He called his friend Les Banos, the Pittsburgh photographer, explained his distress over the corruption in Managua, and said, "Why don't you come down and take pictures?" If not for the Immaculate Reception, Banos replied, he would be there no questions asked, but because the Steelers won he would be covering their next playoff game against the Miami Dolphins on New Year's Eve. Clemente turned to Orlando Cepeda, who was home in Puerto Rico after the most difficult season of his career. Cepeda had been traded from the Atlanta Braves to Oakland the previous June, but underwent knee surgery after only three at-bats with the A's and never got back on the field. After fifteen productive seasons in the big leagues and a total of 358 home runs and 1,261 runs batted in, Cepeda found himself struggling to keep his career alive. Oakland had placed him on waivers at season's end, and not a single club had put in a claim for him. Now, after Christmas, came the deflating news that the A's had given him his unconditional release. That often meant a career was over, but Cepeda, at age thirty-five, was not ready to give up. He wanted to exercise his troublesome legs back into shape, and in any case he loved being in Puerto Rico during the holiday season, and that is why he said, no, sorry, when his friend asked him to come along to Nicaragua. No was not an easy thing to say to Roberto Clemente. "He was angry with me for not going," Cepeda remembered.

The earthquake relief collection site was moved after a few days from the Hiram Bithorn parking lot to a larger lot across the street at Plaza Las Americas because San Juan and Santurce were back playing at the stadium. The Senadores team was a virtual Pirates South, stocked with Clemente's Pittsburgh teammates, including Richie Zisk, Rennie Stennett, Milt May, and Manny Sanguillen. Before a game one night that week, Clemente took a break from his volunteer work and visited the clubhouse, where he immediately fell into the comfortable routine of razzing in a mix of Spanish and English, mostly with Sanguillen, his cheery little brother from Panama.

"Sangy, what position do you play in the winter league?" Clemente asked, fixing a serious stare on Sanguillen. He knew the answer. The sports sections that week had featured stories about how the hot-hitting catcher was learning to play outfield.

"Right field," Sanguillen said. "I play twenty games in right, one in left."

The first crack of a smile showed on Clemente's face. "Sangy, you play left field or go back to catching. You have no chance to take my job."

"I play right field real good now," Sanguillen responded. "Not as good as you, but real close. I may be the best right fielder in the league when you quit."

Now Clemente was laughing. "You never come close, Sangy. Besides, I think I'm a better catcher than you."

When Clemente said something like that, no one could be certain whether he was kidding. He thought he could do anything. He always insisted that he could throw a curveball better than the pitcher Steve Blass. He couldn't, of course, nor could he catch nearly as well as Sanguillen, but that was Clemente. At least he wouldn't feel slighted for not being universally regarded as the best pitcher or catcher in the world. But the very idea of Sangy out there in right challenging his position, that wasn't quite a laughing matter, no more now than it was a month earlier when Edgard Tijerino, the Nicaraguan sportswriter, suggested that a young Cuban outfielder had an arm that could match *El Magnífico*'s. But the beauty of Sanguillen was that he could ease whatever tension Clemente was feeling at the moment. Now Clemente was joking with him again about the monkey that he brought back from Nicaragua after the amateur baseball tournament. At home, he called the monkey Teófilo, but when Sanguillen was around he always joked that the monkey's name was Sangy. Sangy was acting up, he said. Sangy bit one of the kids and went wild at Don Melchor's house and made a mess of all the fruit, fake and real. Had to give him to the zoo. Then Clemente said: I'm going back to Nicaragua, Sangy. Come with me. But Sanguillen couldn't go, either. He had some more baseball games to play in right field.

And there was Osvaldo Gil, his compatriot on the baseball trip to Nicaragua. "Valdy, will you go with me?" Clemente asked, and Gil, without giving it a second thought, said sure. But that night, when he told his wife that he intended to go back to Managua with Roberto Clemente, she fled to the bedroom without saying a word. When

Osvaldo came in, she was crying. She was feeling sad, she told him, because they had just been married a few months when he left for Nicaragua the first time, and now he was leaving again. Gil realized that she was right. The next morning, at Plaza Las Americas, he told Clemente, "I talked to my wife, and I'm not going."

"And you're the one who says we shouldn't listen to the women?" Clemente answered, recalling with a touch of sarcasm how Gil, during their earlier trip to Managua, had teased him so much for reflexively consulting with Vera before making a decision.

"But you're right," Clemente now said to Gil. "You shouldn't go. I'll go by myself."

14

Cockroach Corner

IN THE WIDE WORLD OF AVIATION THERE ARE DARK little corners of desperation. One of them during the early 1970s was a back lot of Miami International Airport known as Cockroach Corner. It was said that you could buy anything for a song at Cockroach Corner, occasionally even planes that had a decent chance of taking flight. The place looked like a mechanical graveyard, creaking with rickety old surplus DC-3s, DC-6s, Lockheed Constellations, and DC-7s, but in fact it was more of a winged bazaar. What were known in the industry as tramp operators did business there, buying, selling, and leasing planes to anyone looking for a cut-rate deal. It was at Cockroach Corner that a twenty-six-year-old operator named Arthur S. Rivera bought another old plane on July 12, 1972. This DC-7, powered by four Curtiss Wright 988 engines with Hamilton Standard propellers, would double Rivera's cargo fleet, supplementing his twin-engine DC-3 in hauling goods between San Juan, his home base, and other Caribbean islands.

Rivera had obtained a commercial pilot rating four years earlier, but knew nothing about DC-7s, which were more than five times heavier than DC-3s, so he could not fly his plane back to Puerto Rico. It remained at Cockroach Corner until sometime in September, when he finally found a pilot. When they ferried it from Florida to the island, Rivera rode along in the right seat as copilot. They parked the aircraft at a cargo ramp at San Juan International Airport on Isla Verde, and there it remained throughout the fall. Word soon spread about Rivera's folly, the only DC-7 at the airfield. The plane had a registration number, N500AE, but seemed anything but airworthy. Among other deficiencies, its No. 3 propeller was said to be feathered, indicating engine

309

malfunction. "It was never seen to fly, and everybody wondered what Mr. Rivera was going to do with the plane. That probably included Mr. Rivera," Michael Pangia, a Justice Department aviation lawyer, observed later. What Rivera did was spruce up the exterior. He gave the fuselage a new paint job of silvery white and added the bravado touch of a lightning bolt, orange with black trim, that ran horizontally along both sides above the windows and zigzagged below the cockpit. The same color scheme was applied to the tips of the propellers, creating the effect of tiger stripes. With that superficial remodeling, Rivera placed advertisements in the local newspapers, announcing that his outfit—he called himself the American Air Express Company—had a DC-7 available for lease. The phone in his home office on Loiza Street in Santurce did not ring off the hook.

On the Saturday morning of December 2, Rivera and a relative, who knew even less about DC-7s than he did, took the plane out for what was called a run-up, meaning they would taxi around the airstrip, warming up the engines, but not try to fly. As practice runs go, this one was a fiasco. Rivera, in the pilot's seat, forgot to close the hydraulic pump bypass, which caused him to lose steering control. He shut down all four engines in an effort to slow the plane's momentum, but it ended up rolling into a drainage ditch. When it came to a stop, the nose of the plane was leaning down and the wings were so low that two propellers touched the ground. It is not every day that a DC-7 plunges into a ditch. Everyone who worked at the airport knew about the "incident" (as it was called, rather than an accident), especially since it blocked the taxiway for several hours and forced air traffic controllers to reroute traffic until heavy equipment was brought in to hoist the plane out of the ditch and tow it ignominiously back to the east ramp. If Federal Aviation Administration officials in San Juan needed a reminder to keep close watch on the comings and goings of Arthur Rivera, this was it, but with his aviation history, one might assume that no further warnings would have been needed.

From the moment he came down from Atlanta and began transporting cargo out of San Juan International in November 1969, Rivera had been a constant irritant to inspectors at the FAA's Flight Standards District Office. Day after day, he offered his DC-3 out for hire as he made island hops from Puerto Rico to St. Thomas to St. Croix and back to San Juan, hauling leisurewear, rugs, dry goods, and luggage. But despite repeated warnings from federal aviation officials, Rivera refused to obtain the proper certification for a commercial operator, acting instead as though he were merely flying the plane for his own personal recreation. This allowed him to avoid more frequent inspections and the far stricter flight standards of commercial aviation. Acting on a complaint from a licensed competitor, the FAA finally launched a formal investigation, compiled a list of sixty-six illegal trips that Rivera had made, and issued an emergency order in August 1970 revoking his pilot's license. In taking that step, the FAA said Rivera's "aviation knowledge and experience was relatively limited" and that he was an "extremely independent and headstrong person who would not take advice."

That characterization was an understatement. To Rivera, the federal regulators were enemy combatants whose sole purpose was to put him out of business. A typical run-in occurred on the Thursday afternoon of April 2, 1970, when he arrived at San Juan International from St. Thomas and parked his DC-3 at its normal spot on the east cargo ramp. Representatives from the Customs Bureau and the FAA were there waiting for him. When Rivera stepped down from the cockpit, inspector Juan L. Villafañe asked to see the papers and manuals of the airplane.

"You people are always picking on me, and on account of that I'm losing a lot of money," Rivera snapped, according to later testimony of the customs officer, Abraham Irizarry. Then Rivera padlocked the door to his plane. When Villafañe noted that a copilot was required for this flight and asked where that person was, Rivera said that he was locked inside the plane. After much haggling, the inspectors made their way in and found 224 pieces of luggage, a load that Rivera had carried for Caribair Airlines, but no copilot. Asked to explain the disappearance, Rivera claimed the copilot "escaped through the hatch." Then, in what the inspectors interpreted as a threat of violence, Rivera said that Villafañe had better watch out if he walked the streets of downtown San Juan.

The chief of the FAA's flight standards office in San Juan then was

William B. Couric, a University of Miami engineering graduate and veteran fighter pilot who flew combat missions in World War II. Couric was such a stickler that his office nickname was Deputy Dog, in honor of the little cartoon character who insisted on doing everything by the book. The Couric v. Rivera relationship took on a bit of a cartoon nature, with the inspector in constant but often frustrating battle to keep the freewheeling pilot on an acceptable course. Couric had counseled Rivera many times before moving to yank his pilot's license, urging him to follow the rules, to no avail. During each discussion, Couric later reported, Rivera would "exhibit a temper and raise his voice." After the emergency order was issued, Rivera simply ignored it, further frustrating Couric. One afternoon Couric confronted Rivera after watching him land his DC-3 at the airport, arriving from what was likely another illegal run. "Why do you continue to fly?" Couric asked. Rivera claimed that he knew nothing about the emergency order. When Couric handed him a copy, Rivera said that he'd worked hard to get his license and would not give it up.

Rather than reform his desperado ways, Rivera went on the offensive. He shadowed Couric around the airfield, occasionally stopping his car to take pictures, as though he were the one doing the enforcement work. There appeared to be no "rhyme or reason" to Rivera's behavior, Couric wrote in a memo to his superiors. "His actions appear irrational and maybe require psychological examination." But Rivera was writing his own memos and letters higher up the chain. He penned what was later described as "a lengthy diatribe" to Alexander P. Butterfield, then FAA administrator in Washington, accusing federal aviation officials of waging a personal campaign to put him out of business. He was just a small businessman trying to follow the American dream, he claimed, while the San Juan investigators were corrupt and taking bribes from his competitors. Aiming even higher, he sent a two-page telegram to President Nixon in which he made the same arguments. There is no evidence that Butterfield or Nixon read Rivera's rants or acted on them in any way, but something did happen in the aftermath that stunned and disappointed Couric and his crew. An appeals court judge, while ruling that Rivera had violated Federal Aviation Regulation 121.3(f) in not having proper certification for commercial flights, nonetheless reduced his penalty from revocation to a 180-day suspension of his pilot's license. The court bought Rivera's argument that the government should not deprive him of his livelihood.

Couric was soon promoted and transferred to another posting in Miami, but Rivera stayed around to live out his dream, eventually expanding his fleet with the DC-7 he found at Cockroach Corner.

The battle of wills between Arthur Rivera and the San Juan regulators was played out in the context of a tragic accident that had jolted the world of aviation safety at the beginning of the decade. On October 2, 1970, at a time when Rivera was ignoring Couric's emergency order, two twin-engine Martin 404s left Kansas carrying members of the Wichita State football team to a game against Utah State in Logan, Utah. The first leg of the flight from Wichita to Denver was uneventful. It was a bright fall day, and on the final leg, the pilot of one of the planes decided to give his passengers a better view of the brilliant autumn colors as they crossed the Continental Divide. He flew into a box canyon, not realizing until too late that he was trapped. The next mountain ridge was approaching too soon for the plane to gain enough altitude to pass over it. The pilot banked sharply to try to turn around but the aircraft stalled and crashed into a forested area near the base of Mount Trelease. All but eight of forty people aboard died, and interest in the disaster was inevitably heightened by the fact that so many college athletes were among the thirty-two dead.

During the investigation, several problems emerged as factors in the crash. The crew had a minimal amount of training on the aircraft, the plane was overloaded, and the pilot made a fatal error by intentionally and unnecessarily flying into a troublesome area. But beyond all that, federal aviation officials came to realize that this case was symptomatic of a larger problem. Air transport companies, especially tramp operators, were using a scheme to get around commercial aviation regulations. In the specific case of Wichita State, the athletic department did not hire a standard airliner for the flight to Utah, but turned to an outfit called Golden Eagle Aviation. In what was known as a "dry lease," Golden Eagle leased the plane to Wichita State, making the university the operator of the plane. In effect it was a deal where Golden Eagle said my right hand will lease you the airplane, so that you are in charge, and my left hand will provide you pilot services. This was cheaper than chartering a commercial airliner, but it also was irresponsible. Companies using dry leases could claim their flights were not commercial operations, since customers who signed the lease were in effect flying themselves—and this allowed everyone involved to avoid the stricter Federal Aviation Regulations for commercial flights. It was only after the Wichita State tragedy that the FAA became fully aware of how endemic this scheme was, particularly in the South and Caribbean, and felt compelled to try to stop it.

Usto E. Schulz, the No. 2 official in FAA flight safety in Washington, said the Wichita State crash "was a matter included for discussion with field division chiefs at a national meeting in 1970 and action was directed from headquarters to effect a coordinated and cooperative effort." Over the next two years, the FAA issued a series of regulatory actions. The final and most comprehensive one was SO 8430.20C, an order drafted by Schulz on September 25, 1972, that came to be known as the Southern Order. The purpose of the order was obvious in the first heading—*Subj: Continuous Surveillance of Large and Turbine-Powered Aircraft.* It was meant for the Southern region of the FAA, which included Cockroach Corner in Miami and Puerto Rico, and read as though it could have been written with Arthur Rivera in mind.

A special sixty-day surveillance program, the order noted, had established beyond doubt that "a considerable number of noncertificated operators of large aircraft and turbine-powered aircraft" were hauling passengers and cargo in violation of federal regulations. To stop this practice, the Southern Order called for continuous surveillance of all aircraft that "cannot be readily identified as bona fide air carriers, commercial carriers, travel clubs, air taxis, or executive operators." In other words, any plane that looked the least bit suspicious. Air traffic controllers were called on to inform Flight Standard District Office inspectors whenever a suspicious plane arrived or departed. Field inspectors were then to see that the pilot was in compliance with commercial regulations, that the plane was airworthy, and that the load was balanced. The most effective investigations would come if the district offices conducted surveillance at odd hours, at nights and weekends. The surveillance was a top priority, the order said, second only to accident investigations.

As it turned out, different districts responded to the order in different ways. San Juan's Flight Standards District Office interpreted the order loosely, asking local air traffic controllers to advise the inspection staff only of "new or strange" incoming flights, not departures.

After Rivera's DC-7 was towed back from the drainage ditch, inspectors under Leonard Davis, who had replaced Couric, examined the aircraft. They determined that it had sustained considerable damage: two blown tires, bent blades on the No. 2 and No. 3 propellers, sudden stoppage of the No. 2 and No. 3 engines, broken hydraulic lines on the right landing gear, and damage to the No. 3 engine oil scoop. Rivera enlisted two mechanics, Rafael Delgado-Cintron and Francisco Matias, who were employed by other airlines at San Juan International, to do some repairs. Delgado-Cintron determined that they only had to replace the two tires and one propeller and file the other propeller back into shape. From his examination, there was no sudden stoppage of engines, which could do severe damage, so Rivera would not have to undertake costly engine replacements. Two weeks after the taxiing incident, on December 17, as Delgado-Cintron and Matias were working on the plane under Rivera's supervision, they encountered FAA inspector Vernon Haynes, who was conducting routine surveillance that day. Haynes suggested to Rivera that it was "high time" for him to replace the engines, noting that they had lived past the lifespan recommended by the manufacturer. But he did not issue a condition notice requiring that engine repairs be made before the next flight, instead marking "satisfactory" and "no further action required" on the FAA inspection forms. The following week, George Mattern, the flight standards office's principal maintenance inspector, also met with Rivera and "discussed with him the possibility of changing engines." This was not mandatory, Mattern said, but made sense.

Two FAA inspectors also talked to Rivera, in the days leading up to Christmas, about doing a test run before taking the DC-7 on any missions. "The airplane ought to be ready for a test hop," one inspector said, after seeing the repair work. But Rivera couldn't do the test hop himself. He still didn't know how to taxi his own plane, let alone fly it.

As New Year's Eve approached, the Clementes were consumed by the earthquake relief effort, working from eight in the morning until past midnight. The activity seemed to take on a momentum of its own, propelling them forward, one task after another, all in a blur. When Roberto wasn't at committee headquarters at Plaza Las Americas, he was traveling around the island, combining baseball clinics for kids with local relief drives. He was on the road when the Super Snoopy left on its second run to Managua, and was even more enraged when he heard that Major Pelligrina and the supplies had been held up again by soldiers at the airport. On the Puerto Rico end, the relief effort was a heartwarming success. They had raised more than $100,000 in cash and checks. Food, clothing, and medical supplies were coming in as quickly as they were going out.

At nine-thirty on the Saturday morning of December 30, Roberto and Vera were both at the south ramp of San Juan International's cargo area as the Super Snoopy was being readied for its third flight to Nicaragua. Mountains of boxes were stacked on the tarmac, far more than could be loaded for this trip. And more supplies were on the way. At the east ramp around the corner, Rafael Delgado-Cintron, the mechanic, was working on Arthur Rivera's DC-7. At about ten o'clock, Delgado-Cintron looked up to see a van approaching with cargo intended for Nicaragua. Apparently, the driver had been directed to the wrong spot to make his delivery, mistaking the DC-7 for the Super Snoopy. Rivera, standing nearby, noticed the van, quickly figured out what was going on, and saw an opportunity. He went to the east ramp, found a group of people standing around, including Roberto Clemente, and told them about the delivery van that had taken a wrong turn. "He came over and introduced himself to us," Vera Clemente recalled. "He told Roberto that he had a plane, a DC-7, for cargo. He was offering his services to us. He gave us two cards and I kept one and Roberto kept one. His business card was white with red lettering and the name was American Air Express Leasing. Arthur Rivera, president. And then two telephone numbers. He said, 'I am available any time today, tomorrow, whenever you need me. I am ready.' Roberto said, 'What time do you think we can leave?' Mr. Rivera said, 'Anytime, whenever you decide.'"

Rivera then invited the Clementes to come see his plane. They drove over to the south ramp—and there stood the DC-7, freshly painted in silvery white with the orange lightning bolt and orange- and black-tipped propellers. A mechanic dressed in a white uniform stood near the steps. Vera stayed below while Roberto climbed inside. It looked okay to him, for the little that he knew about airplanes. Rivera said it was ready for leasing and that he was in no hurry. He would provide the crew, and they would wait in Nicaragua for as long as it took Clemente to do his business, a day or two or three—all for $4,000. Clemente shook hands on the deal, without signing an official lease. Rivera said he would gather a crew and call Clemente later that day when final flight details were arranged.

Roberto and Vera went back to the east ramp, saw off the Super Snoopy, then drove across town to the port at Old San Juan, where volunteer longshoremen were loading more earthquake relief aboard the freighter *San Expedito,* a Panamanian flagship owned by a San Juan packing company. The Clementes were met at the dock by a flock of journalists, including Rosa Sabalones, who took pictures of the scene for the *San Juan Star,* and Efrain Parrilla, who wrote the story. "Clemente told newsmen before sailing that the ship was carrying 210 tons of clothing and 36 tons of food," Parrilla wrote, adding:

> The ship is expected to reach the Nicaraguan port of Blue Field by Wednesday, Clemente said, and the country's National Guard has been advised to provide transportation for the cargo from dockside to Masaya, a town close to Managua.

Masaya is the closest town to Managua that has a hospital and much of the foreign aid pouring into Nicaragua is being taken there, Clemente said.

The Nicaraguan government is pressing the survivors of last Saturday's earthquake to abandon the city in order to avoid the health hazards there and make the work of crews flattening the ruined buildings easier.

Clemente said the ship carried the fourth load of aid sent from the island since the quake. Three other shipments have been made by chartered plane, he said, and another planeload is planned by the committee.

The phrase "another planeload" was a reference to the agreement with Arthur Rivera.

After the news conference at the port, the Clementes drove back to their house in Río Piedras, where Roberto placed a call to the Rauch home in Kutztown. He wanted to make sure that Nevin and Carolyn and her daughters Carol and Sharon were all coming down from Pennsylvania to celebrate New Year's in Puerto Rico. Carol, who had just finished college at Kutztown State as a Spanish major, answered the phone in the kitchen. Roberto often called her and her mother by the same name, Carolina, the name of his hometown. The conversation drifted between English and Spanish, and though some of what Clemente said seemed confusing, at least concerning who would be where, when, his enthusiasm was typical. They would have a big celebration, he said, in honor of Carolina's graduation and his three-thousandth hit and the new year of 1973. He would buy a big juicy pig to be roasted. But that would have to wait until he got back from Nicaragua. He was leaving the next day and would return on New Year's Day. He had to make sure the humanitarian aid was getting to the people. Then, changing his story slightly, he said maybe Carolina should travel to Nicaragua with Vera. They could go shopping. The handicraft clothes in Managua were so beautiful. Wouldn't that be a great graduation gift? A quick trip, maybe an overnight, and then back the next day. Anyway, it was great they were coming and someone would be at the airport in San Juan to get them. Everything would work out.

Life always did with the Clementes, even if it seemed so fluid and spontaneous.

Back at the airport, Arthur Rivera was scrounging. He had a deal, but no crew. He knew that he couldn't fly the DC-7 himself, and there were no pilots in San Juan, at least none that he knew of, who could fly it. He had the name of a qualified pilot in Miami, and placed a call to him but couldn't reach him. A few hours later, a DC-3 happened to arrive from St. Thomas and taxied to a stop near Rivera's plane. The pilot, Jerry C. Hill, noticed the DC-7 as he was walking from the plane to the cargo lounge and said aloud, "I used to fly one of these."

Again, Rivera seized the opportunity. A pilot dropping out of the sky; what a pure stroke of luck. This could be the man to fly Roberto Clemente.

"Hey," Rivera said to Hill. "Want a job?"

15

December 31

VERA CLEMENTE STOOD IN THE KITCHEN FIXING LUNCH.
It was late Sunday morning, the last day of the year, and the house on
the hill was silent. The boys were staying with her mother in Carolina.
Roberto was in the bedroom, shades drawn tight, trying to rest before
his trip to Nicaragua. Angel Lozano, a member of the relief effort who
would accompany Clemente on the mission, had called several times
that morning with the same news. He was near the DC-7 at the cargo
area and nothing was ready; it would be hours before the plane left.
Out the big windows of her kitchen, Vera could look north across the
treetops toward the airport on Isla Verde and the Atlantic Ocean
beyond. The winter sky hung low and gray; the sea looked green. In
the stillness, as she prepared the meal, a song looped around in her
mind. It was the *"Tragedia de Viernes Santo,"* a popular ballad about a
DC-4 that crashed into the ocean on Good Friday 1952 after taking off
from San Juan on the way to New York.

> *Que triste fue el Viernes Santo*
> *Que horas de anguista y dolor*
> *Sufrieron nuestros hermanos*
> *Que volaban a New York*

How sad was Good Friday/ What hours of anguish and pain/ Our brothers suffer/ Who were flying to New York. In the silence, the haunting
lyrics and melody ran through Vera's mind, but it was just a song, it
could have been any song, it could have been "Feliz Navidad," just

something that slipped into the subconscious without her thinking about what it meant.

When lunch was ready, she went to fetch Roberto, who had barely slept. As they ate, they reviewed their plans for the next few days. The Rauches, who were coming to visit from Pennsylvania, had spent the night at Carlos and Carmen Llanos's place in the Bronx and would be catching a flight down to San Juan later in the day. New Year's Eve was a major holiday in Puerto Rico, a time to be with friends and family. There had been so many special days that Roberto had missed lately. He had missed their eighth wedding anniversary on November 14 and then missed Thanksgiving while he was managing the amateur baseball team in Nicaragua. He kept saying that he hated to be separated from his family and yet he kept leaving. Vera didn't directly ask him not to leave again, but the message was there as she cited his absences.

"Don't worry," Roberto said. "When you are healthy and you are happy, every day of life is the same."

"That's true," Vera said. She understood because they thought the same way. He meant that every day of life was special, every day they were together was special, none better than the others. When they were traveling in Europe, without worries, those days were wonderful, but no different. And so many times she had heard him repeat his mantra: If you have a chance to make life better for others, and fail to do so, you are wasting your time on this earth. In going to Managua, she thought, he was doing something good for humanity. She didn't feel great about him leaving on New Year's Eve, but she was not going to make a big deal of it. He'd be back in a day, soon enough.

Jerry Hill, the pilot Arthur Rivera recruited for the trip, had returned to San Juan International Airport at six that morning after a hop to Miami and back. He had not slept overnight, and would need some rest before leaving for Managua. Rather than find a motel, Hill dozed off in the cabin of the DC-7. In his last-minute hunt for a pilot, Rivera had not bothered to check Hill's background. He was not much for going by the book in any case. Hill told him that he loved DC-7s and knew how to fly them, and that was sufficient. The records of the Federal Aviation Administration filled out some of Jerry Carroll Hill's history. He was forty-seven, a veteran pilot who was born in Texas, began flying in California, now lived in Miami, and "seemed to have seen better days," as one report said. He was qualified to captain a DC-7, with about three thousand hours of flying time in the aircraft, two-thirds of that as the pilot in command. But at the time Rivera hired him, he had been furloughed by Airlift International and was in jeopardy of losing his commercial license, facing a hearing on thirteen violations that occurred between October 1971 and January 1972. He was divorced, and his ex-wife wanted nothing to do with him.

This was the pilot, catnapping in the cabin, now entrusted to fly Roberto Clemente and a planeload of humanitarian aid across the Caribbean. Rivera would be the copilot, even though his sum experience amounted to the flight that brought the plane out of Miami's Cockroach Corner and then the incompetent taxiing episode earlier that month. In need of a flight engineer, Rivera first tried to recruit Rafael Delgado-Cintron, the Caribair mechanic, but Delgado-Cintron's boss would not let him off work that day. In desperation, Rivera asked Delgado-Cintron for the number of Francisco Matias, another Caribair mechanic. Matias knew how to fly a single-engine plane but did not have a flight engineer's certificate. As a forty-two-year-old father of four with another baby on the way, he said he could use the extra money moonlighting for Rivera and quickly agreed to join the crew.

The DC-7 was still being loaded while Hill snoozed. At mid-morning, José Fonet, who worked at the airport, climbed inside and woke the captain to tell him that another pickup truck with humanitarian cargo had arrived. Hill was so tired that he expressed no interest in overseeing the last-minute effort. The aircraft was already full, holding one hundred ninety-eight packages of rice, three hundred twelve cartons of evaporated milk, 320 cartons of beans, 70 cartons of vegetable oil, 90 cartons of luncheon meat, and 60 cartons of cornmeal. Now here came another small pickup truck with a final load—16 bags of sugar weighing 60 pounds apiece, plus more rice, beans, milk, sugar, toothpaste, toothbrushes, and medical supplies. Raymond Cintron, a ramp inspector for the airport police, helped load the last-minute cargo with his supervisor. With no space remaining in storage, they stacked it haphazardly in front of a steel mesh net near the bulkhead. Then a large spare tire was placed on top of the load. No attention was paid to the plane's center of gravity. Rafael Vasquez, an airport attendant for Texaco, came by at twelve forty-five to supply five gallons of aircraft oil No. 120. Vasquez said that when he entered the plane he was stunned to see all the "cargo which was not tied down." The plane was not supposed to haul more than 40,000 pounds. The air cargo manifest that Rivera would file with the Bureau of Customs estimated the total weight at 39,288 pounds, but that manifest was a lie. FAA officials later determined that the improperly loaded plane was at least 4,193 pounds over the maximum allowable gross weight.

Sometime after three that afternoon, Rivera called Clemente from the airport and said they were nearly ready. They had prepared a flight plan, the plane was loaded, and they had a full crew. Clemente was at home shining his boots and talking to Vera and his friend Cristobal Colón, the regional sales manager for Goya Food Products who had been helping with the relief effort. Colón, known by his nickname Caguitas, had stopped by the house with his young son, Angel Luis. Time to go, Clemente said, and Caguitas insisted on driving them to the airport. Clemente did not bring a suitcase. He carried what he needed in the alligator-skin briefcase he bought in Nicaragua during the baseball tournament a month earlier. On the ride down the hill toward Isla Verde, Caguitas kept turning to his young son and asking, "Angel Luis, who is sitting beside you?" The toddler would say proudly, "Roberto Clemente."

They arrived at the airport around four and were taken to the cargo ramp. The plane was fueling and there was more paperwork to be done, so Clemente, Vera, and Angel Lozano drove to a nearby restaurant to order food. When they returned, Caguitas Colón seemed alarmed. This was the first time he had taken a good look at the DC-7, and he did not like what he saw. The lightning-bolt paint job of orange with black trim did not impress him. He was concerned with the tires. The landing wheels were so squashed they appeared almost flat, and the nose tire was virtually off the ground. "When I saw all this I complained to Clemente and advised him that the aircraft was unsafe and improperly loaded," Colón said later. He hoped that Clemente would forget about the DC-7 and take a Pan American flight to Miami and go to Nicaragua from there. Vera was standing nearby. As she later recalled, "Roberto said, 'Don't worry. They know what they're doing.'"

There was so much Clemente did not know: Cockroach Corner. Tramp airlines. The FAA's Southern Order. Arthur Rivera's sixty-six transport violations. The ditch incident. Pilot Hill's troubles and lack of sleep. The wholly unqualified copilot and flight engineer. The imbalanced and overweight load. Everything was wrong, but the only physical signs of that were the tires, the tips of the iceberg, and though his friend Caguitas raised the issue, Clemente chose not to worry about the tires. When he said the crew knew what it was doing, Vera believed him. Shortly before five, she said good-bye to Roberto and left with Colón for the other side of the airport, where she had to pick up the Rauches, who would be arriving on a flight from JFK in New York. An earlier plane from New York had arrived already, but the Rauches missed that one, so they would be two hours late.

At 5:30 P.M., according to FAA records, Rivera's DC-7, identified as N500AE, called the air traffic control tower and requested taxi instructions from the Pan American cargo area. The tower cleared the plane to Runway 7.

In the Federal Aviation Administration structure, the air traffic controllers and safety inspectors were under separate fiefdoms. The inspectors of the Flight Standards Office were located in a separate building at the San Juan airport. The air traffic controllers were not enforcers—their duties were demanding enough, handling the flow of planes taking off and landing. When Hill radioed the tower and asked for taxi instructions, it was not up to the traffic controllers to check first whether the plane was airworthy. That was the job of the Flight Standards Office, at least in theory.

It is hard to imagine an aircraft that called out for surveillance more than Arthur Rivera's DC-7 that final day of 1972. As a tramp aircraft purchased at Cockroach Corner in Miami, it seemed to fit the description of planes that were to be watched under the guidelines of the

Southern Order. But Leonard Davis, who ran the Flight Standards Office in San Juan, said that they did not have the manpower to check every departing flight. Office inspectors certainly knew about Rivera and had been watching his plane since the taxiing incident, and had even suggested that he replace one engine and conduct a test flight. But now that Rivera was ready to go, without a new engine, no test flight, a tired pilot, himself as a novice copilot, a mechanic as the flight engineer, a plane so overloaded the tires were slumping, and the famous Roberto Clemente aboard—now there were no Flight Standards inspectors around. It was New Year's Eve. No one was assigned to surveillance that weekend. George E. Mattern, who had arrived in San Juan in October as the general aviation maintenance inspector, was on inspection standby. He had come into work on Saturday to check out another tramp operator and then had been called to the wreckage of a small plane that had crashed on the beach near the Caribe Hilton in Condado, a resort section of San Juan. By Sunday evening, he was back home in Río Piedras. Most of his colleagues were at a New Year's Eve party.

After taxiing to Runway 7, Hill went through final checks in the cockpit. His checks showed a problem with the spark plugs in cylinder No. 5. The plane sat on the runway for twenty-one minutes, then they radioed the control tower and asked for instructions to taxi back from the runway to the Pan Am cargo area. When Hill got out to inspect the spark plugs in the other cylinders, he found that most of them were bad. Hill and the mechanic-cum-flight engineer, Matias, opened the cowling on No. 3 and No. 4 engines and worked on them for more than three hours. Delgado-Cintron, the other Caribair mechanic who could not make the trip, got off work and went over to help. When all the repairwork was done, Delgado-Cintron climbed halfway up the ladder. Clemente handed him a slip of paper on which he had written his home phone number. He asked the mechanic to call his house and tell Vera when and if the plane left for Nicaragua.

As he stood on the ladder, Delgado-Cintron caught a final glimpse of the scene inside: Arthur Rivera sat in the right cockpit seat and Jerry Hill was in the captain's seat. Clemente was sitting on the lower bunk in the cabin, forward of the cargo. Angel Lozano and Francisco Matias stood nearby, not yet in position. In the past few days, Clemente had asked so many friends to come along: Orlando Cepeda, Manny Sanguillen, Osvaldo Gil, but they had all declined. Angel Lozano was the one who had agreed to go. He was thirty-three years old, married with two children, and ran his own trucking company, which hauled provisions for Pueblo Foods. Like Clemente, he had been working long hours every day on the relief effort.

Three and a half hours after the first attempted takeoff, the DC-7 was cleared again to Runway 7. Antonio Ríos, working for Eastern Airlines at Gate 12, saw Rivera's plane as it rolled past his ramp. It must have a lot of cargo, Ríos thought, because "the nose gear was hardly touching the ground."

Seventy-six degrees. Scattered clouds. Visibility twelve miles. Long after sundown, but objects could still be seen in the distance.

"San Juan tower, Douglas five hundred alpha echo ready for departure Runway Seven," Hill reported at nine-eighteen.

"Douglas five nine alpha echo Runway Seven cleared for takeoff," responded the air traffic controller, Dennis A. McHale.

"Roger, that's Douglas five *hundred* alpha echo," Hill said, correcting the number.

"Five hundred alpha echo, okay, you VFR [using visual flight regulations]?"

"Affirmative."

"Okay."

An Eastern Airlines flight radioed from the runway: "Tower, Eastern nine sixty-four ready . . ."

"Okay, Eastern nine sixty . . . uh . . . hold your position just a minute . . . I got a DC-seven taxiing off your right there I think . . ."

"Okay," said the Eastern pilot.

The controller radioed Hill: "Alpha echo, are you behind the jet— can you make your first taxiway there . . . ?"

" . . . the seven twenty-seven go first," responded Hill.

"Okay. Eastern nine sixty-four, he's advised you're in front of him, you can taxi on the runway and cleared for takeoff Runway Seven . . ."

"Okay, cleared for takeoff, nine sixty-four . . . here we go," reported the Eastern pilot.

"And, uh, five hundred alpha echo, taxi into position and hold."

It was nine-nineteen. Gary Cleaveland replaced McHale as ground controller in the air traffic tower.

Thirty seconds later, Cleaveland said: "Douglas five hundred alpha echo, Runway Seven cleared for takeoff."

"Alpha echo, roger."

The Eastern jet was airborne above the ocean by then.

"Eastern nine sixty-four, contact departure, good day," said the controller.

"Nine sixty-four, Happy New Year, sir," responded the Eastern pilot.

At nine-twenty the DC-7 started rolling down Runway 7.

Juan Reyes, an airport security officer, happened to be watching. The plane didn't seem to have the necessary speed to take off, he thought, and "by the sound of the motors it looked like it was making much effort."

Gilberto Quiles, a cleaner for Pan Am, sensed that the plane was in trouble as it rumbled slowly down the runway.

Antonio Ríos, the Eastern employee, noticed how the plane kept rolling down the strip, six thousand, seven thousand, eight thousand feet. As it reached the end of the runway, Ríos heard several loud backfires about five seconds apart on the left wing.

Rafael Delgado-Cintron was near Ríos in the Eastern cargo area. "They were about at the end of the runway . . . I hear like a . . . three backfires . . . changing engine noise and a very big explosion. Then silence."

At the far end of the runway, nearly nine thousand feet from where the takeoff roll began, the plane struggled into the air. Witnesses on the ground could no longer see it after it barely cleared the palm trees at the eastern edge of the airport. From his control tower perch, Cleaveland noticed that the DC-7 was not gaining altitude as it flew about a mile past Punta Maldonado and then banked to the north and out over the ocean. At that point, by his estimate, the plane was no more than two hundred feet above water. It appeared to be descending.

The radio scratched. "Tower, this is five hundred alpha echo coming back around."

Cleaveland could not hear the transmission. "Five hundred . . . uh . . . alpha echo, say again."

Nothing but silence. McHale, tracking on radar, watched as N500AE curved north and then suddenly disappeared from the Brite One display screen.

When the incoming Eastern flight arrived from New York on the passenger side of the airport earlier that evening, Vera was at the gate waiting for her friends Carolyn and Nevin Rauch and their daughters Carol and Sharon. The Rauches were delighted and surprised to see her, considering how late their plane had been and how busy the

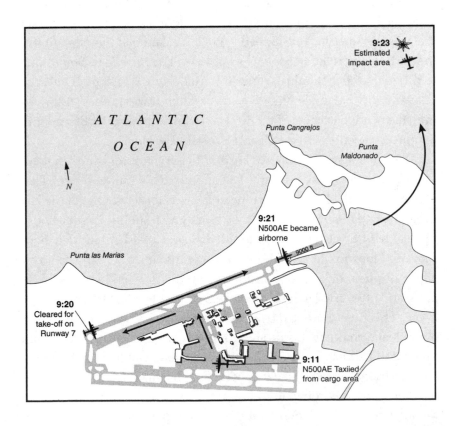

Clementes were with the earthquake relief effort. When they asked about Roberto, Vera said he was probably halfway to Nicaragua. But he would be back the next day if there was no trouble with Somoza, and they would have a great celebration when he returned.

Vera was a warm woman with a contagious laugh and a self-deprecating nature that put people at ease. One of the little jokes she shared with friends was trying to find the right key on her key chain. There were so many keys, for various doors and security systems and gates and she always had to try a few before she found the right one. When they reached the house in Río Piedras, they could hear the telephone ringing as Vera fiddled with the keys. By the time they got inside, the ringing had stopped. "I wonder if that was Roberto," Vera said.

Carolyn and Nevin were hungry and wanted to take Vera out to eat. She was tired, and feeling out of sorts, but they thought it would be good for her. Carolyn called around and found a seafood restaurant that was serving late. Vera agreed to go, but asked that they stop first at the earthquake relief headquarters at Plaza Las Americas. Something told her that she should be there in Roberto's absence. "I felt the responsibility on my shoulders," she said later. It was raining. After visiting the headquarters in Hato Rey and eating dinner at El Pescador in Santurce, they drove to the Zabala house in Carolina.

The boys were asleep. Robertito fussed before going to bed. *"Abuela,* why is Daddy leaving?" he had said to his grandmother. "That plane will crash." Robertito had been anxious for days. One of the last things he had done before they took him away from his parents' house the day before was to sneak into the dressing area behind their bedroom and look in the little dresser drawer divider where his dad usually kept plane tickets. Robertito never liked it when his father flew away, and often tried to hide the tickets in a futile effort to keep him at home. This time there had been no tickets. He had warned his father not to leave, and now his premonition was stronger. Mrs. Zabala told him not to be foolish, everything would be fine. But later, before Vera and her friends arrived, she was overcome by an odd sensation. It felt like her heart was going around in a circle of sadness. She went into the kitchen and cried. Something bad is happening, she thought, but she didn't say anything. Nearby, at his house on Calle Nicolas Aguayo, Melchor Clemente was also haunted by dark feelings. He had had a dream about Momen.

The radio was on at the Zabala house, but it was only background noise, no one was listening. The room was full of people talking. Vera, her mother, her brother Orlando, and his wife. Neighbors. Nevin and Carolyn Rauch and the daughters. A few times Vera thought she heard an announcer say the name Roberto Clemente, but that was nothing out of the ordinary; he was in the news every day for his relief work. The telephone rang constantly. Carol, now fluent in Spanish, answered it once. There was music blaring in the background, and the connection was bad, but she thought she heard something about a plane crash. By the time she handed the phone to Orlando, the caller had hung up. One of Vera's close friends, the godmother to her youngest son, Ricky, called three times. She seemed tentative, evasive, asking how Vera was, then hanging up. The Navarros, Roberto's friends from Carolina, rang the doorbell and paid a visit. They took seats in the living room and didn't talk. It was as though everyone was expecting Vera to know something.

Then Roberto's niece Fafa called. She was coughing, crying. "Are you listening to the news?" she asked Vera. Something about a crash of the airplane going to Nicaragua. At first, Vera was disbelieving, but then Carol took the phone. When word spread through the room the reaction was the same. It couldn't be true. Roberto's plane would have been arriving in Managua by now. "We all said, 'This can't be true! This can't be true!'" Carolyn Rauch remembered. Vera's sister-in-law called the airport and got the first sketchy confirmation. It was a cargo plane with five people bound for Nicaragua. In the far bedroom, Robertito heard his mother's cry and feared the worst.

Vera grabbed her car keys and rushed out the door, followed by Nevin, Carolyn, and Carol. They didn't want her to drive, but she insisted. She knew the way to Roberto's parents' house in El Comandante.

Matino Clemente, Roberto's brother, had been at his father-in-law's house when he heard the news on the radio. He looked outside toward Isla Verde and saw lights flaring in the night sky. He and his brother

Osvaldo reached their parents' house before Vera got there. Melchor and Luisa were asleep. Matino woke his father and took him outside to break the news. The old man was devastated, but not surprised. He had dreamed this, he said. Luisa eventually came out of bed and noticed all the people in her house. What's going on? Matino told her it was a *Paranda,* a spontaneous house call during the holiday season. Then where is the music? Matino huddled with Osvaldo and they decided they had to tell her. She listened without saying a word, then collapsed in deep, sorrowful sobs. December 31. The final day of the year. On that same day eighteen years earlier, Luisa had lost her first-born son, Luis Oquendo.

By the time Vera and the Rauches arrived, the street was buzzing with people. Soon a caravan of cars left for Isla Verde. They drove to the airport. Mass confusion. Sirens wailing, policemen everywhere. Had the plane crashed in Nicaragua? No, on takeoff, here in San Juan. They drove toward the ocean near where the plane might have gone down. In the rain, a crowd was already gathering on Piñones Beach near Punta Maldonado. Police cars were shining headlights into the ocean. Vera knew the area well; it was Roberto's favorite spot to collect driftwood.

Sitting in a car nearby was George Mattern, the FAA inspector. He had been at home in Río Piedras, taking a shower, when his pager went off at about ten that night. He had no phone at his place, so he went out looking for help. Up and down his street, no one was home, they were all out celebrating. Finally, a block away, he found a neighbor who let him use the phone. He called the office and heard about a plane crash. A "newsworthy person" had been aboard. It went down in the Piñones area. Get there as soon as you can. Driving through the back roads along the beach, he ran into his boss, Leonard Davis. Stories were already spreading at the beach. José Ayala of Punta Maldonado had been in bed when he heard a plane flying overhead and the motors sputter and go dead. Gregorio Rivera had seen wreckage floating on the water about a mile out to sea, but a few minutes later it had disappeared.

Vera felt faint; Melchor was getting weak. A nephew took Vera's car keys and drove them home long past two in the morning.

*   *   *

In Puerto Rico, New Year's Eve is one of the biggest nights of the year, celebrated with fireworks, traditional street dancing, and vibrant Latin music. But Orlando Cepeda felt something eerie in the air long before he heard about the crash. "It was quiet and sad. The night felt different. There weren't many people celebrating. No stars were out. Man, nothing happening." Cepeda, who had revered Roberto since he was a bowlegged batboy for the Santurce Cangrejeros in 1954, was with his wife at a brother's house when he got the news. Roberto Clemente cannot die, he thought. And he remembered how Clemente had wanted him to come along on the flight to Nicaragua.

Osvaldo Gil, who had persuaded Clemente to make that first trip to Nicaragua to manage, and who would have accompanied Roberto on the mercy flight had his wife not talked him out of it, was celebrating with his family when word of the crash reached him. In Spanish, Gil is pronounced "heel," and it sounds quite similar to the Spanish pronunciation of the English name Hill. With the first reports listing the names of the five people aboard the DC-7, friends and associates heard the name Hill and feared that Osvaldo was among the dead. He remembered a saying that Clemente had uttered only a few days earlier as they discussed the flight: *Nobody dies the day before.* You die the day you're supposed to.

Caguitas Colón was at a family reunion in his hometown of Caguas at two that morning when a relative told him the news. He had tried to warn Clemente that the plane looked unsafe, to no avail. Now he remembered how Clemente had scoffed at danger with one of his colloquial sayings: *You even die riding a horse.* Colón felt so blue he retreated to his bedroom and would not come out.

Juan Pizarro was on the roof of his house in Castellana Gardens in Carolina, fiddling with his malfunctioning television antenna, when the plane went down. He happened to be looking toward the ocean at the time, and thought he saw an explosion. A few hours later, when he heard that Clemente's plane had crashed, two thoughts rushed into his mind. He remembered when they were teammates on the Pirates and Clemente had told him that he was going to die in a plane crash. But he also thought Clemente absolutely could not die. He had to still be alive.

José Pagan was asleep at the family house in Barceloneta when his father came in and told him the news. The Pirate teammate remembered when Roberto had uncharacteristically fallen asleep on the team plane but jolted awake from a dream saying that a plane had crashed and he had been the only one killed, and how Pagan had tried to soothe him by saying that he often dreamed that he was rich but that didn't make it so. When Pagan's wife, Delia, heard the news, she insisted that they leave immediately for Río Piedras to be with her dear friend, Vera Clemente.

Pedrin Zorrilla, who had signed Clemente to his first contract with Santurce, heard the bulletins on the radio that night at his house in Manatí. The news left him gasping for air. Clemente, he thought, had become more than a baseball player; he was now a symbol, a representation of the Dream of Deeds, the burning pride for Puerto Rico expressed by Zorrilla's poet father: *Land, blood, name, and race.*

Eduardo Valero, a veteran Puerto Rican sports writer, was asleep that night when he received a call from a friend in Virginia. *You know who died? Roberto Clemente.* "It was like a cold water shower," Valero said. But he could never figure it out. "Who in the hell in Latin American culture leaves a family on New Year's Eve? If you find two, let me know the other one. He left his family to go there on New Year's Eve."

Luis Olmo, one of the Three Kings of Puerto Rican baseball, paving the way for Clemente in the major leagues, was with his son's wife's family in Naguabo when he heard the news on the radio. Olmo thought of Clemente as a man of passion for everything in life, and he had a different take on the question raised by Valero. "I don't see any reason for him to be on that plane that night to go to Nicaragua," Olmo said later. "That's the night to be with family. The reason he went, I don't know. That is the night to keep your heart at home."

Vic Power, another of the Three Kings, heard about the plane crash a few minutes before midnight after he had finished dinner with his wife and son at a restaurant in Condado. The last time he had seen Clemente was on the plane returning from Managua after the amateur baseball championships three weeks earlier. Clemente had been quiet during that uneventful flight home, sleeping. Power had been restless, still bothered by that fishbone in his throat. Then Clemente had gone off to run his youth baseball clinics, and Power had returned to manage Caguas. Power could not believe that his friend was gone.

The Pirates had a working relationship with the San Juan Senadores that year, and the team was stocked with young Pittsburgh players. Many of them had gathered on New Year's Eve at a waterfront condo. Chuck Goggin, who had slapped his first major league hit in the same game that Clemente got his three-thousandth, was sitting on the patio deck with Richie Zisk and Bob Johnson shortly after midnight and noticed "a bunch of commotion going on over the ocean, it looked like helicopters and planes" and lights. There were no radios, no phone calls, no one at the party had a clue. They speculated that there must have been a plane crash, or maybe a boat was missing.

Steve Blass and his wife were hosting a party at their house in Upper St. Clair Township, a Pittsburgh suburb. There were eight couples there from the neighborhood, including Dave Giusti and his wife. By two in the morning, everyone had left but the Giustis, who were going to stay and party all night. Then a call came from Bill Guilfoile, the Pirates public relations man. There is an unsubstantiated report that a plane has gone down near Puerto Rico and Clemente was on it, Guilfoile said. My God, Blass thought. Clemente! He's invincible. He doesn't die. He plays as long as he wants to and then becomes governor of Puerto Rico. With the stunning news, Blass and Giusti sobered up quickly. Not knowing what else to do, but wanting to do something, they drove to general manager Joe L. Brown's house in Mount Lebanon, the adjacent township in the South Hills area. Brown let them in and they sat around drinking coffee. As Brown later recalled the scene, the three men "talked about Roberto and cried" as they recalled "the depth of the man and the intelligence of the man and the humor of the man." Clemente never held anything back from the people, Brown thought. He gave them more than they had any right to expect from him. He reminded Brown of a panther, the grace and power of a panther. He would always think of footage from the 1971 World Series of Clemente rounding second and sliding into third, so graceful and strong, such spectacular passion. What a good man.

From there, Blass and Giusti drove across town to Willie Stargell's house, and the three Pirates consoled one another until the sun came up, eventually making their way over to the annual New Year's Day party at the home of Bob Prince. The Gunner had thought about canceling his party after he heard the news, but decided that Roberto would want the party to go on. It did, as a wake.

The fans of Pittsburgh were in shock. On New Year's morning, Ann Ranalli's mother was in the kitchen when she heard a radio report. She ran upstairs to tell her daughter, who three months earlier had taken the streetcar to Three Rivers Stadium and thrown confetti over the right-field railing after Roberto Clemente got his three-thousandth hit. Ann started sobbing. She spent the rest of the day praying that he would be found. "It was really hard," she said later. "He was the Pope to me."

"Adios, Amigo Roberto" read the lights atop Mount Washington. The mayor declared a week of mourning. Richard Santry was home for the holidays during his freshman year at Notre Dame. All through his childhood, Santry had watched Clemente from the Knothole Gang seats in the right-field bleachers. He and his father would stand at the screen and wave and sometimes Clemente would come over to talk to them or throw a ball their way. There are days you remember your whole life, Santry would say decades later. Where you were when JFK was shot. Where you were on 9/11. He would always remember New Year's morning, 1973. "The sound I remember is the bedroom door opening, the creaking of rusty hinges. My mother sat on an empty twin bed and started to poke me a bit. I glanced over at the clock. It was eleven-twenty or so; I had slept pretty good. My mom's first words to me were 'I have some very bad news.' I sat up, and Mom said that Clemente had died in a plane crash. I looked at her, groggy, not quite sure what I heard, waiting for a punch line. What are you talking about? He was on a plane delivering supplies to people in Nicaragua and the plane dropped into the ocean, she said. I was eighteen years old. I went into the bathroom . . . and just sat there and had a cry like a family member or my best friend just died."

Nancy Golding had gone to bed on New Year's Eve with her radio on. Things always seemed louder in the morning, and when she awoke the radio was blaring the news. She was just an average kid in Pittsburgh, and yet she happened to live near Roberto's accountant and the

Clementes had been so kind in letting her into their lives. She had been to their house in Río Piedras and had eaten in their kitchen and had played with their little boys. Roberto Clemente is missing and presumed dead in a plane crash, the radio announcer was saying, and she started screaming. *"Clemente died! Clemente died!"*

In Miami that morning, William Couric, the FAA official who had battled with Arthur Rivera almost daily during his tenure in San Juan, exploded in uncharacteristic fury when he heard the news. How could they let the tramp aircraft from Cockroach Corner ever roll down a runway? "They wouldn't listen to me! They wouldn't listen to me!" he cried. "I tried! I tried so hard to put those people out of business!"

The three Clemente boys, Robertito, Luisito, and Ricky, were brought back to the house in Río Piedras late the next morning. Everything was a blur, but there were a few images they would never forget. Parked cars line both sides of the street all the way up the hill. They are led across the little bridge from the sidewalk to the front gate. A big black bow is on the door. Military police stand at attention at the entryway. The flags of Puerto Rico and the United States frame the doorway. The door opens into a sea of faces. *Oh, there are the kids!* And people rush up to hug and squeeze them. Finally they are taken into a bedroom with their mother and grandparents and their mom starts crying and holds them tight and searches for the words.

16
Out of the Sea

SECONDS AFTER N500AE DISAPPEARED FROM THE RADAR screen, San Juan's air traffic control tower activated the emergency accident notification system, a sequence of twenty telephone calls. The second call went to the U.S. Coast Guard Rescue Center located near the cruise ship piers in Old San Juan, nine miles west of the airport. Since the plane went down in the water, there was little the airport's fire rescue team could do beyond rush to the beachfront and beam spotlights into the dark Atlantic. The search required boats, planes, helicopters, divers—the realm of the Coast Guard and Navy. One Coast Guard vessel and two aircraft went out on the first call after ten that night, but search officers had not yet plotted the Probability of Detection Area so the rescuers were operating on guesswork, literally in the dark, and found nothing.

Not long after sunrise on New Year's Day it became obvious that this was not just a routine search. From Isla Verde to Punta Maldonado, the shore was lined with people who had come to bear witness. The two-lane roads leading to the water became more congested as the day progressed until by afternoon there was a bumper-to-bumper traffic jam of pilgrims flocking toward the place where their hero had fallen.

"That night on which Roberto Clemente left us physically, his immortality began," the Puerto Rican writer Elliott Castro later observed, and here, on Piñones Beach, was the first manifestation of the transformation from man to myth. Although Governor Luis A. Ferré, in his final day in office, had declared a three-day mourning period, in effect acknowledging that Clemente was dead, many Puerto

339

Ricans refused to believe it. The vast crowds at the beach were quiet, expectant. They waited for Roberto to come walking out of the sea. Men carried portable radios, women brought infants; a shout, a sighting of color or shape, and suddenly a line of people were holding hands wading out to take a look. A Coast Guard helicopter landed at the beach and was swarmed by citizens as the false report spread of a body aboard. Vera and her father-in-law, Melchor, returned to the beach and were treated as royalty as they sat in stoic silence, holding hands. Vera wavered between not wanting to believe the accident had happened, desperately holding on to the miracle that her husband was still alive, and more realistically hoping the searchers would find his body or some tangible evidence of his loss. Osvaldo Gil, the family friend who was among those joining Vera at the beach, remembered her saying softly two or three times, "If they could find at least a hand."

Manny Sanguillen, the Pirate catcher from Panama who adored Clemente like an older brother, showed up ready to do anything he could to help the search. He stripped down to his swimming suit and went out with a group of volunteer local divers who focused on the underwater caverns of the coral reef a hundred yards offshore, a likely place for a body to snag. The official Coast Guard and Navy search party included three helicopters, two fixed-wing aircraft, two smaller rescue vessels, and the cutter *Sagebrush*, a 180-foot buoy tender outfitted with a cranelike boom. The effort that day was slowed by rough waters, four- to six-foot swells. While finding no people or bodies, the rescue team recovered the first swath of debris, including seat cushions, life vests, a deflated raft, papers, a nose wheel and strut, two other wheels, and the wallet of Angel Lozano, who had been riding in the cabin near Clemente. They also came across an oil slick under which they suspected they might find the fuselage, but it was growing dark by then so they marked the position of the oil slick to return to it the next day.

At ten on the second day of January, Hernández Colón was sworn in as Puerto Rico's new governor. Less than a month earlier, Clemente had brought back a red and white hammock from Nicaragua as a gift for his political friend. Now the great ballplayer's loss cast a dark shadow over the inaugural ceremony. All the musical festivities that were to be held that night at La Fortaleza were canceled. Before the swearing-in began, the cutter *Sagebrush*, on its way out to the crash site, cruised by within sight of supporters gathering at the capital grounds. At the start of the program, there was a minute of silence in memory of Clemente. In his speech, Hernández Colón said of him, "Our youth have lost an idol and an example; our people have lost one of their glories." The governor was following the lead of Puerto Rico's newspapers, who that morning had published their editorial eulogies. "Off the field," the *San Juan Star* wrote of Clemente, "he was a complicated, intense man who felt a special burden to use his fame and prestige for noble ends . . . He was a unique man, a shining example for the rest of us. A man who thrilled and entertained us with his athletic exploits and ennobled and inspired us with his humanism."

In the early afternoon, another rumor buzzed through the large crowd that had gathered at the beach for a second consecutive day. Someone had seen a body floating in the water fifty yards from shore a mile west of Punta Maldonado. But a search of the area came up with nothing. It could have been a log, a scrap of debris, even a fish. The Coast Guard station in San Juan was being deluged with calls from people saying they could help, even from thousands of miles away. "It seemed like every psychic and seer all over the world was calling in, telling us they had heard from Roberto," remembered Captain Vincent Bogucki, then commander of the Coast Guard unit in San Juan. "They might say he was on a small island and okay but needed help. We had a lot of unasked for leads . . . that to some extent we followed."

Captain Bogucki was feeling pressure from all sides. President Nixon was interested in Clemente, and that meant top Coast Guard officials in Washington had to know about the search and were requesting constant updates from San Juan. In Puerto Rico, the plane crash had surpassed even the inauguration as the dominant news story, and every official from the governor on down wanted to make sure that everything possible was being done to find the plane and its occupants. Deep into the second day with no results, Vera contacted Captain Bogucki and asked him to come to her house in Río Piedras. She wanted to know what he was doing, and why he wasn't doing more. He talked about the possibility of getting another plane, but did not feel he could tell Mrs. Clemente the cold truth, which was this: The Coast Guard is in the business of search and rescue, not salvage. Bogucki and his men had already privately reached the grim conclusion that there was nothing to rescue, and probably not much in the way of human remains to recover. As one of Bogucki's officers, Lieutenant John Parker, later explained, "If a plane breaks up badly and if bodies break loose, it is rare to recover them. Why? The sharks. They are hungry. It is a shark-infested area." None of this could be said to the widow. Bogucki told Mrs. Clemente that he would try to add another plane to the search and invited her to visit the Coast Guard Rescue Center to see for herself how diligently his crew was working.

As Bogucki was leaving the Clemente house, he looked across the room and noticed that Vera had brought in her own seer. "I saw the figure from the rear, and she had a robe on," Bogucki said later. "I wasn't invited to meet this person." This seer was among those claiming that Clemente was still alive. Her supernatural signs were telling her that he was dazed and walking through the streets of La Perla, a poor waterfront neighborhood nestled below Old San Juan. Fernando González, the rookie Pirate infielder from Arecibo, happened to be at the Clemente house then and left with a scouting party of friends and relatives. "We went to La Perla to look for him," González said later. "And we never found him."

It was not mythmaking but pure baseball that led Jack Lang's colleagues in the press corps to start calling his home in Huntington Station, Long Island, that night. "I'm way ahead of you. That's the first thing I thought of," Lang told one caller. What others wanted to suggest to him, and what he had already thought of, was that the Baseball Writers Association of America, of which he was secretary-treasurer, should take the extraordinary step of immediately inducting Clemente into the Hall of Fame, foregoing the requirement that a player be inactive for five years before being eligible for enshrinement. Certain statistical achievements virtually ensured a place in Cooperstown, and one of those was three thousand hits. Clemente died with precisely that number, along with his .317 career average and closetful of Gold

Gloves as the finest right fielder of his generation. Lang had already talked to commissioner Bowie Kuhn about waiving the waiting period. It had happened only once before in baseball history, when Lou Gehrig was chosen by acclamation in 1939 while he was dying of amyotrophic lateral sclerosis. Eleven weeks after Lang started the process, the BBWAA would overwhelmingly vote Clemente into Cooperstown, making him the first Latin American player among the game's all-time elite. Ninety-three percent of 424 writers would support him, with most of the others saying they did not want to break the five-year requirement.

Clemente had never been an easy case for baseball writers. For eighteen seasons, he had burned with resentment about being underappreciated and called a hypochondriac and quoted in broken English. His fury had helped motivate him on the diamond, even as it confused the men in the press box. Yet he was usually willing to admit when he was wrong, and was so much more earnest and committed than most ballplayers that by the end he had earned the respect of those he fought with the most. Now, after the first news cycle of stories about the plane crash, they were all writing more personal columns praising and trying to explain this complicated man. Many of them repeated the dramatic cycle of anger, understanding, and loss.

"I remember the first time I ever spoke to him, the day he shouted at me, the anger streaming out of those fierce black eyes and washing over me so that I could almost feel its heat," wrote Phil Musick in the *Pittsburgh Press.* " 'You writers are all the same,' he yelled at Byron Yake of the AP and me, the passion in his voice freezing the few people left in the Pirate clubhouse. 'You don't know a damn thing about me.' I had hollered back, scared clear through at watching the fury rise in his face, afraid to back down." Musick then went on to remember a day, much later, when he had felt comfortable enough to needle Clemente as the old man—"and he laughed, and for a moment we weren't natural enemies. And when I heard he was dead, I wished that sometime I had told him I thought he was a hell of a guy. Because he was, and now it's too late to tell him there were things he did on a ball field that made me wish I was Shakespeare."

Milton Richman of UPI, who covered Clemente's entire career, said he had seen all sides of the complex man. "You had to be around him a while to see both sides. I've seen him when he'd rail up at a newsman's perfectly innocent question, and as a guest at his home in Río Piedras, Puerto Rico, as well as on other occasions, I've seen him when he was one of the most hospitable, helpful and cooperative individuals ever to wear a major league uniform."

"Roberto," wrote David Condon in the *Chicago Tribune*, "was kind, generous, considerate, and humble about his own abilities . . . Yet Roberto was a man of mighty wrath. One day in the spring training camp he cut loose with language that humbled the thunder as he berated writers for overkill in their idolatry for American-born baseball players. Because he was speaking from his heart and his argument was credible, Roberto offended no one that afternoon."

Milton Gross of the *New York Post* wrote that he was indeed once offended by Clemente, but then won over again. A few years earlier, Gross had conducted a long interview with Clemente at training camp in Bradenton. After his article appeared, he received a handwritten letter from Clemente. "I give you two hours of my time, and you write horseshit story about me. I don't want to talk to you no more if you write horseshit stories. I don't want you to write about me no more." The letter left Gross angry and confused. His column about Clemente had been "a positive one in which I attempted to correct some of the unfair raps on Clemente, particularly the tale that he was a malingerer." Gross wrote Clemente back demanding to know what he objected to in the piece. Weeks later, he encountered Clemente in the visitors locker room at Shea Stadium. Clemente said that he had based his first angry letter on what a friend from New York had told him about the story. Now that he had read the story himself, he said, "I find out that you did not write what my friend said. So now I apologize to you for the letter and I tell my friend he is no longer my friend because he does not tell me the truth."

"It was a rare moment in my years in sports; a player admitting that he may have been wrong," Gross declared in his sports page eulogy two days after the crash. "Clemente didn't need me but he felt it incumbent upon himself to tell me that he had done me an injustice."

On that night of January 2, as Jack Lang first contemplated Clemente's place in the Hall of Fame and his colleagues were writing their newspaper requiems, President Nixon mentioned in a conversation with aide Charles Colson that the White House should work with the sports world to organize a Roberto Clemente Memorial Fund. Nixon already had released a taped statement on Clemente—calling him "one of the greatest baseball players of our time" and "a generous and kind human being"—and had written a personal $1,000 check to donate to the cause. There was a nobility to the Clemente story that seemed lacking in other matters Nixon and Colson were dealing with then, Vietnam and Watergate. Nixon that day was obsessed by suspicions that Henry Kissinger, his National Security Adviser, had been telling newspaper friends that he privately questioned the President's decision to bomb Hanoi during Christmas. Get the Secret Service to check Kissinger's telephone logs, Nixon told Colson, according to biographer Richard Reeves, and Colson came back with the delicious report that Kissinger had spent hours talking to columnist Joseph Kraft even while insisting to Colson that he would never talk to "that son-of-a-bitch."

The next morning, January 3, presidential aide Richard A. Moore followed up on the Clemente issue. In a memorandum to chief of staff H. R. Haldeman, Moore suggested that the President meet later that day with a delegation from the Pittsburgh Pirates. Moore said that he had talked with the team president, Dan Galbreath, who told him that he liked Nixon's idea of a memorial fund. If the President had the time, Galbreath and a few players could be in the Oval Office that very afternoon. "The visit would be in time for the television news shows and would be a superb kickoff for the project," Moore noted. "In the course of telling the press about the memorial, Galbreath or a player could allude to the fact that the President already made a generous contribution himself." At the end of his memo, Moore added a special note: "Colson wholeheartedly endorses meeting with the President."

During their discussions that day, Haldeman and Nixon had Colson on their minds, but not in the context of the death of Roberto Clemente. They were discussing the role Colson and former attorney general John Mitchell had played in the Watergate bugging. Nixon asked, "Does Mitchell know that Colson was involved, and does Colson know that Mitchell was involved?" and Haldeman answered, "I think the answer is yes to both," On the other matter, Haldeman liked the idea of the President seeing the Pirates delegation. He initialed a box in Moore's memo approving a ten-minute meeting at quarter to four that afternoon.

An hour beforehand, Moore was ushered into the Oval Office to brief the President. He brought in a list of talking points for Nixon:

A) *Clemente was chosen by the President for his postwar National League All-Star Team.*

B) *Apart from baseball, Clemente was known for his year-round service to good causes and his love of Puerto Rico, where he was virtually a folk hero. He was aboard the airplane because he had heard that a previous shipment [to Managua] had been diverted by profiteers and he wanted to make certain that the clothing and food reached the people in need. Clemente had been the chief organizer in raising $150,000 plus tons of clothing and foodstuffs.* [In citing "profiteers," the memo avoided saying that these were the sons and relatives of General Somoza, a great Nixon fan who had recently sent a letter supporting the President for the Nobel Peace Prize.]

C) *Members of the club and other Pittsburgh friends will fly to Puerto Rico in a chartered plane tomorrow for a special memorial service.*

D) *Clemente, thirty-eight, was National League batting champion four times in eighteen seasons, named twelve times to the All-Star team, most valuable player in NL in 1966, and MVP in 1971 World Series.*

E) *Daniel Galbreath's father, John Galbreath, has met the President at All-Star games and sports dinners. He named a racehorse Roberto in honor of Clemente.*

At three forty-three, Galbreath was escorted into the Oval Office along with pitchers Steve Blass and Dave Giusti, who had slept little since they first received word of the plane crash. Television cameramen and the White House photographer were ushered in and out of the room.

Nixon impressed everyone with his detailed knowledge of Clemente and the Pirates roster. They talked until a few minutes after four.

By that hour in the choppy Atlantic waters about a mile and half off Punta Maldonado, dragging operations by the *Sagebrush* had brought a body to the surface. It was identified as the pilot, Jerry Hill, and transferred to Centro Médico Hospital in Río Piedras. The autopsy conducted by forensic pathologist Nestor A. Loynaz revealed the overwhelming corporal trauma occupants of the plane experienced when the plunging DC-7 hit the water, which was much like hitting a brick wall at two hundred miles an hour. Hill's body was broken everywhere: multiple fractures of the head and face; multiple fractures of the ribs and sternum; completely broken spinal column; multiple fractures of the tailbone; complete amputation of right leg; broken left leg; cavities in the stomach and diaphragm; ruptured aorta; ruptured bladder. Manny Sanguillen had seen the body on the recovery boat before it was flown to the hospital and the devastation of it convinced Sangy that he would never find his friend Roberto alive.

Early the next morning, a chartered jet left Pittsburgh carrying more than sixty members of the Pirates family to a memorial service for No. 21 in Puerto Rico. The contingent included manager Bill Virdon and most of the players and coaches and many wives, former managers Danny Murtaugh and Harry Walker, John and Dan Galbreath, general manager Joe L. Brown, baseball commissioner Bowie Kuhn, Marvin Miller and Richard Moss of the players association, and Preston Pearson, representing the Pittsburgh Steelers, who on the day Clemente died had lost an NFL playoff game to the Miami Dolphins. The plane was "real quiet going down," Richie Hebner recalled, though Pearson happened to be sitting near Dock Ellis, the irrepressible pitcher, who could not stop talking. The baseball men were all dressed in black. After they filed off the plane and assembled in San Juan International's lobby for a press conference, Joe L. Brown stepped to the microphone. Addressing the bustling throng of local writers, television crews, and onlookers, Brown showed his deep respect for Clemente, yet also sounded as though Roberto's real family had arrived at last to tell these people about him.

"We would like to get on with it, please. Ladies and gentlemen, when you are ready, we'll get started," Brown began. "I'd like to say a few words first. Gentlemen, please. I don't want your attention as far as the camera's concerned, we'd just like a little quiet, please. I'd like to say a few things first. This plane from Pittsburgh contains many of Roberto's closest and dearest friends. There is one purpose in their visit: to show their love and respect for Vera and the Clemente family. We ask your cooperation in keeping this as a family affair. There perhaps might be some questions. I will try to answer them before you ask them . . . I'm sure you are going to ask about memorial services for Roberto. They will be held at three-thirty this afternoon. . . . If you want to take pictures of friends or family entering or leaving the church, you are certainly free to do so. But no pictures inside. I think there is no way to handle a thing of this sort except to tell you that behind me are part of Roberto's family. If you care to talk to them, if you care to take their picture, I'm sure they'll be happy, not happy, but they will accommodate you."

Commissioner Kuhn followed with a brief, well-received lament: "It is a very sad event to be here in Puerto Rico for this service for Roberto. Very sad for baseball, for Puerto Rico. He was a truly great man in every way."

Dan Galbreath described his meeting in the Oval Office with President Nixon, just as the President's aides had hoped. "I thought it was going to be a perfunctory meeting but we talked with the President for twenty-five minutes," Galbreath said. "He showed a genuine concern over Clemente and displayed a remarkable knowledge of Clemente the athlete and the humanitarian. His manner was not that of a passing gesture. He said that he and Mrs. Nixon were donating a thousand-dollar check . . . on behalf of Roberto's memorial fund."

When an island reporter told Galbreath about Clemente's interest in using some abandoned San Juan Naval Station property for his sports city dream, the team president promised to pass the information along to the White House.

Bill Virdon said these were the only circumstances he could think of that would make him return to Puerto Rico without enjoying it. Danny Murtaugh, his predecessor, was nearly at a loss for words. He recalled the first time he had seen Clemente in 1955 and had said to himself then that he was watching a kid who was going to be one of the greatest ballplayers of all time. Gene Clines said Roberto was like a big brother to him. Al Oliver said Clemente was the strongest inspiration in his baseball career. Steve Blass said he would never forget Roberto as long as he lived. The room fell quiet as Willie Stargell spoke. For nearly a decade, Stargell had been the other pillar on the Pittsburgh team. He towered over Clemente physically, but always looked up to him.

"I'll tell you, it's really hard to put into words all the feelings that I have for Robby," Stargell said. "Since I've been with him I've had a chance to know a really dynamic man who walked tall in every sense you can think of. He was proud, he was dedicated. He was in every sense you can determine a man. And I think going the way he went really typifies how he lived. Helping other people without seeking any publicity or fame. Just making sure that he could lend a hand and get the job done. . . . The greatness that he is, we all know the ballplayer that he is. For those who did not know him as a man they really missed a fine treat for not knowing this gentleman. I had the opportunity to play with him, to sit down and talk about the things that friends talk about. And I am losing a great friend. But he will always remain in my heart."

The baseball delegation filed into two buses for the short ride from the airport to the central plaza in Carolina and the memorial mass led by Archbishop Luis Aponte Martínez at San Fernando Roman Catholic Church. Crowds lined the streets into town, and thousands of *carolinenses* filled the plaza, much as they had only eight years earlier when Roberto and Vera had been married in the same stone chapel. Mourners entering the church were handed programs with an artist's rendering of Clemente and the words of his mother's spiritual refrain: *Only God makes man happy. Life is nothing. Everything ends. Only God makes man happy.* Steve Blass, speaking for his teammates at the service, read a poem that Pirates press man Bill Guilfoile gave him, a slightly reconfigured version of an ode to another baseball hero who had died young, Lou Gehrig. Blass was more afraid in the pulpit than he had ever felt on the mound. All the way down on the plane, all he thought about was whether he could do this. The poem had the sentimentalism of 1930s sports journalism, when writers often expressed themselves in rhyme, but Blass infused the words with sincerity and choked up several times during his reading. *Let this be a silent token/Of Lasting friendship's gleam/And all that we've left unspoken/ Your pals on the Pirates team.* As Blass faltered, so too did many in the audience. "Blass is one of the funniest guys you'd ever want to meet," recalled trainer Tony Bartirome. "Yet it brought tears to your eyes when a guy like that was up there crying." Not a dry eye among the Pirates delegation, recalled Joe L. Brown.

Manny Sanguillen skipped the service because he preferred to be in a boat off Punta Maldonado all day helping the search teams. Sangy kept churning and bobbing in the dismal sea; an expression of loss deeper than any public statement. Eight Navy scuba divers were on the scene, going deep in pairs fifteen minutes at a time. They found small, scattered pieces of aircraft in 120 feet of water and were able to recover parts of the forward cockpit. About two-hundred yards away, the cutter *Sagebrush* appeared to locate larger pieces of wreckage; the divers would have to wait until the next day to confirm it. There were also reports of another body floating in a coral pocket closer to shore, but turbulent waters kept divers away at first, and when they reached the area there was nothing.

In keeping with her daily ritual, Vera had returned to Piñones Beach in the morning with friends and relatives. She was there for the commotion over the body sighting. No sign of Roberto, dead or alive, only rags and sticks. On the way back, she got trapped in a traffic jam on the clogged roads and never made it to the memorial mass in Carolina. It was not a funeral or burial mass that she missed, there was no body to bury, and there would be another memorial service a few days later, at the stadium, open to everyone. Vera did reach the house on the hill in time to host the Pittsburgh delegation early that evening. She was standing in the lush living room, surrounded by relatives, as she greeted the visitors one by one, expressing thanks to each of them.

Les Banos, the team photographer, had worried on the plane about what he would say when he saw Vera. "I thought about it all the way," he said later. "Then I saw her and said, 'I've lost my best friend.' And she said, 'So have I.'" The evening was soft and calm. From the balcony of the house, visitors could see the ocean where the DC-7 had gone down. Steve Blass had felt so much already, but from a distance. This was the real thing. "Vera is there. The boys are there. The emotions are like a raw vein." Dock Ellis, always with something to say, was now somber and shaken. Al Oliver had contained himself throughout the day. Now he thought about how Clemente had to die for people to realize what an uncommon man he was, and how Roberto reminded him of his father, who had died on the very day that Scoop, as he was known, got called up to the major leagues. Clemente and his dad were strong individualists who carried themselves with dignity and talked about life the same way. "I probably have not broke down more than once or twice in life, but I was hurt bad," Oliver said later. "The team went over to the house and reality set in. I was just standing there thinking about it. All of a sudden tears started rolling."

By the end of that weekend the search team, reinforced with more divers and sophisticated sonar and salvage equipment, had located most everything that was to be found. First they came across significant portions of the cockpit, with the pilot seat attached, instruments and electrical wiring dangling freely, along with some fuselage sections and melted medical equipment. Behind the pilot seat, divers recovered a shirt and trousers with a wallet inside that belonged to Jerry Hill. Then they found the tail section intact, from the tip to the large cargo loading doors, with the tail number N500AE clearly visible. About 150 feet away from the tail they encountered a twenty-five-foot section of one wing, with the landing gear attached and in the down position.

Following an underwater line perpendicular to the tail section, they spotted three engines, all separated from the wings. The No. 1 engine showed nothing unusual. On the No. 2 engine, two propellers were bent and one sheared off. These remnants offered more clues to National Transportation Safety Board investigators in determining the cause of the crash. Arthur Rivera's DC-7 was a death trap even before it rolled down Runway 7, but it appeared from the wreckage clues that there were some final errors. Trying to fly a previously damaged and untested plane that was overloaded and imbalanced, it seemed that Hill had overboosted the engines, pushing them beyond their limits. His crewmates, who were to monitor the instruments and throttles and perhaps could have prevented the overboosting, were not trained for the task.

The seers and psychics were less effective zeroing in on Roberto Clemente. Rumors and false sightings continued. They were no closer to finding him than was his youngest son, little Ricky, who picked up the telephone and pretended that he was talking to his father. No closer than the mourners who started rowing out from the beach to spread flower petals in the sacred water. Vic Power had been convinced that his friend was alive until he saw a photograph of some more debris collected from the wreckage. There was the briefcase Clemente had bought in Nicaragua during their baseball trip, with the little alligator head he thought looked funny and wanted to cut off. Ohhh, baby, Power said, he's gone. That was January 6, Three Kings Day. Later that day, Power joined his fellow ballplayers at the annual Puerto Rico winter league All-Star game at Hiram Bithorn Stadium. The game was conducted in honor of Clemente, the greatest Latino player of them all.

The long, bleak week was closing, and at the end, after his people by the thousands lined the Atlantic shore in expectation that Clemente would walk out of the sea, and thousands more made pilgrimages up the hillside to shuffle past his house like a shrine, and the seers said that he was alive but dazed, and President Nixon got involved at the White House, and Pittsburgh comrades arrived in Puerto Rico to show their grief and solidarity, and the U.S. Coast Guard, with all its boats and planes and divers and equipment, slowly dragged up the wreckage and debris, searching in a Probability of Detection Area stretching for miles—at the end, finally, on a coral reef a mile east of Punta Maldonado, they found one sock, and Vera knew it was Roberto's. One sock, that's all, the rest to sharks and gods.

Myth and Memory

Three decades after Clemente's death, an official at San Juan's leading art museum suggested that he would be an interesting subject for an exhibition. After some grumbling from the Museo de Arte de Puerto Rico's board of directors—what does baseball have to do with art? they asked—the project moved forward and two avant-garde designers, Nestor Barretto and Jorge Carbonell, were brought in to create the exhibition. Barretto and Carbonell were interested in art and culture, politics and sociology, but had little knowledge of baseball and less of Clemente. They were, in fact, the perfect team for the assignment. Clemente represents more than baseball, and though he was a singular person, he also represents more than himself. In life he was a work of art; in death he has become a cultural icon. During the early stages of the project, Barretto and Carbonell spread the word that they were looking for any art related to Clemente. Soon enough they were overwhelmed by the breadth and depth of material. Thousands of people from Puerto Rico and all corners of the United States came forward with thousands of objects: paintings, murals, cards, gloves, shrines, carvings, statues, gadgets, photographs, songs. The stories that accompanied each collection were spiritual, poetic, and the stuff of myth.

The mythic aspects of baseball usually draw on clichés of the innocent past, the nostalgia for how things were. Fields of green. Fathers and sons. But Clemente's myth arcs the other way, to the future, not the past, to what people hope they can become. His memory is kept alive as a symbol of action and passion, not of reflection and longing. He broke racial and language barriers and achieved greatness and died a hero. That word can be used indiscriminately in the world of sports, but the classic definition is of someone who gives his life in the service of others, and that is exactly what Clemente did. He was also the greatest of the early Latino players in a game that is increasingly dominated

353

by Spanish-speaking athletes. Ramirez, Martinez, Rodriguez, Pujols, Rivera, Ortiz, Beltran, Tejada, Guerrero—these are the names of baseball today, among the 204 Latinos who opened the 2005 season on major league rosters, about one-quarter of all players. Puerto Rico itself has mostly moved on to basketball and other faster-paced sports, leaving the baseball obsession more to the Dominican Republic and Venezuela, but the story of how Clemente was the best among them is passed along from generation to generation, country to country.

At Clemente's sweetest moment of glory, in the dugout after his Pittsburgh Pirates won the 1971 World Series, he brought pride to all of Latin America by choosing to speak in Spanish to honor his parents back home. Thirty-four years later, when another Latino, Ozzie Guillen, the Venezuelan manager of the champion Chicago White Sox, stood atop the baseball world, he too paid homage, revealing that in the study of his house he kept a shrine to the one baseball figure he honored above all others, Roberto Clemente. For many years after Clemente's death, Tony Taylor, the Cuban infielder, made a point of walking young Latino teammates out to the right field wall whenever they visited Pittsburgh to give them a history lesson about the great Clemente. He is your heritage, Taylor would tell them, but more than that he is what you can become.

Acknowledgments

This book is dedicated to my father, who died last year at age eighty-six before I could finish it. Everything I love and know about baseball, I learned from him. He was born in Boston, but taught me never to root for the Red Sox because they were the last team to integrate. He spent most of his youth on Coney Island in Brooklyn, which made him a Dodgers fan, and family legend has it that he was holding me and listening on the radio when Bobby Thomson hit *the* home run, and dropped me in disgust—or maybe he just threw some crackers. He stopped rooting for the Bums when they traded Jackie Robinson and moved West. When we lived in Detroit, he became a Tigers fan. My mother would know that he'd gone to a game when he came home with mustard on his shirt. Once he was at Briggs Stadium watching them play the Red Sox, and with Detroit winning but Boston threatening late in the game, the bases loaded and Ted Williams at the plate, he screamed, "Walk him! Walk him!" seconds before a grand slam came crashing toward his seat in the outfield bleachers. Many of my favorite adolescent memories in Wisconsin are of the two of us listening to Braves or Cubs games on the radio. He liked the soft voice of Lou Boudreau. He liked Rico Carty and Denis Menke and Felipe Alou and Adolfo Phillips and Whale No. 1 and sweet-swinging Billy Williams. He said that Henry Aaron hit the ball harder than any player he ever saw. He had absolutely no use for the Yankees, though he liked Mickey Mantle and Derek Jeter and Joe Torre. He always rooted for the underdog, which meant that he had a soft spot for teams like the Pittsburgh Pirates, which is partly why Roberto Clemente became my favorite player.

Whatever baseball mistakes are in this book, and I'm sure some earnest baseball lover will find them, my dad would have caught. My mother, Mary Maraniss, who also loves baseball—perhaps out of necessity, though she prefers Mozart to Moe Drabowsky—read the manuscript alone this time, but with her usual editing grace. She and I both achingly wish that she could have fought over each page with my father. My son, Andrew Maraniss, learned to love baseball from his grandpa, and went on to work in the major leagues, and is the type of true blue Milwaukee Brewers fan who might never forgive Rick Manning for how he ruined Paul Molitor's hitting streak. It was wonderful that Andrew could be at my side at times on my one baseball book. The Yankees v. Red Sox rivalry is played out in our family by my daughter, Sarah, who apparently has come to love Jeter and A-Rod and New York, and her husband, Tom Vander Schaaff, who has excellent taste in all other matters yet remains loyal to Boston.

There are many other people to acknowledge. Palmira Rojas, organizer and interpreter extraordinaire, was an amazing guide in Puerto Rico. In helping me go through scores of Spanish-language documents, I couldn't have had a more thorough and accurate translator than Sandra Alboum. Patricia Rengel of Madison did a marvelous job translating chapters from Pedro Chamorro's *Richter 7*. Adria Fernández in Managua, Lisa Margot Johnson in Pittsburgh, Jim Shelton in Fort Myers, and Madonna Lebling in Washington were terrific in helping me track down clippings. Dale Petroskey and Bill Francis were of great assistance at the National Baseball Hall of Fame, as was Jeff Flannery, manuscript librarian at the Library of Congress, and Laura J. Brown at the Federal Aviation Administration. Ramiro Martínez in San Juan, Dwayne Reider in Pittsburgh, Squire Galbreath in Columbus, and Mike Pangia in Washington all were generous in opening up their incredible personal collections related to different aspects of Roberto Clemente's life and death.

Also pointing me in the right direction, reading parts of the manuscript, or providing moral support were Nelson Briles (who died too young), Javier Velez-Arocho, Daniel Rolleri, Luis Ferré, George de Lama, Dawn Law, Chad Schmidt, Gene Collier, Scott Higham, Paul Schwartzmann, Len Coleman, Brad Snyder, Mark London, Howard Fineman, Tom Hinger, Barbara and Ned Nakles, Roy McHugh, Myron Cope, Bill Nunn Jr., Jim Warren (Yankee fan, but eagle-eyed), Michael Weisskopf (lover of Sherm Lollar and Jungle Jim Rivera), Beth and

Michael Norman (despite their Yankee bobble heads), John Feinstein, Carol Rigolot and the Henry House crew at Princeton, the sixteen students of HUM 440, Juliet Eilperin, Edith Eglin, John McPhee, Whitney Gould, scribbler pals Rick Atkinson (a Mays and Marichal man) and Anne Hull, Chip Brown, Bob Woodward, Jim Maraniss, Gigi Kaeser, Scott Garner, Jean and Mike Alexander, Dick and Maryann Porter, Jim Rowen, Paul Soglin, Kim Vergeront, and Andy Cohn. This is in no way an authorized biography, but Vera Clemente and her sons were gracious and helpful throughout the process. People often say that Doña Vera is the sweetest person in the world, and I agree. Rafe Sagalyn, my agent and fellow rotisserie baseball owner for twenty years, was supportive from the beginning. Many thanks to James Shokoff (for making some great baseball-related catches in the manuscript), Simon & Schuster's David Rosenthal (big baseball guy), Carolyn Reidy, Victoria Meyer, Aileen Boyle, my wonderful team of Rebecca Davis and Roger Labrie, Serena Jones, Leah Wasielewski, Kathleen Rizzo, and Carolyn Schogol. I can't think of anyone I'd rather write books for than my editor, Alice Mayhew, who brings a Clemente-like passion to her profession.

And finally, this book has been blessed by two beauties. My wife, Linda, was the first to read every chapter, her eye, wit, and love of life as sharp and clear as ever. I'm sure she appreciated the fact that unlike my last sports book, when we moved to Green Bay for a winter to research Vince Lombardi, winters this time took us to Puerto Rico. They say that writing a book is like giving birth, but of course that is ridiculous; how would I or any man know? What I do know is that as much as this book means to me it doesn't compare with the arrival this year of our first granddaughter, the huggable redheaded bundle named Heidi. We were lucky to live nearby for the first six weeks of her life, and the reward of finishing a day of writing was doubled by the prospect of a Heidi fix. May she someday enjoy listening to a ball game on the radio like the great-grandfather she sadly missed, the sweet-swinging lefty first baseman from Coney Island's Abraham Lincoln High, Elliott Maraniss.

Madison, Wisconsin
September 2005

Notes

The Library of Congress might seem an unlikely place to conduct research for a book on a baseball player, but it was invaluable in the hunt for information on Roberto Clemente. Using its occasionally cranky microfilm machines but incomparable collection of newspapers, I was able to pore over old copies of a geographically and sociologically diverse group of papers that covered Clemente at various times, including the *San Juan Star, Montreal Gazette, New York Times, New York Herald Tribune, San Francisco Chronicle, Milwaukee Journal, Los Angeles Times, Chicago Tribune, Philadelphia Inquirer, Pittsburgh Post-Gazette, Pittsburgh Press, Pittsburgh Sun-Telegraph,* and *Pittsburgh Courier,* the influential black weekly that opened up a fascinating new world to me by writing about Clemente and major league baseball from a detailed and uniquely black perspective. In addition, the papers of Branch Rickey Jr. are archived at the Manuscript Division of the Library of Congress. The historic patina of those papers comes from Rickey's key role in integrating baseball by bringing Jackie Robinson to the Brooklyn Dodgers, but he moved on to the Pittsburgh Pirates after that and ran the club when Clemente arrived as a rookie in 1955. Rickey was a meticulous note keeper, and his papers and records were of enormous help in providing the feel of baseball, the Pirates, and Clemente during that era.

Other important research sources included the National Baseball Hall of Fame, which maintains file cabinets of clippings, photographs, and archival material on Clemente; the National Archives at College Park, which houses the presidential papers of Richard Nixon and other materials related to the Nicaraguan earthquake that led Clemente to his death; the Harvey S. Firestone Memorial Library at Princeton University, for its collection of African American newspapers; the Carimar Design and Research studio in Old San Juan, for its special archive on the art and mythology of Clemente; Darby Dan farm in Columbus, Ohio, for the personal archives of former Pirates owner John W. Galbreath and his son, former team president Dan Galbreath; public libraries in Pittsburgh, Managua, and Fort Myers; the newsroom morgues at San Juan's *El Nuevo Día,* the *Washington Post, Chicago Tribune,* and *New York Daily News;* and the personal collections of Ramiro Martínez, the family of Pedrin Zorrilla, Duane Reider, Caguitas Colón, Les Banos, Roy McHugh, and most of all, the home files and memorabilia of Clemente's widow, Vera.

Tracking down records related to the fatal plane crash at times seemed like a futile effort—only the sparest documents were available at the Federal Aviation Administration and in the dockets of various courts that heard the ensuing lawsuit. Then, one day in March 2004, I visited the office of aviation lawyer Michael Pangia, who had worked for the U.S. Department of Justice in the 1970s and represented the government in the case. After talking with Pangia for several hours, he took me downstairs to a closet and hauled out two large boxes marked "Clemente"—and inside were copies of all the depositions and transcripts from the trial as well as the internal reports from the FAA and National Transportation Safety Board. Gold mine, as reporters like to say.

Along with the documentary record, scores of individuals were interviewed for this book. They include: Vera Clemente, Roberto Clemente Jr., Luis Clemente, Matino Clemente, Osvaldo Gil, Caguitas Colón, Vic Power (Victor Pellot), Juan Pizarro, Luis Olmo, Enrique Zorrilla, Diana Zorrilla, Rosa Semprit, Fernando González, Orlando Cepeda, Tony Taylor, Eduardo Valero, Ramiro Martínez, Roy McHugh, Myron Cope, Bill Nunn Jr., George Kiseda, Joe L. Brown, Steve Blass, Richie Hebner, Al Oliver, Bob Veale, Donn Clendenon, Nelson Briles, José Pagan, Don Leppert, Tony Bartirome, Les Banos, Chuck Goggin, Gene Garber, Harding Peterson, Bob Friend, Dick Schofield, Nick Koback, Gene Freese, Ferguson Jenkins, Juan Marichal, Earl Weaver, Paul Blair, Sparky Anderson, Gaylord Perry, Monte Irvin, Don Zimmer, Preston Pearson, Joan Whitman, Chico Fernández, Glenn Cox, Len Harsh, John Yarborough, Pat McCutcheon, Ann Ranalli King, Bruce Laurie, Howard Fineman, Juliet Schor, Richard Santry, Richard Moss, Carolyn Rauch, Squire Galbreath, Carol Bass, Anthony Jilek, Maurice J. Williams, Frederick Zugibe, Hart Achenbach, Nancy Golding, Jorge Carbonell, Nestor Barretto, Bernard Heller, John Heller, Bev Couric, Chico Azocar, Juanita Modale, Stuart Speiser, Jon Hoffman, Gary Czabot, John Parker, Mike Pangia, Vincent Bogucki, Paul Kutch, Chuck Tomasco, Duane Reider, Eliezer Rodriguez, George Shamoon, and Rex Bradley.

1: SOMETHING THAT NEVER ENDS

PAGE

3 *It was long past midnight:* Ints. Osvaldo Gil, Vera Clemente, Juan Pizarro.

3 *In one bad dream:* Int. Vera Clemente. During their years together, Roberto and Vera often talked about dreams, and decades later she could remember the discussions vividly, as well as some of her own long-ago dreams, including one about the monkey they brought back from Nicaragua.

4 *So much had happened since Gil:* Int. Osvaldo Gil.

6 *Martín the Crazy is not that crazy:* Int. Matino Clemente.

6 *Not only Clemente and his ballplayers: La Prensa,* November 10, 1972; Program, XX Campeonato Mundial de Béisbol Aficionado.

6 *Hughes occupied the entire:* Glenn Garvin, *Reason,* March 2000; Jay Mallin, *The Great Managua Earthquake,* Broadway: New York, 1972; Drosnin, *Citizen Hughes,* Henry Holt: New York, 1985; ints. Osvaldo Gil, Vic Power.

7 *On the fifteenth:* Int. Osvaldo Gil; UPI, November 15, 1972; *Novedades,* November 16, 1972; *La Prensa,* November 16, 1972. The *Novedades* account read as though Somoza's publicist had written it, which was essentially the case: "Thousands of Nicaraguans saw once more General Somoza surrounded in the middle of his people, confirming with his presence the love that the public has for him . . ."

8 *Clemente took to the people:* Ints. Vera Clemente, Vic Power, Osvaldo Gil; *Do You Remember?* Clemente in Nicaragua with San Juan Senators in 1964, Edgard Tijerino, *La Prensa.* Tijerino wrote of the San Juan team that year: "The lineup that Puerto Rico presented could not be more impressive: Horace Clarke on second, José Pagan at short, Clemente in right field, Julio LaBoy and Orlando Cepeda alternating in left, Reynaldo Oliver and Marical Allen patrolling center . . . and a strong staff headed by Juan Pizarro, Luis Arroyo, Palillo Santiago, and Warren Hacker."

9 *This trip went no better: San Juan Star,* November 16–30, 1972; ints. Vic Power, Osvaldo Gil.

9 *With outfielder Julio César Roubert:* Int. Osvaldo Gil.

9 *His longtime friend from Puerto Rico:* Int. Vic Power.

10 *One morning, reading* La Prensa: Ints. Osvaldo Gil, Vic Power; Edgard Tijerino, *La Prensa,* "Standing Up, Clemente Bats."

11 *Tijerino was now "oh for two":* Edgard Tijerino, The Last Interview; int. Osvaldo Gil.

13 *There he met a wheelchair-bound:* Ints. Osvaldo Gil, Vera Clemente.

14 *One day in the old city:* Int. Vera Clemente.

14 *Clemente flew back to Puerto Rico:* Ints. Vic Power, Osvaldo Gil, Vera Clemente.

15 *All seemed well back home:* Ints. Vera Clemente, Luis Clemente, Vic Power.

2: WHERE MOMEN CAME FROM

PAGE

17 *This was the summer of 1934:* Ints. Matino Clemente, Vera Clemente.

18 *The story has been told:* Int. Vera Clemente.

18 *Runaway slaves, known as* cimarrones: Este Silencio, Lydia Milagros González, Instituto Cultura Puertorriqueña, 1998; *Home: A Celebration of Roberto Clemente's Spirit and Passion,* San Juan, 2003.

19 *Sugar was then nearing the end: Economic Existence, Sugar and Labor:* 1928–1930s. 35th Annual Report of the governor of Puerto Rico; *Farr's Manual of Sugar Companies.* Department of Labor 1934, Report on Sugar Industry.

19 *By the standards of Depression-era Carolina:* Ints. Matino Clemente, Vera Clemente.

21 *Momen was his nickname:* Int. Matino Clemente.

21 *"When I was a little kid":* "A Conversation with Roberto Clemente," Sam Nover, WIIC-TV, October 8, 1972. For all his confrontations with reporters, Clemente got along well with Nover. "Well, I tell you one thing, I tell you the truth, I don't like lots of writers," Clemente told Nover. "I think if I was a writer, one thing I would try to do is have a good relationship with the players. I never criticize a writer that I think is sincere in what he is writing. But a lot of these writers, they go to you, and they put the interview in a way that they sound like and you don't exactly say that, see?"; Ints. Matino Clemente, Rosa Semprit.

22 *Melchor was a regular figure:* Ints. Matino Clemente, Orlando Cepeda, Vera Clemente, Rosa Semprit.

24 *The Cangrejeros were grittier:* Ints. Enrique Zorrilla, Juan Pizarro, Diana Zorrilla, Matino Clemente; Thomas E. Van Hyning, *The Santurce Crabbers.*

24 *Irvin said later that he enjoyed:* Int. Monte Irvin.

24 *When he could, Momen caught the bus:* Conversation with Clemente; Ints. Matino Clemente, Juan Pizarro, Monte Irvin.

25 *Cáceres developed a friendship:* Cáceres, *Reader's Digest,* July 1973.

26 *Zorrilla scribbled the name:* Ints. Enrique Zorrilla, Diana Zorrilla.
26 *When Campanis filled out:* Zorrilla family scrapbooks, Clemente family collection.
28 *The Three Kings, in a sense: Chicago Tribune, El Imparcial, San Juan Star, El Nuevo Día, Pittsburgh Courier, Sporting News;* Ints. Eduardo Valero, Ramiro Martínez, Osvaldo Gil, Luis Olmo, Vic Power.
36 *Five major league teams expressed:* Zorrilla family archives, Vera Clemente family scrapbooks; ints. Diana Zorrilla, Luis Olmo, Matino Clemente.
38 *His first bats were variations:* Hillerich & Bradsby records maintained by Rex Bradley.

3: DREAM OF DEEDS

PAGE

39 *Before Momen left home:* Int. Matino Clemente. It was a family ritual every spring that his brothers Matino and Andres would drive Roberto to the airport for his flight to Florida.
39 *It is hard to imagine: Montreal Gazette,* Canadian Press dispatch, April 1, 1954.
40 *Momen was the youngest player: Montreal Gazette:* Int. Chico Fernández.
41 *The International Baseball League lived up: Montreal Gazette,* April 15, 1954, International League to Open with two New Teams April 20; Playing the Field, Dink Carroll, *Montreal Gazette,* April 20, 1954. Carroll wrote of the Sugar Kings: "The big name in Cuban baseball today is Roberto Maduro, president of the Sugar Kings. We met him at the Baseball Writers Dinner in New York in February and noted that he spoke English without any trace of an accent." "I should." He smiled. "I graduated from Cornell University." Tom Meany, *Collier's,* July 1954.
43 *"made some sparkling":* Lou Miller, *Montreal Gazette,* May 1, 1954.
43 *There was talk:* The discussion began in New York and made its way to Montreal in a May 5 column by Dink Carroll. If Amoros made the club, Carroll wrote, "the Dodgers would have five Negroes in the lineup on a day that Don Newcombe or Joe Black was pitching. The suggestion was that this was one too many . . ."
45 *The rooming house offered beds:* Ints. Chico Fernández, Joan Whitman, Glenn Cox.
46 *At night, Clemente would pour out:* Int. Chico Fernández.
49 *Havana was not home for Momen:* Ints. Ramiro Martínez, Chico Fernández; *Montreal Gazette.*

50 *Andy High visited Montreal: Montreal Gazette;* int. Chico Fernández.

52 *Rickey sent Haak up to Montreal:* Int. Howie Haak; Kevin Kerrane, *Dollar Sign on the Muscle;* ints. Chico Fernández, Glenn Cox.

54 *Even the batboy:* Ints. Don Zimmer, Orlando Cepeda; Zorrilla family archive.

55 Foreigners: make space: Enrique Zorrilla, "Dream of Deeds"; Zorrilla family archives.

55 *Mays was embraced joyously:* Tom Meany, "Señor Mays Hit in San Juan," *Collier's,* January 7, 1955; Zorrilla family archive; int. Don Zimmer.

56 *Clemente admired Mays:* Ints. Orlando Cepeda, Enrique Zorrilla, Vic Power, Eduardo Valero, Monte Irvin, Luis Olmo; Zorrilla family archive.

56 *At eleven on the Monday morning of November 22:* Notice No. 29, Office of the Commissioner, October 29, 1954; C-41-54, National League of Professional Baseball Clubs, Warren C. Giles President, November 3, 1954; UP, November 22, 1954; UP November 23, 1954. "The Puerto Rican Negro batted only .257 in eighty-six games at Montreal last season, where he was used chiefly for defensive purposes, but impressed the Pirates and several other teams with his brilliant play this fall in the Puerto Rican winter league."

57 *Herman Franks's lineup card:* Ints. Don Zimmer, Orlando Cepeda, Enrique Zorrilla, Zorrilla family archives; Thomas E. Van Hyning, *The Santurce Crabbers.*

58 *When the road trip was over:* Ints. Matino Clemente, Vera Clemente. Luis was a schoolteacher. His wife, Victoria Carrasquillo, was fearful of the operation and tried to talk him out of it. He was buried at the Cementerio Municipal de Rio Grande.

4: THE RESIDUE OF DESIGN

PAGE

59 *All of this was overseen by:* Branch Rickey Papers, Manuscript Division, Library of Congress, Washington, D.C. (LCMD); Arthur Mann, *Branch Rickey, American in Action; Branch Rickey's Little Blue Book;* Galbreath Collection, Darby Dan.

61 *With aide-de-camp Blackburn:* Memorandum of Game, January 18, 1955. Following Game in Havana, Cuba, Between Cienfuegos and Havana, Branch Rickey Papers, LCMD.

61 *He kept his own scorecard:* Ruben Gomez pitched that day, and Clemente was bracketed in the lineup by Don Zimmer batting second

and Buster Clarkson at cleanup. Harry Chiti was behind the plate. Rickey, in characteristic acerbic fashion, was not impressed: "Had no life, looked slow in his physical actions, and I could not help thinking that he was somewhat indifferent about his work."

62 *it appears that this was the first time:* Memorandum of Game Between Santurce and Ponce at San Juan, Puerto Rico, on January 25, 1955, Branch Rickey Papers, LCMD.

64 *"The other is Ron Necciai":* Branch Rickey Papers, LCMD. According to Branch Rickey's *Little Blue Book* Necciai once struck out twenty-seven opponents in an Appalachian League game.

65 *On his way back to Pittsburgh:* "Mack, Rickey Meet at Terry Park," *Fort Myers News-Press,* January 29, 1955; int. Len Harsh. The *News-Press* was published seven days a week. "I was the whole sports department," Harsh recalled a half-century later. "And filled in covering the police beat on Sunday nights."

67 *Clemente and other black prospects:* Ints. Len Harsh, John Yarborough, Pat McCutcheon, Bob Veale.

69 *to young Clemente the prevailing culture:* Sam Nover, "A Conversation with RC," 1972; ints. Vic Power, Ramiro Martínez, Len Harsh.

69 *It is not clear where: Fort Myers News-Press,* January 15, 1955, to April 1, 1955; int. Len Harsh. "He was such a great ballplayer that they respected him," Harsh said of south Florida fans. "He may have done a few things that people thought was hot dog but he was so doggone good it came natural to him. He was as respected as any of them."

70 *"'Roberto, you better'":* Sam Nover, "A Conversation with RC," 1972.

71 *filed regular dispatches: Pittsburgh Courier,* Pittsburgh weekly edition, February 15, 1955, to April 1, 1955.

72 *old man Rickey remained uncertain:* Observations in the game between the Chicago White Sox and the Pittsburgh Pirates, March 23, 1955, Fort Myers, Florida, Branch Rickey Papers, LCMD.

72 *Roberts was another: Pittsburgh Courier,* March 1955; Ronald Barlow, "A True Hometown Hero," *Beaumont News* (Pineland, Texas); *Baseball Almanac; Rich Shrum, Pittsburgh Post-Gazette,* April 25, 2004; Joe Monaco, *Beaumont Enterprise,* May 2, 2004.

75 *only a lost battle:* Ric Roberts, *Pittsburgh Courier,* April 14, 1955. In the column it was noted: "If Jackie Robinson had remained with the Kansas City Monarchs all the years since he joined them back in 1945, he would have earned no more than $35,000. At Brooklyn his income has certainly aggregated more than $252,000! He is the leader in a glittering procession . . ."

75 *Rickey was feeling the harsh sting:* Confidential letter to Mr. Joe
   Bradis of the AP from Branch Rickey, Branch Rickey Papers, July 30,
   1954, LCMD.

76 *Freese liked to tease Clemente:* Int. Gene Freese.

77 *On stationery with a Bing Crosby/Hollywood logo:* Before reaching
   Rickey's desk, Crosby's note was read by the Mahatma's friend and
   aide Ken Blackburn, who added this handwritten message: "Mr. Sisler
   has already written Mr. Crosby re these boys and their clippings . . . Ed McCarrick is also following and will again contact these
   boys when he returns home, K.B."

78 *The fiberglass and plastic batting helmet:* Supplementary Financial
   Information, American Baseball Cap Inc., Branch Rickey Papers,
   June 30, 1962, LCMD.

79 *Two weeks later, after another hot streak:* Bill Nunn Jr, *Pittsburgh
   Courier,* June 16, 1955; int. Bill Nunn Jr.

79 *"he speaks only a little broken English":* *Pittsburgh Courier,* June 16,
   1955; ints. Bill Nunn Jr., George Kiseda, Roy McHugh, Nick Koback.

80 GO TO HILL! NEGRO FAMILY TOLD: *Pittsburgh Courier,* July 2, 1955;
   Pittsburgh Post-Gazette, April 25, 2004. *Courier* reporter George E.
   Barbour began his story: "'I'll throw you out,' Richard Cook, burgess
   of Glenfield, told this 200-pound reporter Monday when he went to
   Cook's office to learn why the latter had advised a Negro family last
   Friday not to move into an all-white residential section."

81 *Clemente's first friend in Pittsburgh:* Ints. Duane Reider, Bill Nunn Jr.,
   Bob Friend; Jim O'Brien, *Remembering Roberto.*

82 *The Garlands had let rooms:* Ints. Vera Clemente, Bill Nunn Jr., Carolyn Rauch.

82 *Looking south and downhill:* Observations of Schenley Park geogra-
   phy and sociology drawn from leisurely tour of the area provided by
   longtime resident Bill Nunn Jr.

83 *with no help from the baseball team:* Stefan Lorant, *Pittsburgh, The
   Story of an American City;* Sports Town, David Shribman, *Pittsburgh
   Post-Gazette,* 2004.

5: ¡ARRIBA! ¡ARRIBA!

PAGE

87 *Bob Prince, the play-by-play announcer:* Ints. Howard Fineman,
   Richard Santry, Bruce Laurie, Myron Cope, Nelson Briles, Bob
   Friend, Harding Peterson; baseballLibrary.com.

89 *Clemente wrote Brown a letter:* February 26, 1960, Duane Reider collection, Pittsburgh, Pennsylvania. Native Pittsburgher Duane Reider, a first-class photographer, has turned the second floor of his firehouse studio into a shrine to Roberto Clemente. Along with a fine collection of photographs, he has accumulated baseballs, letters, even a blue pinstriped suit that Clemente bought in Chicago.

92 *The regular season started on the road: Pittsburgh Post-Gazette, Pittsburgh Press,* April 12–15, 1955.

93 *A face in the crowd:* Int. Howard Fineman. As a native Pittsburgher, who became a national political writer for *Newsweek,* Fineman was fascinated by the role of department stores in the cultural sociology of his hometown: "Pittsburghers had this thing of always being the biggest or best between New York and Chicago. People in Pittsburgh never looked to Philadelphia for anything. As far as we knew, Philadelphia never existed. If you had ambition in Pittsburgh, it was for New York. One of the ways in which Pittsburgh was the training ground was the department store business. What came to be called the Golden Triangle, the central part of downtown Pittsburgh, was compact and Manhattanlike in its own way. And it was a training ground for the guys who would end up running Macy's or whatever. When I was a kid [1950s and early 1960s] there were five department stores in downtown Pittsburgh: Kauffman's, Gimbels, Horns, Frank and Seder, and Rosenbaum's."

94 *During an Easter Sunday doubleheader:* Ints. Bob Friend, Dick Schofield; *Pittsburgh Post-Gazette, Pittsburgh Press,* April 18–22, 1955.

96 *The Pirates were as consistent:* World Champions Pittsburgh Pirates 1960 Statistical Résumé, Pittsburgh Baseball Club, Galbreath Collection, Darby Dan.

96 *One of the paper's weekly features: Pittsburgh Courier,* May–September 1960. In his guest column, utility infielder Gene Baker, who was widely respected by baseball insiders, wrote optimistically about the future of blacks in the game's management. "I'm one of the optimists who like to think the day will come when Negroes are accepted in front-office jobs the same as they are on the playing field. When that day arrives, I would like to be ready to fit into the pattern." Baker went on to become a scout and minor league manager for the Pirates, but never got his full shot at a top job.

97 *"Som' Co-lored people": Pittsburgh Courier,* June 25, 1955. *Courier* sports editor Bill Nunn Jr. followed in the tradition of his father, Bill

Nunn Sr., a longtime editor at the *Courier*. The son played basketball at Westinghouse High School in Pittsburgh and then at West Virginia State, returning to work at the *Courier* in 1948. He was a close friend of most of the black major leaguers, starting with Jackie Robinson. The baseball player guest column began with a regular article under Robinson's byline that was ghost-written by Nunn.

99 *The Pirates had several candidates: Pittsburgh Post-Gazette*, September 2, 1960; *Pittsburgh Courier,* August–September 1960: Ints. Bill Nunn Jr., Roy McHugh, Myron Cope, Bob Friend, Dick Schofield, Joe L. Brown.

101 *Less than a month later: Pittsburgh Post-Gazette, Pittsburgh Press,* August 15–September 15, 1960; *The Incredible Pirates, We Had 'Em All the Way,* LP (Rare Sport films Inc., 1960).

6: ALONE AT THE MIRACLE

PAGE

105 *The last time the Pirates played:* Bob Addie, *Washington Post,* October 5, 1960; Edward Prell, *Chicago Tribune,* October 5, 1960; *Pittsburgh Press,* October 4, 1960.

105 *"We'll fight 'em until our teeth fall out":* Will Grimsley, AP, October 4, 1960.

107 *The Pirates would win:* Int. Bill Nunn Jr.; *Pittsburgh Courier,* October 1960.

107 *Another scouting report got in more digs: Life,* October 5, 1960.

108 *Among those making the trip:* Int. Matino Clemente; *Pittsburgh Courier,* October 1, 1960. In another *Courier* story headlined FIVE TAN PLAYERS READY FOR SERIES, Ric Roberts noted that not since "1950, when the Yankees routed the Phillies in four games, have we seen an all-white World Series. We can be certain that at least one of our heroes will be in the call to arms at Forbes Field on Wednesday, October 5. Over 40,000 Pirate fans will greet his appearance at bat with the Spanish urging *¡Arriba! ¡Arriba!"*

109 *A fellow named Ralph Belcore: Pittsburgh Post-Gazette, Pittsburgh Press,* AP, October 5, 1960.

109 *"Only in Pittsburgh":* Red Smith, *New York Herald Tribune,* October 5, 1960.

110 *A telegram had been taped:* Branch Rickey Papers, LCMD; *Pittsburgh Press,* October 6 1960.

111 *Law had the stuff: San Francisco Chronicle, Chicago Tribune, New York Herald Tribune, New York Times,* October 4–7, 1960; *The Incred-*

ible Pirates, LP; ints. Bob Friend, Roy McHugh, Harding Peterson, Bill Nunn Jr., Dick Schofield.

112 *"Any questions?":* *Pittsburgh Post-Gazette,* Dick Groat, October 6, 1960.

113 *The first-inning rally:* Account of Game 1 drawn from ints. Bob Friend, Harding Peterson, Dick Schofield, Roy McHugh, Joe L. Brown; *The Incredible Pirates,* LP; *Baseball Classics, 1960 World Series* (Rare Sportsfilms Inc.); articles in the *Pittsburgh Press, Pittsburgh Post-Gazette, San Francisco Chronicle, New York Times, New York Herald Tribune, Pittsburgh Courier, Chicago Tribune, New York Post,* and *Washington Post.*

115 *It rained all that night: Pittsburgh Post-Gazette, New York Times, New York Herald Tribune, Pittsburgh Press, Washington Post,* October 7, 1960.

116 *"I don't blame Danny":* Int. Bob Friend.

116 *In the mess of this slaughter: New York Herald Tribune, Washington Post,* October 7, 1960; *The Baseball Encyclopedia;* Ralph Berger, *The Baseball Biography Project,* SABR.

117 *The batting star: New York Times, New York Herald Tribune, Chicago Tribune, Pittsburgh Post-Gazette, Pittsburgh Press, Pittsburgh Courier,* October 7, 1960; int. Dick Schofield.

119 *"If you quit on the Pirates now":* Don Hoak column, *Pittsburgh Post-Gazette,* October 9, 1960.

120 *For the critical fourth game:* Game account drawn from columns by Vern Law, Don Hoak, and Pennsylvania Governor David Lawrence in *Post-Gazette; Washington Post, New York Times, New York Daily News, Chicago Tribune, Pittsburgh Press,* October 10, 1960; ints. Bob Friend, Dick Schofield, Joe L. Brown.

122 *Bob Friend was ready:* Int. Bob Friend; Don Hoak column *Pittsburgh Post-Gazette,* October 12, 1960.

122 *In the locker room after the game:* Ted Meir, Associated Press, published in *San Juan Star,* October 12, 1960. The *Star* article ran under the headline: CASEY ADMITS ROBERTO IS GOOD RIGHT FIELDER.

123 *The focus of the world: Washington Post, New York Times, New York Herald Tribune, Chicago Tribune,* October 12, 1960.

124 *"The fellow who did the most throwing": New York Times,* October 13, 1960.

125 *The thirteenth of October:* Account of Game 7 of World Series and postgame drawn from *Baseball Classics, 1960 World Series; The Incredible Pirates,* LP; ints. Bob Friend, Dick Schofield, Harding Peterson, Joe L. Brown, Roy McHugh, Myron Cope, Bill Nunn Jr., Howard Fineman, Matino Clemente; *Pittsburgh Post-Gazette, Pitts-*

burgh Courier, Pittsburgh Press, New York Times, New York Daily News, New York Herald Tribune, Washington Post, San Francisco Chronicle, Chicago Tribune.

135 *Nunn noticed that Clemente:* Ints. Matino Clemente, Bill Nunn Jr.; Bill Nunn Jr., *Pittsburgh Courier,* October 22, 1960. After describing Clemente's actions in the clubhouse and during the walk to his car, Nunn's concluding paragraph read: "And as the auto pulled away from the curb and Clemente sat back and relaxed, it was obvious that here was a player who had enjoyed his victory celebration a lot better on the streets of Pittsburgh than in the clubhouse he shares with his teammates."

7: PRIDE AND PREJUDICE

PAGE

137 *Handmade welcome-home placards:* San Juan Star, October 17, 1960. HOME FROM BATTLE read the cutline above a *Star* photograph accompanying the front-page story that showed Clemente kissing his mother.

138 *There was only one small note:* Jim Douglas, ROBERTO SAYS HE'S NOT SURE HE'LL PLAY HERE, *San Juan Star,* October 17, 1960.

140 *The winner was indeed a Pirate:* Ints. Matino Clemente, Vera Clemente, Roy McHugh, Myron Cope, Bill Nunn, Jr., Bob Friend, Dick Schofield, Joe L. Brown; *San Juan Star,* November 18–19, 1960, *Pittsburgh Post-Gazette;* Sam Nover, "A Conversation with RC," 1972.

141 *"My father was a boy":* Int. Enrique Zorrilla.

142 *Power and Clemente were fast friends:* Ints. Vic Power, Matino Clemente, Luis Olmo, Eduardo Valero; Zorrilla family archive; Thomas E. Van Hyning, *The Santurce Crabbers.*

143 *On the day he reached Fort Myers: New York Times,* March 2, 1961.

144 *Wendell Smith, the influential black sportswriter:* Wendell Smith papers, National Baseball Hall of Fame, Cooperstown, New York; Brian Carroll, Wendell Smith's "Last Crusade," 13th Annual Cooperstown Symposium on Baseball and American Culture, National Baseball Hall of Fame; Jack E. Davis, "Baseball's Reluctant Challenge," *Journal of Sports History,* Summer 1992; *Pittsburgh Courier,* March 26, 1961; *Chicago's American,* January–August 1961. In an April 3, 1961, *Chicago's American* article, "What a Negro Ballplayer Faces Today in Training," Smith wrote: "To the average white player, the six weeks spent training is merely a blink of pleasant time in a ballplayer's life, but

to his Negro teammate it is an eternity of humiliations and frustrations."

148 *Clemente was described as "bitter":* Bill Nunn Jr., *Pittsburgh Courier,* April 15, 1961.

148 *"So I say to Joe Brown":* Sam Nover, "A Conversation with RC," 1972.

149 *When the Fort Myers Boosters Club: Fort Myers News-Press,* March 8, 1961.

149 *When the Fort Myers Country Club: Fort Myers News-Press,* March 27, 1961. Manager Danny Murtaugh said he shot his "best round ever," a 104, which was said to be a few strokes better than Joe L. Brown, "who had a few difficulties": ints. Bob Friend, Dick Schofield.

150 *Change was slow: Pittsburgh Courier,* May 20, 1961; Wendell Smith columns in *Chicago's American,* April–August 1961; Carroll, *Wendell Smith's Last Crusade.*

151 *Clemente was not to be ignored: New York Times, Fort Myers News-Press,* March 28–29, 1961, *New York Times,* March 29, 1961.

151 *Sisler's first breakthrough:* Sisler hitting analysis, Branch Rickey Papers, LCMD; *Fort Myers News-Press,* March 10–30, 1961.

152 *But by 1961 he was using:* Hillerich & Bradsby bat documents maintained by Rex Bradley; int. Rex Bradley.

155 *The All-Star setting offered: Pittsburgh Courier,* AP, *San Francisco Chronicle, Pittsburgh Post-Gazette, Pittsburgh Press,* July 11–12, 1961.

157 *A trivial manifestation: New York Times, Chicago's American, Pittsburgh Courier,* August 1, 1961; ints. Bill Nunn Jr., Bob Friend.

159 *One night that August:* Jack Hernon, "Roamin Around," *Pittsburgh Post-Gazette,* August 13, 1961. In that same sports section, the *Post-Gazette* ran a photo of Smoky Burgess, Dick Groat, Clemente, and Bill Virdon holding a bat that read 1,000 hits. Clemente had reached the 1,000-hit club a week earlier, Burgess a day earlier, and Virdon needed four more hits to join them.

160 *This was not just Clemente's rise:* Ints. Orlando Cepeda, Vic Power, Eduardo Valero, Osvaldo Gil, Matino Clemente, Luis Olmo; *El Imparcial, San Juan Star,* October 8–10, 1961. A front-page photograph on October 10 showed Cepeda and Clemente inside Sixto Escobar stadium, waving to the crowd. Clemente kept his sore right elbow at his side and waved with his left.

8: FEVER

PAGE

163 *On a December day in 1963:* Narrative of Clemente-Zabala courtship drawn from several interviews with Vera Clemente and Matino Clemente; also M. I. Caceres, *Reader's Digest,* July 1973.

168 *To Steve Blass, a rookie pitcher:* Int. Steve Blass.

169 *First base that year:* Int. Donn Clendenon.

170 *The Tobs had a rivalry:* Ints. Bob Veale, Donn Clendenon.

171 *He had become:* Int. Tony Taylor.

172 *"'Clemente's a mean man'":* Sam Nover, "A Conversation with RC," 1972.

173 *"I always had a theory":* Int. Steve Blass.

173 *Leppert placed the blame:* Int. Don Leppert.

174 *"it becomes a vicious circle":* Myron Cope, *Sports Illustrated,* March 7, 1966.

175 *"He'd crawl in a shell":* Bill Mazeroski, *Sport,* November 1971.

176 *Clemente took offense:* Int. Roy McHugh.

176 *"Everybody in that clubhouse":* Int. Tony Bartirome.

177 *The Pirates were in the middle: Pittsburgh Post-Gazette, Pittsburgh Press, San Juan Star.*

178 *In his ellipses-dotted:* Al Abrams, *Pittsburgh Post-Gazette,* July 7–8, 1964.

179 *The trip was a success:* Int. Vera Clemente.

180 *Rickey scouted for general manager:* Branch Rickey Papers, LCMD.

181 *Groat went on to hit .292:* Halberstam, *October 1964,* pp. 33-36.

182 *Here, in Carolina:* Ints. Vera Clemente, Matino Clemente; *San Juan Star,* November 15, 1964.

183 *One woman in New York:* Letter to RC, Duane Reider collection, Pittsburgh, Pennsylvania.

184 *Clemente organized a group:* Ints. Vera Clemente, Juan Pizarro; *San Juan Star,* February 4, 1965; *San Juan Star,* February 15, 1965.

184 *What was wrong?* Ints. Vera Clemente, Juan Pizarro, Eduardo Valero, Ramiro Martínez, Joe L. Brown, Matino Clemente.

9: PASSION

PAGE

187 *Every move Clemente made:* Ints. Bruce Laurie, Howard Fineman, Rex Bradley, Roy McHugh, Richard Santry, Donn Clendenon; Jim Murray, *Los Angeles Times,* October 15, 1971.

190 *During the first two months: Pittsburgh Post-Gazette, Pittsburgh Press,*

May 3–7, 1965. On May 3, in his "Sidelights on Sports" column, Al Abrams wrote from St. Louis: "The 'Hat' went into a monumental rage. He not only banged and threw things around in the small cubicle in which the visiting players dress, he let his men know in the most earthy and sulphuric language at his command that he is far from pleased with the way they were playing."

193 *The malarial funk was long forgotten:* Ints. Vera Clemente, Luis Clemente.

194 *During a home stand late in September:* Int. Gene Garber.

195 *Home now was a funky modernist house:* Observations of Clemente home in Rio Piedras. Ints. Vera Clemente, Roberto Clemente Jr. The ponds in the front became filled with frogs that were collected by neighborhood children.

195 *One visitor that winter:* Ints. Myron Cope, Roy McHugh, Vera Clemente; Myron Cope, *Sports Illustrated,* March 7, 1966.

198 *A few days after Cope left:* Brown letter, Duane Reider collection, Pittsburgh, Pennsylvania.

199 *she wrote a note to Phil Dorsey:* Duane Reider collection, Pittsburgh, Pennsylvania.

200 *The truth was he had a temper:* Account of the punch incident drawn from ints. Bernard Heller, John Heller; *Philadelphia Inquirer, Pittsburgh Post-Gazette,* May 7–9, 1966.

202 *The punch seemed more instinctive: Pittsburgh Post-Gazette,* May 6, 1963; *Baseball Classics, 1960 World Series;* Ints. Vic Power, Juan Pizarro, Luis Olmo, Ramiro Martínez.

203 *Carol Brezovec would only see:* Ints. Carol Brezovec (Bass), Carolyn Rauch, Vera Clemente.

207 *"So the story goes":* Int. Steve Blass.

208 *"When you have the world's best base runner":* Int. Gaylord Perry.

208 *making it feel more like home:* Ints. José Pagan, Vera Clemente.

209 *"Sore arm, my foot!": New York Daily News,* September 18–19, 1966.

210 *You have to visit me:* Ints. Carol Brezovec (Bass), Vera Clemente, Roberto Clemente Jr.

10: A CIRCULAR STAGE

PAGE

213 *Ask him how he felt:* Ints. Tony Bartirome, Bob Veale, Steve Blass, Myron Cope, Roy McHugh, Harding Peterson, Les Banos. The training room, Bartirome recalled, "was like a playroom. Everybody'd come in there, not for treatment, just to screw around."

217 *One nagging concern:* Flight time calculated from Pirates 1968 schedule and 1968 national flight records; ints. Vera Clemente, Bob Veale,
José Pagan, Juan Pizarro.

219 *He bought his cologne:* Int. Les Banos.

219 *When a sales clerk met:* Sam Nover, "A Conversation with RC," 1972;
int. Vera Clemente.

220 *Al Oliver, a black teammate:* Int. Al Oliver.

221 *What Clemente admired:* Sam Nover, "A Conversation with RC,"
1972.

221 *The Clementes spent twenty-two days:* Int. Vera Clemente

222 *"Love and hate":* Pittsburgh Press, April 14, 1969; ints. Roy McHugh,
Juliet Schor; Bill Mazeroski, *Sport,* November 1971.

224 *No National League pitcher wanted:* Int. Ferguson Jenkins, Tony Taylor; Bill Curry and George Plimpton, *One More July,* 1978.

226 *One other event that season:* Ints. Vera Clemente, Matino Clemente;
Bill Christine, *Roberto,* 1973.

228 *The most significant event in baseball:* Minutes of Executive Board
Meeting, Major League Baseball Players Association, Sheraton Hotel,
San Juan, Puerto Rico, December 13–14, 1969; int. Dick Moss; *San
Juan Star,* December 12–15, 1969; *New York Times,* December 14–15,
1969.

233 *Listening in on the conversation:* Int. Enrique Zorrilla.

235 *"I don't know why they invited me":* Int. Nancy Golding.

237 *In Pittsburgh two days later: Pittsburgh Post-Gazette, Pittsburgh
Press,* July 15–18, 1970.

237 *July 24 was Roberto Clemente night:* Account of night drawn from
ints. Vera Clemente, Luis Clemente, Matino Clemente, Roy
McHugh, Al Oliver, Richie Hebner, Howard Fineman, Ramiro
Martínez; Martínez's tape-recording of speeches, July 24, 1970; *Pittsburgh Post-Gazette, Pittsburgh Press,* July 23–25, 1970.

11: EL DÍA MÁS GRANDE

PAGE

241 *In Baltimore on the eve:* Ints. Vera Clemente, Carolyn Rauch.

242 *"I'm never sorry": San Francisco Chronicle, Baltimore Sun, Chicago
Tribune, Pittsburgh Post-Gazette, New York Times,* October 5–9, 1971.

243 *"Anger, for Roberto Clemente":* Roy McHugh, *Pittsburgh Press,* October 15, 1971; int. Roy McHugh.

244 *Russo and Youse returned: Baltimore Sun,* October 9, 1971.

245 *Game 1, on the Saturday afternoon:* Game account drawn from ints. Steve Blass, Al Oliver, Richie Hebner, Nellie Briles, José Pagan, Roy McHugh, Joe L. Brown, Tony Bartirome, Harding Peterson, Earl Weaver, Paul Blair, Vera Clemente; *Baltimore Sun, Washington Post, New York Times, Pittsburgh Post-Gazette, Pittsburgh Press, Chicago Tribune,* October 10, 1971.

246 *No bad clams at the restaurant:* Ints. Vera Clemente, Carolyn Rauch.

247 *"I had the ball and he was sliding":* Int. Richie Hebner.

248 *the baseball writers had all quit:* David Condon, *Chicago Tribune,* Arthur Daley, *New York Times,* Jim Murray, *Los Angeles Times,* October 11–12, 1971.

249 *Clemente could not sleep:* Ints. Vera Clemente, Steve Blass.

250 *"look what we got":* Ints. Tony Bartirome, Steve Blass.

250 *Cuellar hurried his throw:* Int. Earl Weaver.

251 *"Guess I missed a sign":* Pittsburgh Post-Gazette, New York Times, Baltimore Sun,* October 13, 1971.

253 *It only lasted an inning:* The best account of the all-black Pirate lineup is by Bruce Markesun, a researcher at the National Baseball Hall of Fame, on the baseballguru.com Web site.

254 *Rice called it foul:* Int. Don Leppert; *Pittsburgh Post-Gazette, Baltimore Sun, Washington Post, New York Times,* October 14, 1971.

255 *The fans could not see it:* Int. Nellie Briles; *Pittsburgh Press, Baltimore Sun, San Francisco Chronicle,* October 15, 1971.

256 *"The rest of us were just players":* Int. Steve Blass.

256 *The prince was a pip: Newsday, New York Times, New York Daily News, Pittsburgh Press, Baltimore Sun, Chicago Tribune, San Francisco Chronicle, Los Angeles Times,* October 15, 1971.

259 *Clemente could not have performed better:* Ints. Earl Weaver, Paul Blair, Roy McHugh, Tony Bartirome, José Pagan; *Baltimore Sun, Pittsburgh Post-Gazette,* October 16, 1971.

261 *As the taxi hurtled north:* Ken Nigro, *Baltimore Sun,* October 17, 1971.

262 *Blass was even more effective:* Ints. Steve Blass, Earl Weaver, Richie Hebner, Nellie Briles, Les Banos, José Pagan, Joe L. Brown, Tony Bartirome; *Los Angeles Times, Baltimore Sun, Pittsburgh Press, Pittsburgh Post-Gazette, Chicago Tribune, New York Times,* October 17, 1971.

264 *"En el día más grande":* Ramiro Martínez tape collection. (In two closets in his condominium in the San Juan suburbs, Martínez maintains the world's largest archive of audio and videotapes of Clemente. Many of them were recorded by Martínez in his capacity as a radio

announcer. He was a Zelig-like character who seemed to always be at Clemente's side whenever something important was happening.)

265 *At the White House: Pittsburgh Post-Gazette, Baltimore Sun;* Nixon tapes, National Archives at College Park. Nixon-Rogers exchange uncovered and transcribed by James C. Warren of the *Chicago Tribune,* a leading expert on the voluminous Nixon tapes.

266 *Three days later, on the afternoon of October 20:* Ramiro Martínez archive; *New York Times,* October 21, 1971; Roger Kahn; ints. Stuart Speiser, Vera Clemente.

12: TIP OF THE CAP

PAGE

269 *Momen was a fanatic about crabs:* Int. Roberto Clemente Jr.

269 *They visited Caracas:* Clemente family collection, travel documents: Int. Vera Clemente.

271 *"I think the World Series":* Ramiro Martínez tape collection.

272 *Clemente chose to live:* Ints. Richie Hebner, Fernando González, Al Oliver.

273 *Also hanging around was Roy Blount Jr.:* C. R. Ways, *New York Times Magazine,* April 9, 1972.

274 *In his letter to Vera:* Duane Reider collection, Pittsburgh, Pennsylvania. The letter was handwritten on Pirate City stationery.

275 *the 1972 team was even looser:* Ints. Steve Blass, Tony Bartirome, Les Banos, Richie Hebner, Al Oliver, Nellie Briles.

277 *"Hey, Roberto," Sanguillen called out:* Int. Fernando González.

278 *"We stayed and we talked":* Int. Carolyn Rauch.

279 *Barely half that many: Pittsburgh Post-Gazette, Pittsburgh Press;* ints. Richie Hebner, Tony Bartirome, Steve Blass, Matino Clemente, Les Banos, Nellie Briles; Tom Seaver, Recollection at Hall of Fame gathering at National Geographic Society, Washington, D.C., February 2003.

280 *The next morning at eleven:* Account of Clemente's three-thousandth hit drawn from ints. Ann Ranalli King, Steve Blass, Richie Hebner, Nellie Briles, Tony Bartirome, Les Banos, Roy McHugh, Chuck Goggin, Bill Nunn Jr.; *El Nueva Día,* (Luis Ramos); *Pittsburgh Press; Pittsburgh Post-Gazette,* September 30, 1971 and October 1, 1971; Ramiro Martínez tape collection (Felo Martínez broadcasts). In explaining why Clemente was her favorite player, Ann Ranalli, who later married the sportswriter Peter King, said: "You never felt like he was playing a media game. He always seemed to be his own person, on and off the field, which was admirable. Pittsburgh was not a great baseball town,

nor particularly supportive of the team. I happened to be a fan and had more enthusiasm and he was the centerpiece of the games."

284 *the surest evidence that he intended:* Int. Rex Bradley, Hillerich & Bradsby bat archives.

286 *the night before he left:* Int. Al Oliver.

13: TEMBLOR

PAGE

287 *Three days before Christmas:* Nixon Presidential Papers, National Archives, Nicaragua file, Telegram, December 22, 1972. A stamp next to the White House logo says: Ambassador/ Hand-Carry/President. The telegram is addressed to Mr. Howard Hughes/Intercontinental/ Hotel/Managua, Nicaragua. It was copied to R. Woods/R. Price/J. Andrews/ R. Ziegler/H. Klein.

289 *Holiday revelers were out strolling:* Account of first moments of earthquake drawn from int. Anthony Jilek; Nixon Presidential Papers, Nicaragua file, National Archives; Pedro Chamorro, *Richter 7* (translation, Patricia Rengal); *Washington Post, New York Times,* December 24, 1972; Nicholas Daniloff, UPI, Washington, D.C., December 23, 1972.

291 *The Clementes, at their house:* Ints. Vera Clemente, Ramiro Martínez, Osvaldo Gil.

292 *The disaster relief effort was underway:* Southern Command News, Quarry Heights, Canal Zone, January 5, 1973; Situation Report, Staff Communications Division, Department of the Army, Nicaragua, National Archives at College Park.

293 *American soldiers arriving:* Int. Gary Czabot.

293 *the attention of President Nixon:* President Nixon's Daily Diary, Nixon Presidential Papers, National Archives, Washington, D.C. (NARA), December 23, 1972. The diary entries: 9:35—The President had breakfast; 11:07 The President talked with his senior White House physician, Major General Walter Tkach; 12:53 The President talked long distance with his Assistant for National Security Affairs, Henry A. Kissinger, in Washington, D.C.; 1:05 The President had lunch. The President watched the Oakland Raiders–Pittsburgh Steelers football game on television.

293 *Fourth and ten:* Ints. Myron Cope, Bill Nunn Jr., Les Banos; *Pittsburgh Post-Gazette, Pittsburgh Press,* December 24, 1971.

295 *"I don't know what":* Ints. Osvaldo Gil, Vera Clemente; Ramiro Martínez archive.

295 *President Nixon took breakfast at eight forty-five:* President Nixon's Daily Diary, Nixon Presidential Papers, Nicaragua file, NARA; Memorandum for Al Haig, Subject: Nicaragua Earthquake, National Security Council, NARA, December 24, 1972.

296 *In San Juan, Clemente and Ruth Fernández:* Ints. Vera Clemente, Osvaldo Gil, Ramiro Martínez; Ramiro Martínez tape collection.

297 *Pedro Chamorro circled Managua:* Pedro Chamorro, *Richter 7*.

298 *Clemente spent the day:* Ints. Vera Clemente, Osvaldo Gil; Ramiro Martínez tape collection.

299 *Howard Hughes, after refueling stops: Times of London, New York Times, Miami Herald,* AP, December 24–26, 1971.

301 *the greed of Somoza:* Ints. Osvaldo Gil, Vera Clemente, Ramiro Martínez.

302 *Bianca, then only twenty-two:* Kurt Jacobsen, "A Conversation with Bianca Jagger, Human Rights Advocate," *Logos Journal,* Fall 2003.

303 *Once the plane touched down:* Ints. Dr. Hart Achenbach, Dr. Frederick Zugibe; Hart Achenbach, M.D., *Tales of the Curious Traveler.*

304 *President Nixon placed a call:* Int. Maurice J. Williams; President Nixon's Daily Diary, Nixon Presidential Papers, NARA.

304 *Come with me:* Ints. Les Banos, Orlando Cepeda, Chuck Goggin, Vera Clemente, Osvaldo Gil.

14: COCKROACH CORNER

PAGE

309 *you could buy anything for a song:* Ints. Mike Pangia, Jon Hoffman, Stuart Speiser.

310 *As practice runs go:* Pangia memo, Pangia archive, Federal Aviation Administration, U.S. Department of Justice.

310 *From the moment he came:* National Transportation Safety Board Report, Douglas DC-7CF Accident, Aircraft Accident File Contents, San Juan, Puerto Rico, December 31, 1972.

312 *Couric was such a stickler:* Int. Bev Couric (wife of William Couric); National Transportation Safety Board (NTSB), Aircraft Accident File.

312 *Rivera went on the offensive:* NTSB, Alexander P. Butterfield, FAA, vs. Arthur S. Rivera, Docket SE-1399.

313 *The battle of wills:* Ints. Stuart Speiser, Jon Hoffman, Mike Pangia; Speiser Brief (50 pp.), U.S. District Court; Lawsuit (p. 382); FAA Report of Investigation, May 11, 1970, Compliance and Security Office.

314 *Usto E. Schulz:* Schulz trial testimony: Vera Christina Zabala de Clemente et al., Plaintiff, vs. McDonnell Douglas Corp. et al., and other consolidated cases, Defendants. Transcript of trial heard before the Honorable Juan R. Torrulella, U.S. District Judge sitting in San Juan, Puerto Rico, November 1975.

314 *that came to be known:* Department of Transportation, FAA, Southern Region, September 25, 1972, Pangia archive.

315 *Rivera enlisted two mechanics:* NTSB Air Accident File, depositions of Rafael Delgado-Cintron and Francisco Matias.

316 *the Clementes were consumed:* Ints. Vera Clemente, Osvaldo Gil; Air Accident File, Delgado-Cintron deposition. U.S. District Court trial testimony, Vera Zabala de Clemente, November 1975.

317 *The Clementes were met at the dock:* Int. Vera Clemente; *San Juan Star,* December 30, 1972.

318 *Roberto placed a call:* Ints. Carolyn Rauch, Carol Brezovec (Bass), Vera Clemente.

319 *Back at the airport:* NTSB Air Accident File, Delgado-Cintron, Matias depositions.

15: DECEMBER 31

PAGE

321 *Vera Clemente stood in the kitchen:* Int. Vera Clemente; lyrics of song by Trio Vegabajeño.

322 *Jerry Hill, the pilot Arthur River recruited:* Transcript of crash trial, testimony Delgado-Cintron, Matias, Vera Clemente; NTSB Air Accident File depositions.

323 *The aircraft was already full:* cargo manifest filed with FAA, San Juan, NTSB Air Accident File, Pangia archive.

324 *Clemente was at home:* Ints. Vera Clemente, Cristobal Colón; testimony, transcript, Vera Clemente, United States District Court for the District of Puerto Rico, civil numbers 778–73, 779–73, 999–73, 1000–73, 1096–73.

325 *At 5:30 P.M., according to FAA records:* Air Accident File, History of Flight; Pangia Memo, Pangia archive; transcript, George E. Mattern testimony, U.S. District Court.

326 *Clemente handed him:* NTSB, Statement of Interview with Rafael Delgado-Cintron. The mechanic was likely the last person outside the plane to see Clemente alive. "The stairs were already on the way [out] but he put it back and said good-bye to everybody and . . . Mr. Cle-

mente asked for a favor to call his wife and gave me the telephone [number]. Did you see where he was seated? Yes, he was seated on the bunk forward of the cargo."

327 *"San Juan tower, Douglas":* NTSB Air Accident File, Transcript of Air Traffic Control, December 31, 1972.

328 *The plane didn't seem:* NTSB Air Accident File, Statement of Witness—Juan Reyes, Gilberto Quiles, Antonio Ríos, Rafael Delgado-Cintron, Dennis A. McHale, Gary Cleaveland.

329 *The Rauches were delighted:* Ints. Carolyn Rauch, Carol Brezovec (Bass), Vera Clemente.

332 *Matino woke his father:* Int. Matino Clemente, Carolyn Rauch, Carol Brezovec (Bass), Vera Clemente; testimony transcript, George E. Mattern, United States District Court for the District of Puerto Rico, civil numbers 778–73, 779–73, 999–73, 1000–73, 1096–73.

333 *"It was quiet and sad":* Reaction to news of the crash drawn from Ints. Orlando Cepeda, Osvaldo Gil, Cristobal Colón, Juan Pizarro, Enrique Zorrilla, Diana Zorrilla, Eduardo Valero, Luis Olmo, Vic Power, Chuck Goggin, Steve Blass, Joe L. Brown, José Pagan, Ann Ranalli, Richard Santry, Nancy Golding, Bev Couric, Vera Clemente, Luis Clemente.

16: OUT OF THE SEA

PAGE

339 *a sequence of twenty telephone calls:* Facility Accident Notification Record, January 1, 1973, Aircraft Ident N500AENTSB Air Accident File; Department of Transportation, U.S. Coast Guard Telecommunications Center, Sitrep 1, January 1, 1973.

339 *"That night on which Roberto Clemente":* Elliott Castro, *Home: A Celebration of Roberto Clemente's Spirit and Passion,* Museo de Arte de Puerto Rico.

340 *Vera wavered between:* Ints. Vera Clemente, Osvaldo Gil, Carolyn Rauch.

340 *The effort that day was slowed:* U.S. Coast Guard sitrep, January 1–2, 1973; AP, January 1, 1973; *San Juan Star, El Nuevo Día,* January 1–3, 1973; Ints. John Parker, Vincent Bogucki, Fernando González, Vera Clemente.

342 *It was not mythmaking:* Newsday, AP, *Pittsburgh Press, Chicago Tribune, New York Post,* January 3–4, 1973.

345 *President Nixon mentioned:* Account of the White House and Roberto Clemente drawn from President Nixon's Daily Diary, Nixon Presidential Papers, NARA, Statement About the Death of Roberto Clemente;

Memorandum for the President from: Richard A. Moore, January 3, 1973; Memorandum for H. R. Haldeman from Richard A. Moore, January 3, 1973; Richard Reeves, *President Nixon: Alone at the White House.*

347 *By that hour in the choppy Atlantic:* Instituto de Medicina Legal, Centro Medico Hospital, Rio Piedras, Puerto Rico, Autopsy No. 31-ML-73.

347 *Early the next morning:* Ints. Richie Hebner, Al Oliver, Preston Pearson, Les Banos, Steve Blass, Vera Clemente, Ramiro Martínez, Eduardo Valero, Fernando González; transcript of press conference drawn from Ramiro Martínez tape collection.

351 *By the end of that weekend:* U.S. Coast Guard Telecommunications Center, Sitreps 5–6; NTSB Air Accident File; ints. Osvaldo Gil, Vic Power, Vera Clemente.

Lifetime Record of Roberto Clemente

YR.	CLUB	CLASS	G	AB	H	2B	3B	HR	RBI	AVG.
1954	Montreal	AAA	87	148	38	5	3	2	12	.257
1955	Pittsburgh	NL	124	474	121	23	11	5	47	.255
1956	Pittsburgh	NL	147	543	169	30	7	7	60	.311
1957	Pittsburgh	NL	111	451	114	17	7	4	30	.253
1958	Pittsburgh	NL	140	519	150	24	10	6	50	.289
1959	Pittsburgh	NL	105	432	128	17	7	4	50	.296
1960	Pittsburgh	NL	144	570	179	22	6	16	94	.314
1961	Pittsburgh	NL	146	572	201	30	10	23	89	.351
1962	Pittsburgh	NL	144	538	168	28	9	10	74	.312
1963	Pittsburgh	NL	152	600	192	23	8	17	76	.320
1964	Pittsburgh	NL	155	622	211	40	7	12	87	.339
1965	Pittsburgh	NL	152	589	194	21	14	10	65	.329
1966	Pittsburgh	NL	154	638	202	31	11	29	119	.317
1967	Pittsburgh	NL	147	585	209	26	10	23	110	.357
1968	Pittsburgh	NL	132	502	146	18	12	18	57	.291
1969	Pittsburgh	NL	138	507	175	20	12	19	91	.345
1970	Pittsburgh	NL	108	412	145	22	10	14	60	.352
1971	Pittsburgh	NL	132	522	178	29	8	13	86	.341
1972	Pittsburgh	NL	102	378	118	19	7	10	60	.312
18 YRS	ML. TOTALS		2433	9454	3000	440	166	240	1305	.317

National League Batting Champion: 1961, 1964, 1965, 1967

Puerto Rico Winter League Batting Champion: 1956–57, .396

National League MVP: 1966

World Series MVP: 1971

National League Outfield Assist Leader: 1958 (22); 1960 (19); 1961 (27); 1966 (17); 1967 (17)

National League All-Star: 1960–67, 1969–71

Gold Glove: 1961–72

Selected Bibliography

The sourcebook I turned to more than any other was an old battered green copy of *The Baseball Encyclopedia: The Complete and Official Record of Major League Baseball,* published by Macmillan and edited by David Biesel, Audra Chastain, Lawrence S. Graver, Jane Herman, Fred Honig, Casey-Kwang-Chong Lee, Fred C. Richardson, and Eleanor Widdoes, with Joseph L. Reichler as the special editorial consultant. This encyclopedia was my primary source of statistics for every major league ballplayer ranging from Roberto Clemente to Mose J. (Chief) Yellowhorse. It has been revised many times since, but I used the 1976 edition, which was sufficient for all the players in Clemente's life. Every time I reached for this heavy book it was with anticipation and a certain measure of delight, although it hurt like crazy when it fell on my foot.

It was Clemente's nature to honor those who paved the way before him, and in that spirit I would like to make special mention of Bruce Markesun, a true baseball man, for his earlier book, *Roberto Clemente: The Great One,* and to Kal Wagenheim, whose love and deep knowledge of Puerto Rico and baseball shines through in his many books about the island and in his *Clemente!* I also benefited from the Clemente works of Phil Musick, Bill Christine, and Jim O'Brien. The most beautiful and in many ways most penetrating publication on Clemente is *Home: A Celebration of Roberto Clemente's Spirit and Passion,* which accompanied an extraordinary exhibit at the Puerto Rico Museum of Art.

Information posted on the Internet must be considered with caution, but over the course of my research I found there were three absolutely reliable and first-rate sources only a click away. The Baseball Almanac (baseball-almanac.com) is a bountiful source of accurate schedules and box scores. The Baseball Library (baseballLibrary.com) supplies accurate mini-biographies and day-by-day chronologies. In addition, the famed Society for American Baseball Research, home to the sport's insatiable band of intellectuals, has graciously made more and more of its reports available on the Web.

BOOKS

Baldassaro, Lawrence, *The American Game,* Carbondale, Ill.: Southern Illinois University Press, 2002.

Barretto, Nestor and Jorge Carbonell, *Home: A Celebration of Roberto Clemente's Spirit and Passion,* San Juan: Museo de Arte de Puerto Rico, 2002.

Brosnan, Jim, *The Long Season,* New York: Harper & Row, 1960.

Carrion, Arturo Morales, *Puerto Rico: A Political and Cultural History,* New York: Norton, 1983.

Chamorro, Pedro, *Richter 7,* Managua, Nicaragua: Ediciones El Pez y la Serpenta, 1981.

Christine, Bill, *Roberto!* Pittsburgh: Stadia Sports Publishing, 1973.

Cope, Myron, *Broken Cigars,* Englewood Cliffs, N.J.: Prentice-Hall, 1968.

———, *Double Yoi!,* Pittsburgh: Sports Publishing LLC, 2002.

Cruz Baez, Angel David, *Atlas Puerto Rico,* Miami: Cuban American National Council, 1997.

Einstein, Charles, *Willie's Time,* New York: Lippincott, 1979.

Gonzalez Echevarria, Roberto, *The Pride of Havana,* New York: Oxford University Press, 1999.

Halberstam, David, *October 1964,* New York: Villard Books, 1994.

Kerrane, Kevin, *Dollar Sign on the Muscle,* New York: Simon & Schuster, 1984.

Lorant, Stefan, *Pittsburgh: The Story of an American City,* Derrydale Press, 1999.

Mann, Arthur, *Branch Rickey: American in Action,* New York: Houghton Mifflin, 1957.

Markesun, Bruce, *Roberto Clemente: The Great One,* Pittsburgh: Sports Publishing LLC, 2001.

Marsh, Irving T., *Best Sports Stories of 1961,* New York: Dutton, 1961.

Morales Carrion, Arturo, *Puerto Rico: A Political and Cultural History,* New York: Norton, 1983.

Musick, Phil, *Reflections on Roberto,* Pittsburgh: Pittsburgh Associates, 1994.

———, *Who Was Roberto?* Garden City, N.Y.: Associated Features, 1974.

O'Brien, Jim, *Remember Roberto,* Pittsburgh: James O'Brien Publishing, 1994.

Pittsburgh Pirates 1956, New York: Big League Books, 1956.

Pittsburgh Pirates 1957, New York: Big League Books, 1957.

Pittsburgh Pirates 1958, New York: Big League Books, 1958.

Pittsburgh Pirates 1959, New York: Big League Books, 1959.

Rickey, Branch, and John J. Monteleone, *Branch Rickey's Little Blue Book*, New York: Macmillan, 1995.

Robinson, Jackie, *I Never Had It Made*, New York: Putnam, 1972.

Rodriguez-Mayoral, Luis, *Aun Eschucha Las Ovaciones*, Carolina, P.R.: Ciudad Deportiva, 1987.

Shribman, David, *Sports Town*, Pittsburgh: *Pittsburgh Post-Gazette*, 2004.

Speiser, Stuart M., *Lawsuit*, New York: Horizon Press, 1980.

Thomas, Clarke M., *Front-Page Pittsburgh*, Pittsburgh: University of Pittsburgh Press, 2005.

Van Hyning, Thomas E., *The Santurce Crabbers*, Jefferson, N.C.: McFarland & Company, 1999.

Wagenheim, Kal, *Clemente!* New York: Praeger, 1973.

———, *Puerto Rico: A Profile*, New York: Praeger, 1970.

Wendel, Tim, *The New Face of Baseball*, New York: HarperCollins, 2003.

MAGAZINE ARTICLES

Caceres, M. I., *The Unforgettable Roberto Clemente, Reader's Digest*, July 1973, 113–117.

Cohn, Howard, *Roberto Clemente's Problem, Sport*, May 1962, 54–56.

Cope, Myron, *Aches and Pains and Three Batting Titles, Sports Illustrated*, March 7, 1966, 76–80.

Feldman, Jay, *Clemente Went to Bat for All Latino Players, Smithsonian*, September 1993, 128–136.

Mazeroski, Bill, *My 16 Years with Roberto Clemente, Sport*, November 1971, 60–63.

Milagros González, Lydia, *Este Silencio*, San Juan: Instituto Cultura Puertorriqueña, 1998.

Sanguillen, Manny, *Manny Sanguillen Remembers Roberto Clemente, Baseball Digest*, May 1973, 40–42.

Ways, C. R., *Nobody Does Anything Better than Me in Baseball, Says Roberto Clemente, New York Times Magazine*, April 9, 1972, 38–48.

Steve Wulf, *Arriba Roberto, Sports Illustrated*, December 29, 1992, 114–128.

Index

About the Author

David Maraniss is an associate editor at the *Washington Post* and the author of critically acclaimed and bestselling books: *They Marched into Sunlight, When Pride Still Mattered,* and *First in His Class.* He won the 1993 Pulitzer Prize for National Reporting and has been a Pulitzer finalist three other times. He lives in Washington, D.C., and Madison, Wisconsin, with his wife, Linda. They have two grown children.